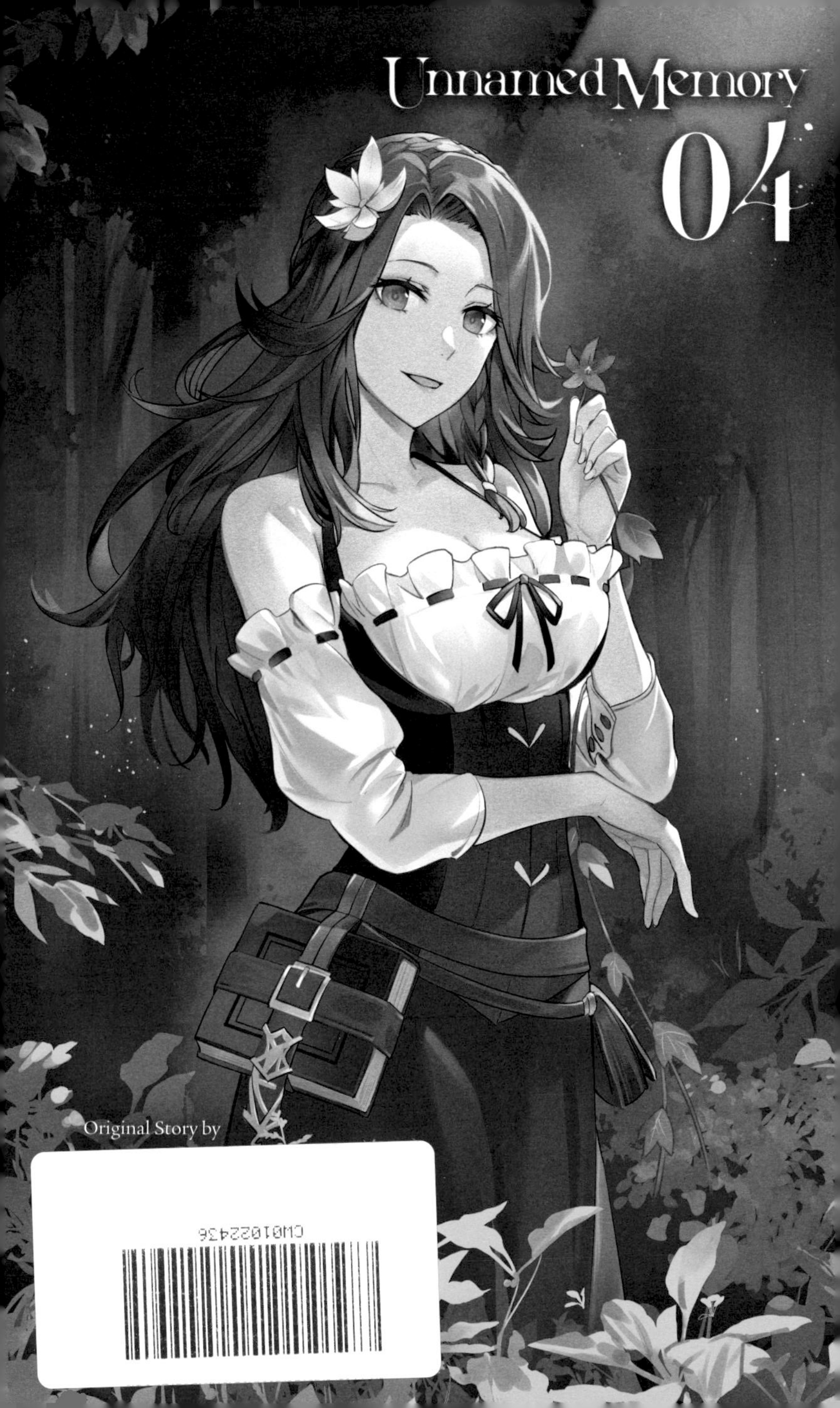
Unnamed Memory
04
Original Story by

~ The Lands of *Unnamed Memory* ~

Cuscull
Tayiri
Irsheut
Cezar
Tarviga
Druza
Old
Tuldarr
Yarda
Farsas
Mensanne
\<Tower\>
Gandona
\<Castle\>
Magdalsia

CONTENTS

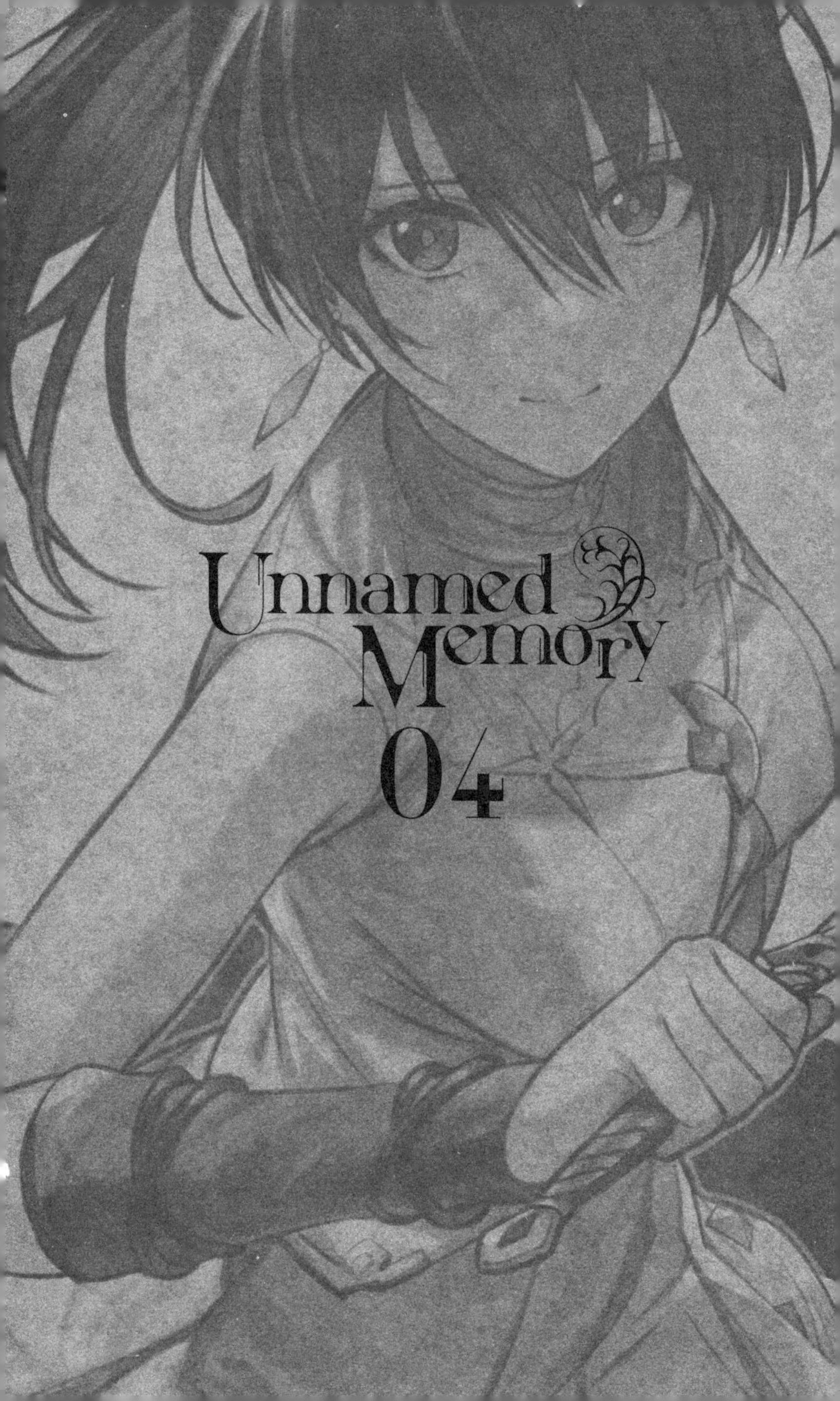
Unnamed Memory
04

CHARACTERS

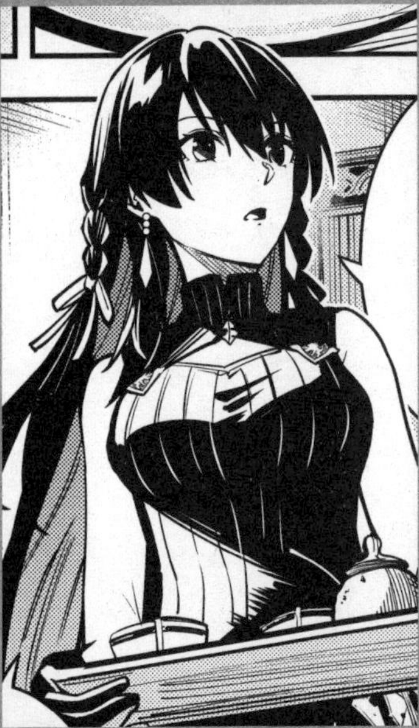

Tinasha

A.k.a. the Witch of the Azure Moon. The mainland's mightiest, currently Oscar's protector.

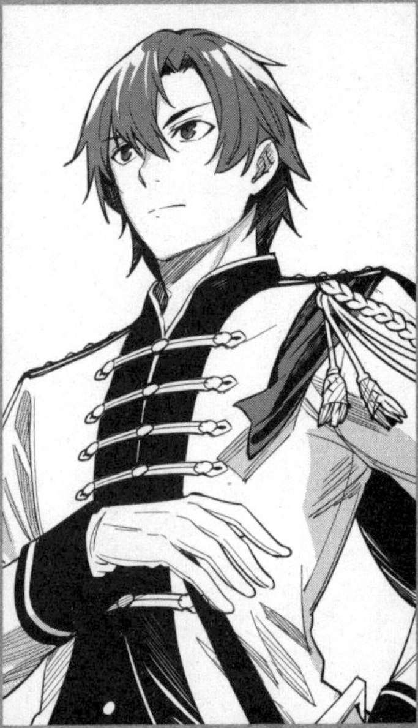

Oscar

Crown Prince of the Kingdom of Farsas. Wields the legendary royal sword Akashia, which nullifies magic.

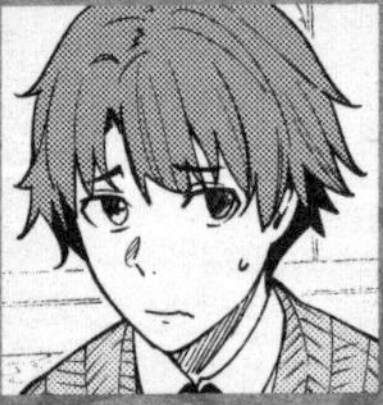

Lazar

Oscar's childhood friend and retainer. Gets run through the wringer.

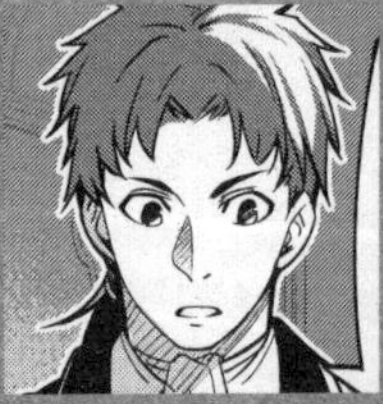

Als

An officer of Farsas. The most influential among the officer corps.

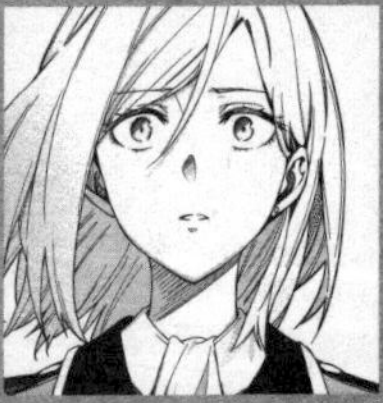

Meredina

Als's childhood friend and an accomplished swordswoman herself.

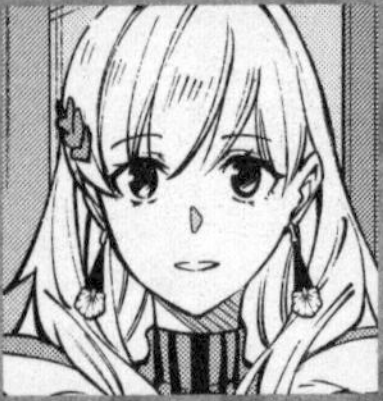

Sylvia

A mage of Farsas. Kind-hearted, slightly ditzy.

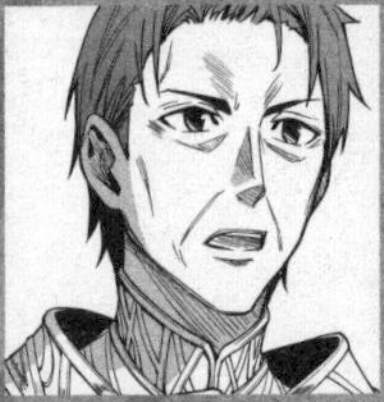

Kevin

Oscar's father and King of Farsas.

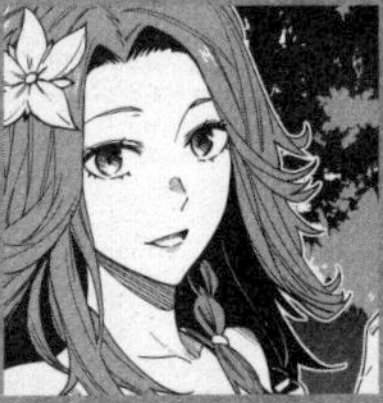

Lucrezia

A.k.a. the Witch of the Forbidden Forest. Tinasha's old friend.

Chapter 16.5: A Dream in the Forest ①

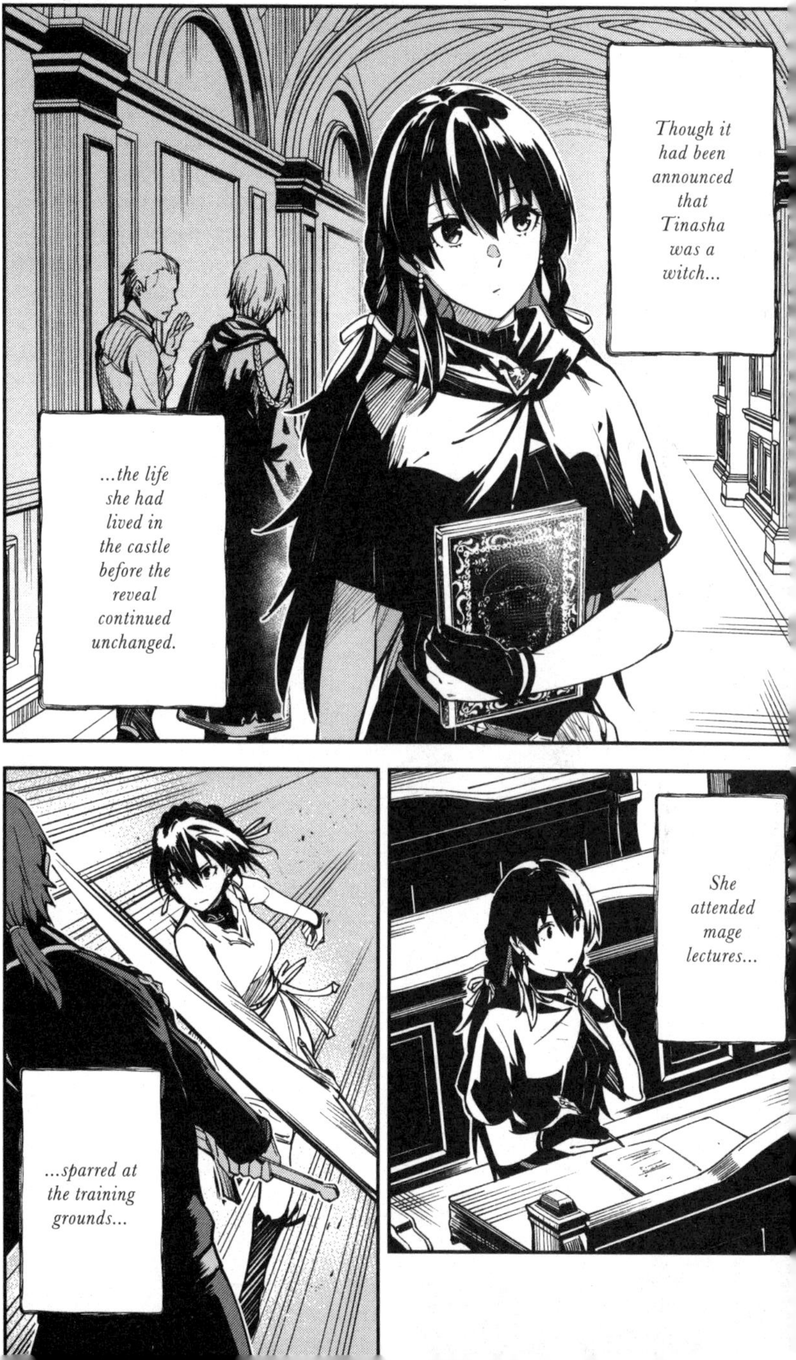
Though it had been announced that Tinasha was a witch...
...the life she had lived in the castle before the reveal continued unchanged.
She attended mage lectures...
...sparred at the training grounds...

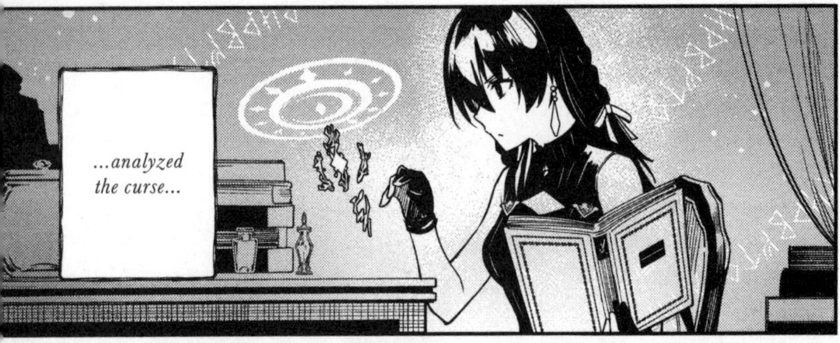
...analyzed the curse...

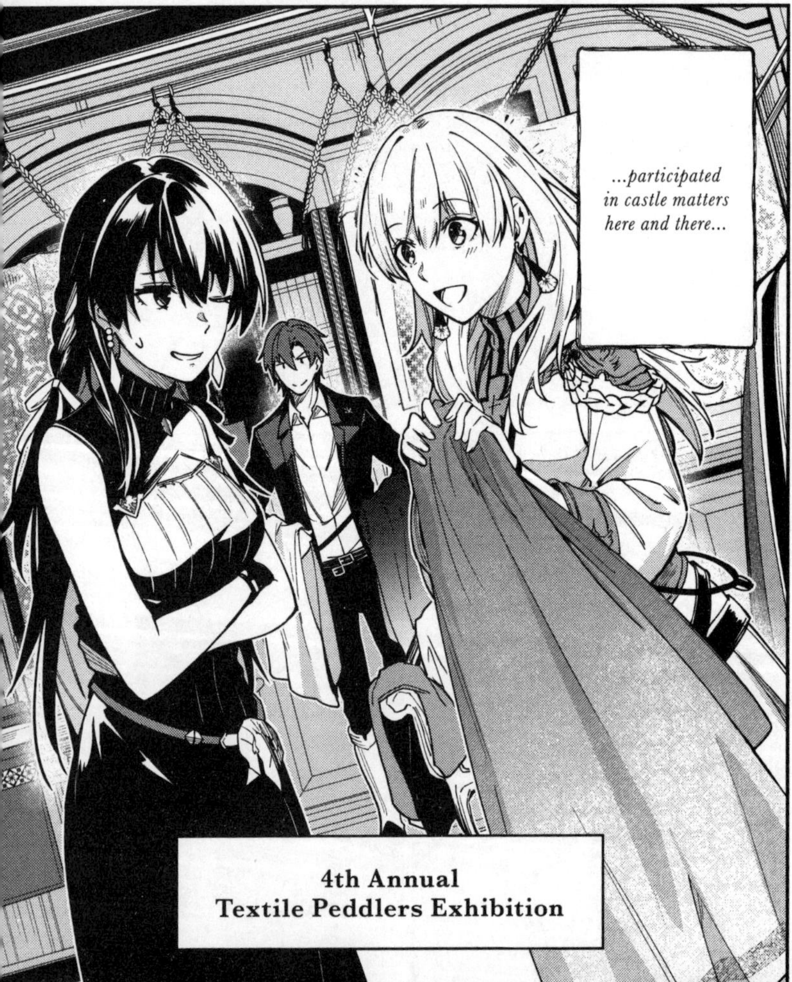
...participated in castle matters here and there...
4th Annual Textile Peddlers Exhibition

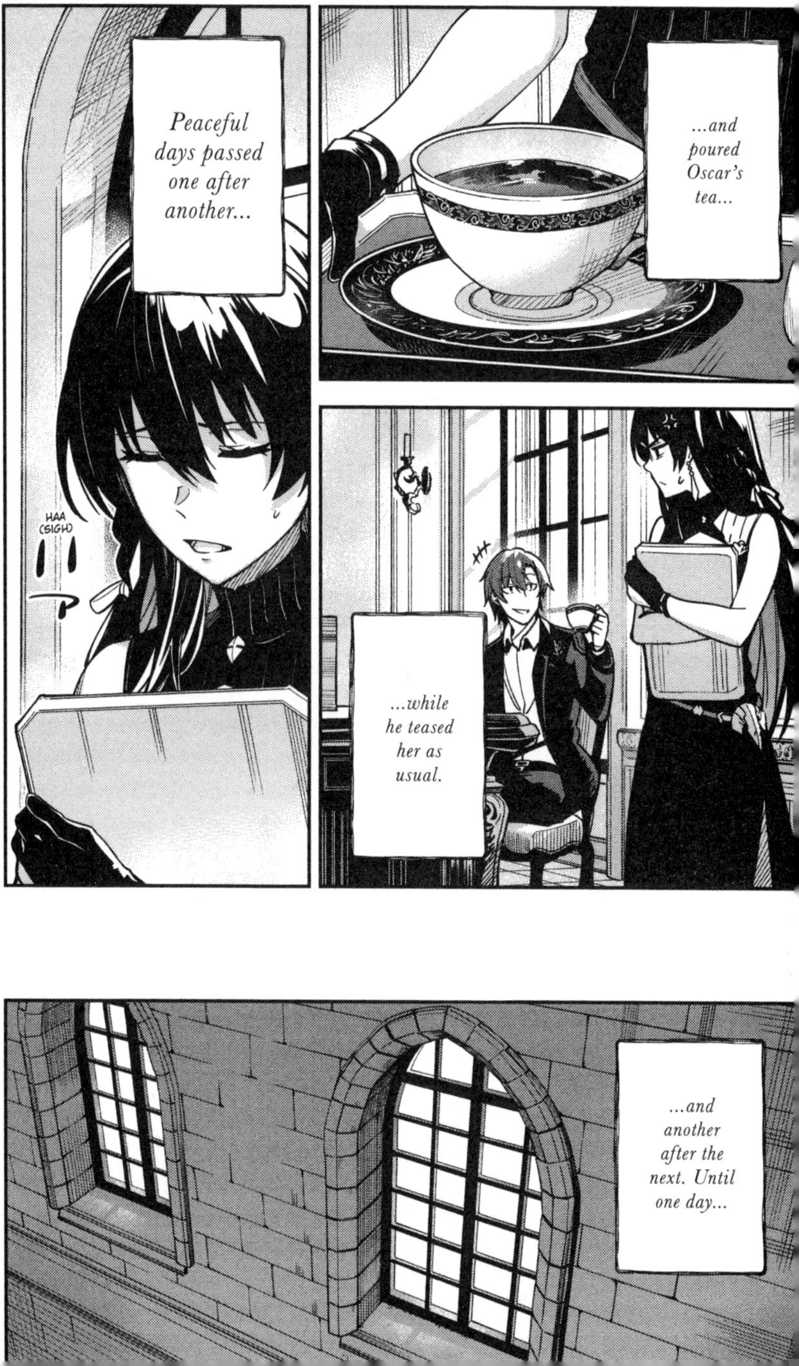
...and poured Oscar's tea...
...while he teased her as usual.
Peaceful days passed one after another...
HAA (SIGH)
...and another after the next. Until one day...

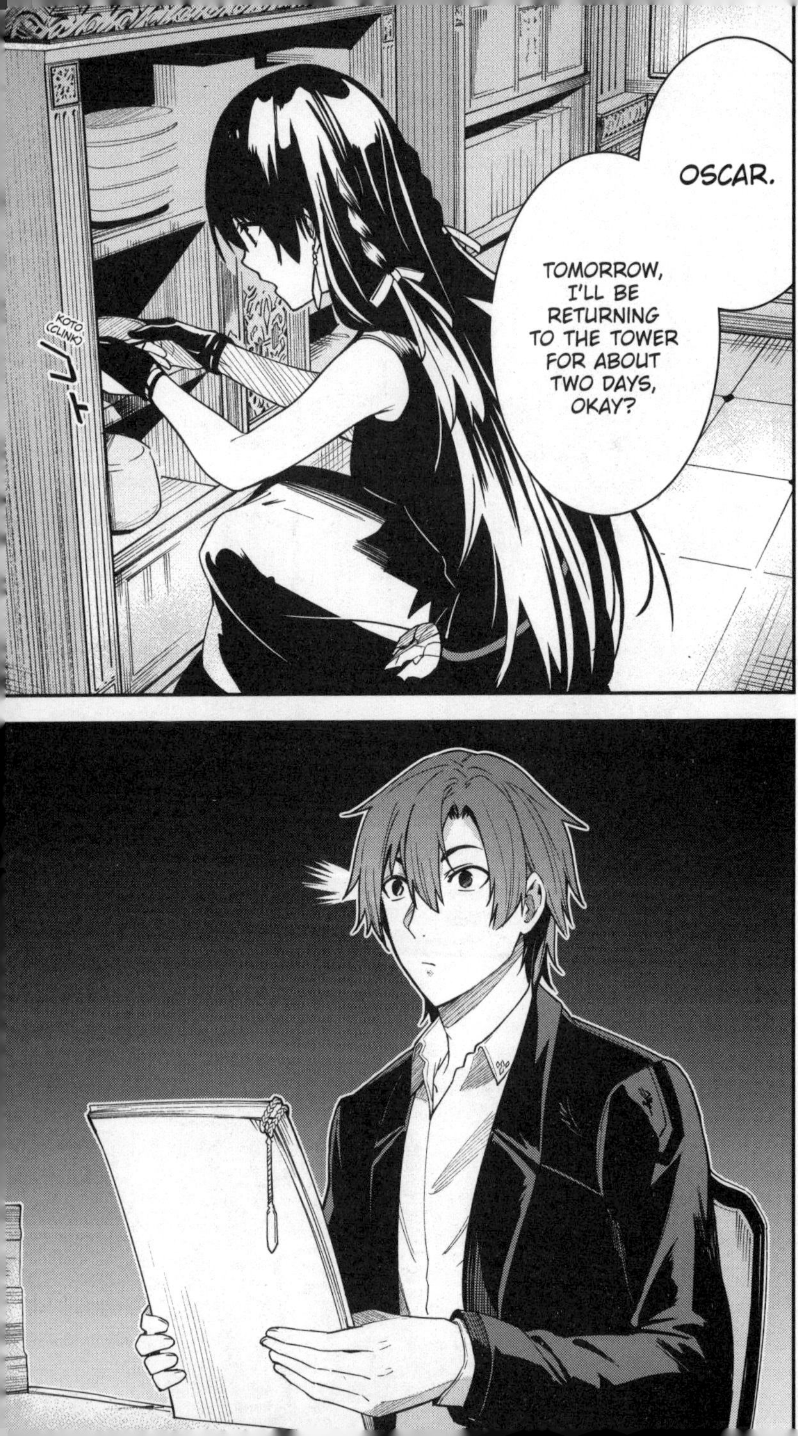
OSCAR.
TOMORROW, I'LL BE RETURNING TO THE TOWER FOR ABOUT TWO DAYS, OKAY?
KOTO (CLINK)

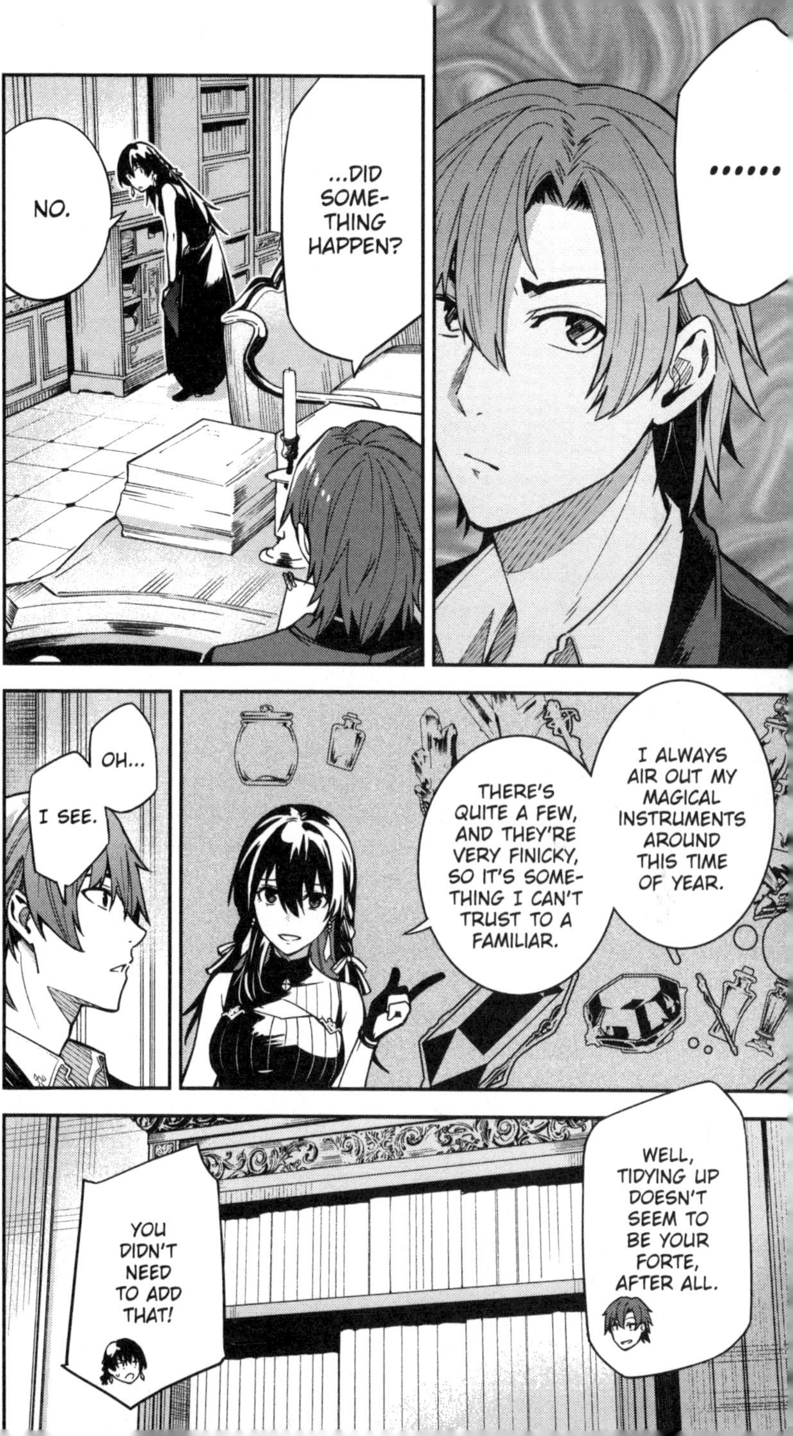
......
...DID SOMETHING HAPPEN?
NO.
I ALWAYS AIR OUT MY MAGICAL INSTRUMENTS AROUND THIS TIME OF YEAR.
THERE'S QUITE A FEW, AND THEY'RE VERY FINICKY, SO IT'S SOMETHING I CAN'T TRUST TO A FAMILIAR.
OH...
I SEE.
WELL, TIDYING UP DOESN'T SEEM TO BE YOUR FORTE, AFTER ALL.
YOU DIDN'T NEED TO ADD THAT!

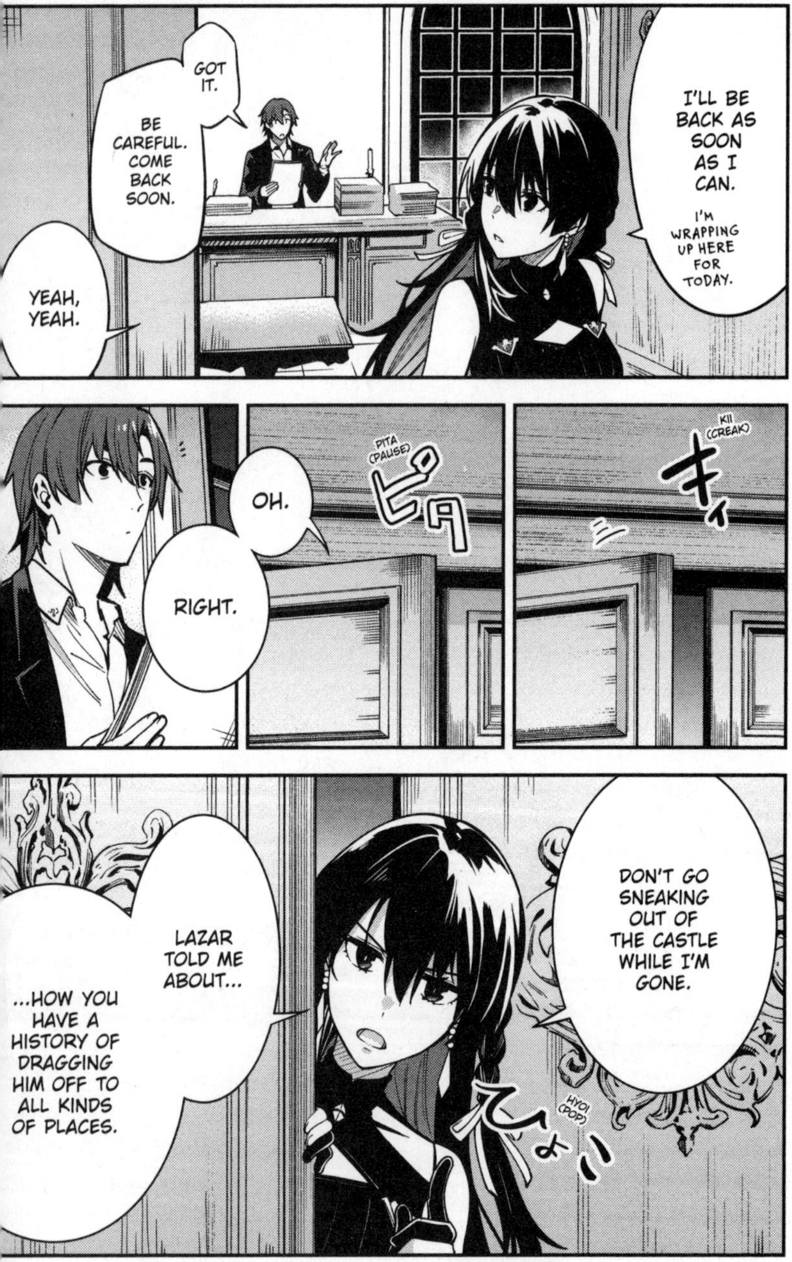
I'LL BE BACK AS SOON AS I CAN.
I'M WRAPPING UP HERE FOR TODAY.
GOT IT.
BE CAREFUL. COME BACK SOON.
YEAH, YEAH.
KII (CREAK)
キィ
PITA (PAUSE)
ピタ
OH.
RIGHT.
DON'T GO SNEAKING OUT OF THE CASTLE WHILE I'M GONE.
HYOI (POP)
ひょい
LAZAR TOLD ME ABOUT...
...HOW YOU HAVE A HISTORY OF DRAGGING HIM OFF TO ALL KINDS OF PLACES.

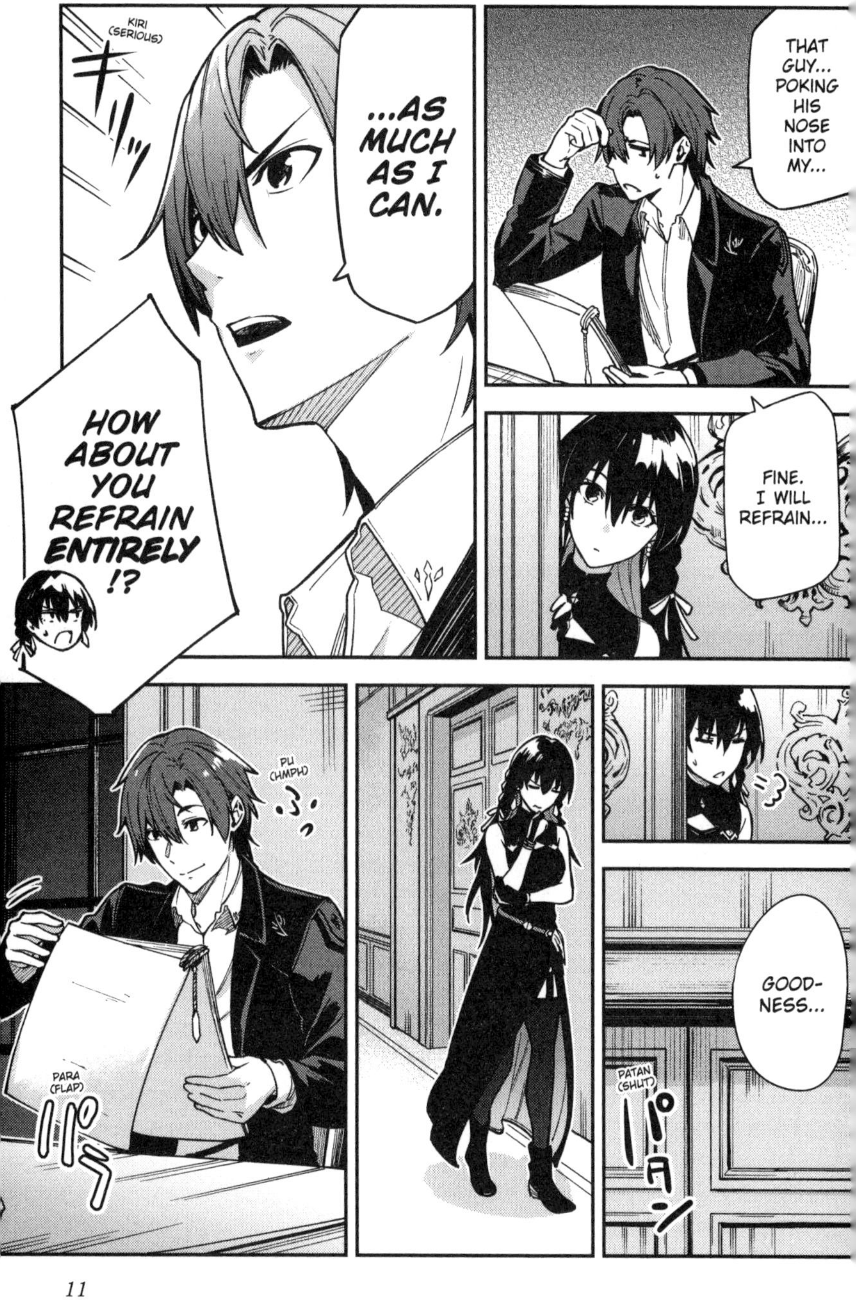
THAT GUY... POKING HIS NOSE INTO MY...
FINE. I WILL REFRAIN...
KIRI (SERIOUS)
...AS MUCH AS I CAN.
HOW ABOUT YOU REFRAIN ENTIRELY!?
GOODNESS...
PATAN (SHUT)
PU (HMPH)
PARA (FLAP)

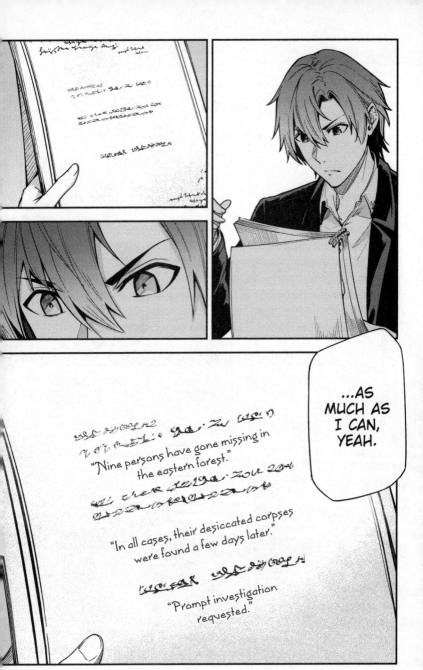

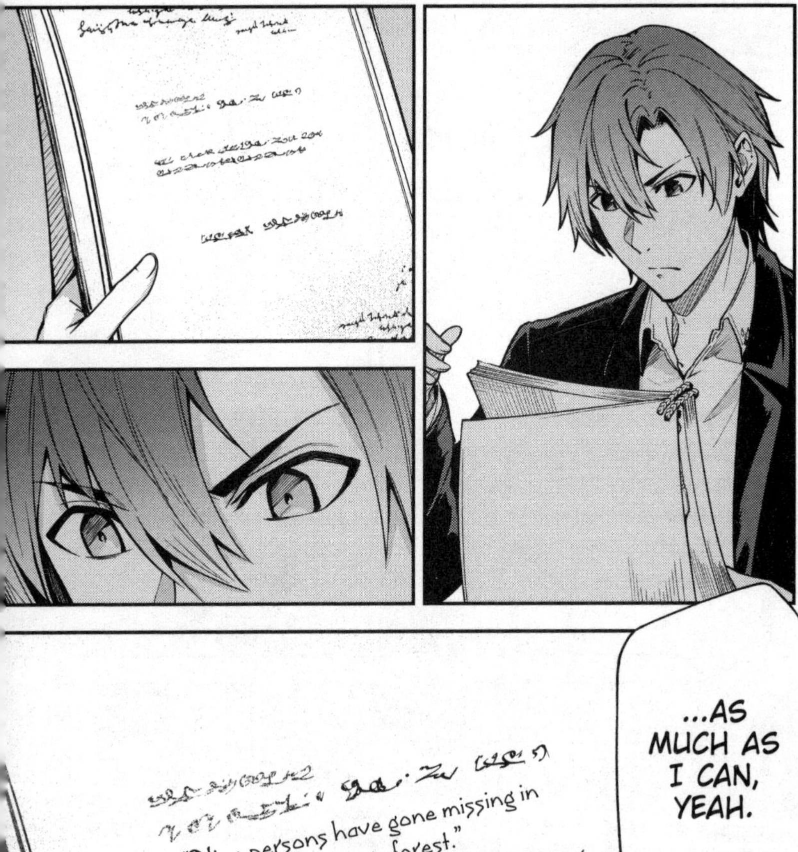
...AS MUCH AS I CAN, YEAH.
"Nine persons have gone missing in the eastern forest."
"In all cases, their desiccated corpses were found a few days later."
"Prompt investigation requested."

Unnamed Memory

Unnamed Memory

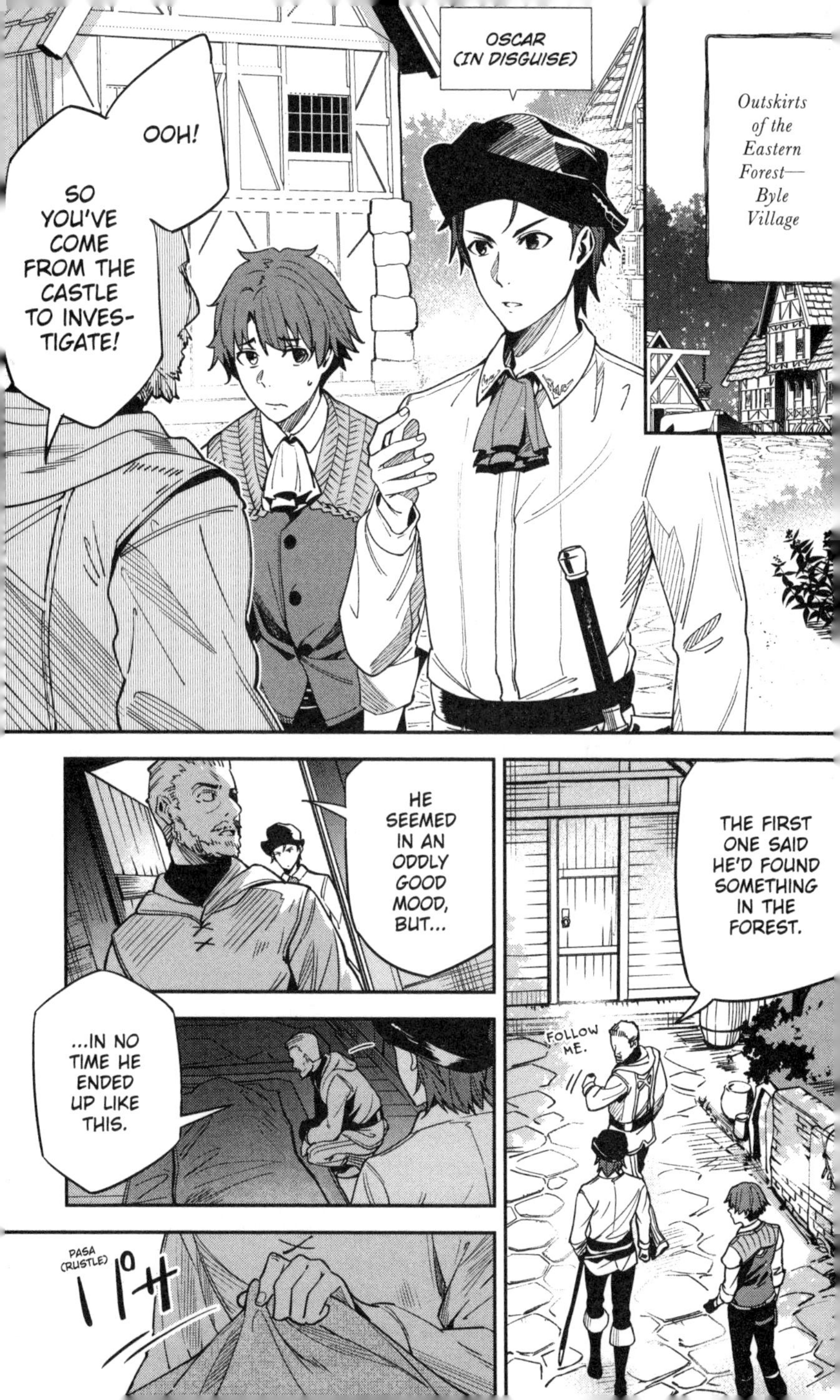
Outskirts of the Eastern Forest—Byle Village
OSCAR (IN DISGUISE)
OOH!
SO YOU'VE COME FROM THE CASTLE TO INVESTIGATE!
THE FIRST ONE SAID HE'D FOUND SOMETHING IN THE FOREST.
FOLLOW ME.
HE SEEMED IN AN ODDLY GOOD MOOD, BUT...
...IN NO TIME HE ENDED UP LIKE THIS.
PASA (RUSTLE)

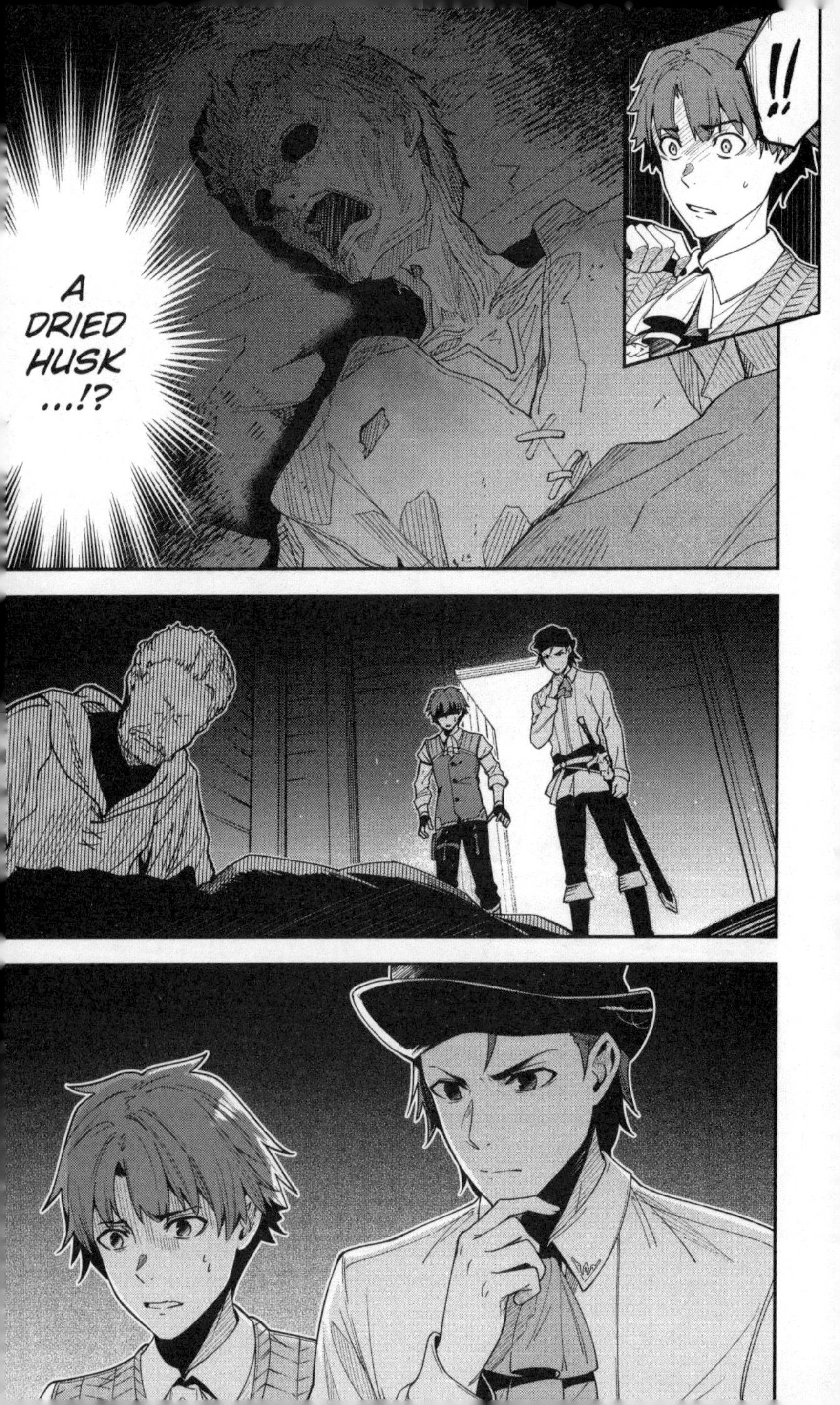
!!
A DRIED HUSK ...!?

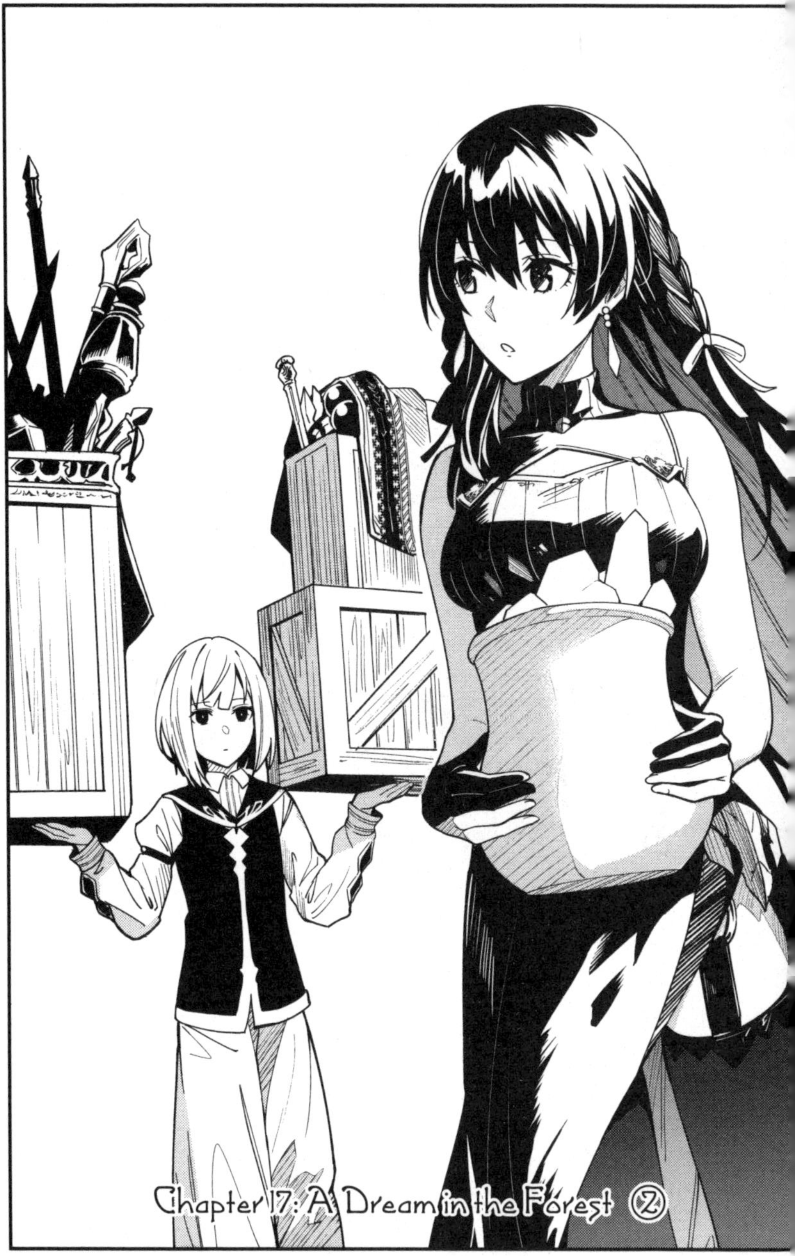
Chapter 17: A Dream in the Forest ②

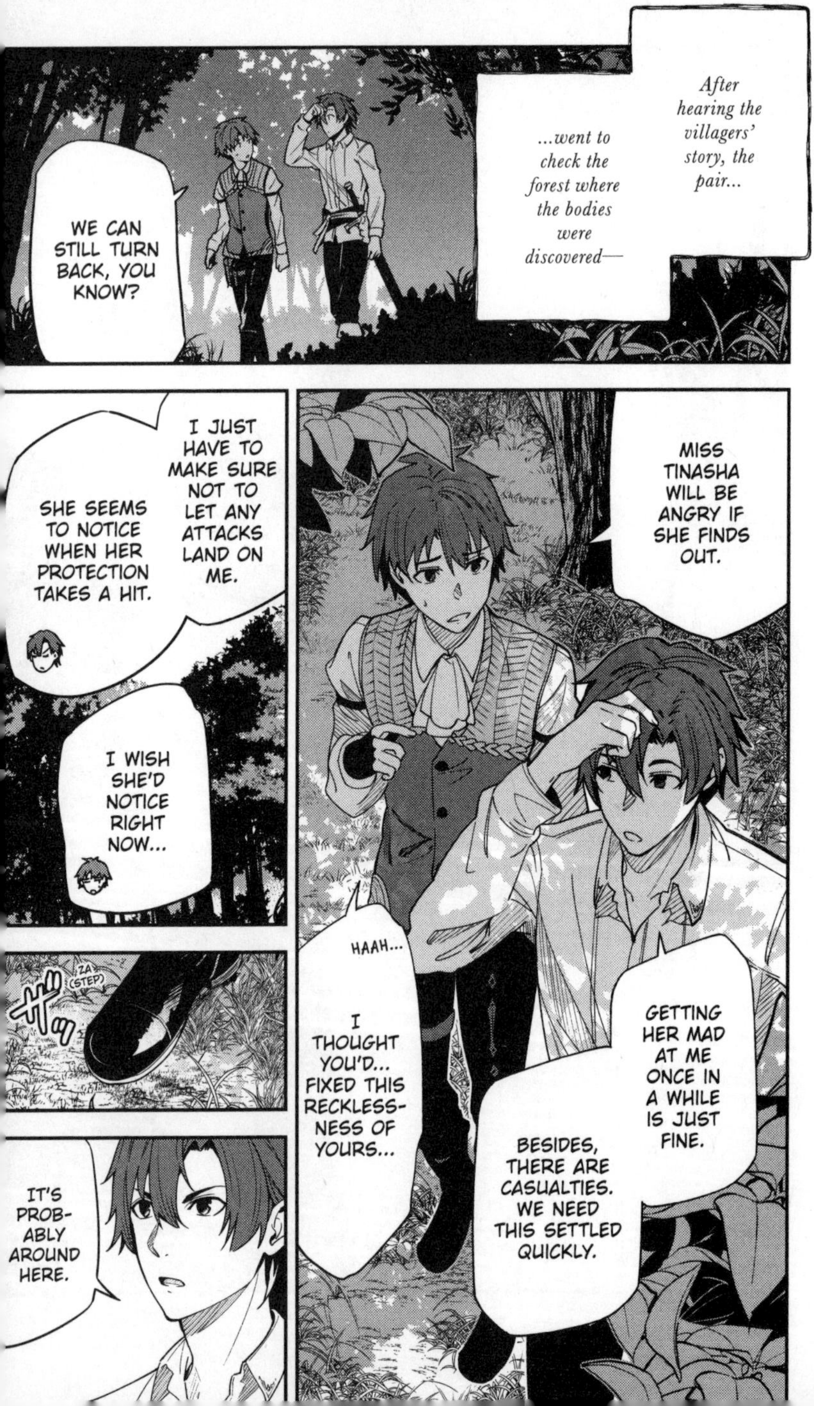
After hearing the villagers' story, the pair...
...went to check the forest where the bodies were discovered—
WE CAN STILL TURN BACK, YOU KNOW?
MISS TINASHA WILL BE ANGRY IF SHE FINDS OUT.
GETTING HER MAD AT ME ONCE IN A WHILE IS JUST FINE.
BESIDES, THERE ARE CASUALTIES. WE NEED THIS SETTLED QUICKLY.
HAAH...
I THOUGHT YOU'D... FIXED THIS RECKLESS-NESS OF YOURS...
I JUST HAVE TO MAKE SURE NOT TO LET ANY ATTACKS LAND ON ME.
SHE SEEMS TO NOTICE WHEN HER PROTECTION TAKES A HIT.
I WISH SHE'D NOTICE RIGHT NOW...
ZA (STEP)
IT'S PROB-ABLY AROUND HERE.

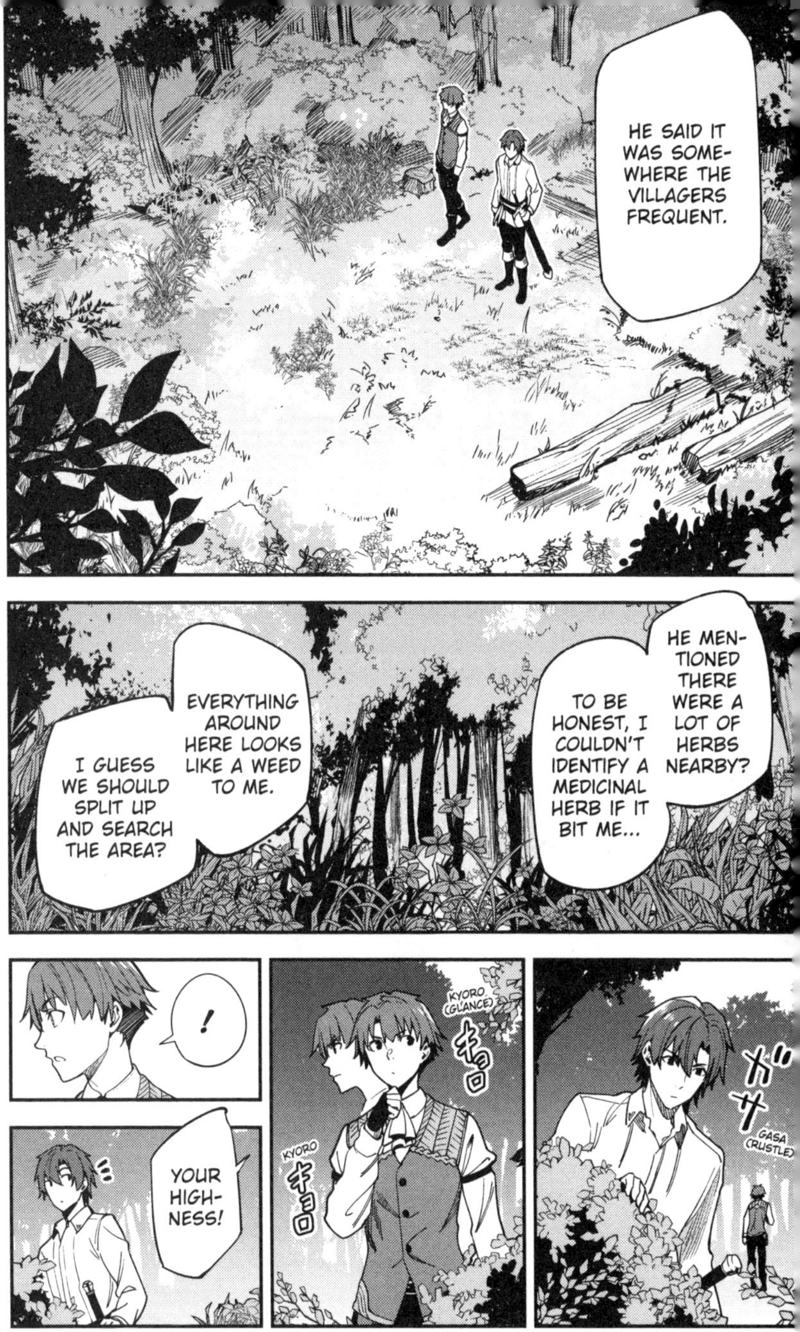
HE SAID IT WAS SOME-WHERE THE VILLAGERS FREQUENT.
HE MEN-TIONED THERE WERE A LOT OF HERBS NEARBY?
TO BE HONEST, I COULDN'T IDENTIFY A MEDICINAL HERB IF IT BIT ME...
EVERYTHING AROUND HERE LOOKS LIKE A WEED TO ME.
I GUESS WE SHOULD SPLIT UP AND SEARCH THE AREA?
ガサ
GASA (RUSTLE)
KYORO (GLANCE)
キョロ
KYORO
キョロ
!
YOUR HIGH-NESS!

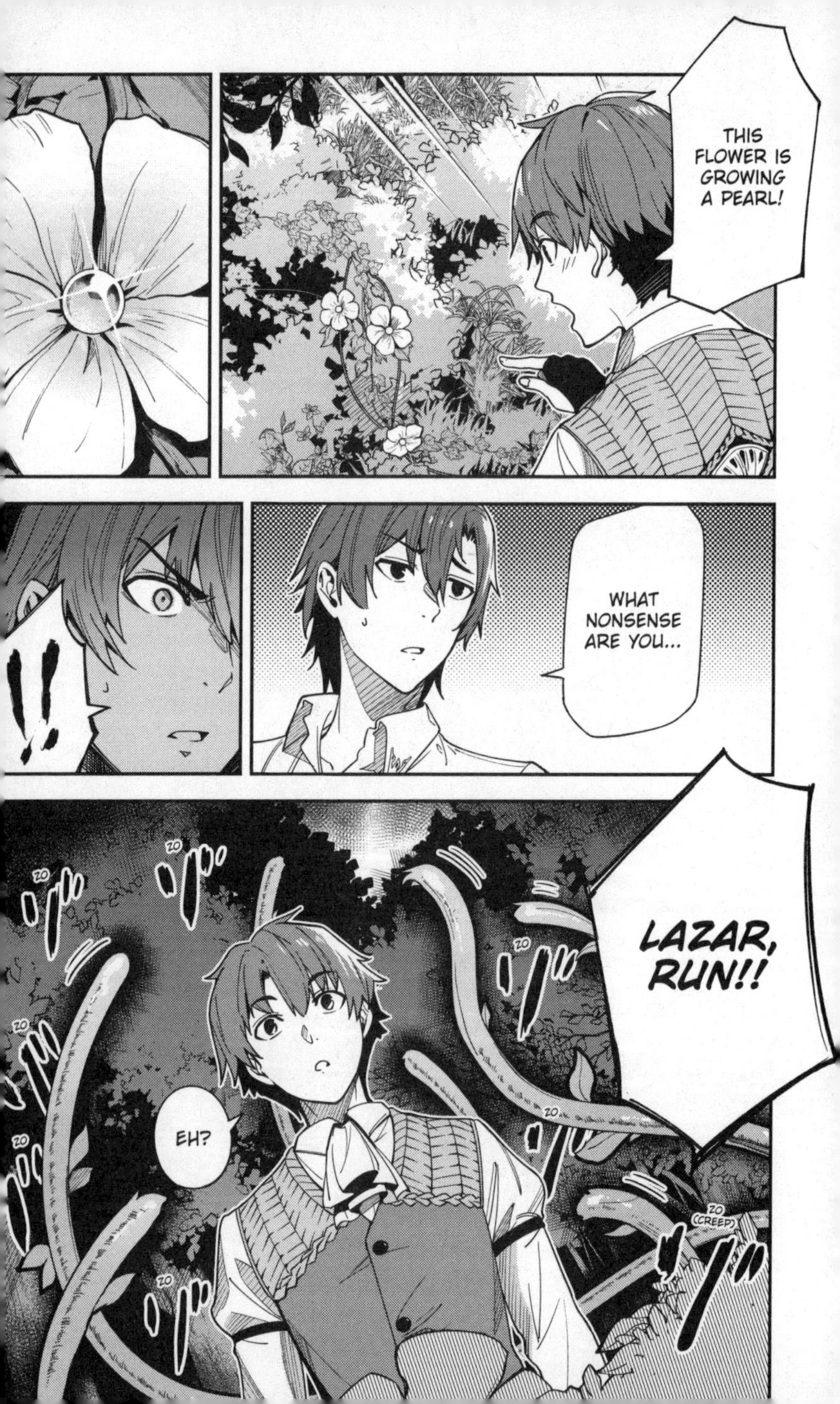
THIS FLOWER IS GROWING A PEARL!
WHAT NONSENSE ARE YOU...
!!
LAZAR, RUN!!
ZO
ZO
ZO (CREEP)
ZO
EH?
ZO
ZO
ZO
ZO

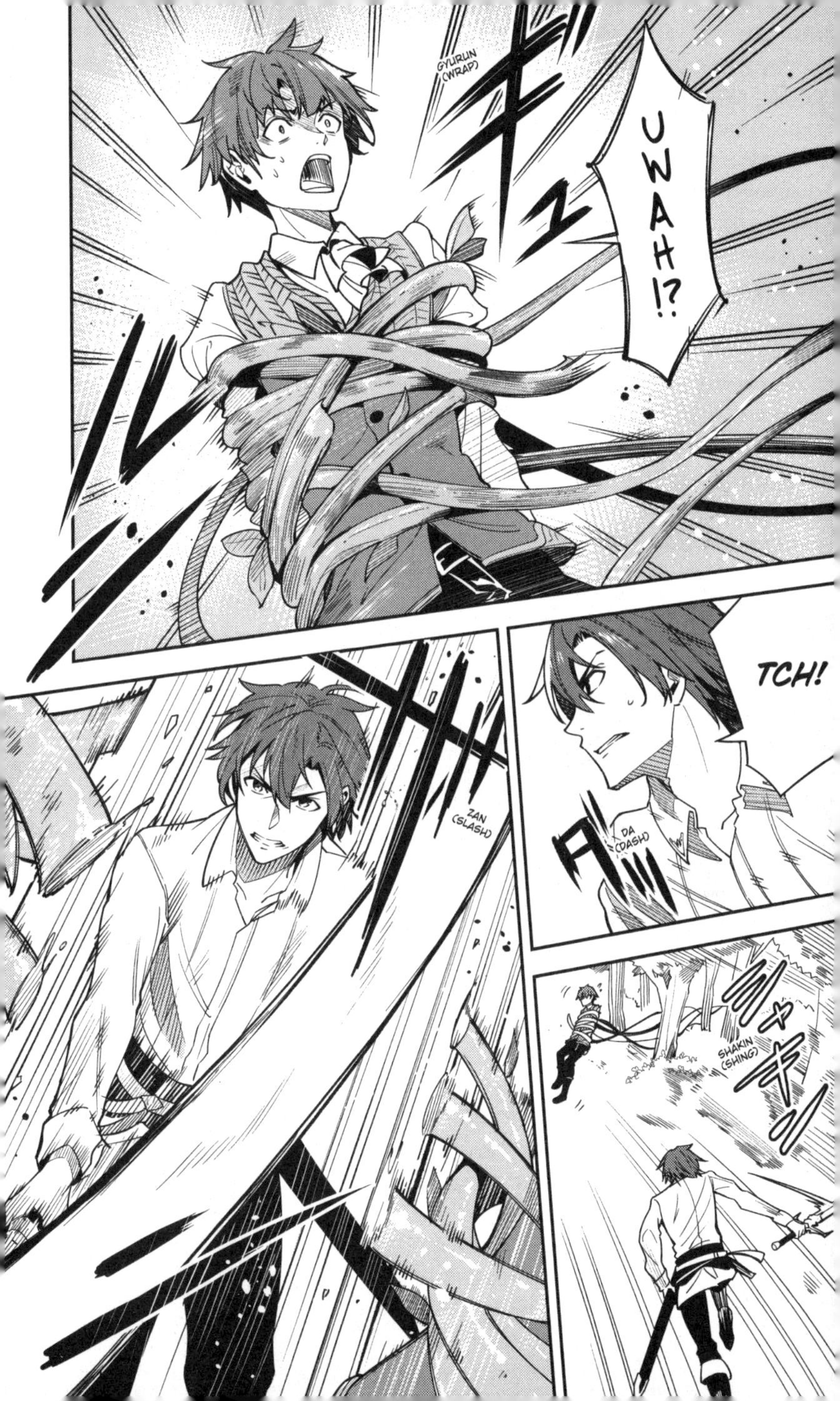
UWAH!?
GYURUN (WRAP)
TCH!
DA (DASH)
ZAN (SLASH)
SHAKIN (SHING)

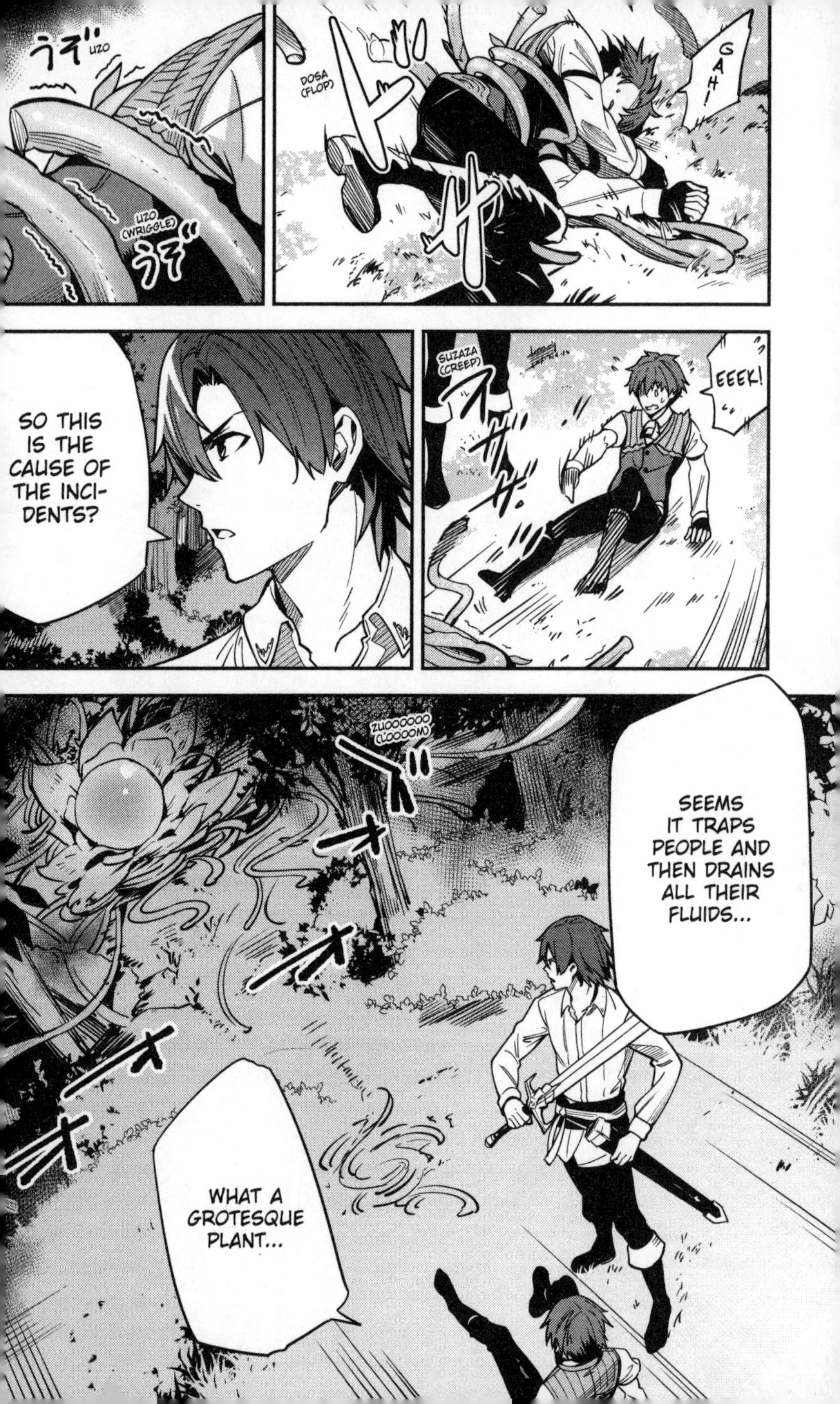

GAH!
DOSA (FLOP)
うぞ UZO
UZO (WRIGGLE)
うぞ
EEEK!
SUZAZA (CREEP)
SO THIS IS THE CAUSE OF THE INCI-DENTS?
ZUOOOOOO (LOOOOM)
SEEMS IT TRAPS PEOPLE AND THEN DRAINS ALL THEIR FLUIDS...
WHAT A GROTESQUE PLANT...

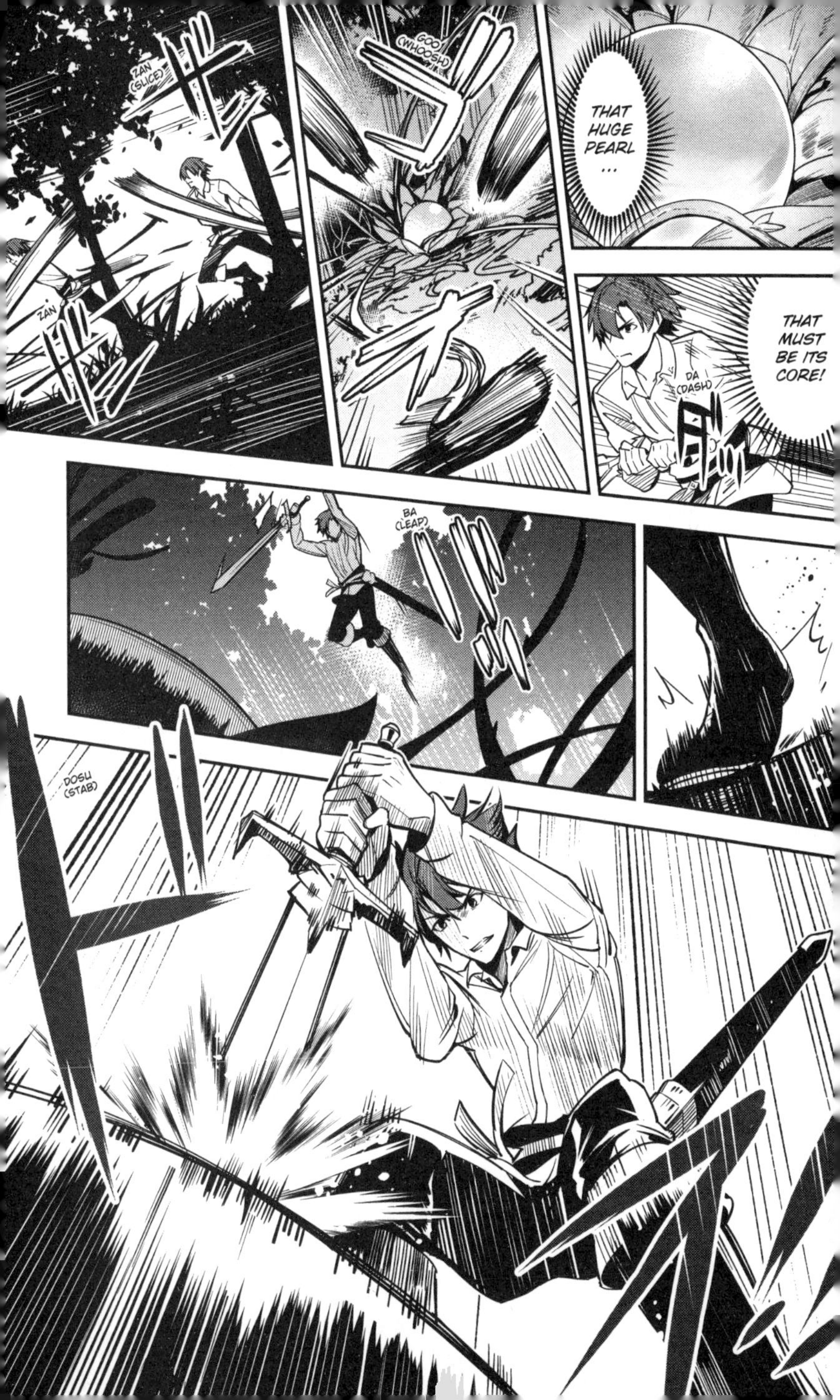

THAT HUGE PEARL ...
THAT MUST BE ITS CORE!
DA (DASH)
GOO (WHOOSH)
ZAN (SLICE)
ZAN
BA (LEAP)
DOSU (STAB)

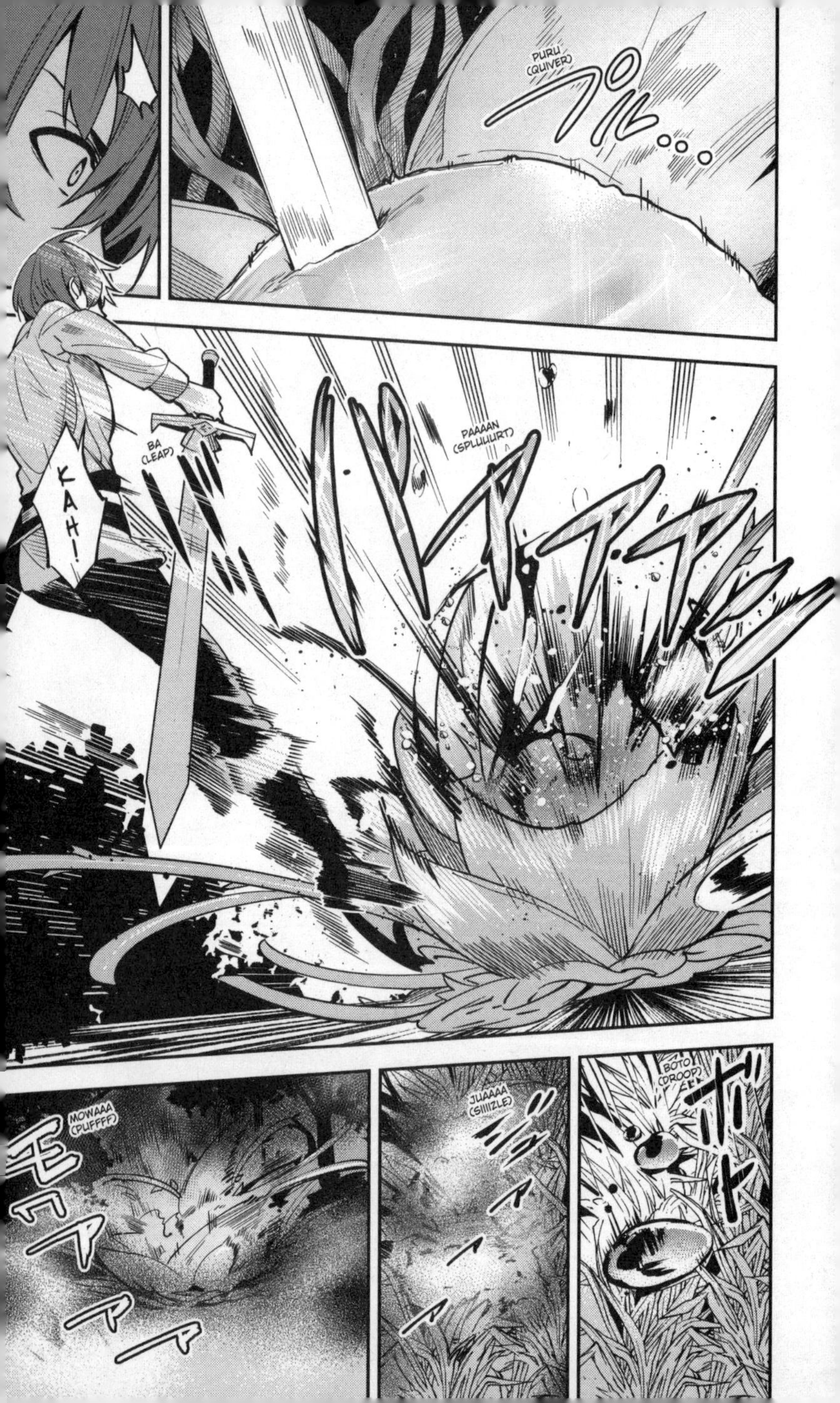
PURU (QUIVER)
PAAAAN (SPLUHURT)
BA (LEAP)
KAHI!
BOTO (DROOP)
JUAAAA (SIIIIZLE)
MOWAAA (PUFFFF)

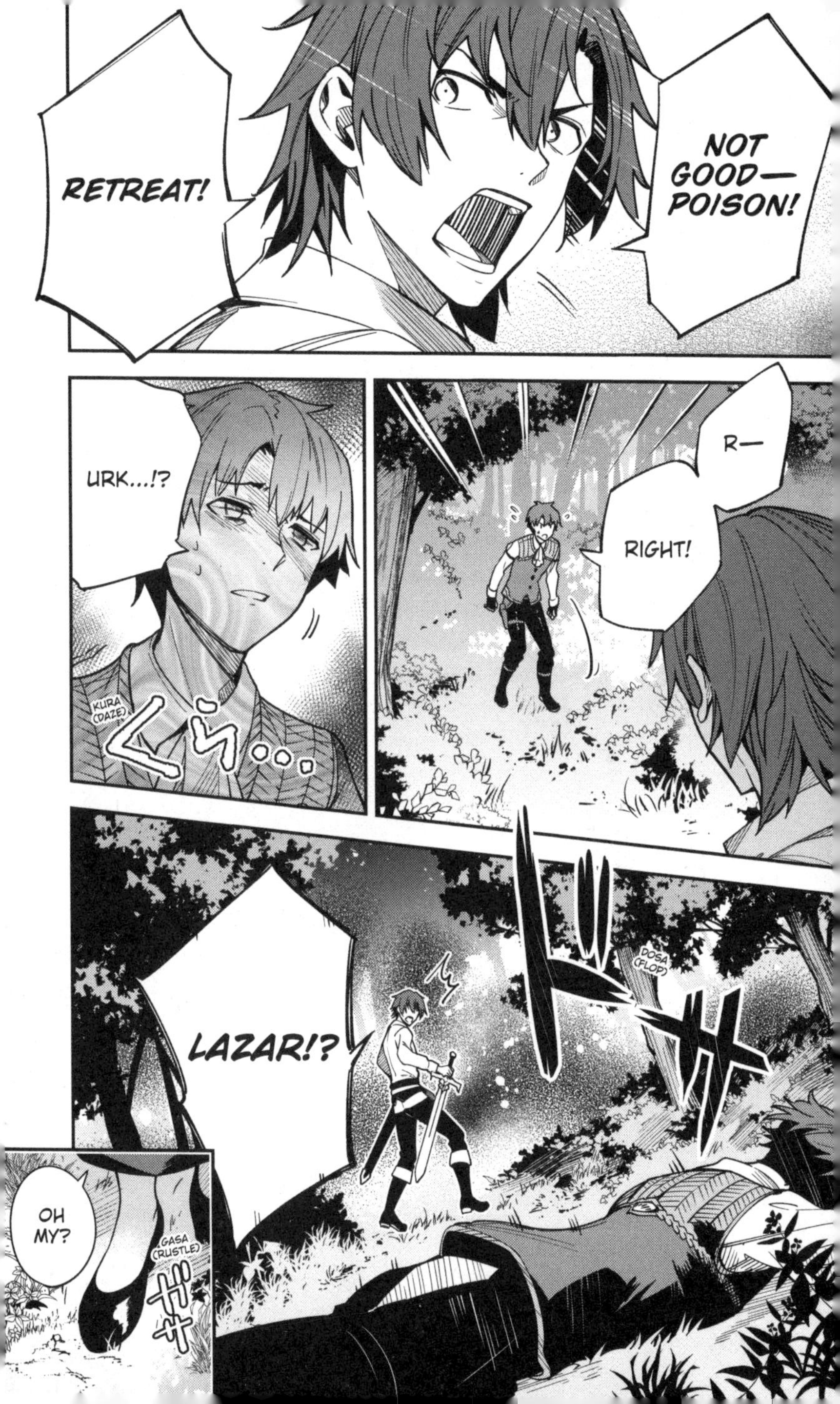
NOT GOOD— POISON!
RETREAT!
R—
RIGHT!
URK...!?
KURA (DAZE)
DOSA (FLOP)
LAZAR!?
OH MY?
GASA (RUSTLE)

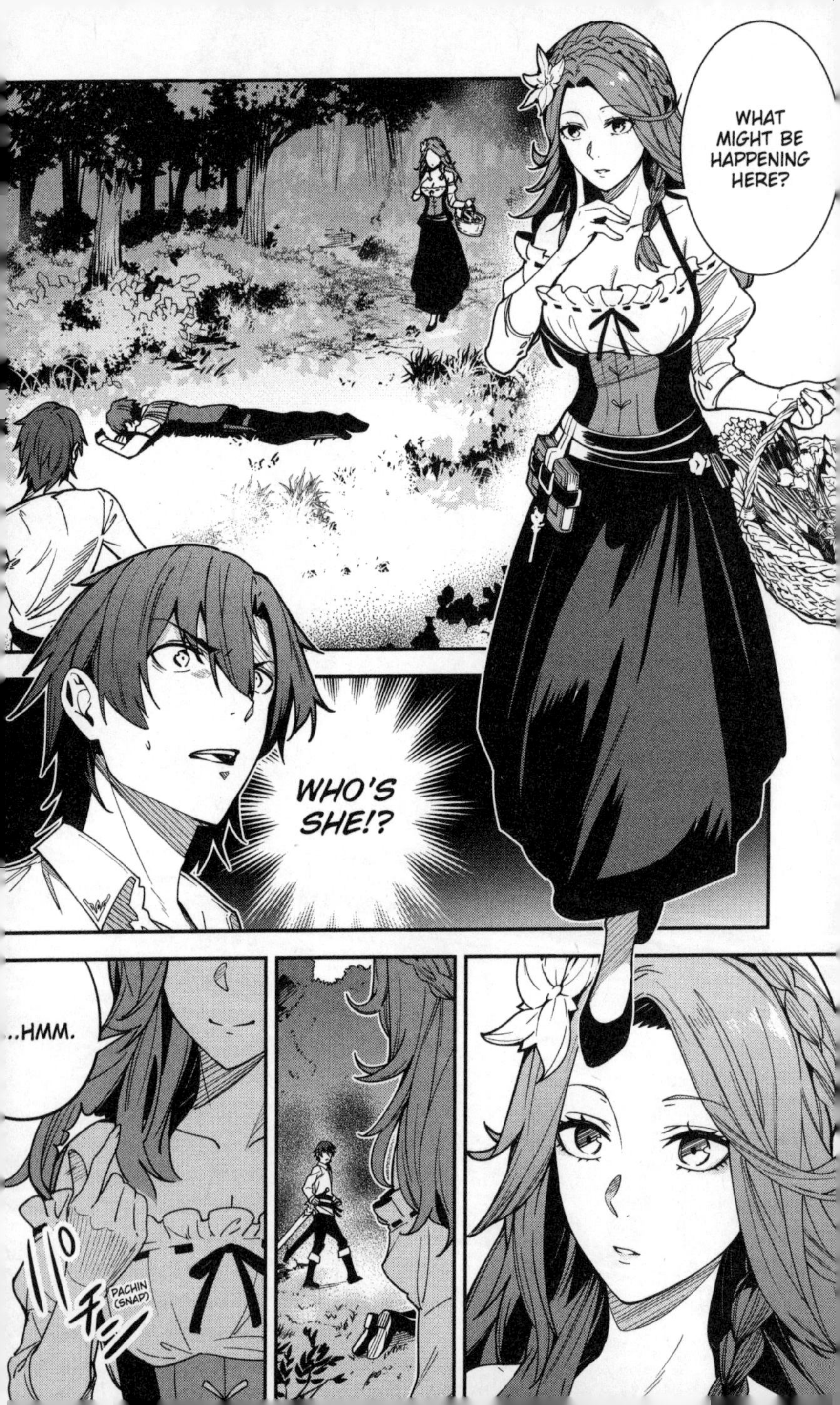

WHAT MIGHT BE HAPPENING HERE?
WHO'S SHE!?
...HMM.
パチン
PACHIN (SNAP)

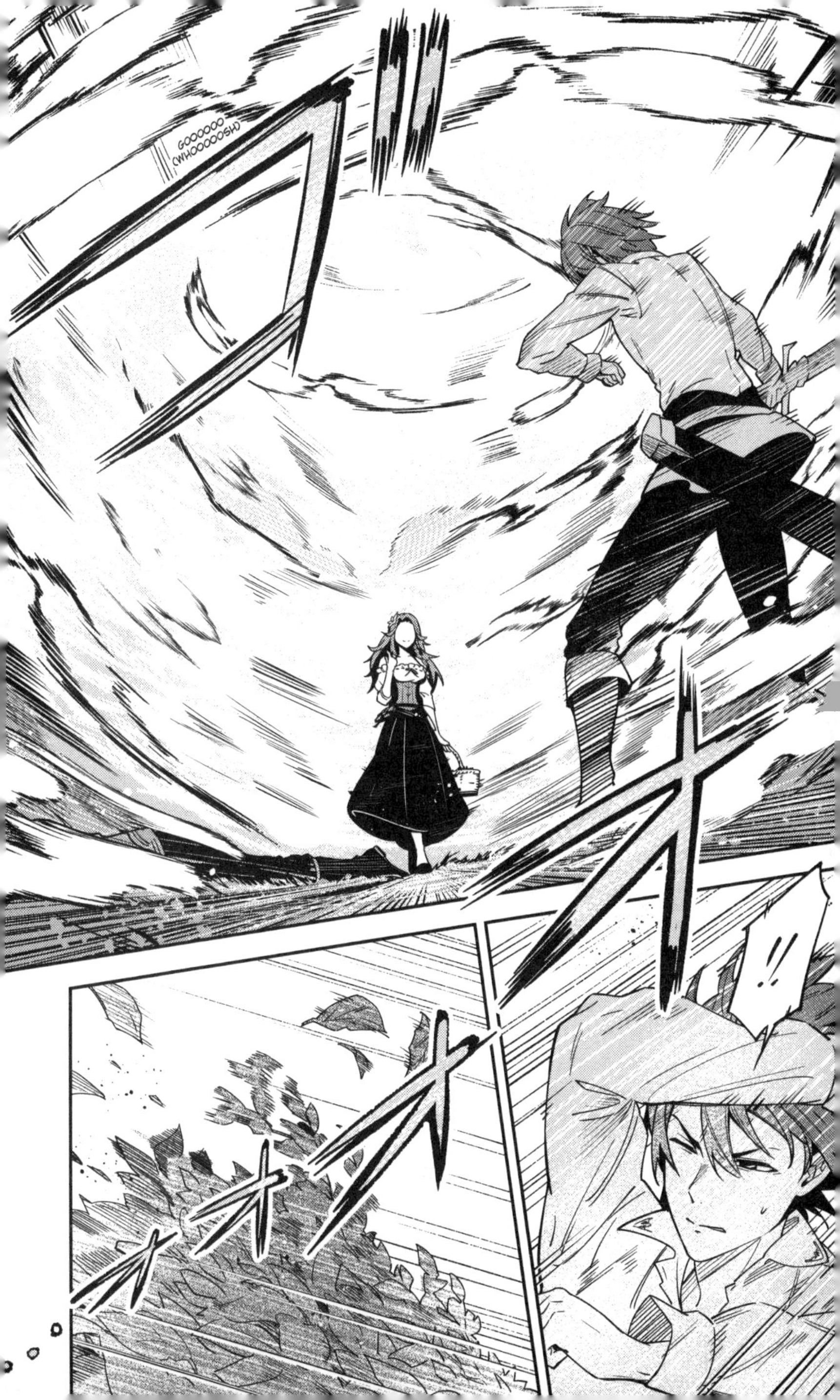
GOOOOOO (WHOOOOOOSH)
!!

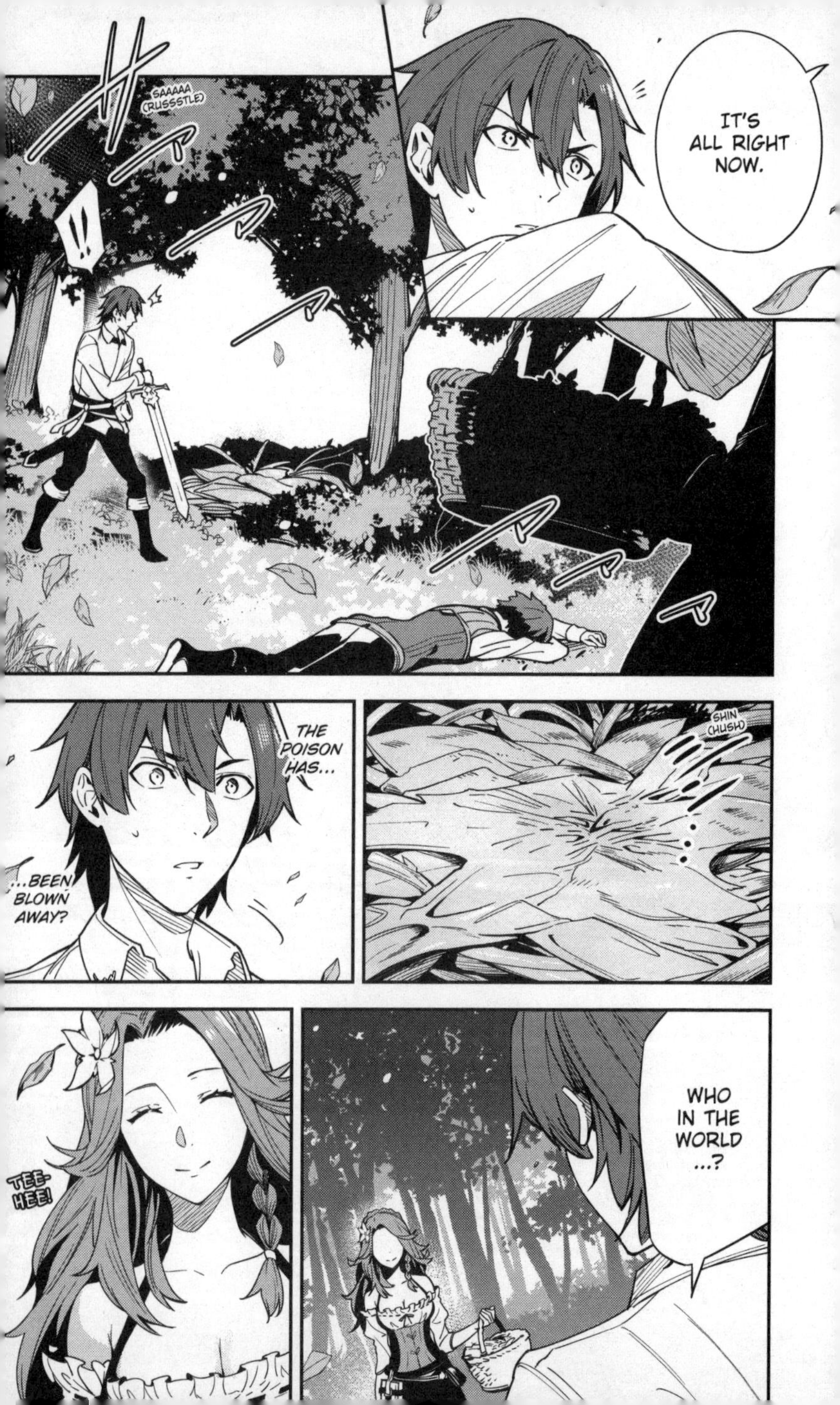
IT'S ALL RIGHT NOW.
SAAAAA (RUSSSTLE)
!!
SHIN (HUSH)
THE POISON HAS...
...BEEN BLOWN AWAY?
WHO IN THE WORLD ...?
TEE-HEE!

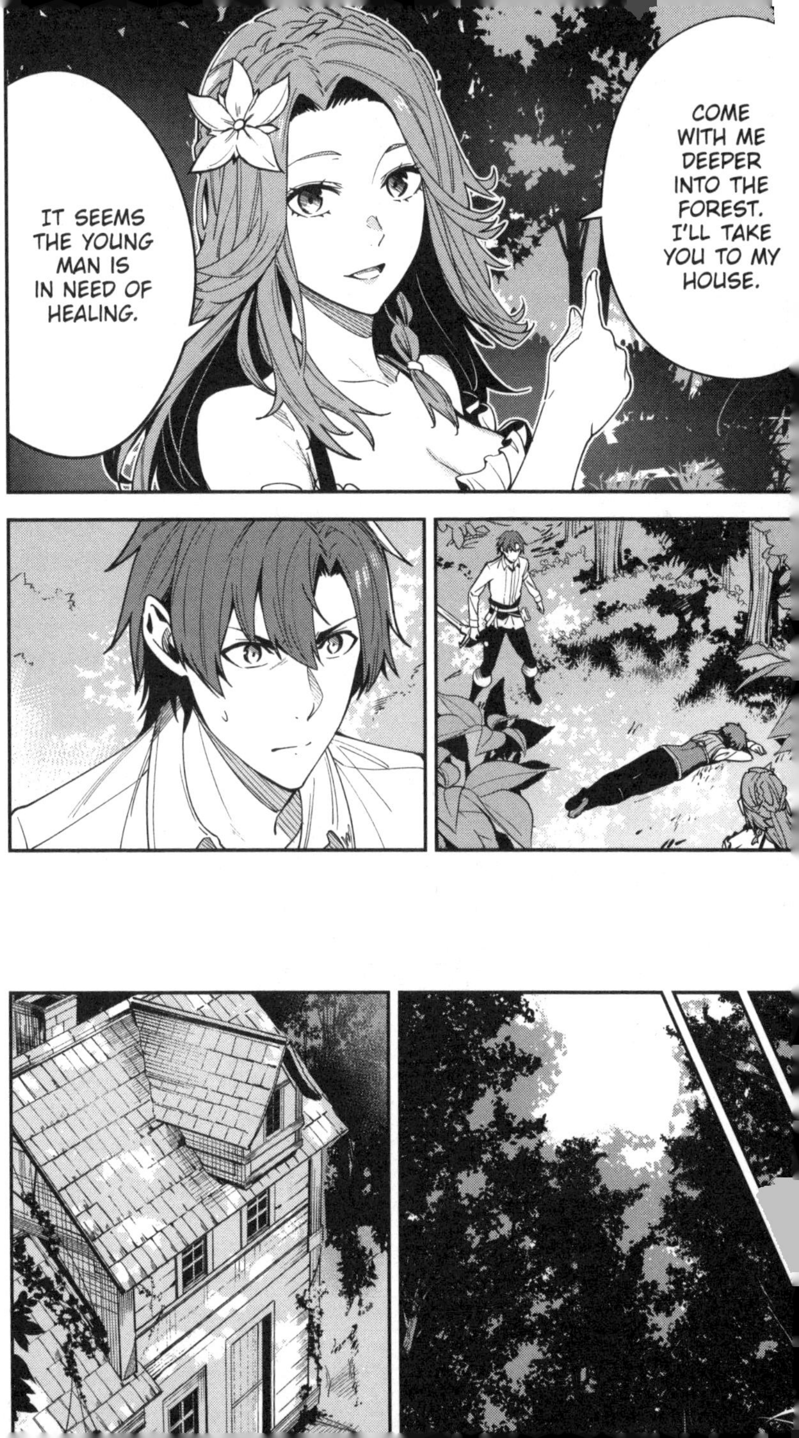
COME WITH ME DEEPER INTO THE FOREST. I'LL TAKE YOU TO MY HOUSE.
IT SEEMS THE YOUNG MAN IS IN NEED OF HEALING.

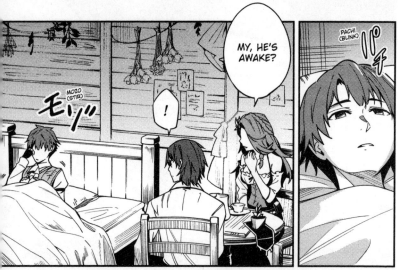

PACHI (BLINK)
パチ
MY, HE'S AWAKE?
!
MOZO (STIR)
モゾ
HOW DO YOU FEEL?
YOUR HIGHNESS... I...
SEEMS THERE WAS A MIASMA BACK THERE TOO.
SORRY I DIDN'T NOTICE.
NO, I'M...
...QUITE SORRY MYSELF.

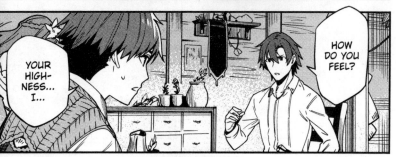

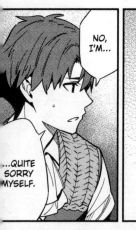

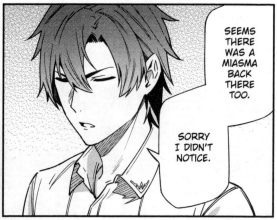

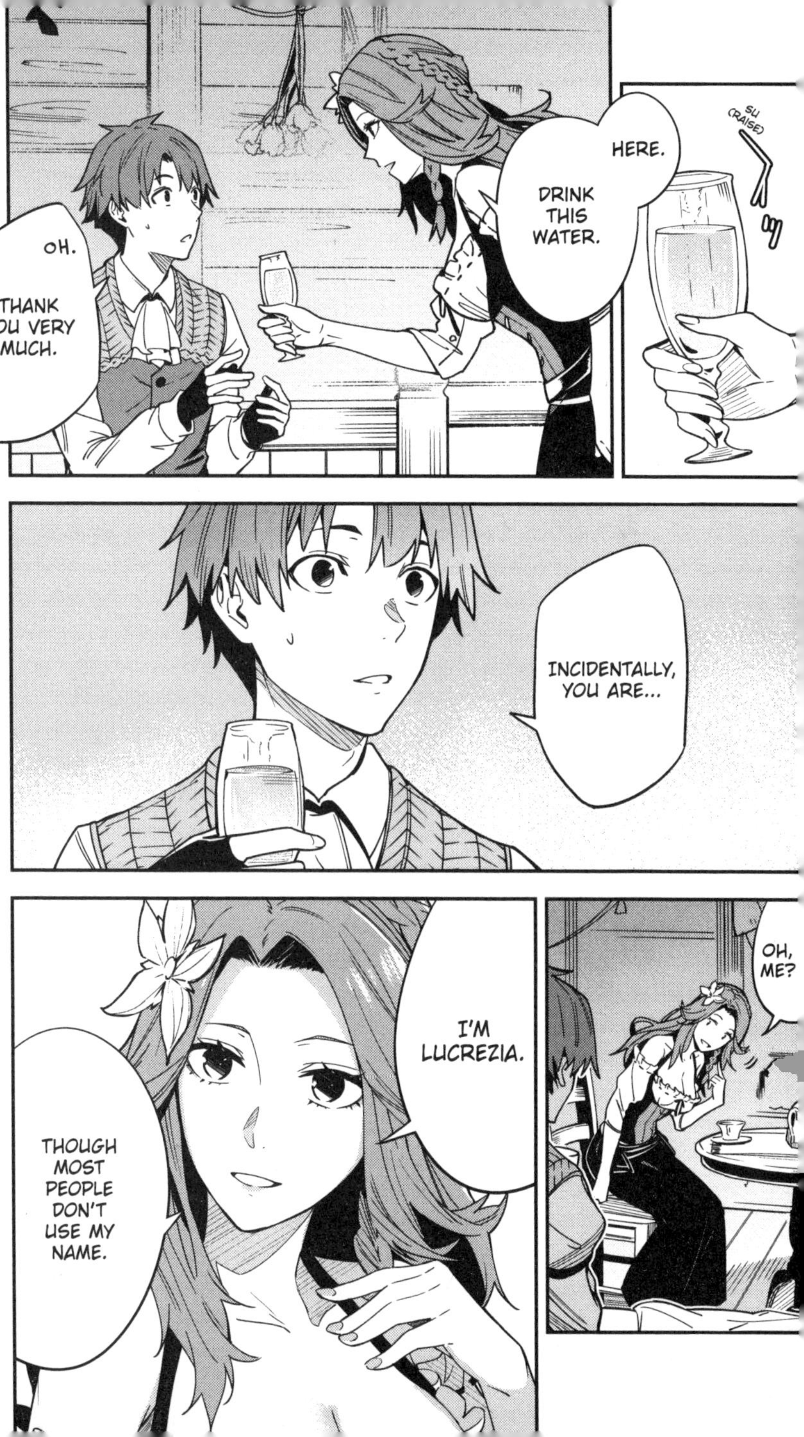
SU (RAISE)
HERE.
DRINK THIS WATER.
OH.
THANK YOU VERY MUCH.
INCIDENTALLY, YOU ARE...
OH, ME?
I'M LUCREZIA.
THOUGH MOST PEOPLE DON'T USE MY NAME.

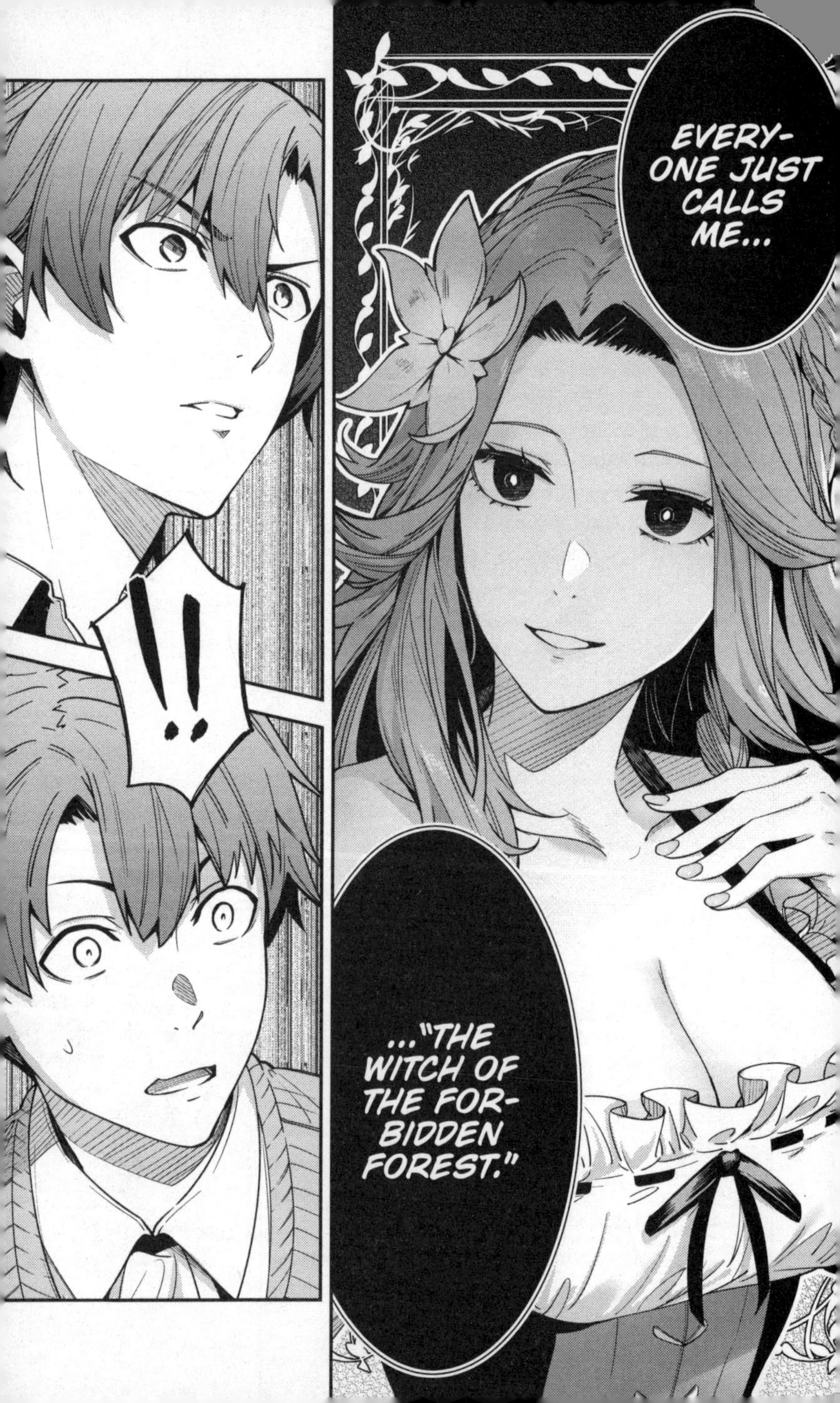
EVERY-ONE JUST CALLS ME...
..."THE WITCH OF THE FOR-BIDDEN FOREST."
!!

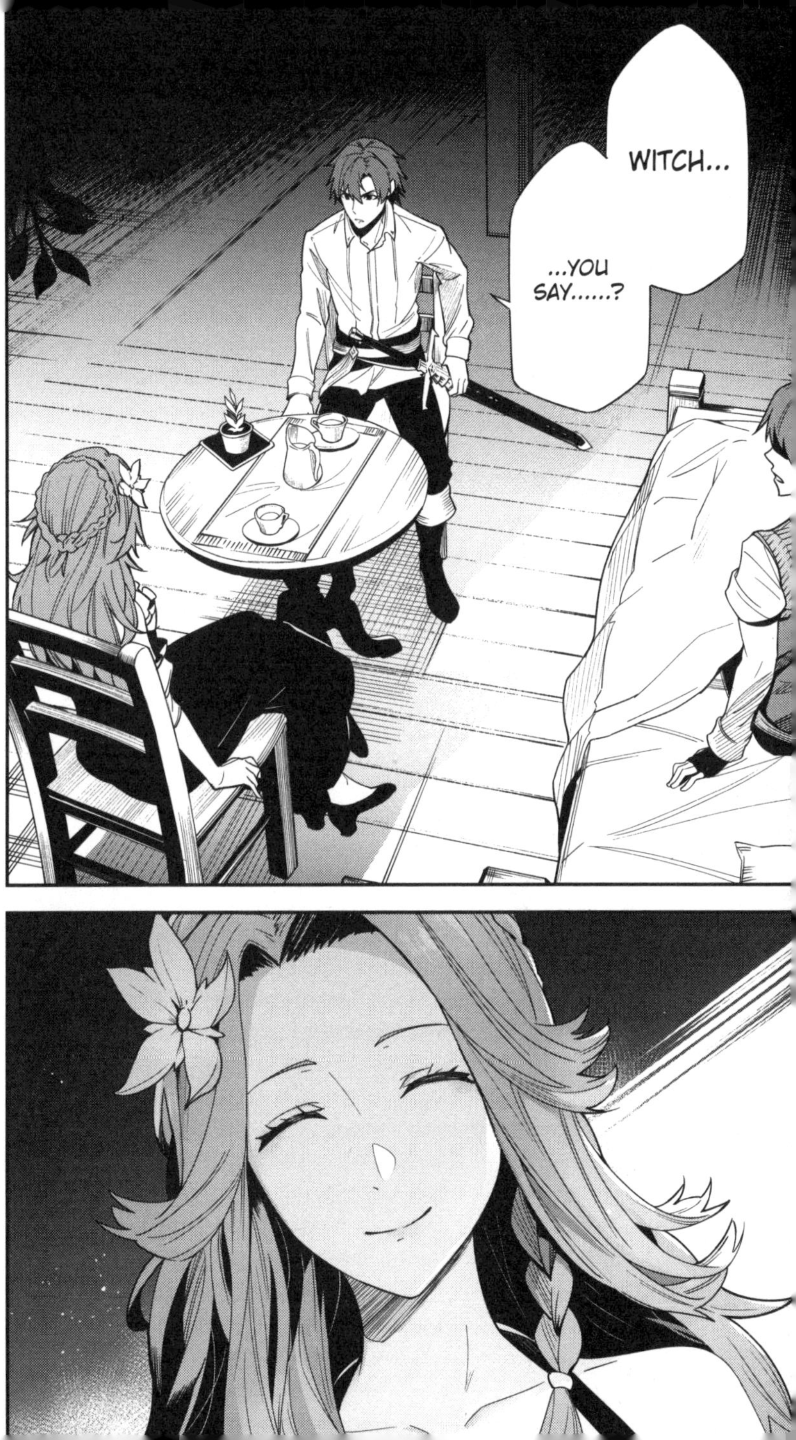
WITCH...
...YOU SAY......?

Unnamed Memory

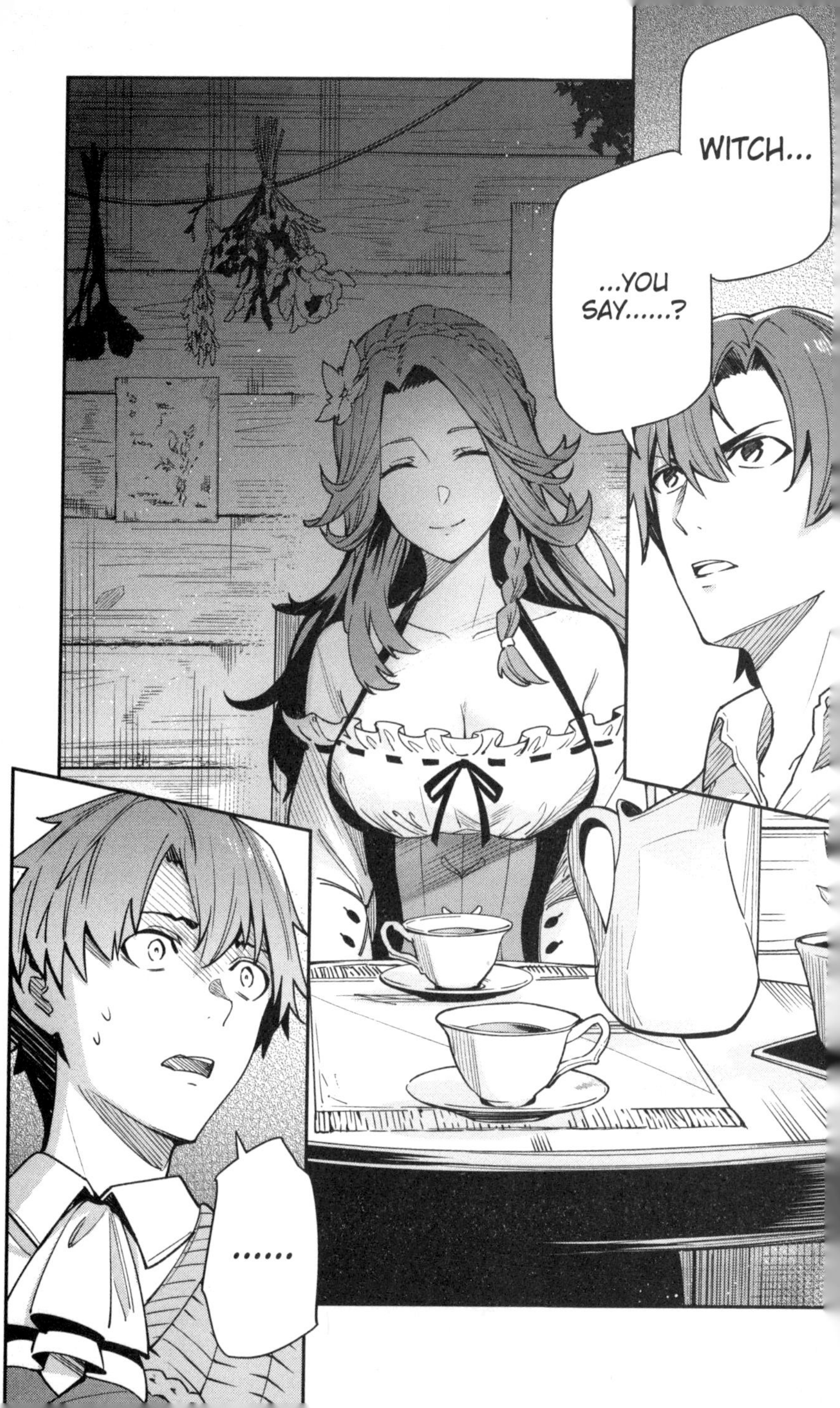
WITCH...
...YOU SAY......?
......

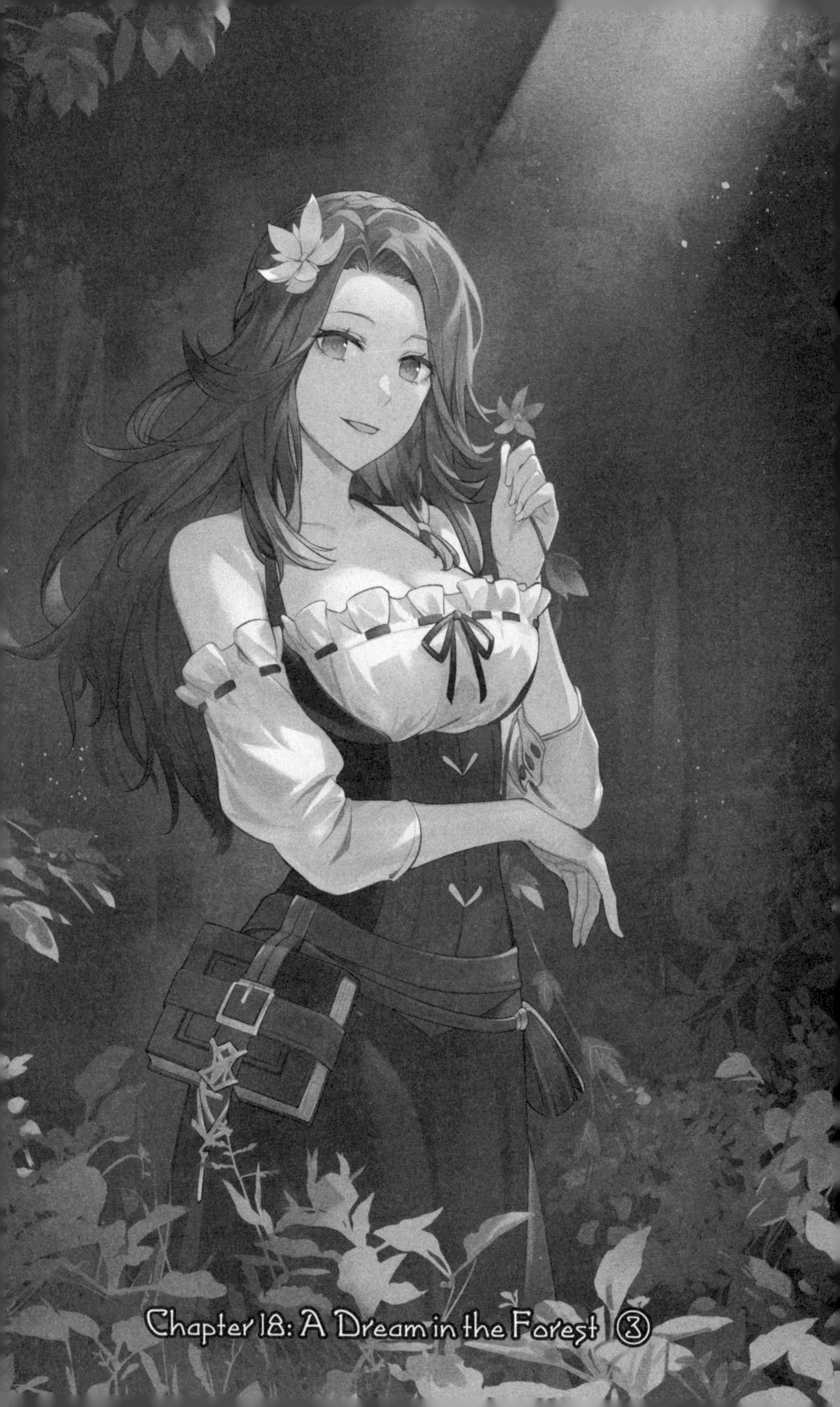

Chapter 18: A Dream in the Forest ③

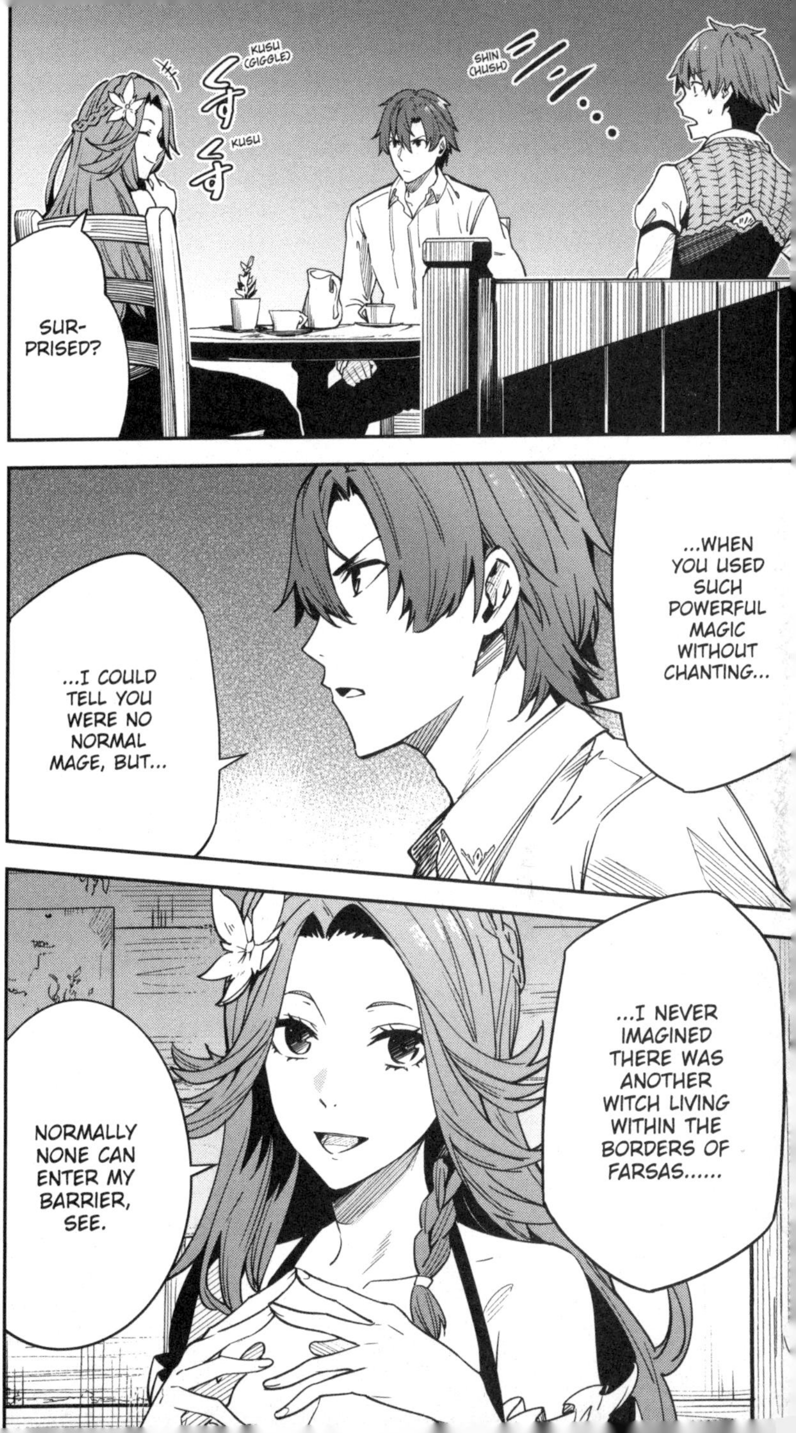
SHIN (HUSH)
KUSU (GIGGLE)
くすくす
KUSU
SUR-PRISED?
...WHEN YOU USED SUCH POWERFUL MAGIC WITHOUT CHANTING...
...I COULD TELL YOU WERE NO NORMAL MAGE, BUT...
...I NEVER IMAGINED THERE WAS ANOTHER WITCH LIVING WITHIN THE BORDERS OF FARSAS......
NORMALLY NONE CAN ENTER MY BARRIER, SEE.

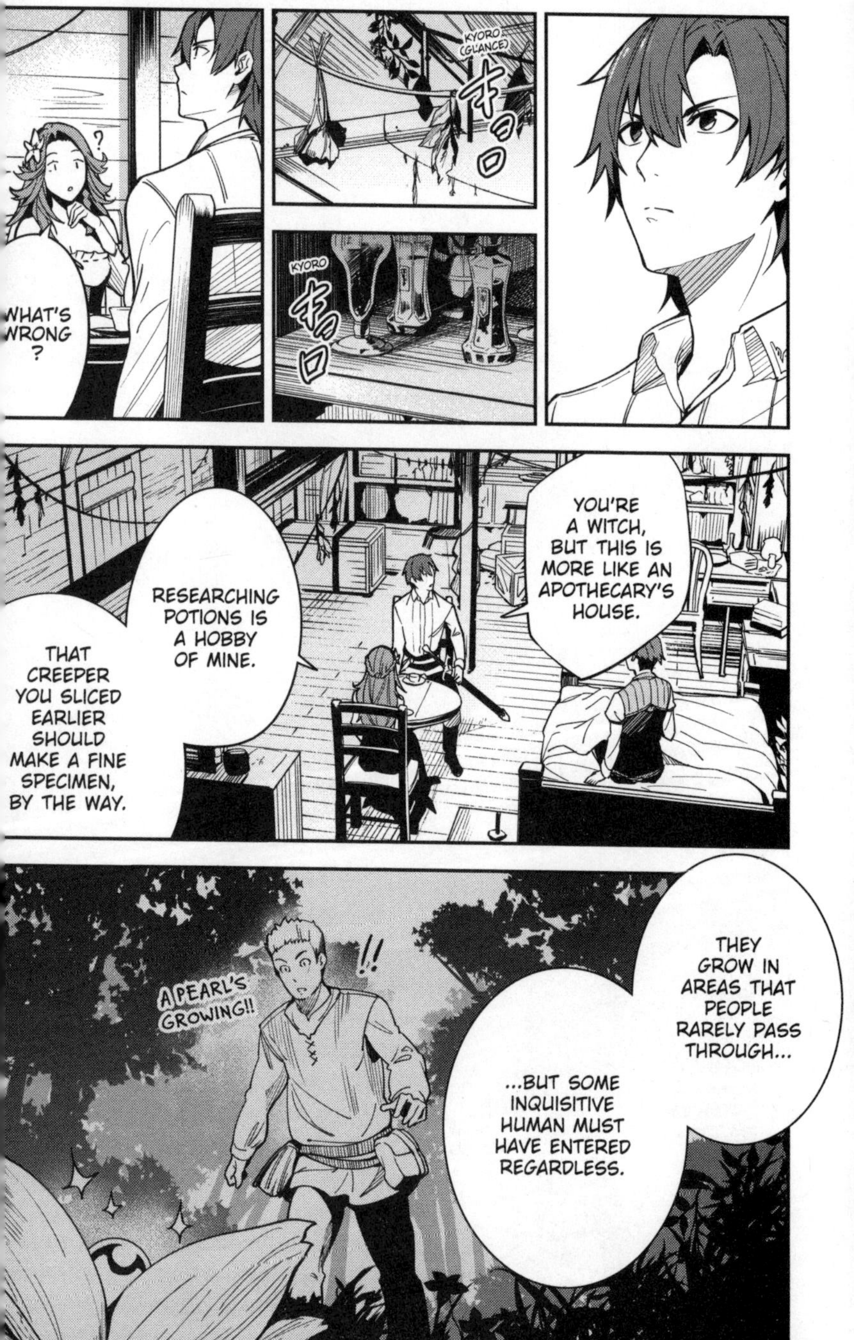
KYORO (GLANCE)
キョロ
KYORO
キョロ
?
WHAT'S WRONG?
YOU'RE A WITCH, BUT THIS IS MORE LIKE AN APOTHECARY'S HOUSE.
RESEARCHING POTIONS IS A HOBBY OF MINE.
THAT CREEPER YOU SLICED EARLIER SHOULD MAKE A FINE SPECIMEN, BY THE WAY.
THEY GROW IN AREAS THAT PEOPLE RARELY PASS THROUGH...
...BUT SOME INQUISITIVE HUMAN MUST HAVE ENTERED REGARDLESS.
!!
A PEARL'S GROWING!!

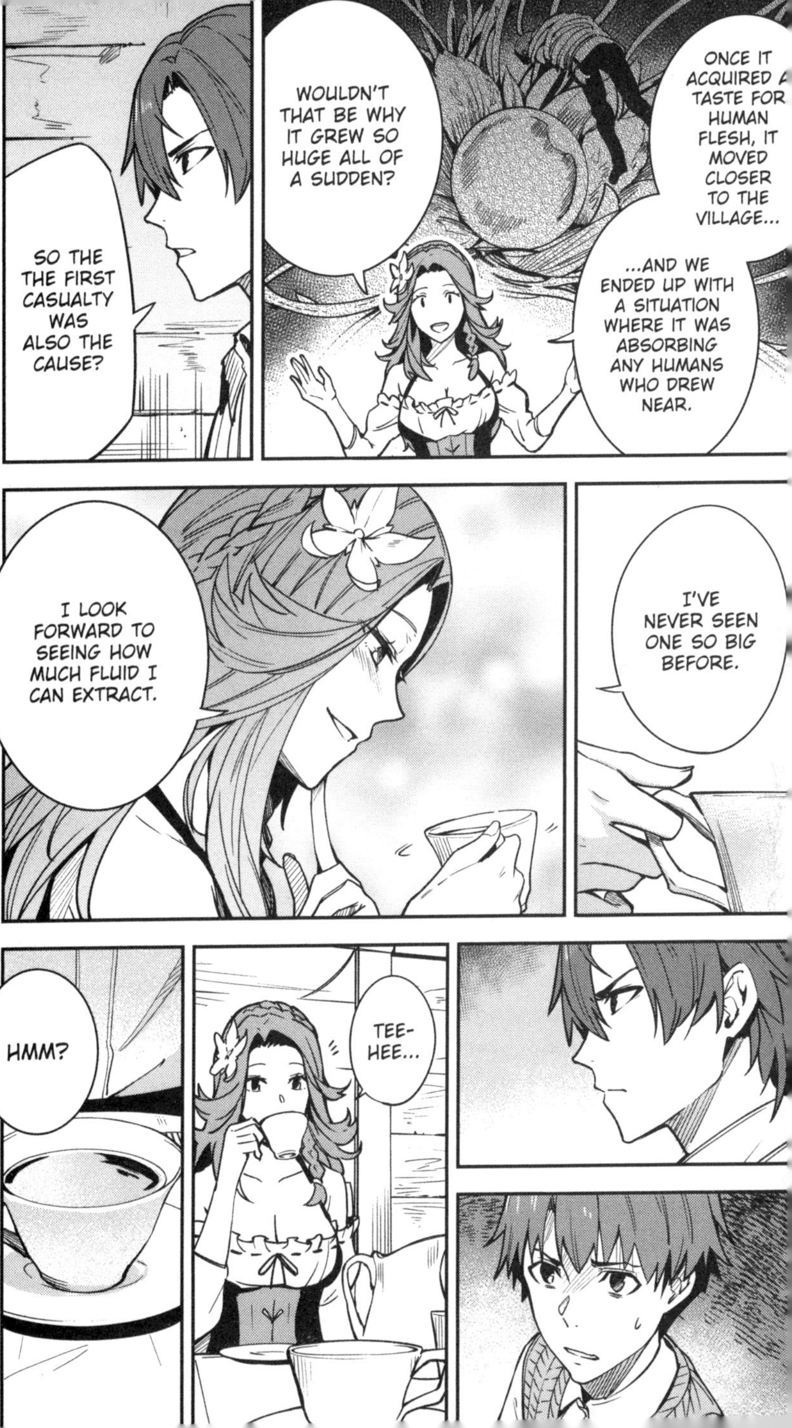
ONCE IT ACQUIRED A TASTE FOR HUMAN FLESH, IT MOVED CLOSER TO THE VILLAGE...
WOULDN'T THAT BE WHY IT GREW SO HUGE ALL OF A SUDDEN?
...AND WE ENDED UP WITH A SITUATION WHERE IT WAS ABSORBING ANY HUMANS WHO DREW NEAR.
SO THE THE FIRST CASUALTY WAS ALSO THE CAUSE?
I'VE NEVER SEEN ONE SO BIG BEFORE.
I LOOK FORWARD TO SEEING HOW MUCH FLUID I CAN EXTRACT.
TEE-HEE...
HMM?

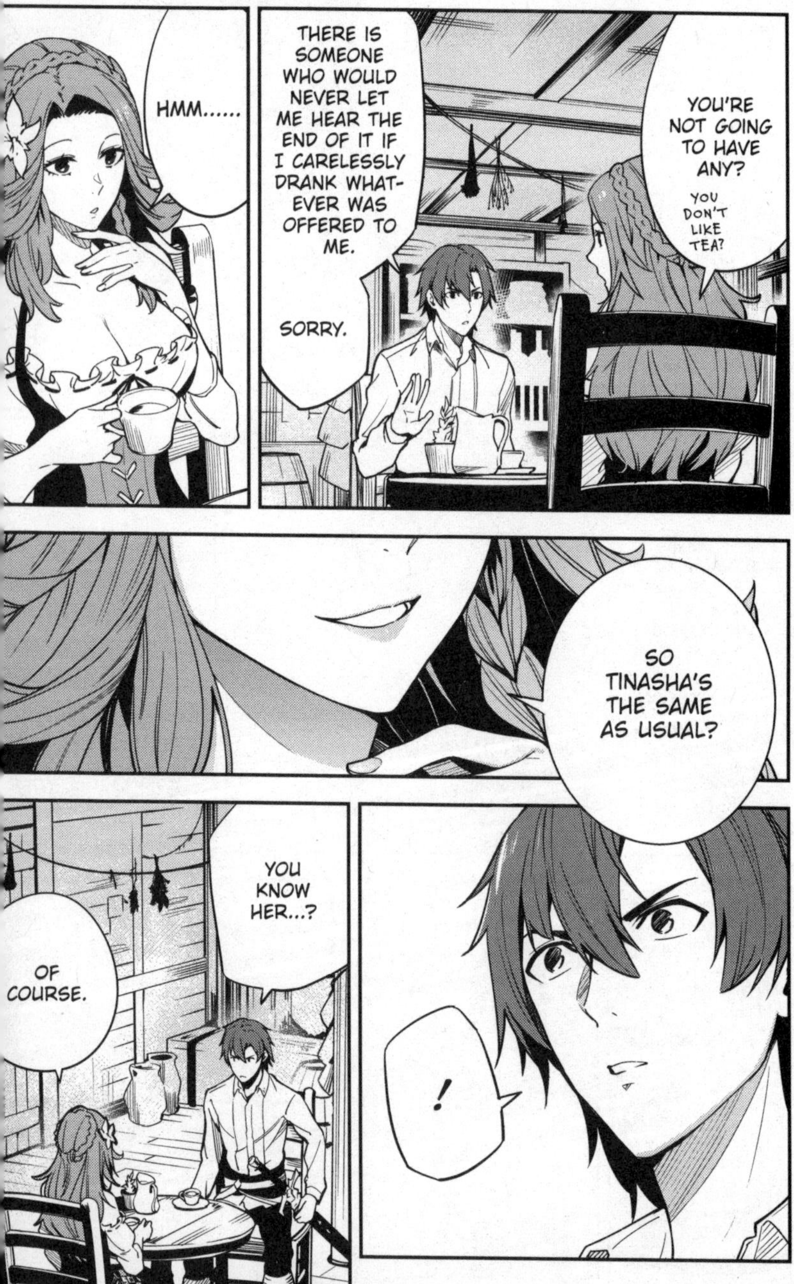
YOU'RE NOT GOING TO HAVE ANY?
YOU DON'T LIKE TEA?
THERE IS SOMEONE WHO WOULD NEVER LET ME HEAR THE END OF IT IF I CARELESSLY DRANK WHATEVER WAS OFFERED TO ME.
SORRY.
HMM......
SO TINASHA'S THE SAME AS USUAL?
!
YOU KNOW HER...?
OF COURSE.

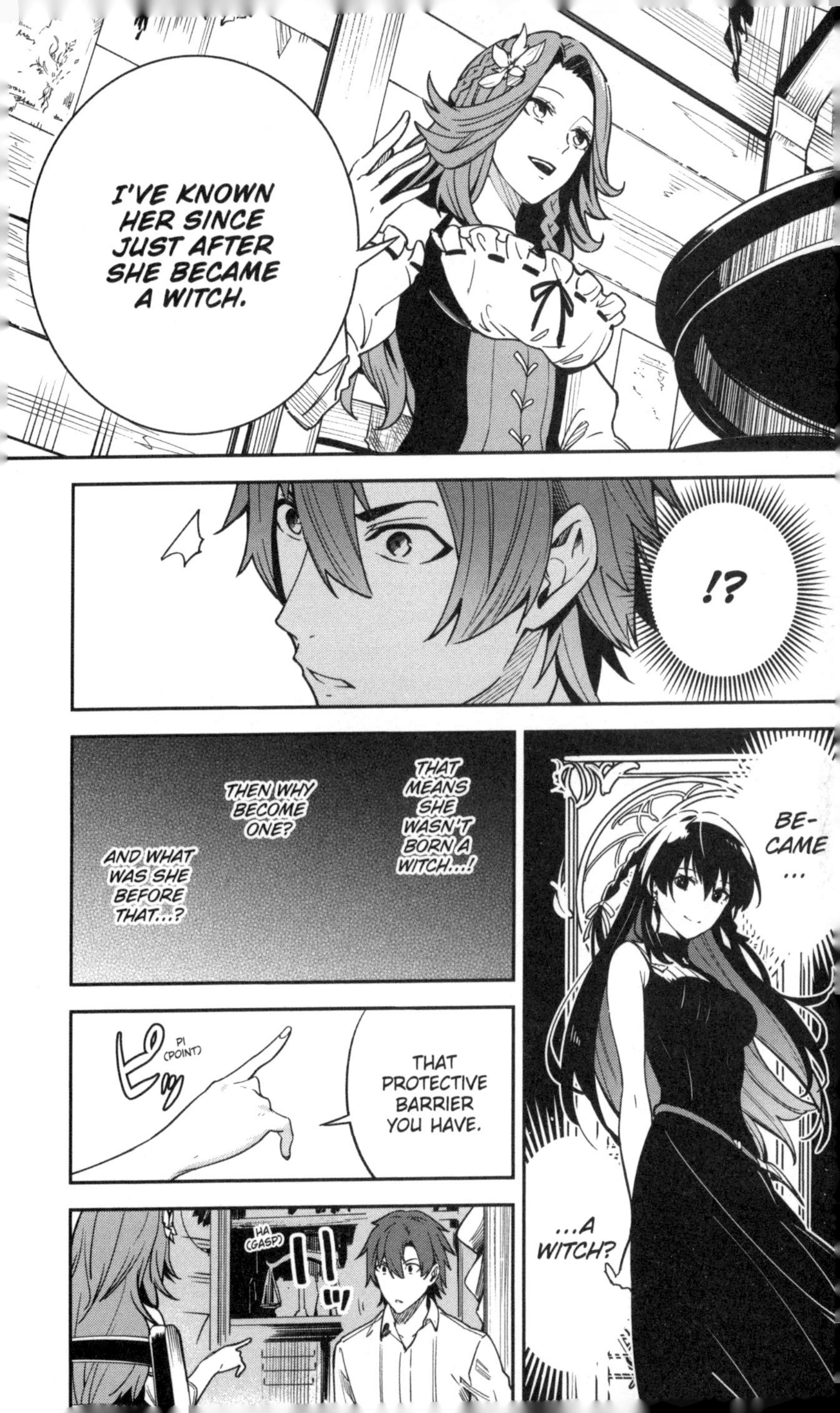
I'VE KNOWN HER SINCE JUST AFTER SHE BECAME A WITCH.
!?
BE-CAME...
...A WITCH?
THAT MEANS SHE WASN'T BORN A WITCH...!
THEN WHY BECOME ONE?
AND WHAT WAS SHE BEFORE THAT...?
THAT PROTECTIVE BARRIER YOU HAVE.
PI (POINT)
HA (GASP)

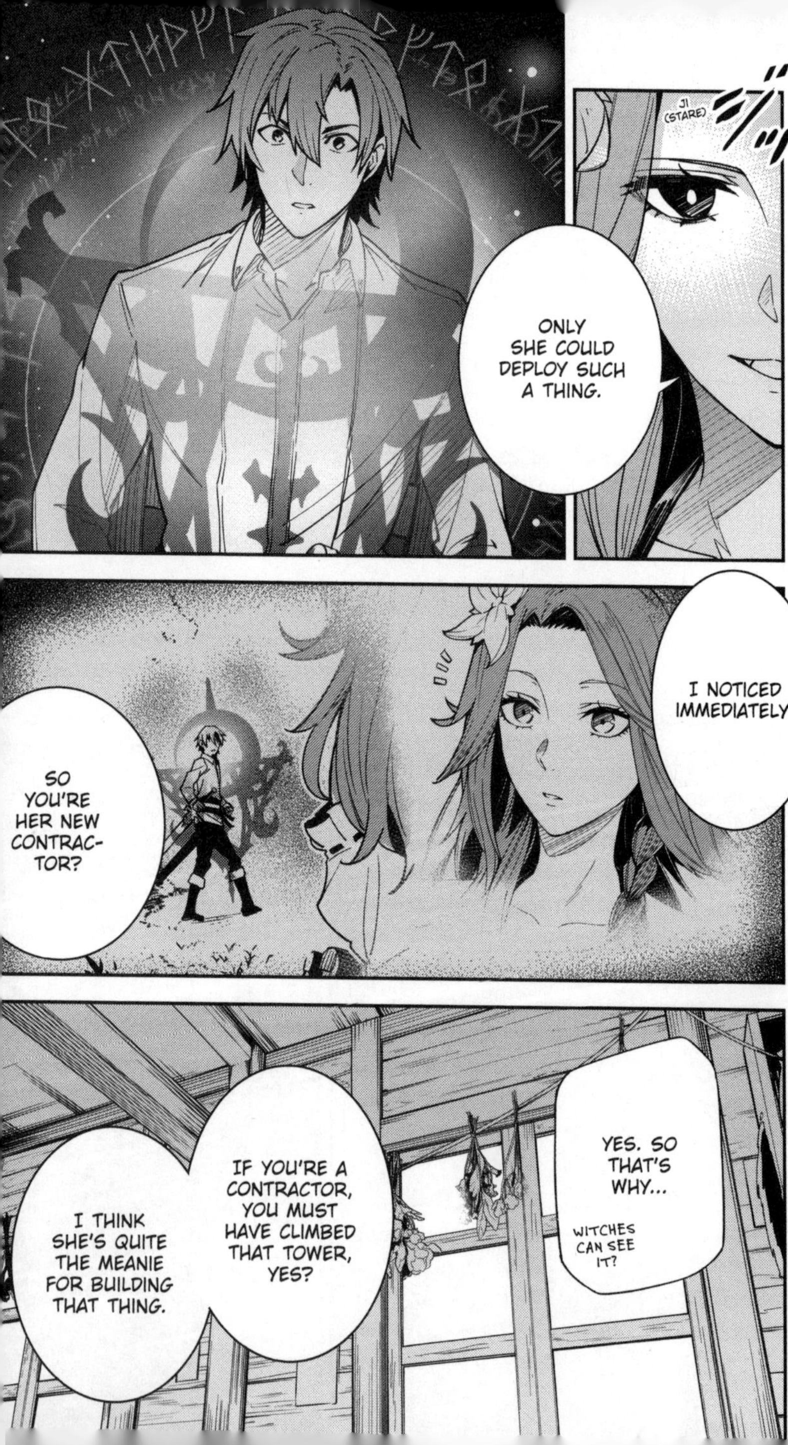

JI (STARE)
ジッ
ONLY SHE COULD DEPLOY SUCH A THING.
I NOTICED IMMEDIATELY.
SO YOU'RE HER NEW CONTRAC-TOR?
YES. SO THAT'S WHY...
WITCHES CAN SEE IT?
IF YOU'RE A CONTRACTOR, YOU MUST HAVE CLIMBED THAT TOWER, YES?
I THINK SHE'S QUITE THE MEANIE FOR BUILDING THAT THING.

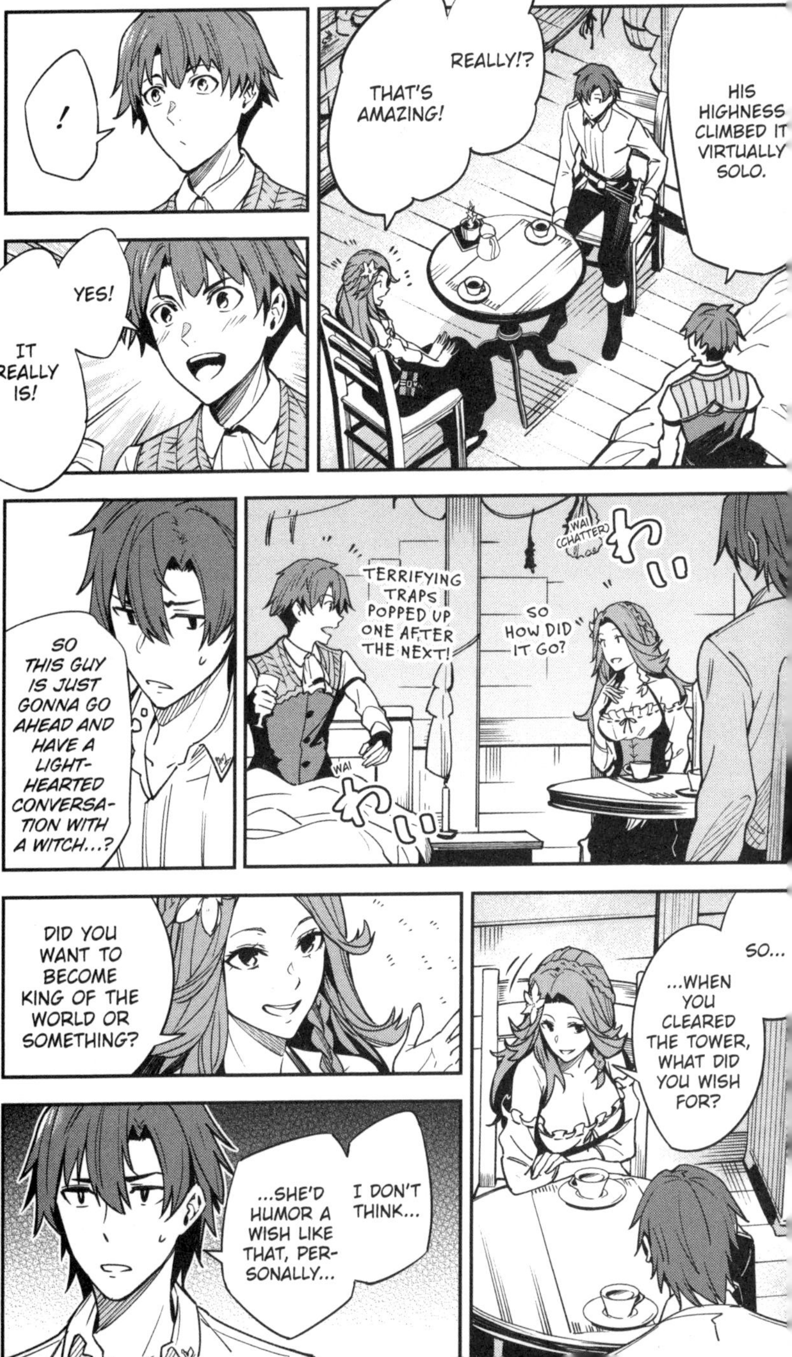
HIS HIGHNESS CLIMBED IT VIRTUALLY SOLO.
REALLY!?
THAT'S AMAZING!
!
YES!
IT REALLY IS!
WAI (CHATTER)
SO HOW DID IT GO?
TERRIFYING TRAPS POPPED UP ONE AFTER THE NEXT!
WAI
SO THIS GUY IS JUST GONNA GO AHEAD AND HAVE A LIGHT-HEARTED CONVERSA-TION WITH A WITCH...?
SO...
...WHEN YOU CLEARED THE TOWER, WHAT DID YOU WISH FOR?
DID YOU WANT TO BECOME KING OF THE WORLD OR SOMETHING?
I DON'T THINK...
...SHE'D HUMOR A WISH LIKE THAT, PER-SONALLY...

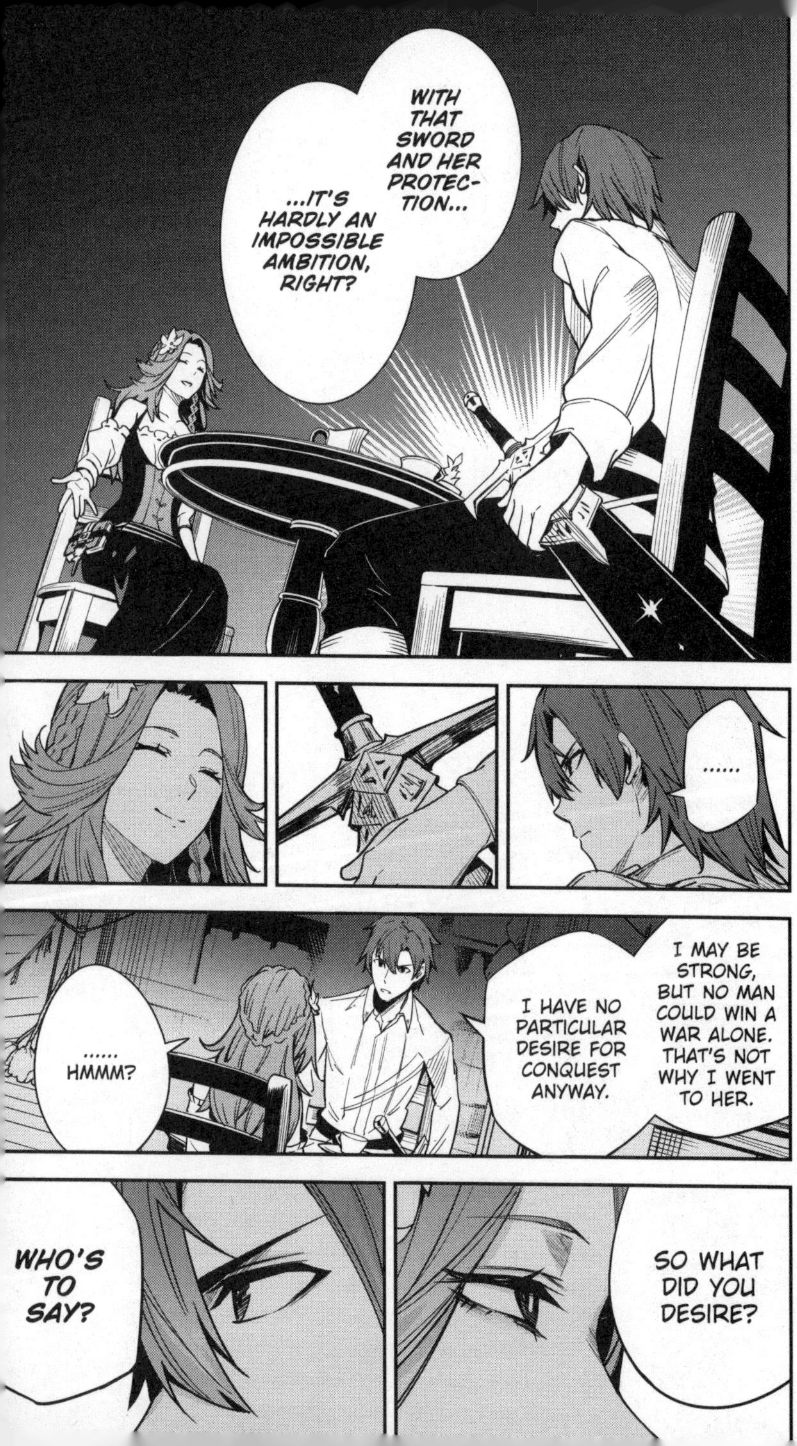
WITH THAT SWORD AND HER PROTECTION...
...IT'S HARDLY AN IMPOSSIBLE AMBITION, RIGHT?
......
I MAY BE STRONG, BUT NO MAN COULD WIN A WAR ALONE. THAT'S NOT WHY I WENT TO HER.
I HAVE NO PARTICULAR DESIRE FOR CONQUEST ANYWAY.
...... HMMM?
SO WHAT DID YOU DESIRE?
WHO'S TO SAY?

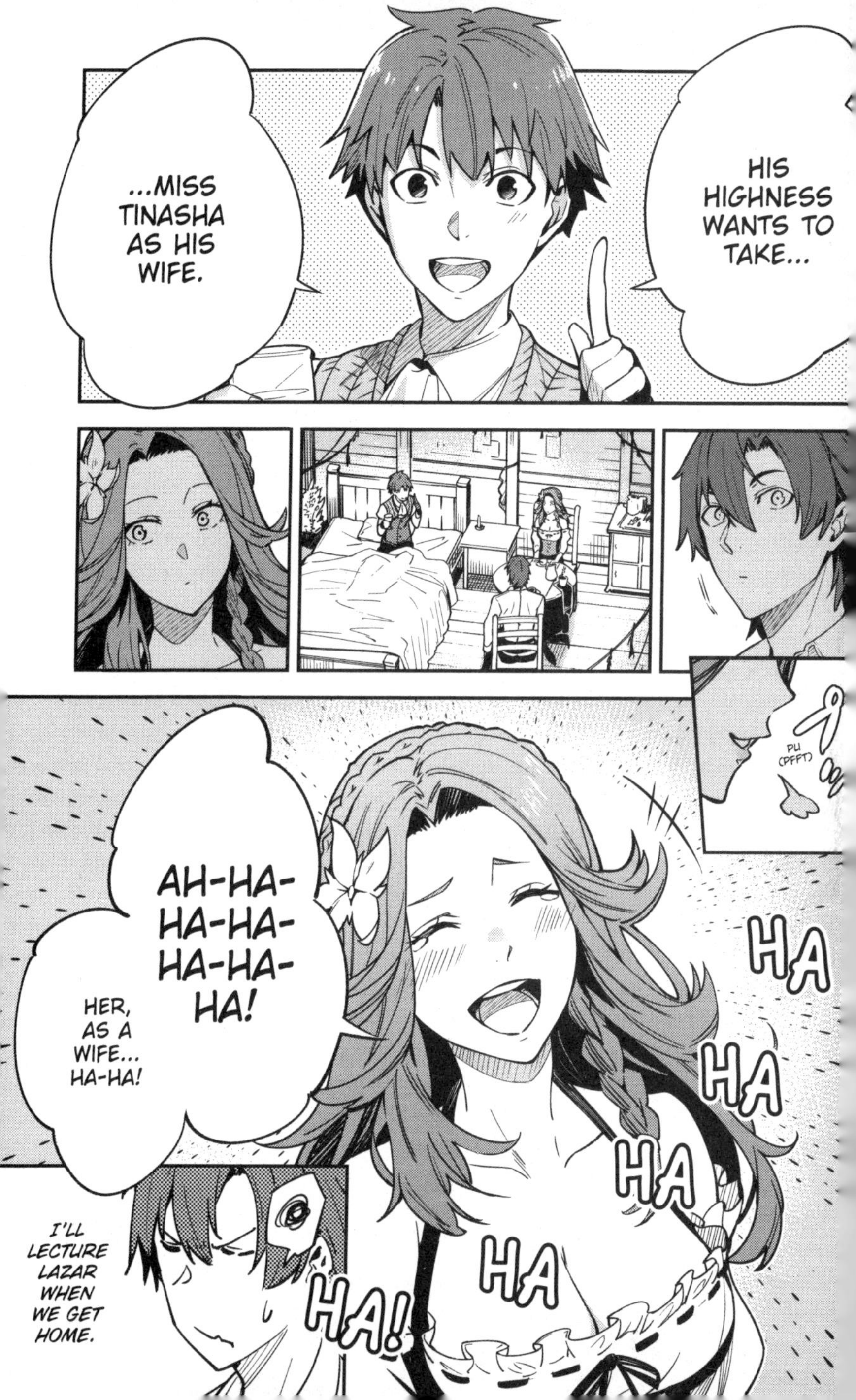

HIS HIGHNESS WANTS TO TAKE...
...MISS TINASHA AS HIS WIFE.
PU (PFFT)
AH-HA-HA-HA-HA-HA-HA!
HER, AS A WIFE... HA-HA!
HA
HA
HA
HA
HA!
I'LL LECTURE LAZAR WHEN WE GET HOME.

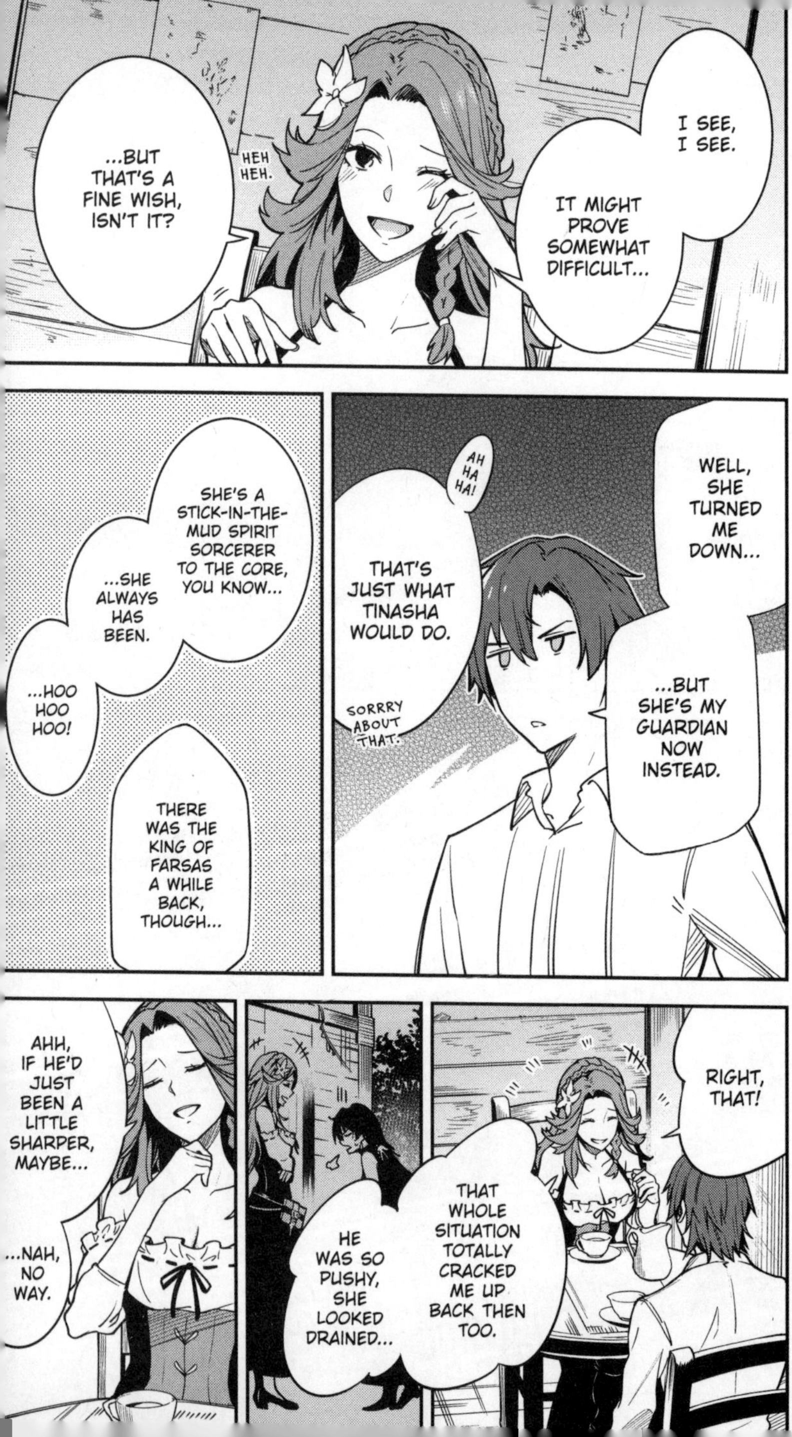
I SEE, I SEE.
IT MIGHT PROVE SOMEWHAT DIFFICULT...
HEH HEH.
...BUT THAT'S A FINE WISH, ISN'T IT?
WELL, SHE TURNED ME DOWN...
...BUT SHE'S MY GUARDIAN NOW INSTEAD.
AH HA HA!
THAT'S JUST WHAT TINASHA WOULD DO.
SORRRY ABOUT THAT.
SHE'S A STICK-IN-THE-MUD SPIRIT SORCERER TO THE CORE, YOU KNOW...
...SHE ALWAYS HAS BEEN.
...HOO HOO HOO!
THERE WAS THE KING OF FARSAS A WHILE BACK, THOUGH...
RIGHT, THAT!
THAT WHOLE SITUATION TOTALLY CRACKED ME UP BACK THEN TOO.
HE WAS SO PUSHY, SHE LOOKED DRAINED...
AHH, IF HE'D JUST BEEN A LITTLE SHARPER, MAYBE...
...NAH, NO WAY.

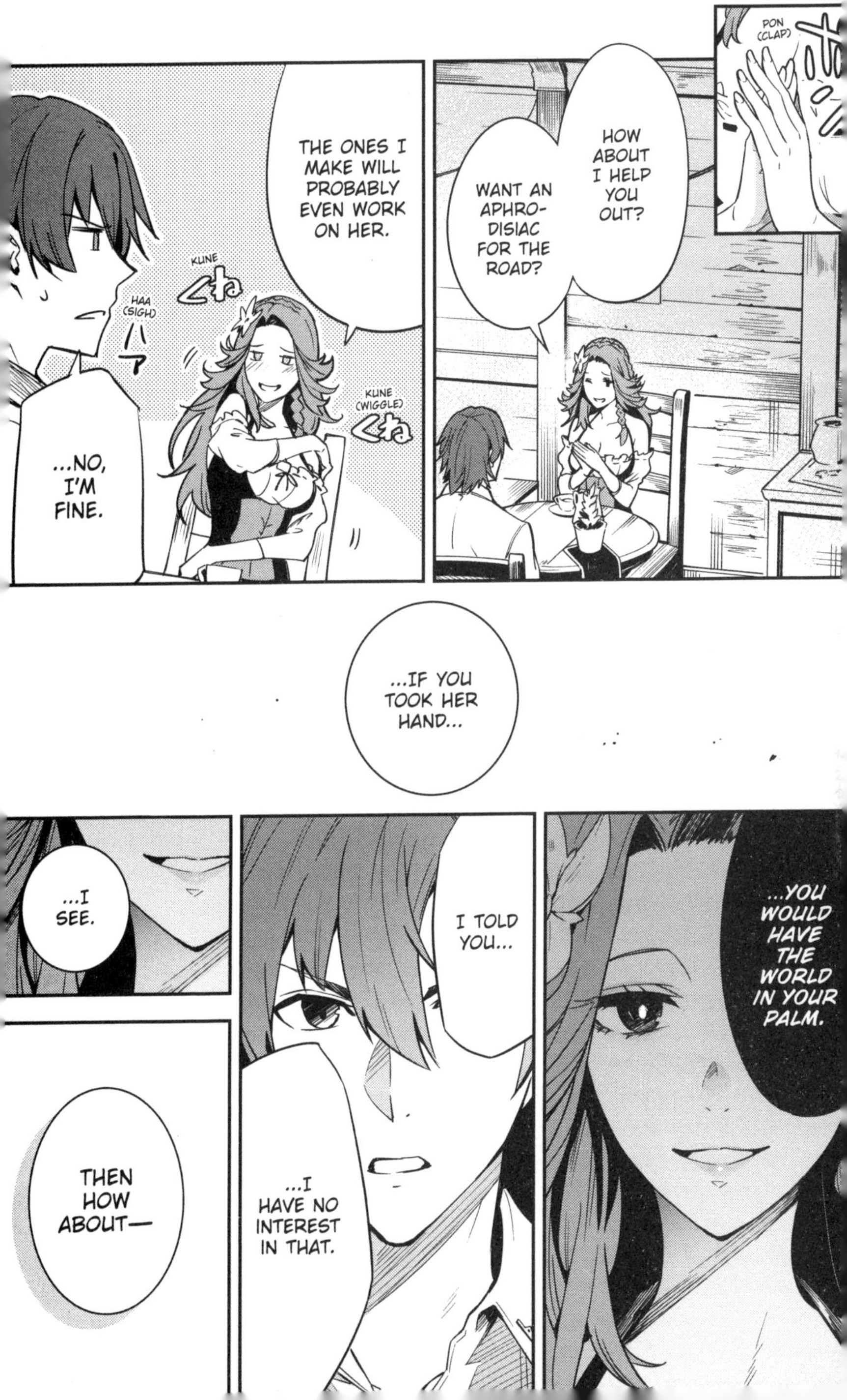
PON (CLAP)
HOW ABOUT I HELP YOU OUT?
WANT AN APHRO-DISIAC FOR THE ROAD?
THE ONES I MAKE WILL PROBABLY EVEN WORK ON HER.
KUNE
KUNE (WIGGLE)
HAA (SIGH)
...NO, I'M FINE.
...IF YOU TOOK HER HAND...
...YOU WOULD HAVE THE WORLD IN YOUR PALM.
I TOLD YOU...
...I HAVE NO INTEREST IN THAT.
...I SEE.
THEN HOW ABOUT—

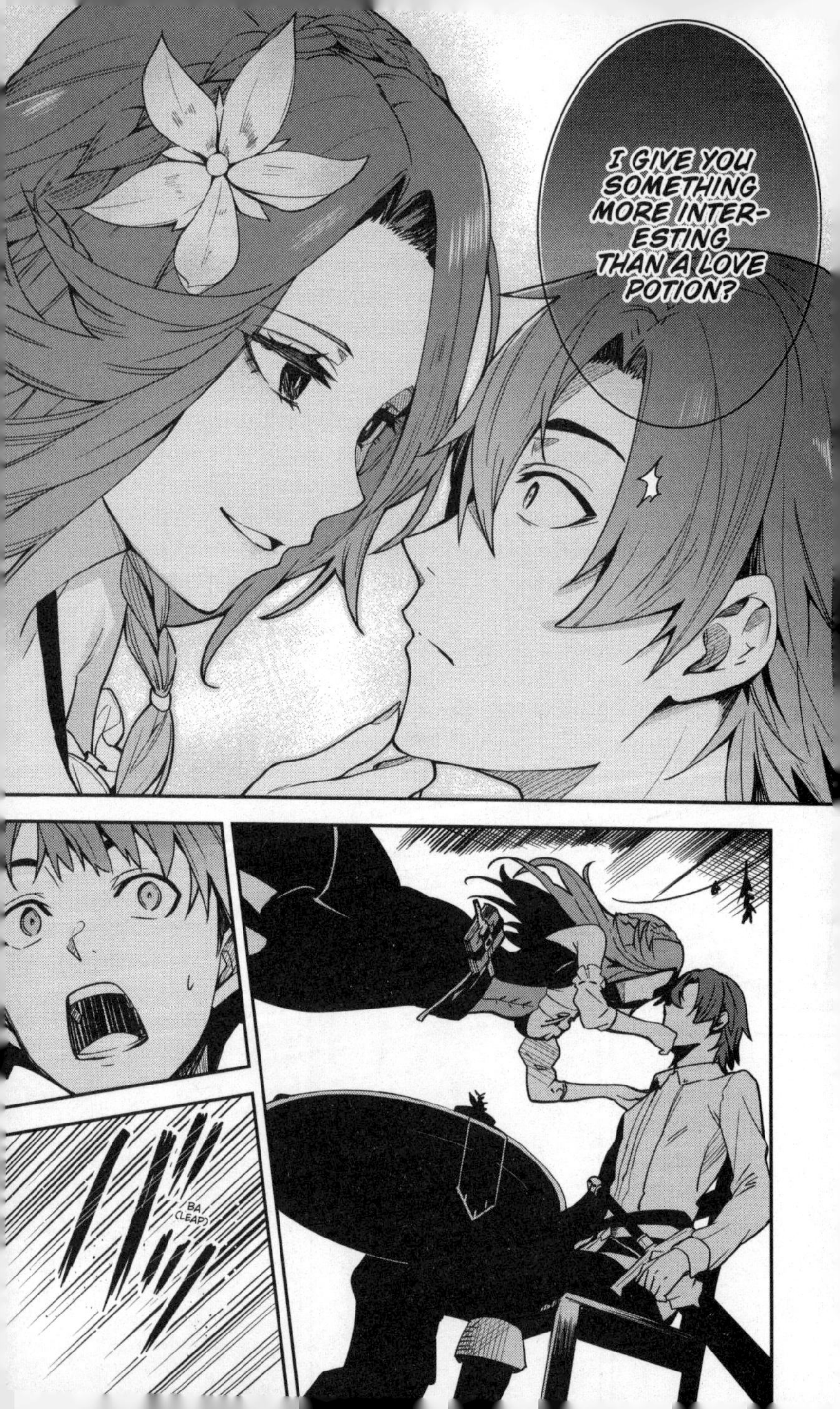
I GIVE YOU SOMETHING MORE INTER-ESTING THAN A LOVE POTION?
BA (LEAP)

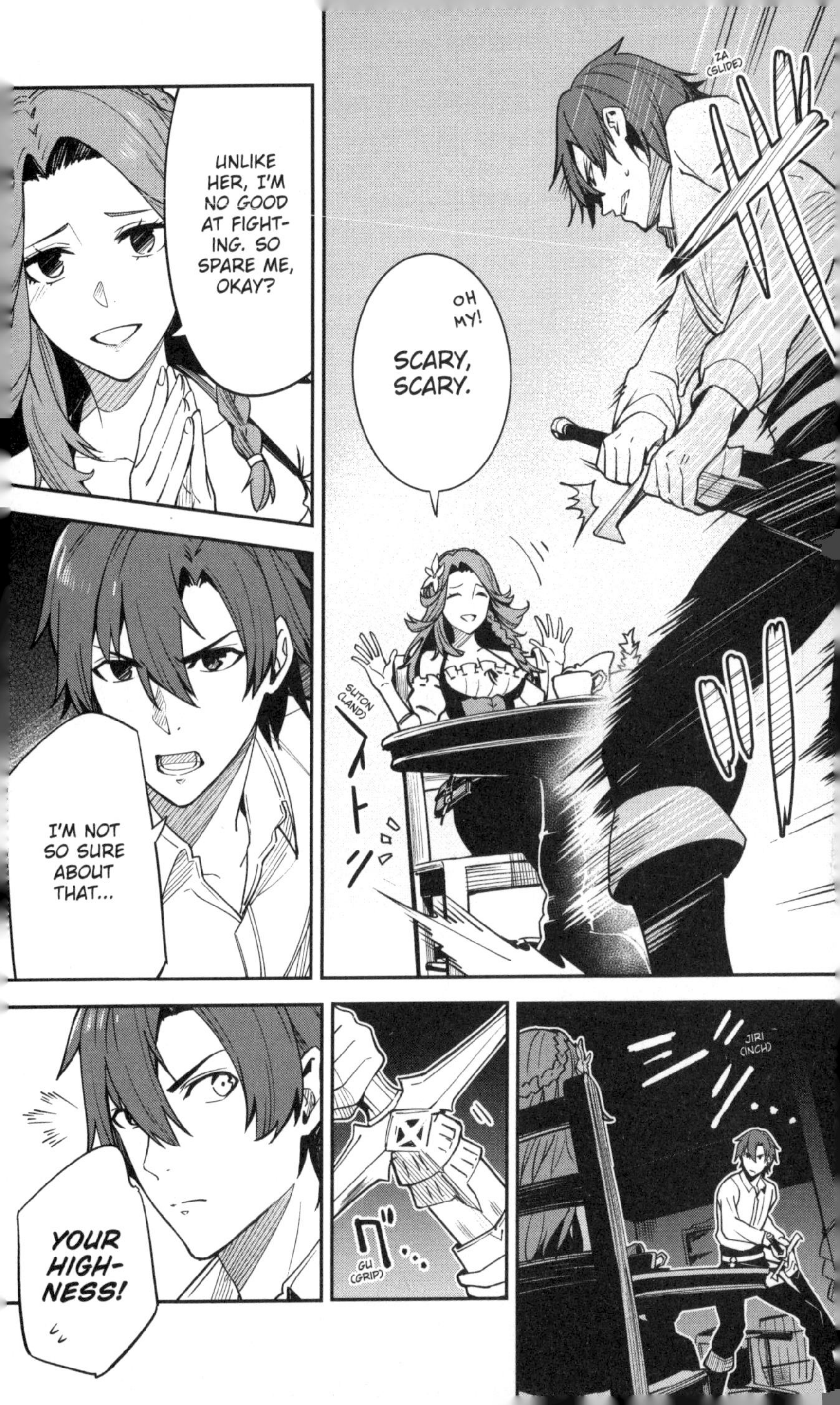
ZA (SLIDE)
OH MY!
SCARY, SCARY.
SUTON (LAND)
UNLIKE HER, I'M NO GOOD AT FIGHTING. SO SPARE ME, OKAY?
I'M NOT SO SURE ABOUT THAT...
JIRI (INCH)
GU (GRIP)
YOUR HIGHNESS!

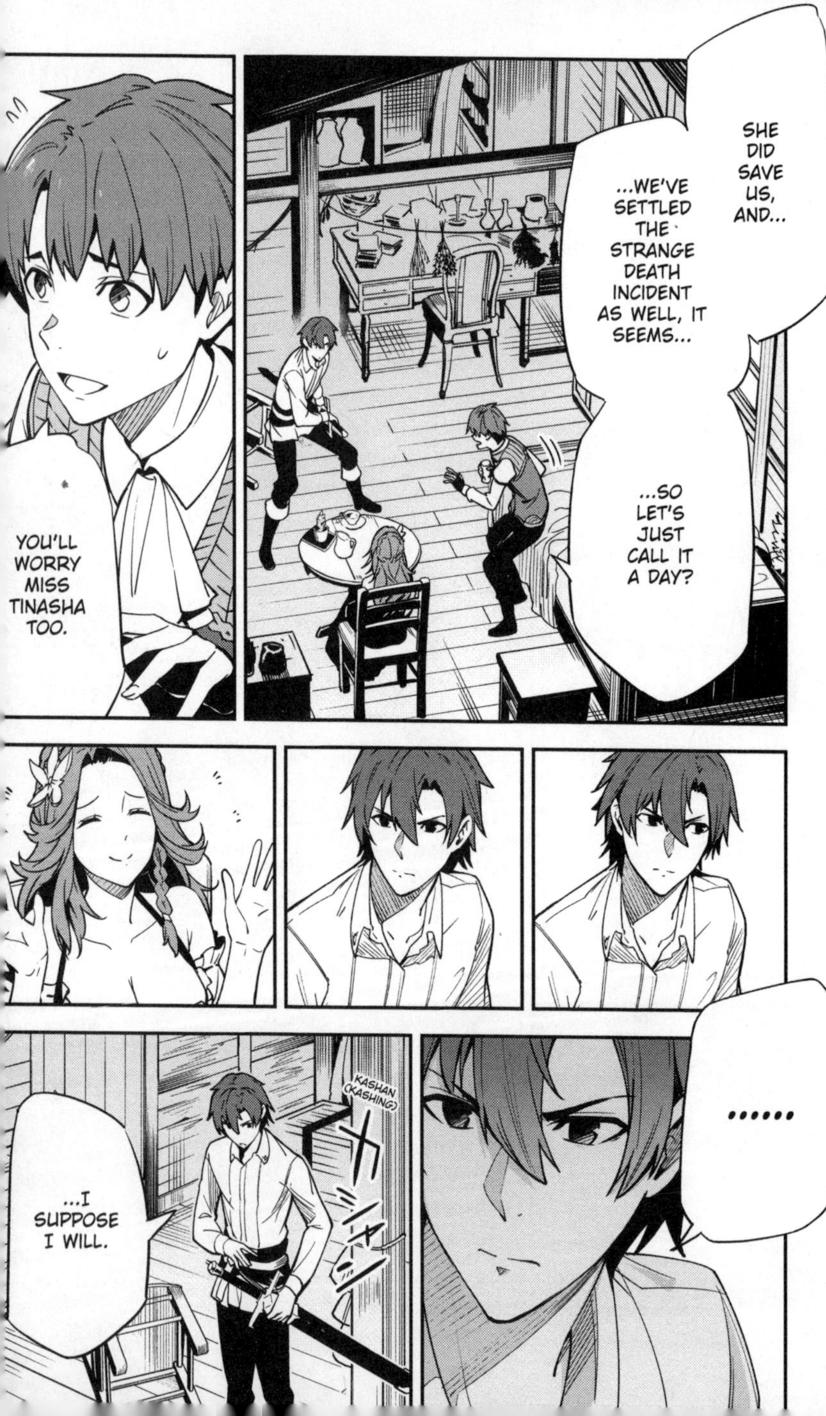

SHE DID SAVE US, AND...
...WE'VE SETTLED THE STRANGE DEATH INCIDENT AS WELL, IT SEEMS...
...SO LET'S JUST CALL IT A DAY?
YOU'LL WORRY MISS TINASHA TOO.
......
KASHAN (KASHING)
...I SUPPOSE I WILL.

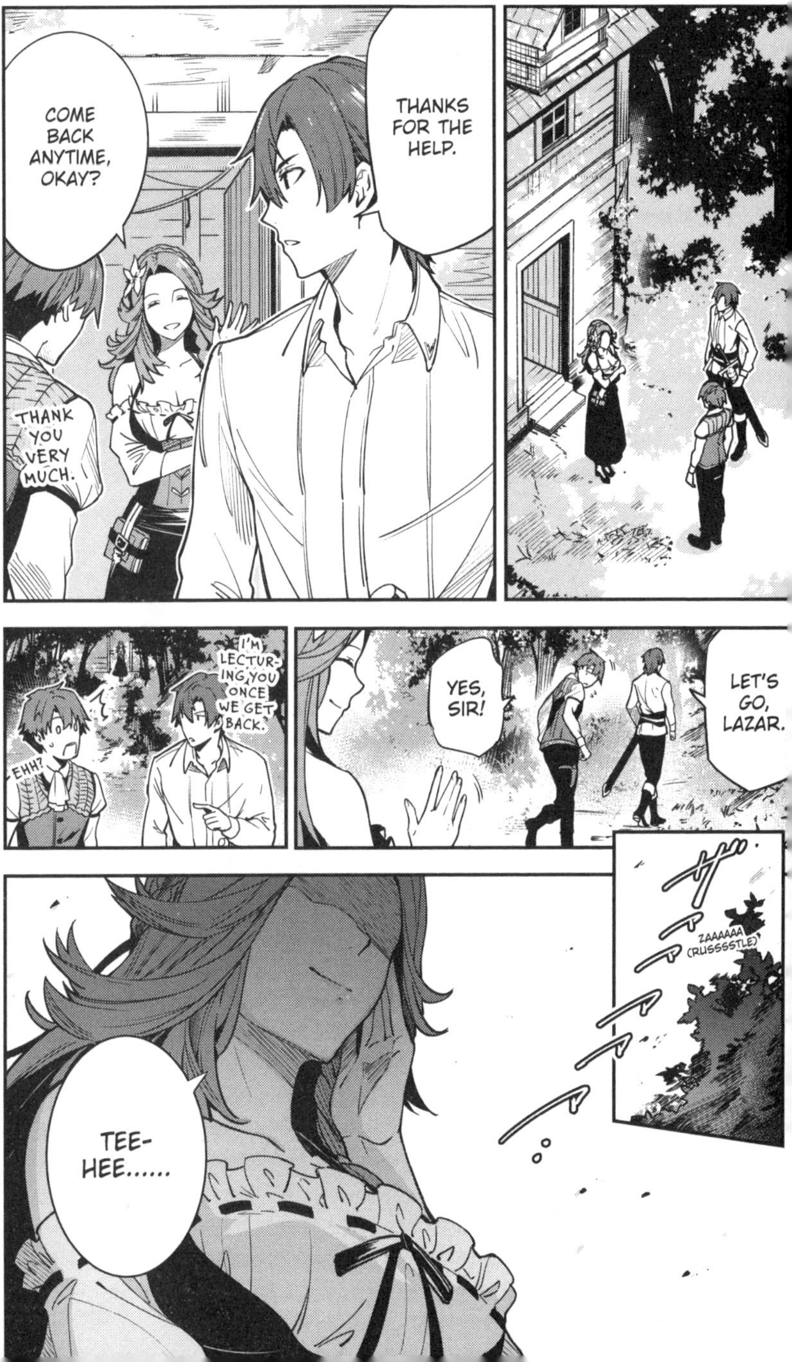
THANKS FOR THE HELP.
COME BACK ANYTIME, OKAY?
THANK YOU VERY MUCH.
LET'S GO, LAZAR.
YES, SIR!
I'M LECTURING YOU ONCE WE GET BACK.
EHH?
ZAAAAAA (RUSSSSTLE)
TEE-HEE......

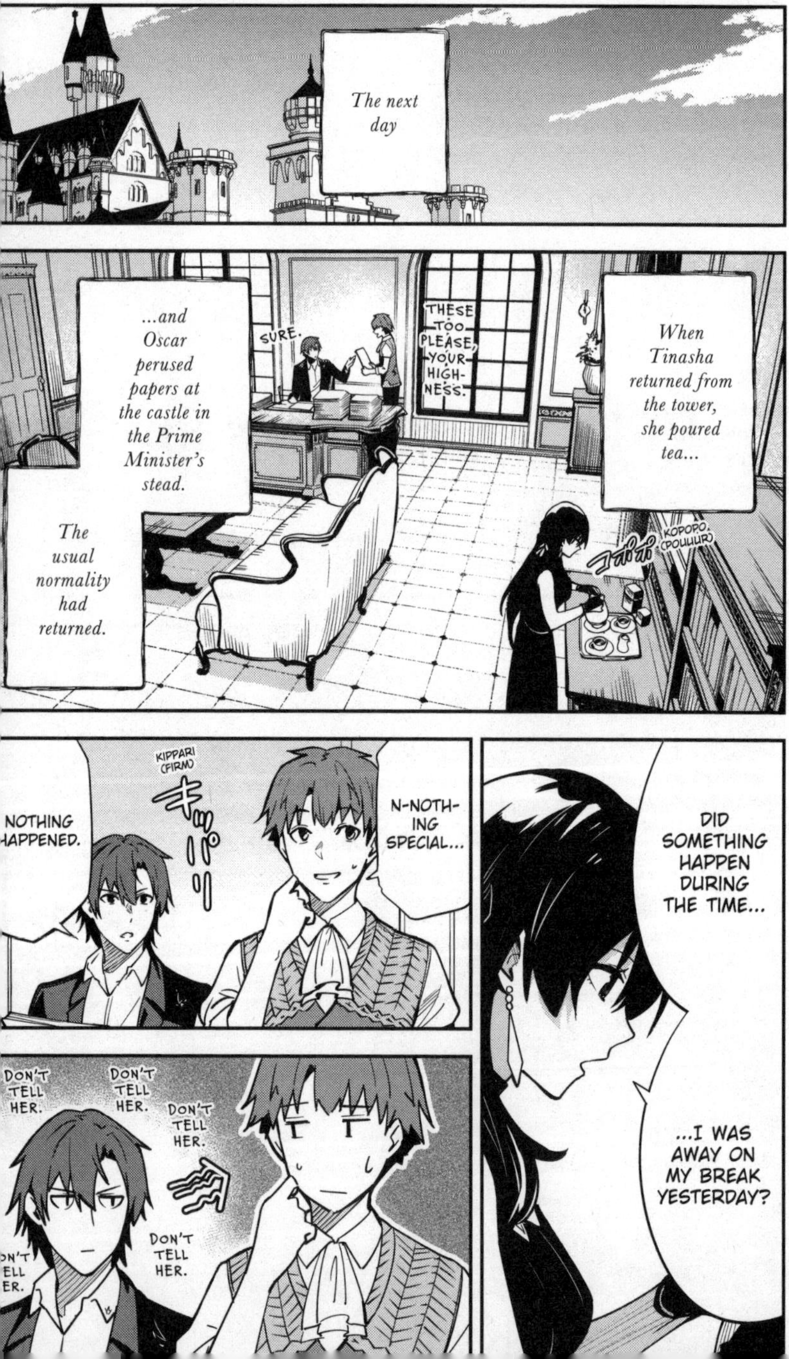
The next day
When Tinasha returned from the tower, she poured tea...
KOPOPO (POUUUR)
THESE TOO PLEASE, YOUR HIGHNESS.
SURE.
...and Oscar perused papers at the castle in the Prime Minister's stead.
The usual normality had returned.
DID SOMETHING HAPPEN DURING THE TIME...
...I WAS AWAY ON MY BREAK YESTERDAY?
N-NOTHING SPECIAL...
KIPPARI (FIRM)
NOTHING HAPPENED.
DON'T TELL HER.
DON'T TELL HER.
DON'T TELL HER.
DON'T TELL HER.

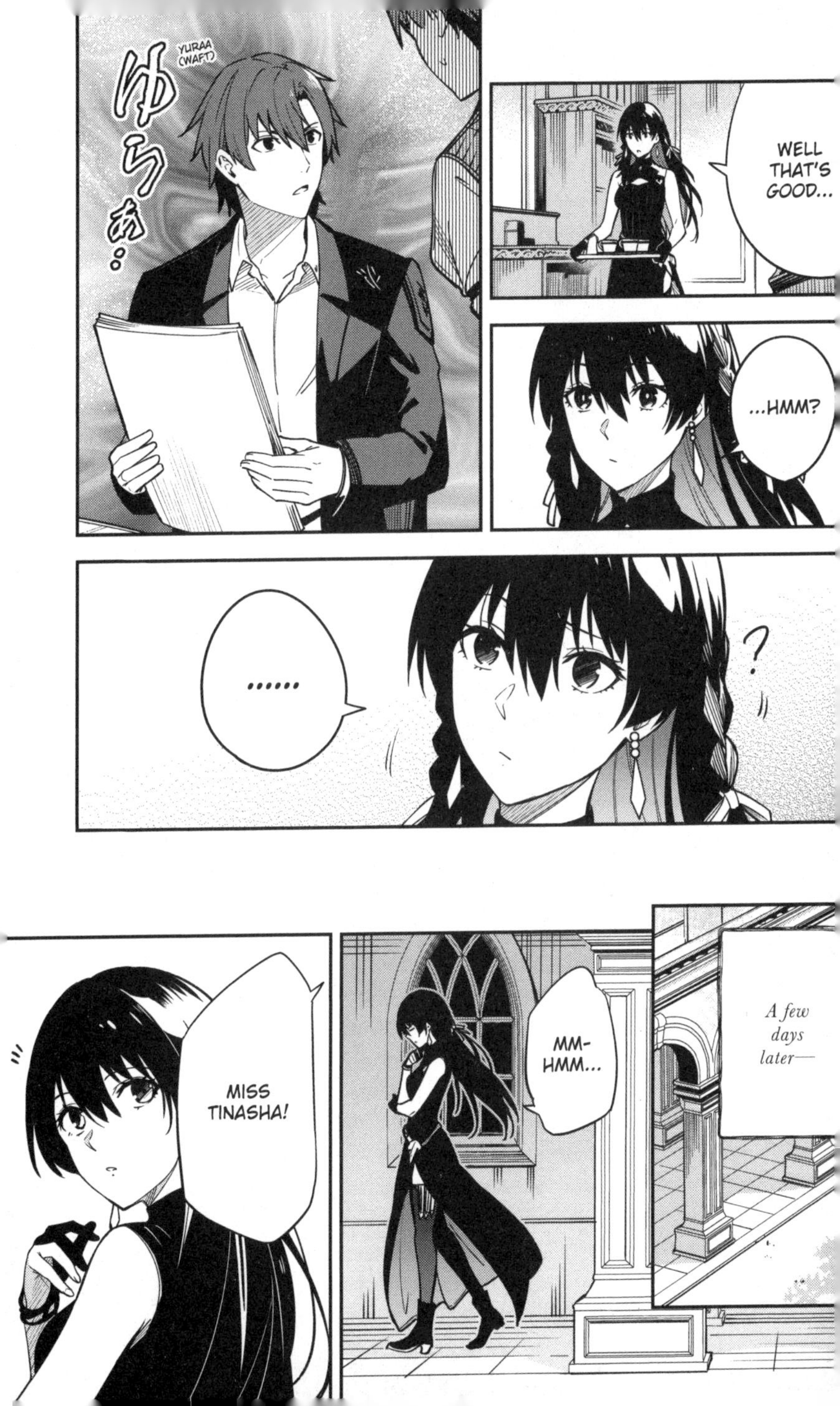
WELL THAT'S GOOD...
...HMM?
ゆらぁ。
YURAA (WAFT)
......
?
A few days later—
MM-HMM...
MISS TINASHA!

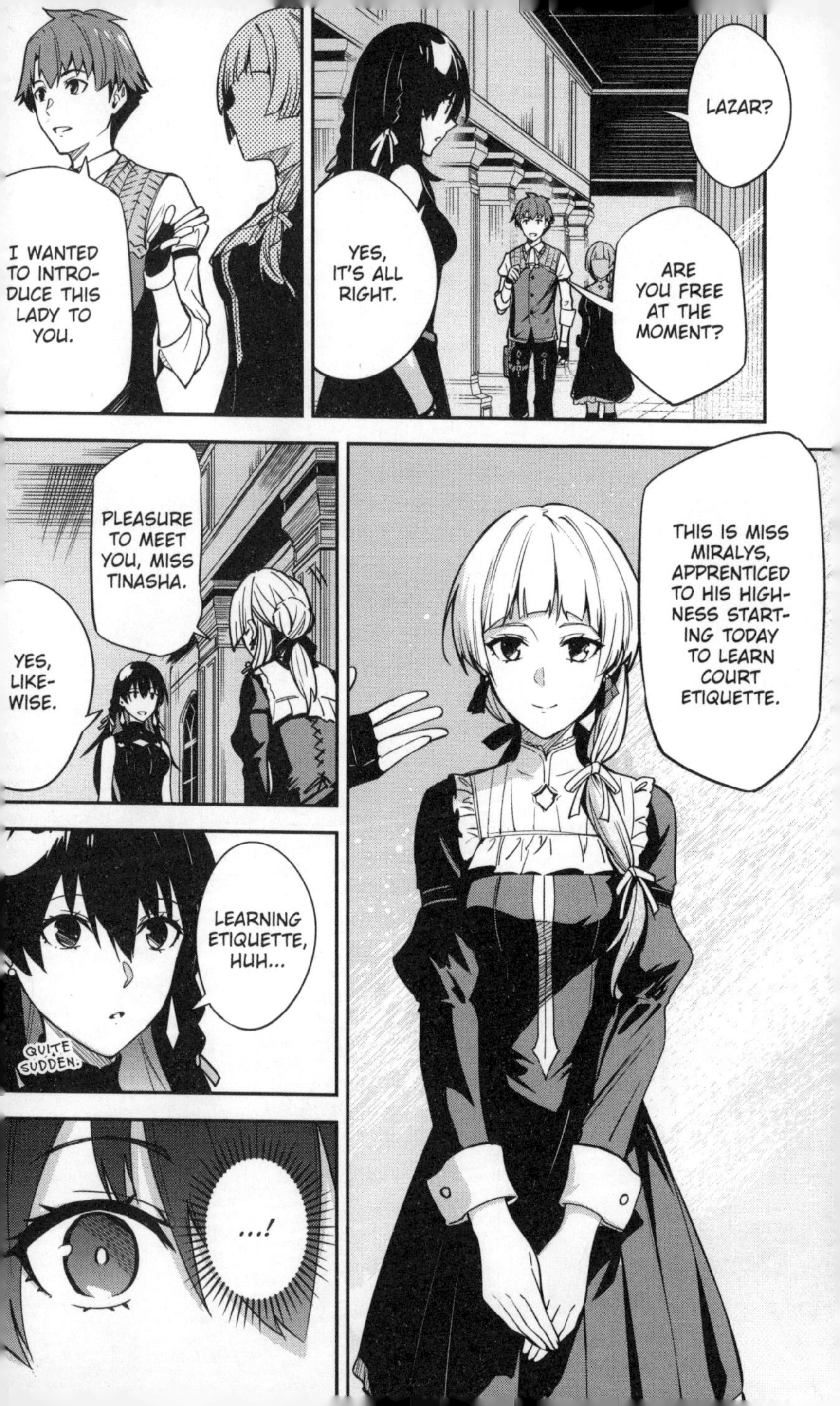
LAZAR?
ARE YOU FREE AT THE MOMENT?
YES, IT'S ALL RIGHT.
I WANTED TO INTRODUCE THIS LADY TO YOU.
THIS IS MISS MIRALYS, APPRENTICED TO HIS HIGHNESS STARTING TODAY TO LEARN COURT ETIQUETTE.
PLEASURE TO MEET YOU, MISS TINASHA.
YES, LIKEWISE.
LEARNING ETIQUETTE, HUH...
QUITE SUDDEN.
...!

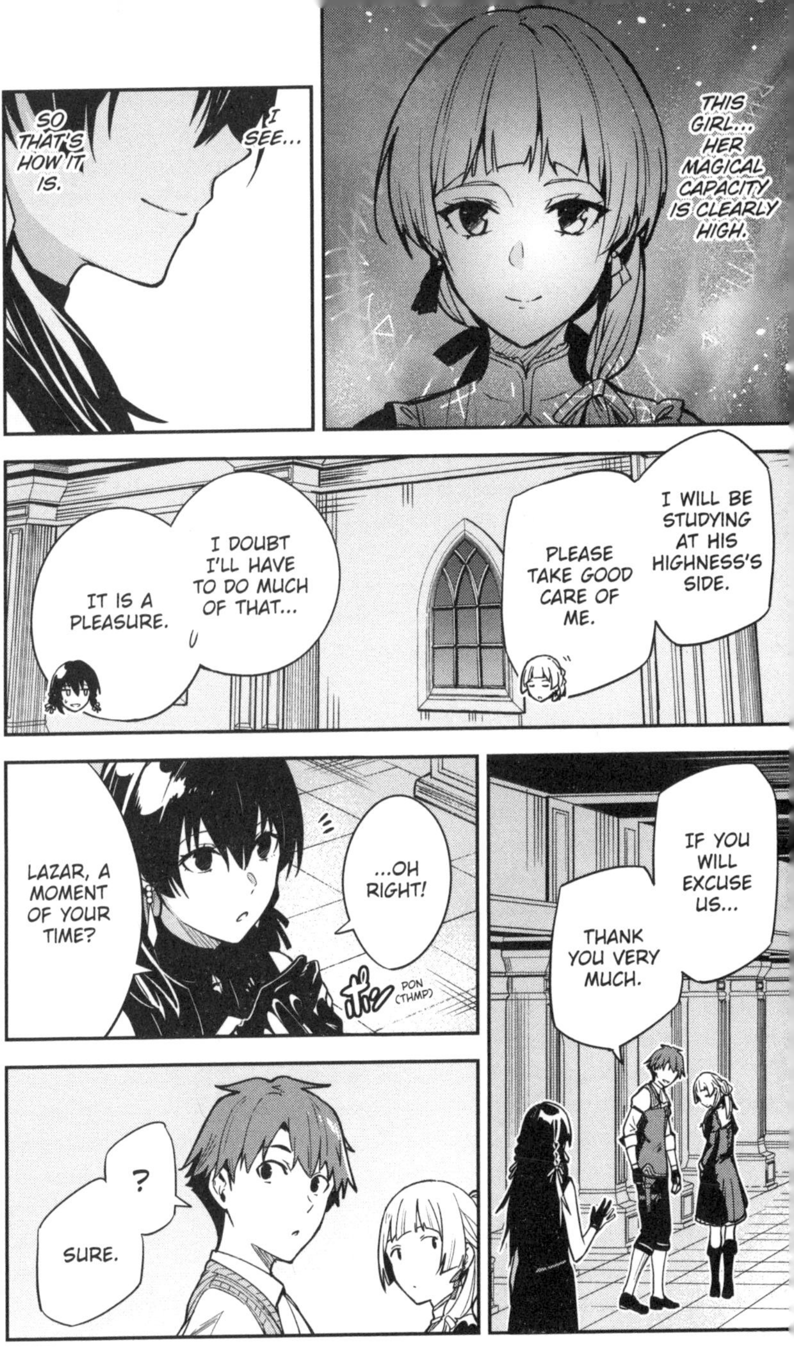
THIS GIRL... HER MAGICAL CAPACITY IS CLEARLY HIGH.
I SEE...
SO THAT'S HOW IT IS.
I WILL BE STUDYING AT HIS HIGHNESS'S SIDE.
PLEASE TAKE GOOD CARE OF ME.
I DOUBT I'LL HAVE TO DO MUCH OF THAT...
IT IS A PLEASURE.
IF YOU WILL EXCUSE US...
THANK YOU VERY MUCH.
...OH RIGHT!
PON (THMP)
LAZAR, A MOMENT OF YOUR TIME?
?
SURE.

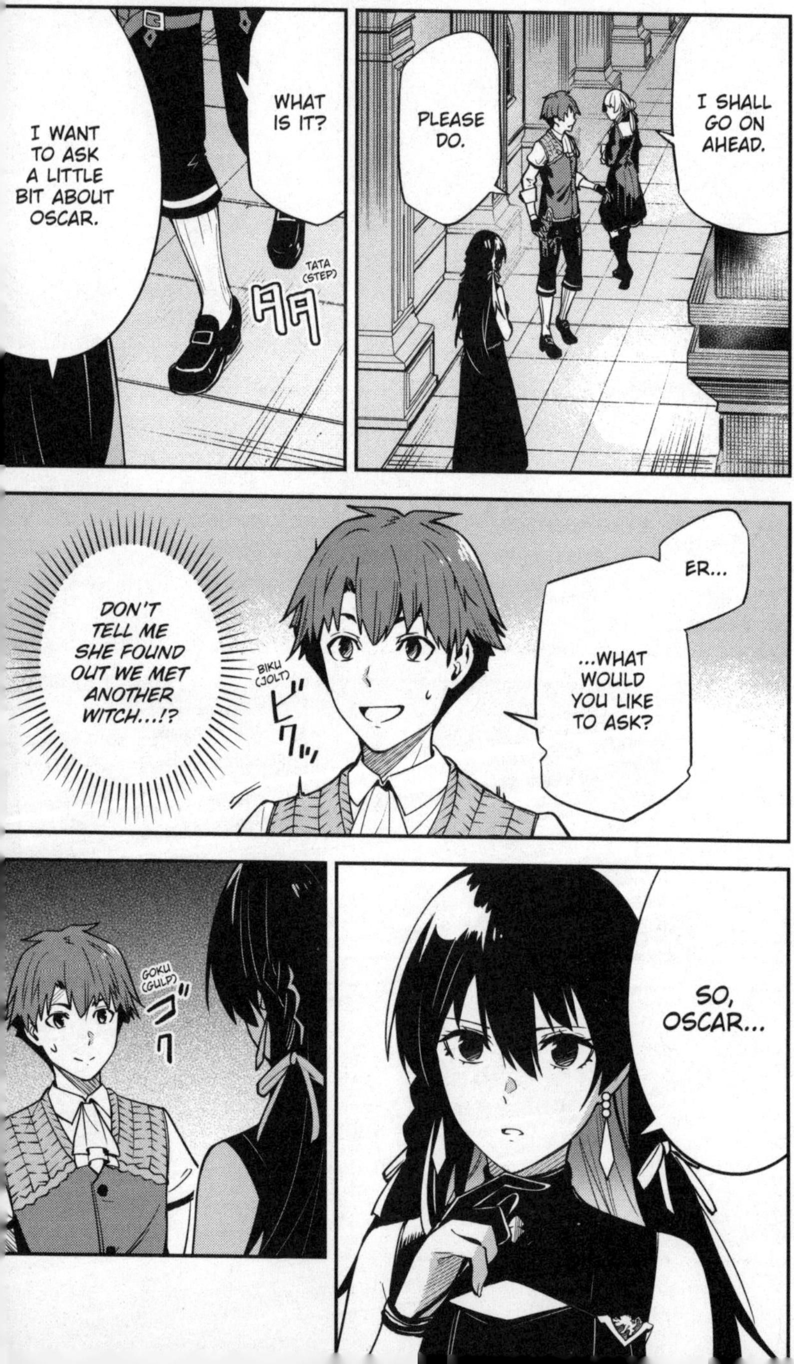
I SHALL GO ON AHEAD.
PLEASE DO.
WHAT IS IT?
TATA (STEP)
I WANT TO ASK A LITTLE BIT ABOUT OSCAR.
ER...
...WHAT WOULD YOU LIKE TO ASK?
BIKU (JOLT)
DON'T TELL ME SHE FOUND OUT WE MET ANOTHER WITCH...!?
SO, OSCAR...
GOKU (GULP)

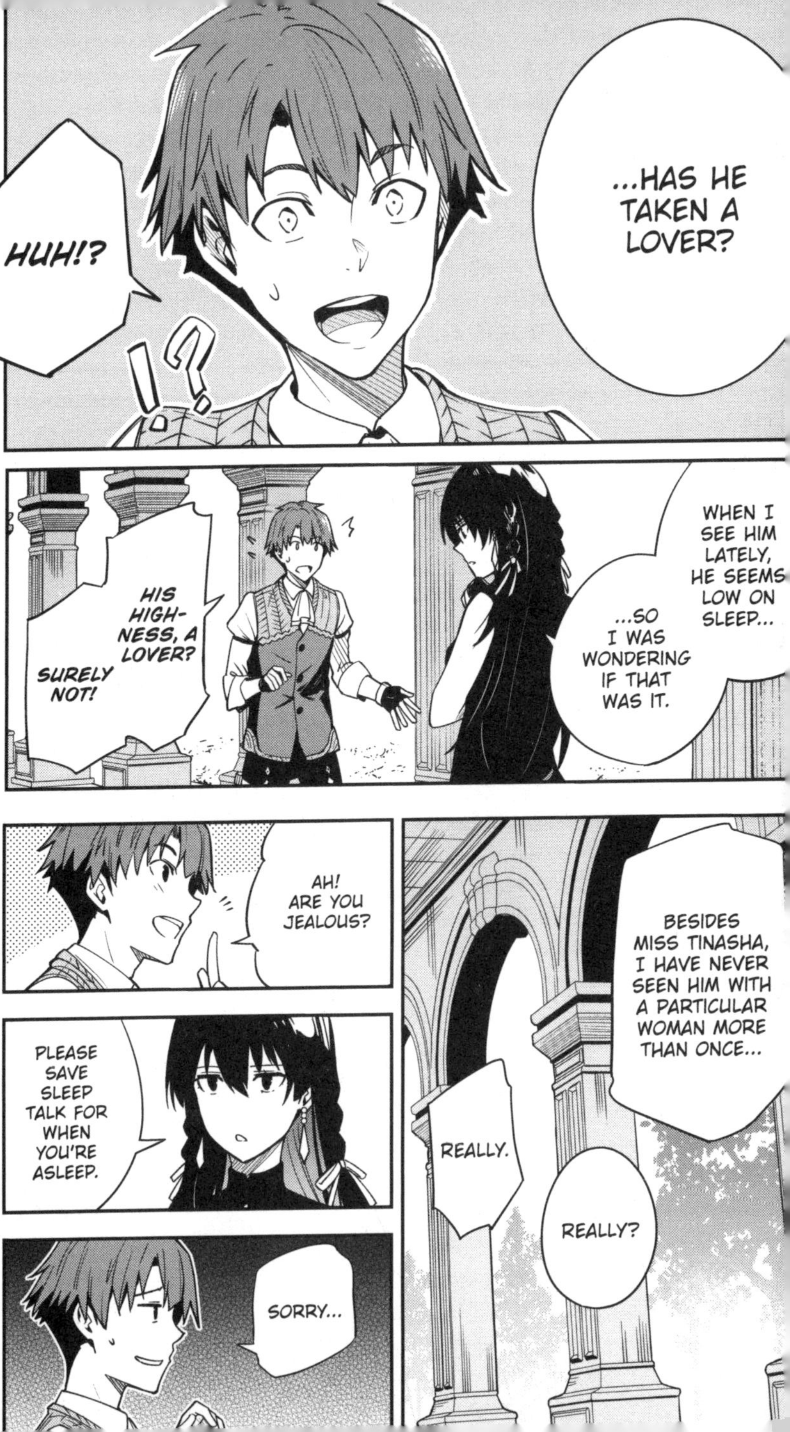
...HAS HE TAKEN A LOVER?
HUH!?
WHEN I SEE HIM LATELY, HE SEEMS LOW ON SLEEP...
...SO I WAS WONDERING IF THAT WAS IT.
HIS HIGHNESS, A LOVER?
SURELY NOT!
BESIDES MISS TINASHA, I HAVE NEVER SEEN HIM WITH A PARTICULAR WOMAN MORE THAN ONCE...
REALLY.
REALLY?
AH! ARE YOU JEALOUS?
PLEASE SAVE SLEEP TALK FOR WHEN YOU'RE ASLEEP.
SORRY...

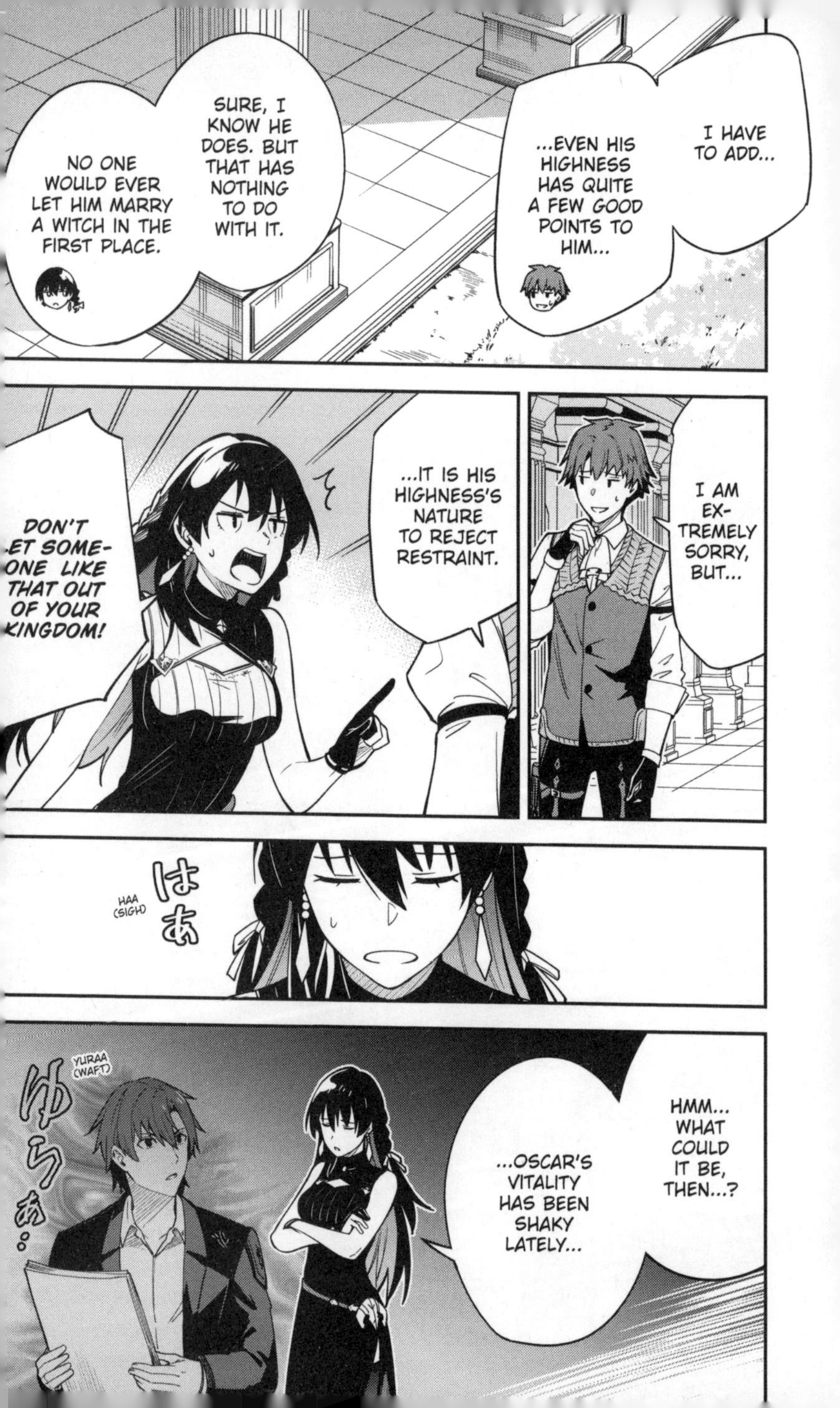
I HAVE TO ADD...
...EVEN HIS HIGHNESS HAS QUITE A FEW GOOD POINTS TO HIM...
SURE, I KNOW HE DOES. BUT THAT HAS NOTHING TO DO WITH IT.
NO ONE WOULD EVER LET HIM MARRY A WITCH IN THE FIRST PLACE.
I AM EXTREMELY SORRY, BUT...
...IT IS HIS HIGHNESS'S NATURE TO REJECT RESTRAINT.
DON'T ET SOME-ONE LIKE THAT OUT OF YOUR KINGDOM!
はあ
HAA (SIGH)
HMM... WHAT COULD IT BE, THEN...?
...OSCAR'S VITALITY HAS BEEN SHAKY LATELY...
ゆらあ。
YURAA (WAFT)

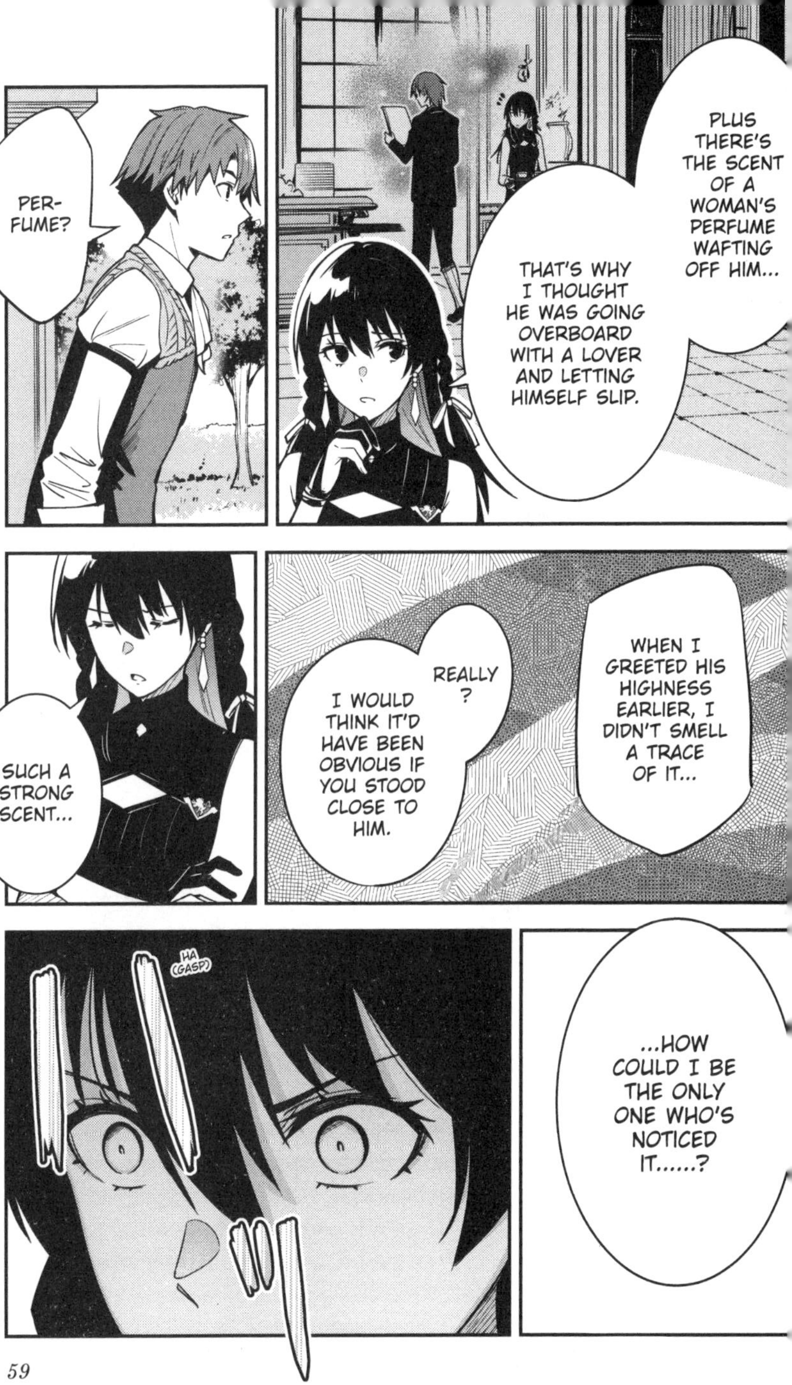
PLUS THERE'S THE SCENT OF A WOMAN'S PERFUME WAFTING OFF HIM...
THAT'S WHY I THOUGHT HE WAS GOING OVERBOARD WITH A LOVER AND LETTING HIMSELF SLIP.
PER-FUME?
WHEN I GREETED HIS HIGHNESS EARLIER, I DIDN'T SMELL A TRACE OF IT...
REALLY?
I WOULD THINK IT'D HAVE BEEN OBVIOUS IF YOU STOOD CLOSE TO HIM.
SUCH A STRONG SCENT...
...HOW COULD I BE THE ONLY ONE WHO'S NOTICED IT......?
HA (GASP)

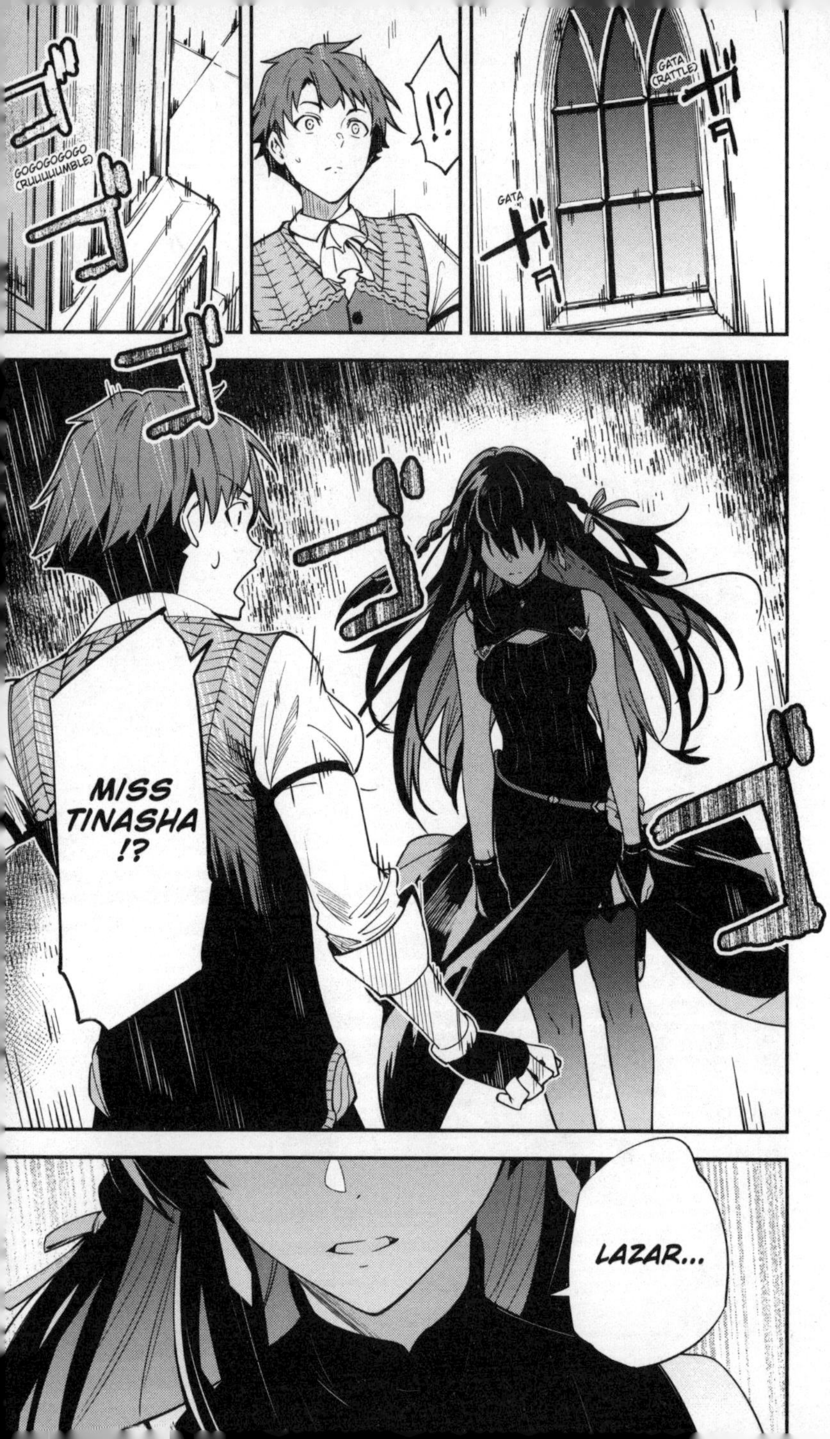
GATA (RATTLE)
GATA
!?
GOGOGOGOGO (RUUUUUMBLE)
MISS TINASHA !?
LAZAR...

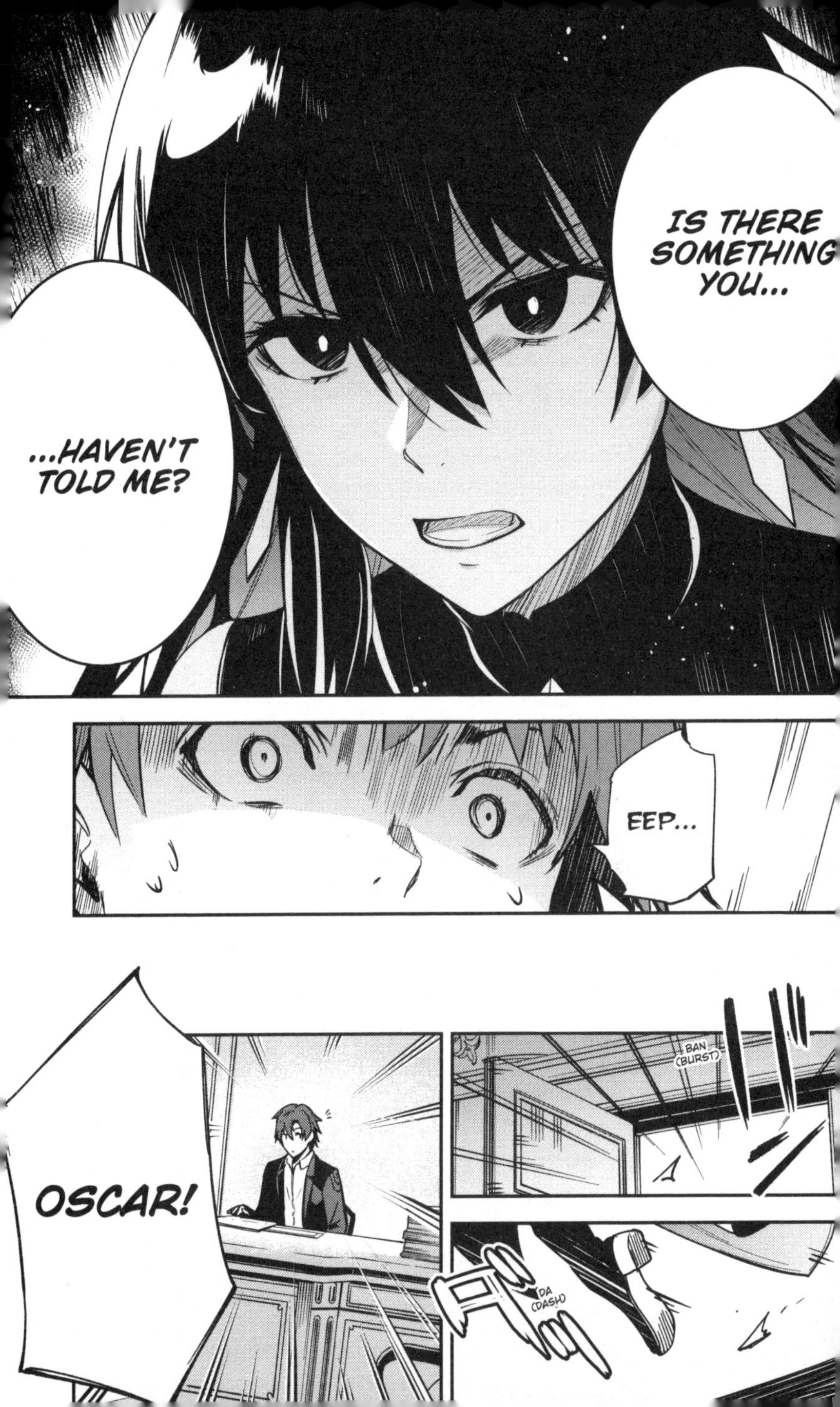
IS THERE SOMETHING YOU...
...HAVEN'T TOLD ME?
EEP...
BAN (BURST)
DA (DASH)
OSCAR!

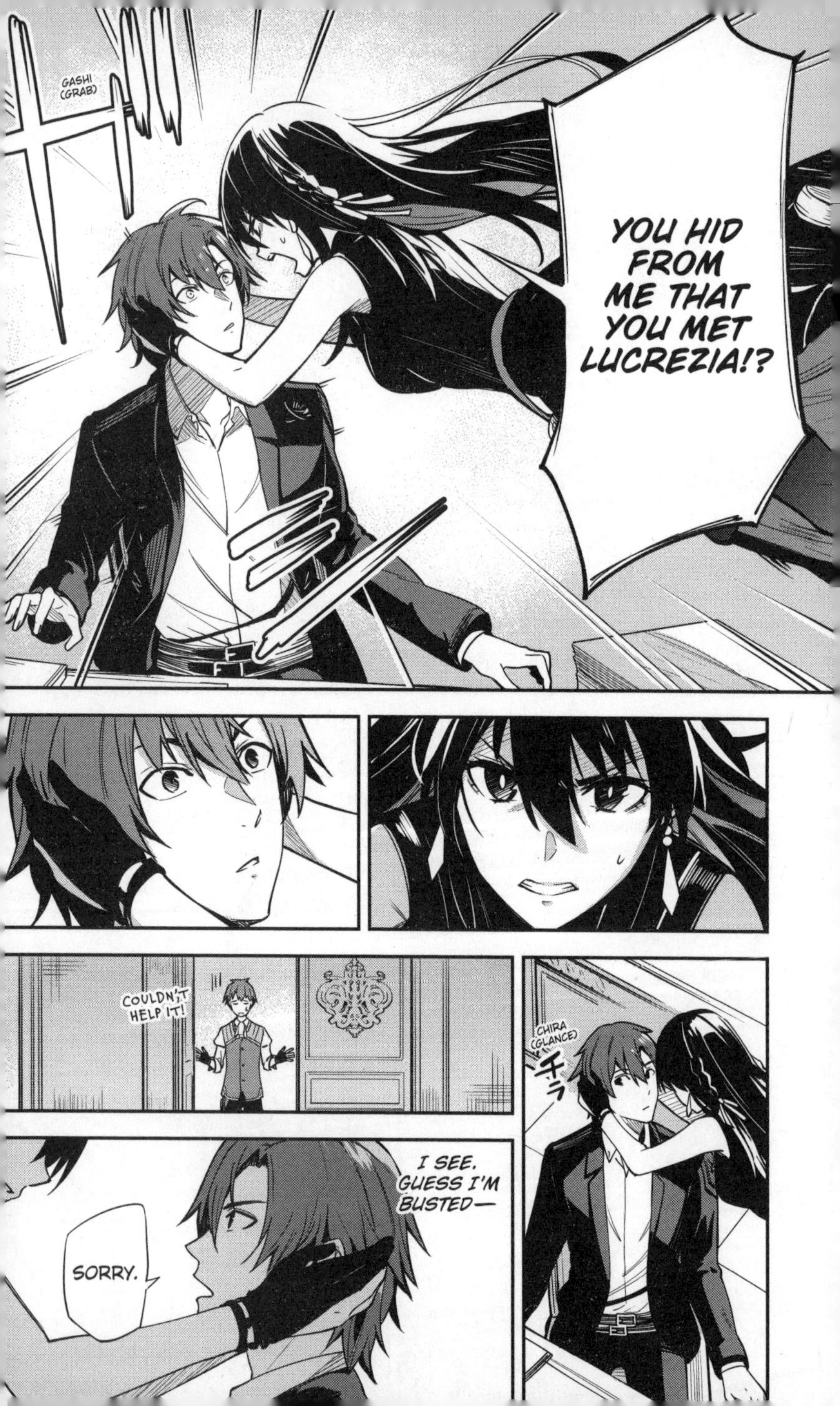
YOU HID FROM ME THAT YOU MET LUCREZIA!?
GASHI (GRAB)
CHIRA (GLANCE)
チラ
COULDN'T HELP IT!
I SEE. GUESS I'M BUSTED—
SORRY.

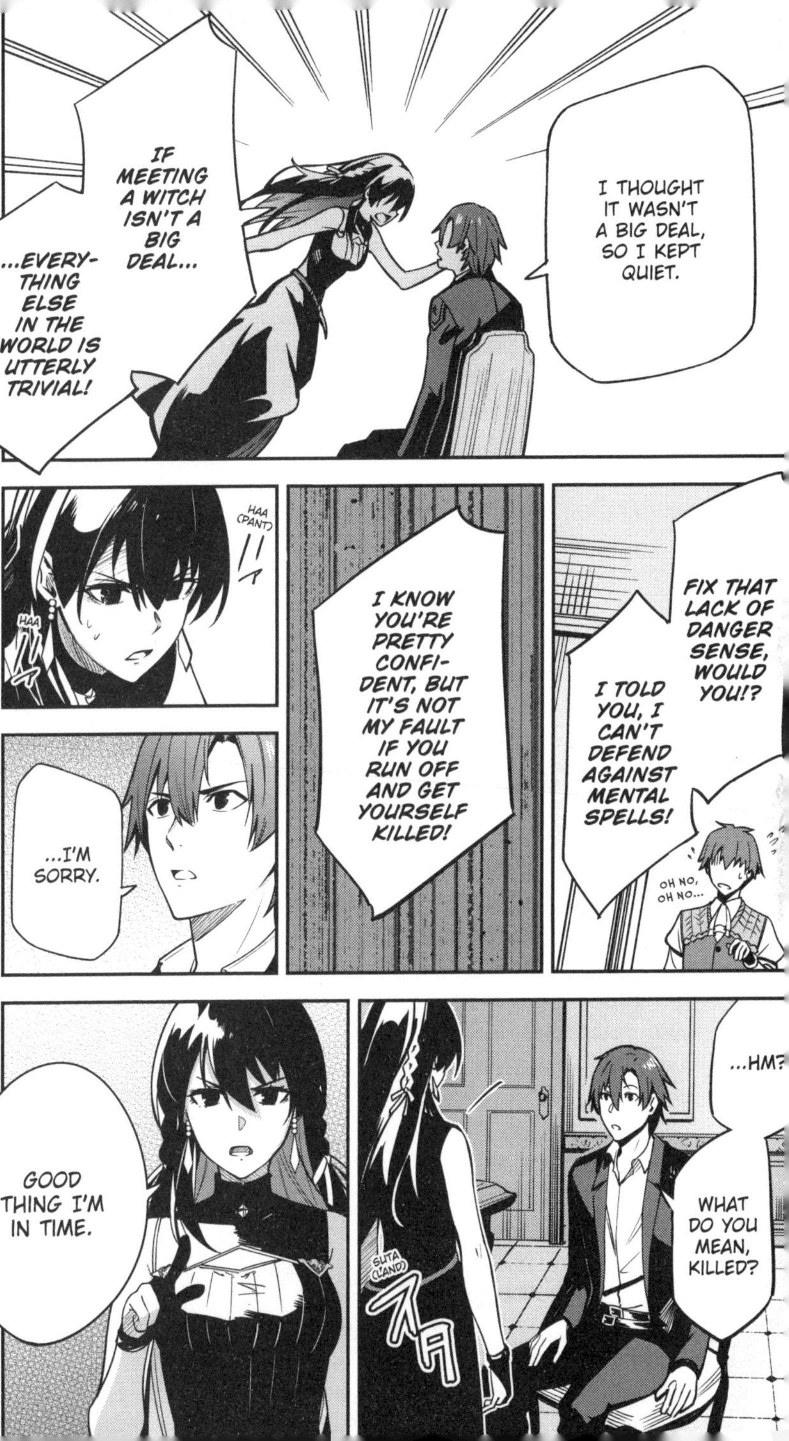
I THOUGHT IT WASN'T A BIG DEAL, SO I KEPT QUIET.
IF MEETING A WITCH ISN'T A BIG DEAL...
...EVERY-THING ELSE IN THE WORLD IS UTTERLY TRIVIAL!
FIX THAT LACK OF DANGER SENSE, WOULD YOU!?
I TOLD YOU, I CAN'T DEFEND AGAINST MENTAL SPELLS!
OH NO, OH NO...
I KNOW YOU'RE PRETTY CONFI-DENT, BUT IT'S NOT MY FAULT IF YOU RUN OFF AND GET YOURSELF KILLED!
HAA (PANT)
HAA
...I'M SORRY.
...HM?
WHAT DO YOU MEAN, KILLED?
SUTA (LAND)
GOOD THING I'M IN TIME.

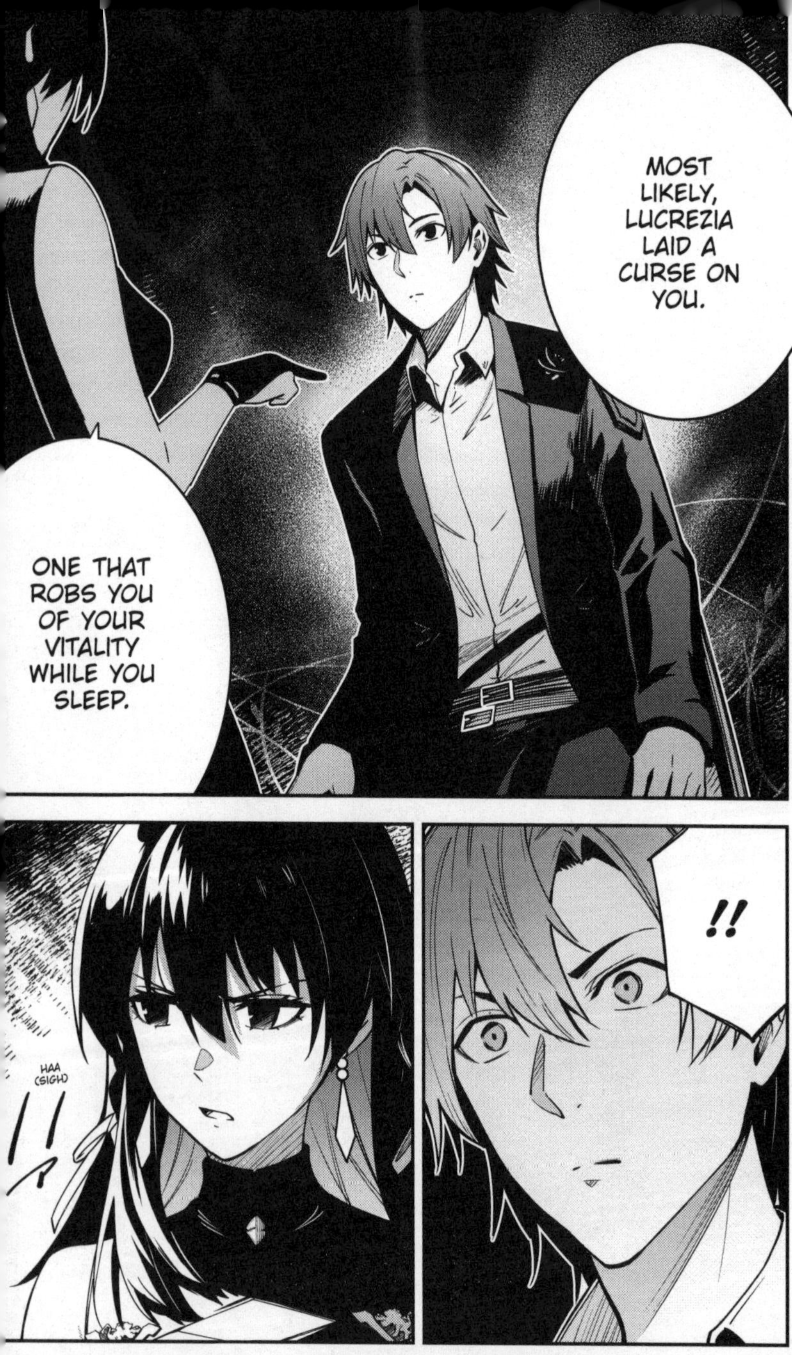
MOST LIKELY, LUCREZIA LAID A CURSE ON YOU.
ONE THAT ROBS YOU OF YOUR VITALITY WHILE YOU SLEEP.
!!
HAA (SIGH)

Unnamed Memory

Unnamed Memory

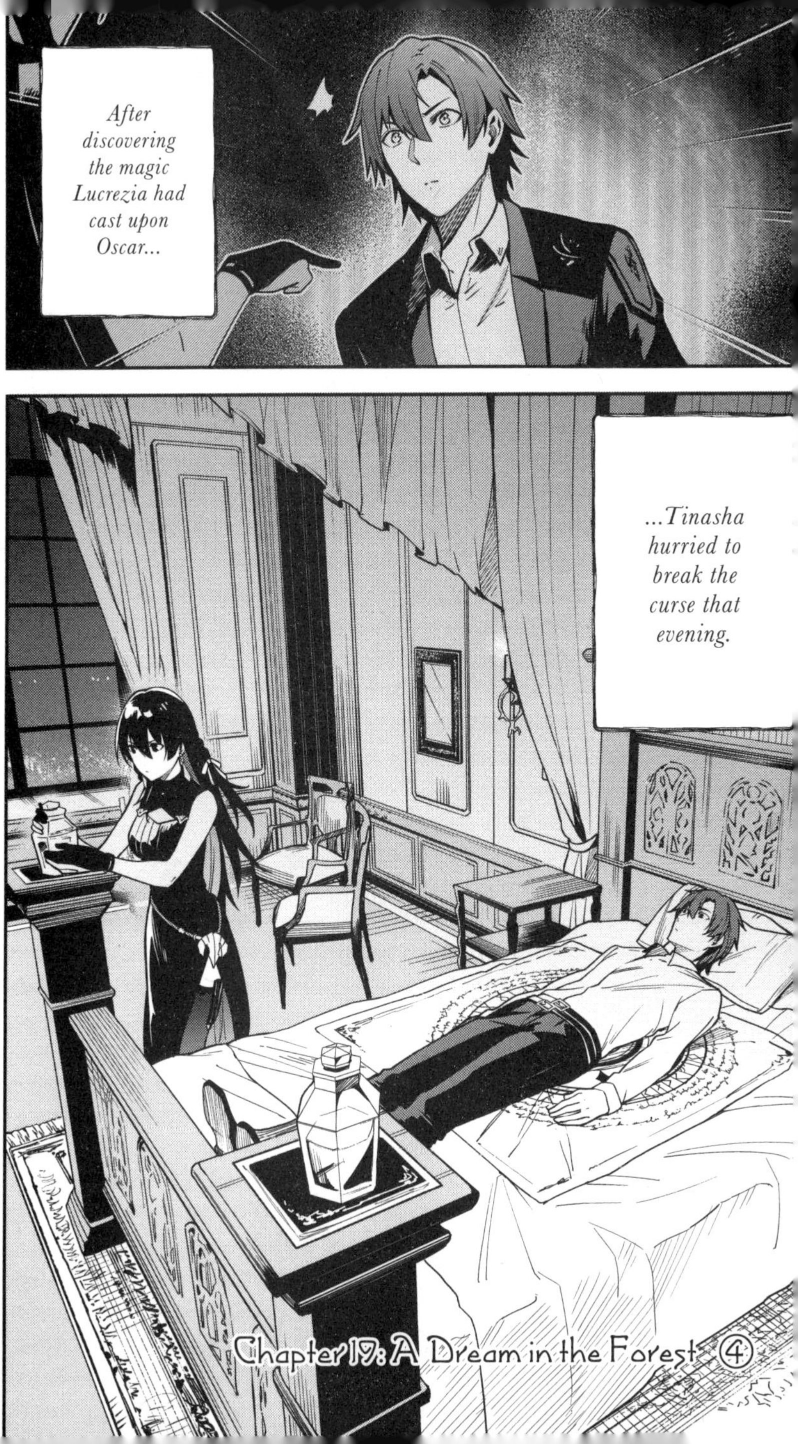
After discovering the magic Lucrezia had cast upon Oscar...
...Tinasha hurried to break the curse that evening.
Chapter 19: A Dream in the Forest ④

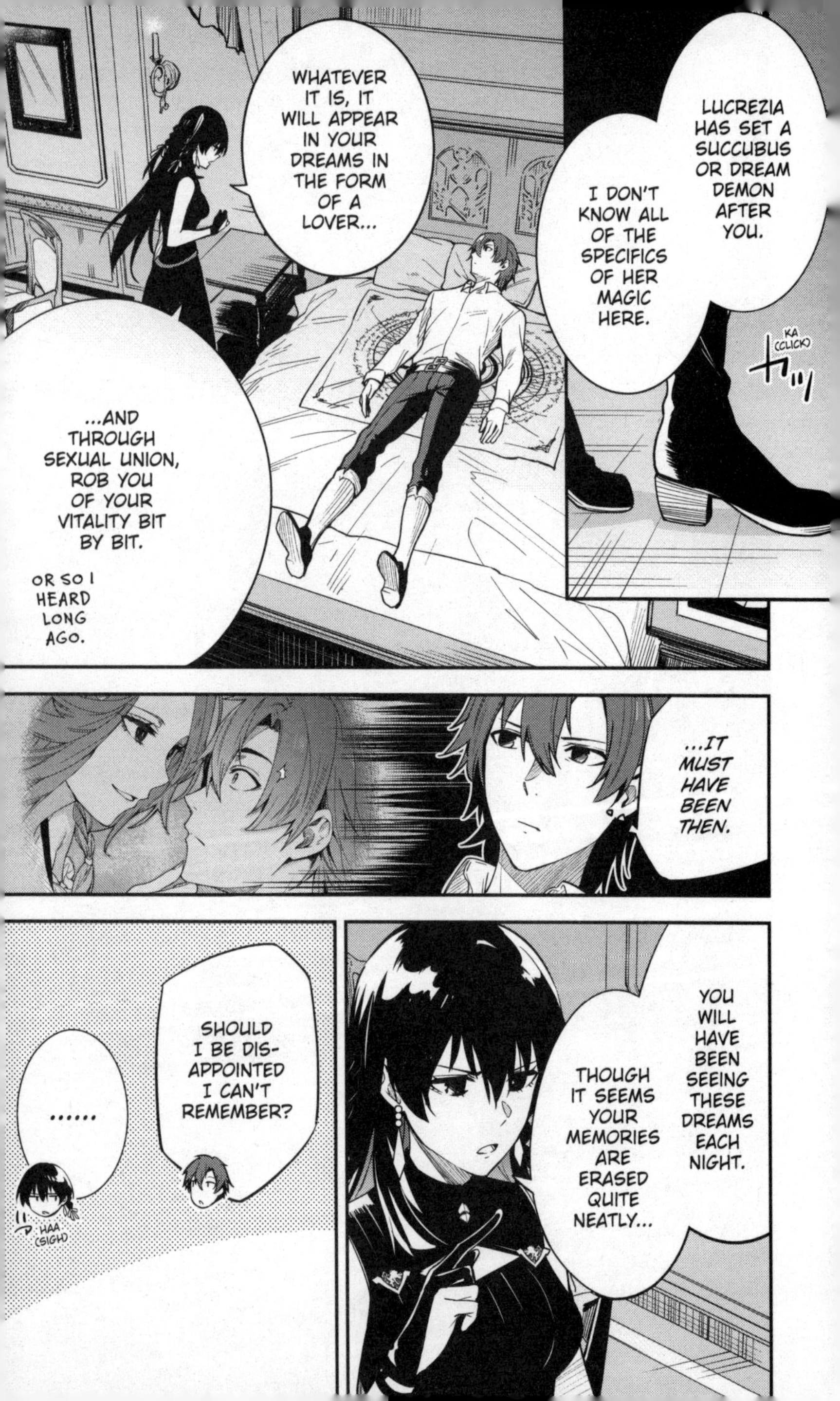

LUCREZIA HAS SET A SUCCUBUS OR DREAM DEMON AFTER YOU.
I DON'T KNOW ALL OF THE SPECIFICS OF HER MAGIC HERE.
KA (CLICK)
WHATEVER IT IS, IT WILL APPEAR IN YOUR DREAMS IN THE FORM OF A LOVER...
...AND THROUGH SEXUAL UNION, ROB YOU OF YOUR VITALITY BIT BY BIT.
OR SO I HEARD LONG AGO.
...IT MUST HAVE BEEN THEN.
YOU WILL HAVE BEEN SEEING THESE DREAMS EACH NIGHT.
THOUGH IT SEEMS YOUR MEMORIES ARE ERASED QUITE NEATLY...
SHOULD I BE DIS-APPOINTED I CAN'T REMEMBER?
......
HAA (SIGH)

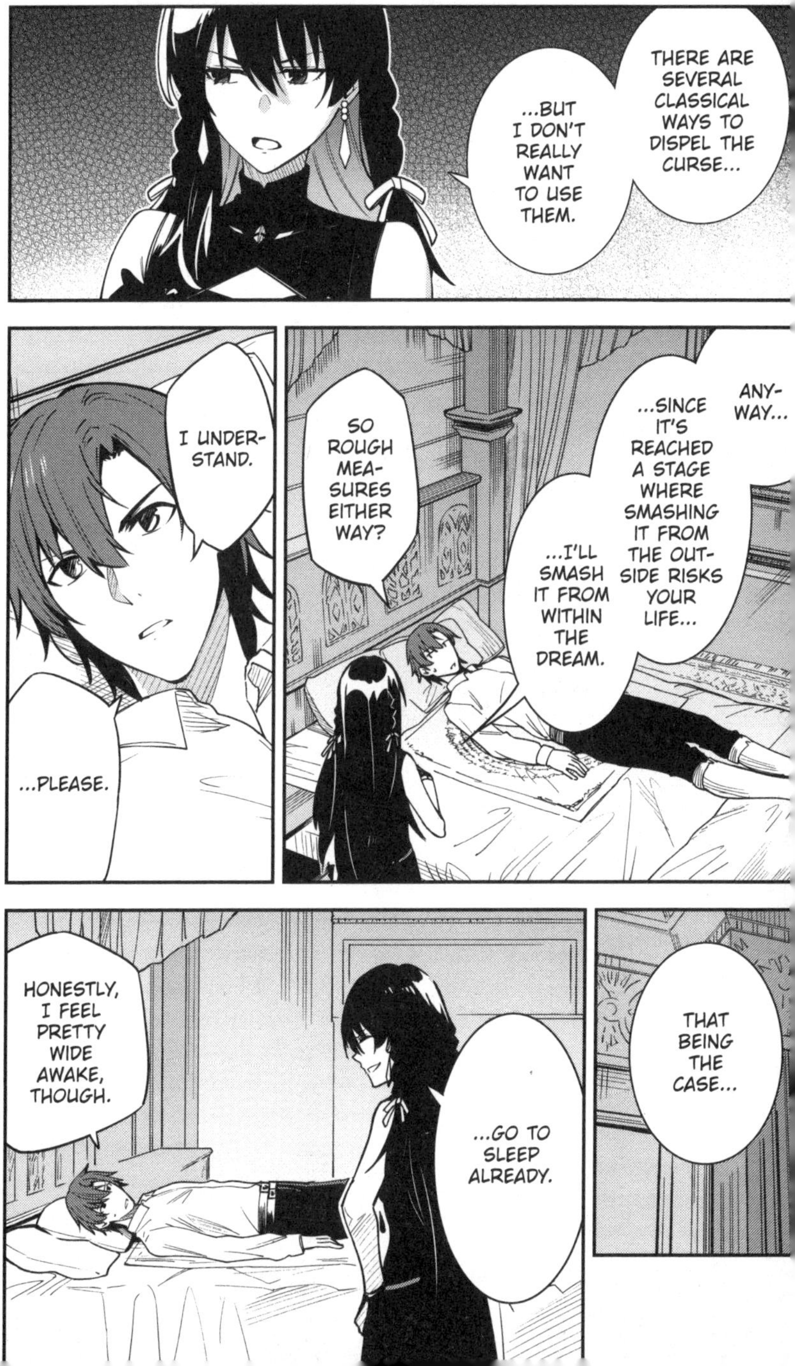
THERE ARE SEVERAL CLASSICAL WAYS TO DISPEL THE CURSE...
...BUT I DON'T REALLY WANT TO USE THEM.
ANY-WAY...
...SINCE IT'S REACHED A STAGE WHERE SMASHING IT FROM THE OUT-SIDE RISKS YOUR LIFE...
...I'LL SMASH IT FROM WITHIN THE DREAM.
SO ROUGH MEA-SURES EITHER WAY?
I UNDER-STAND.
...PLEASE.
THAT BEING THE CASE...
...GO TO SLEEP ALREADY.
HONESTLY, I FEEL PRETTY WIDE AWAKE, THOUGH.

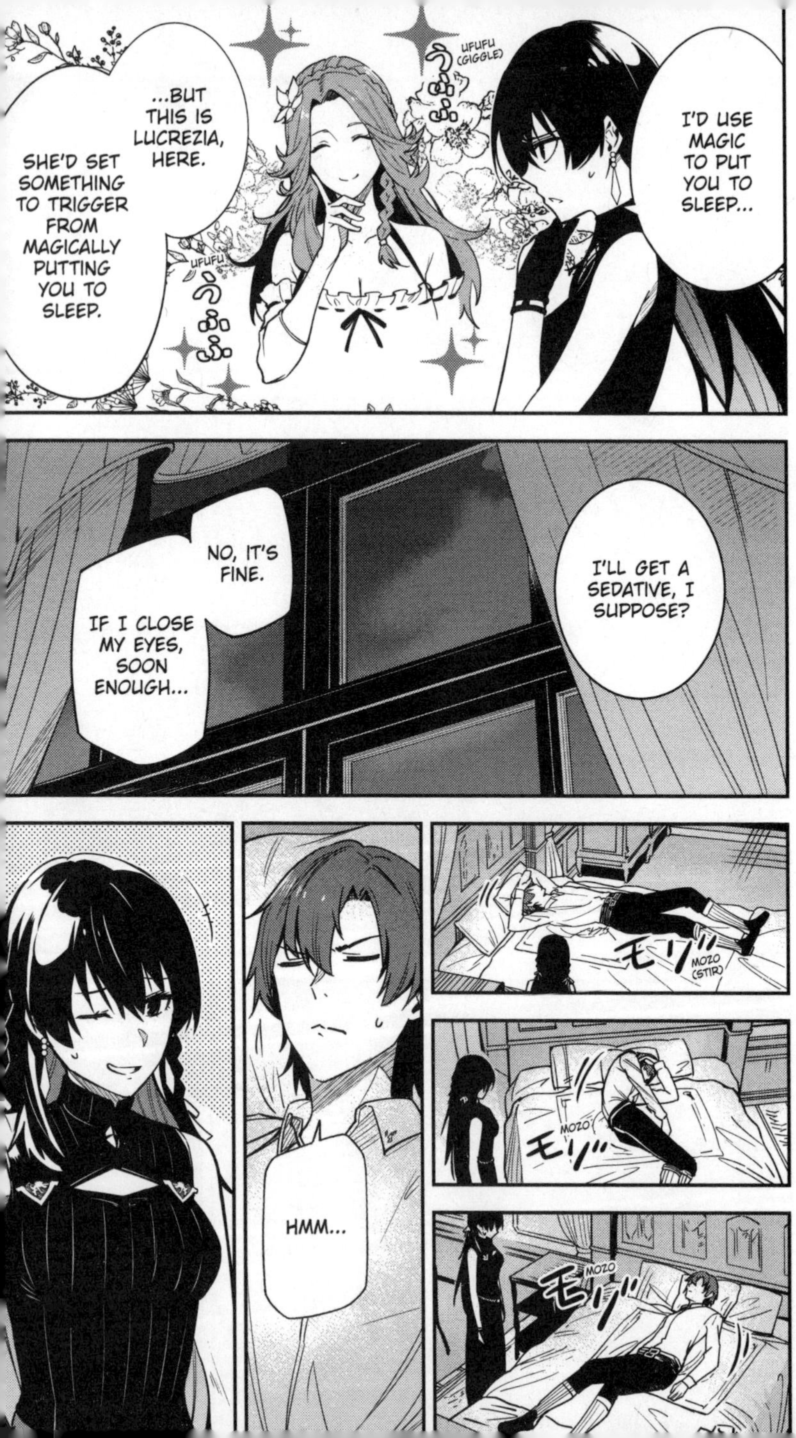
I'D USE MAGIC TO PUT YOU TO SLEEP...
うふふ
UFUFU (GIGGLE)
...BUT THIS IS LUCREZIA, HERE.
SHE'D SET SOMETHING TO TRIGGER FROM MAGICALLY PUTTING YOU TO SLEEP.
うふふ
UFUFU
I'LL GET A SEDATIVE, I SUPPOSE?
NO, IT'S FINE.
IF I CLOSE MY EYES, SOON ENOUGH...
モゾ
MOZO (STIR)
モゾ
MOZO
モゾ
MOZO
HMM...

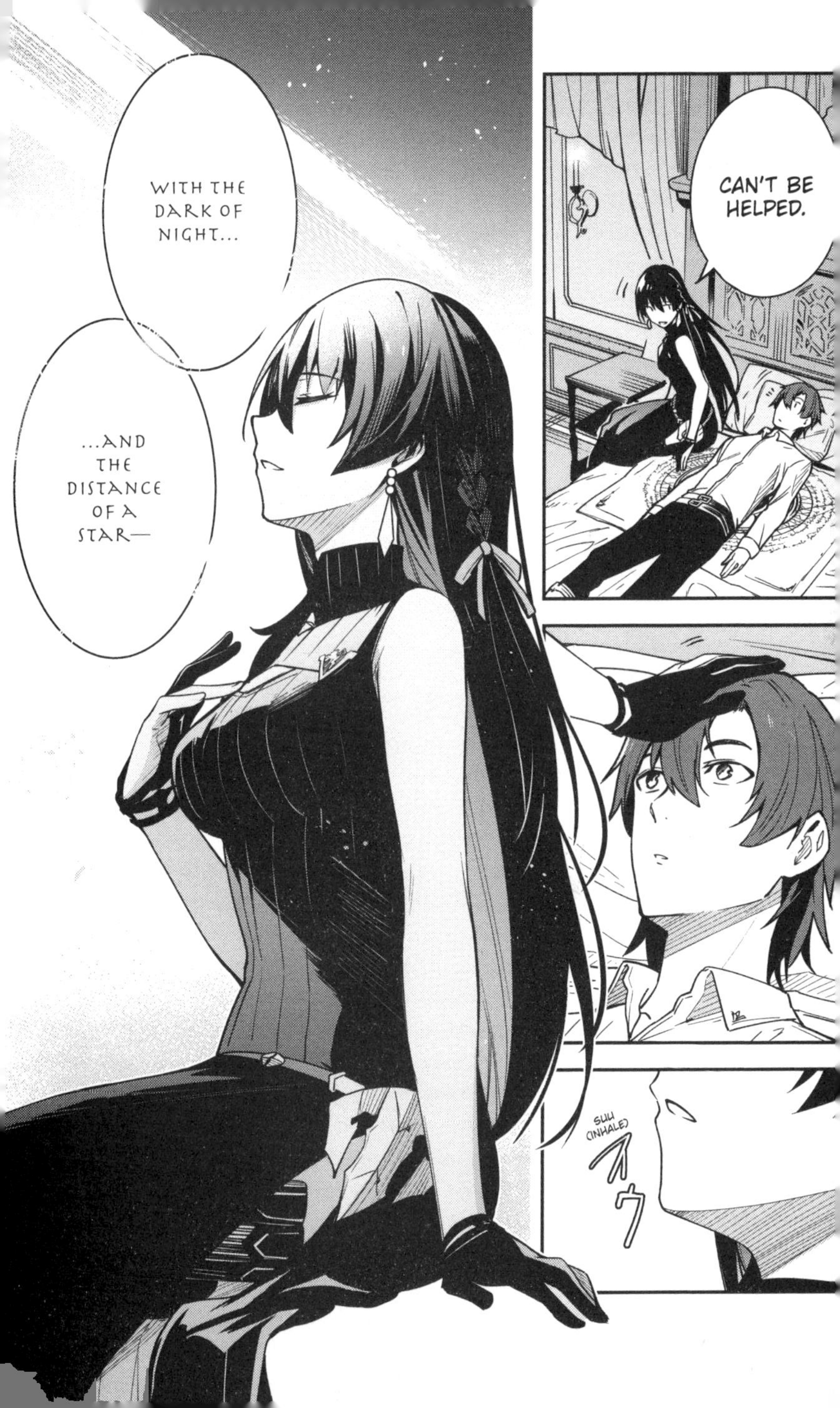
CAN'T BE HELPED.
SUU (INHALE)
WITH THE DARK OF NIGHT...
...AND THE DISTANCE OF A STAR—

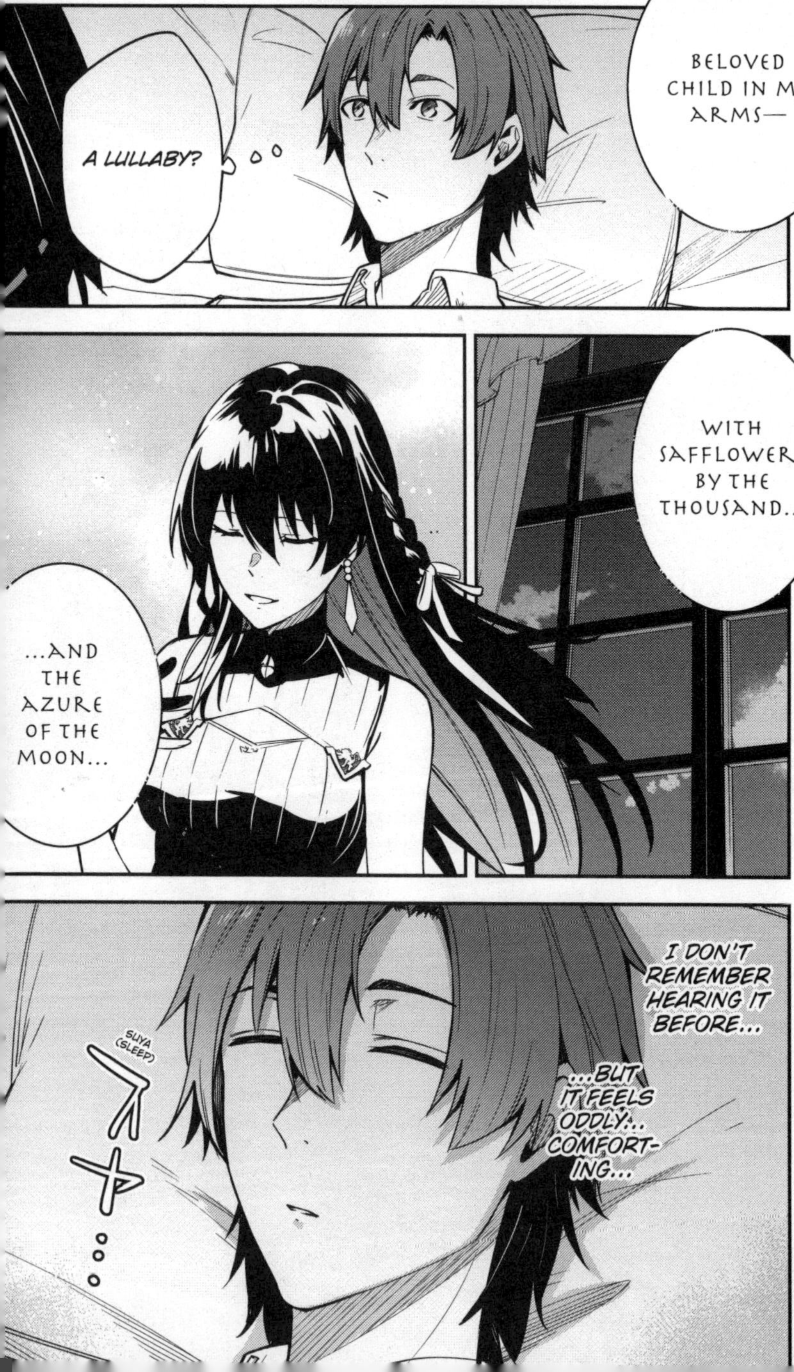
BELOVED CHILD IN MY ARMS—
A LULLABY?
WITH SAFFLOWERS BY THE THOUSAND...
...AND THE AZURE OF THE MOON...
I DON'T REMEMBER HEARING IT BEFORE...
...BUT IT FEELS ODDLY... COMFORTING...
SUYA (SLEEP)

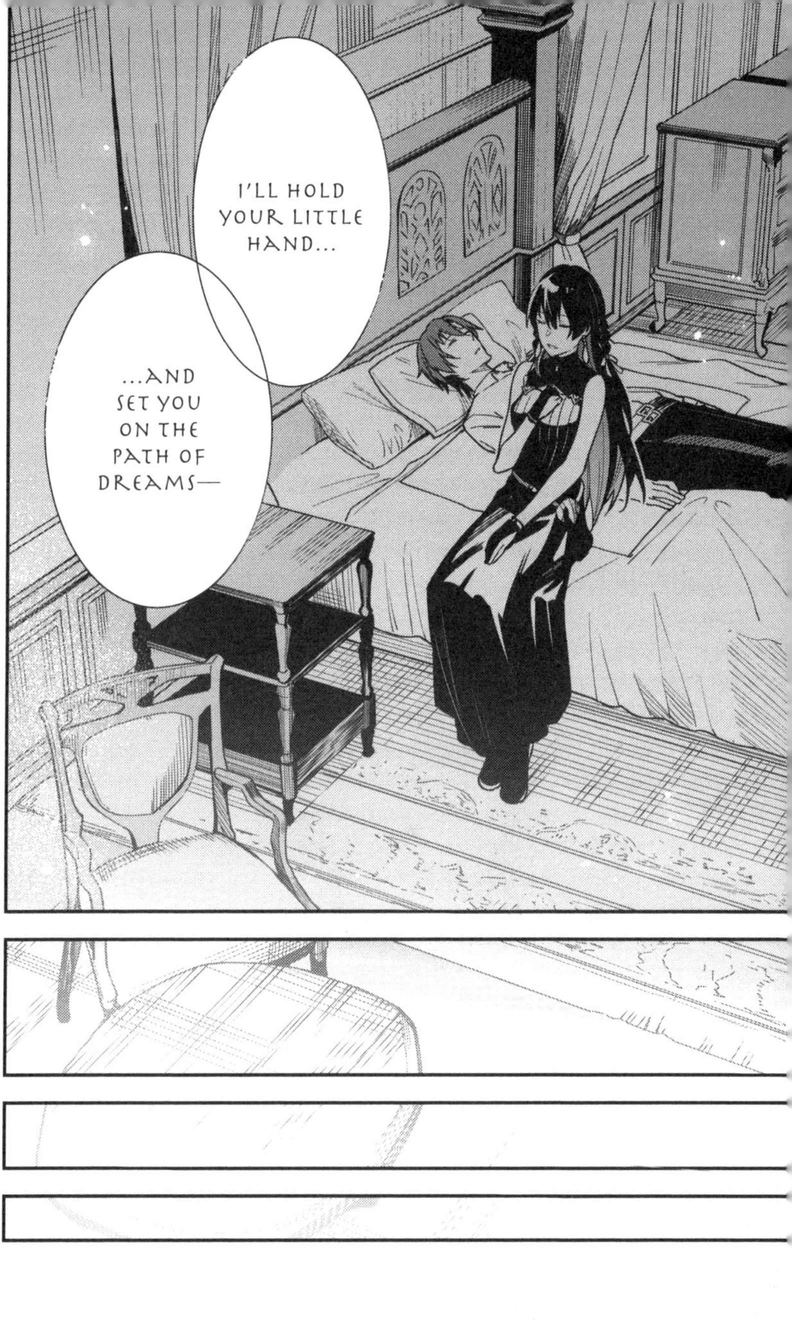
I'LL HOLD YOUR LITTLE HAND...
...AND SET YOU ON THE PATH OF DREAMS—

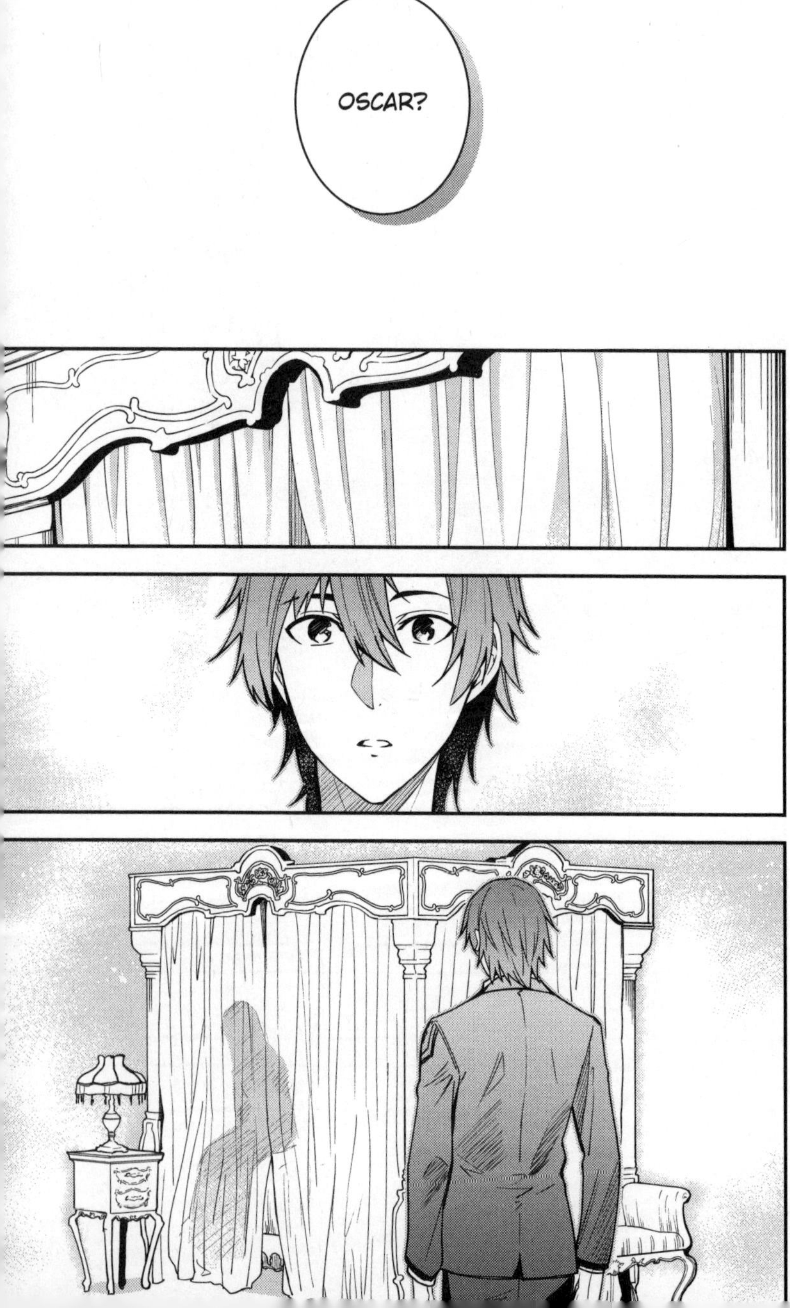
OSCAR?

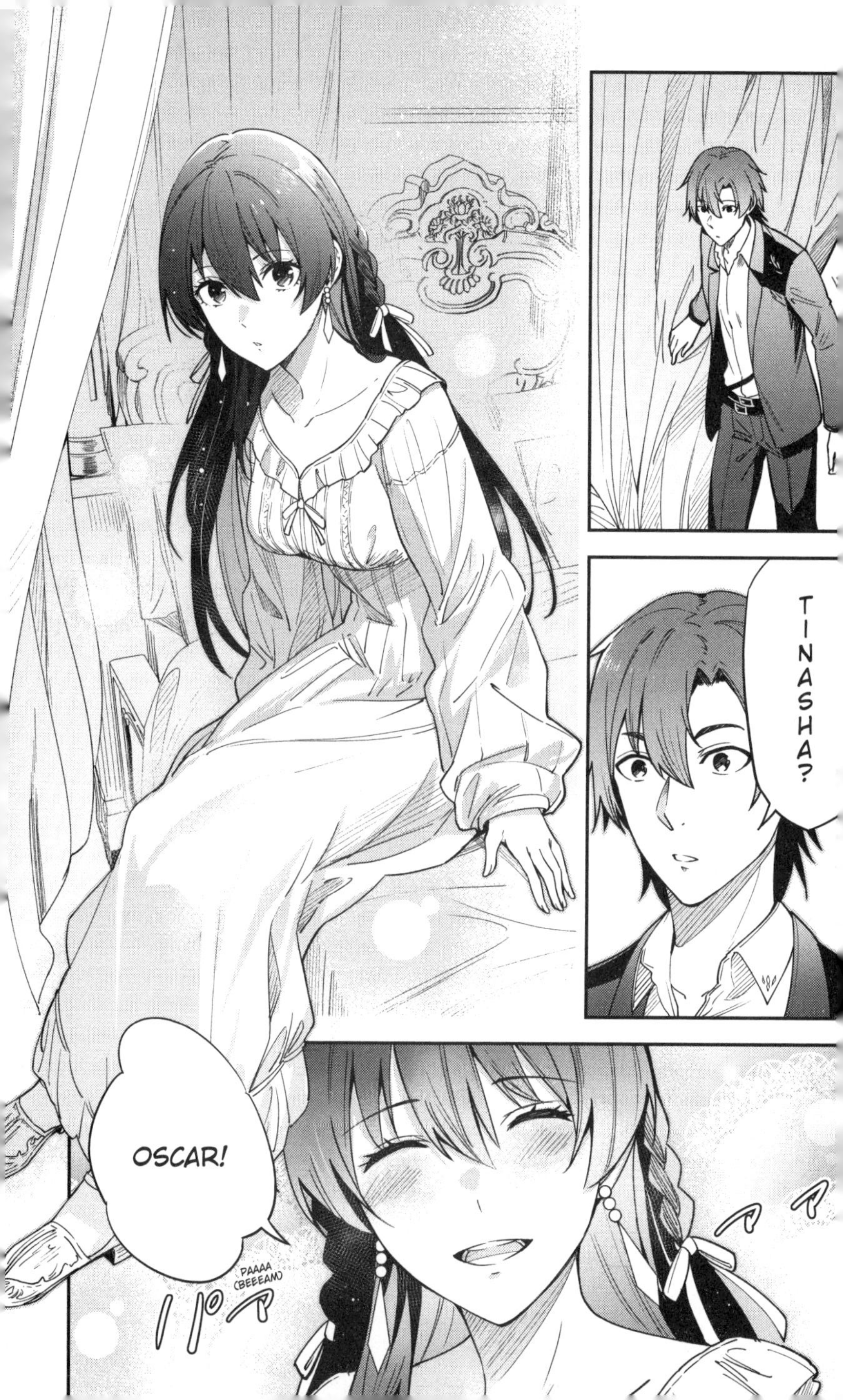
TINASHA?
OSCAR!
パァ
PAAAA (BEEEAM)

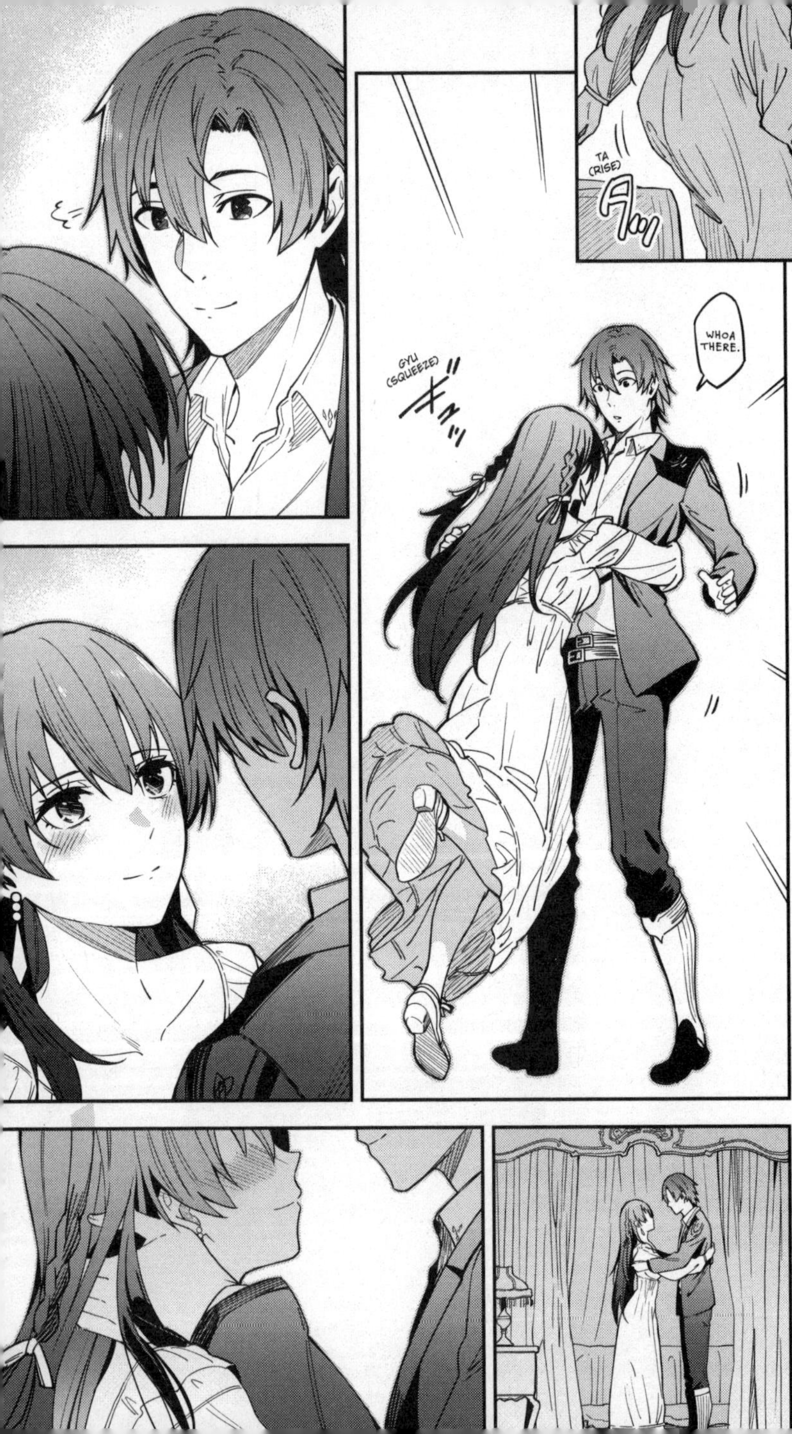
TA (RISE)
WHOA THERE.
GYU (SQUEEZE)

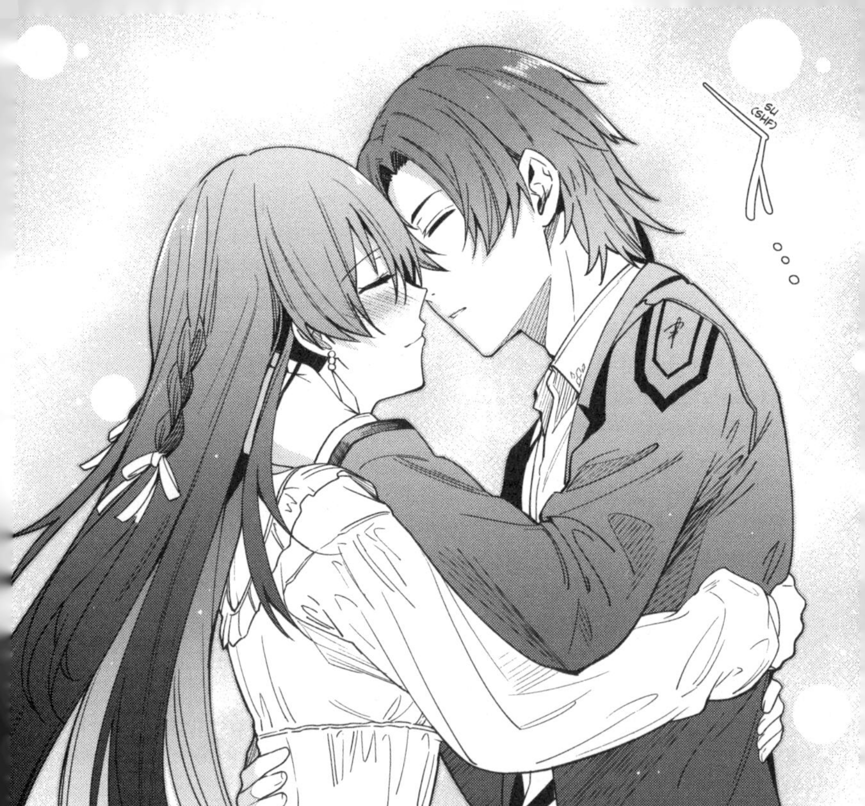
SU (SHF)

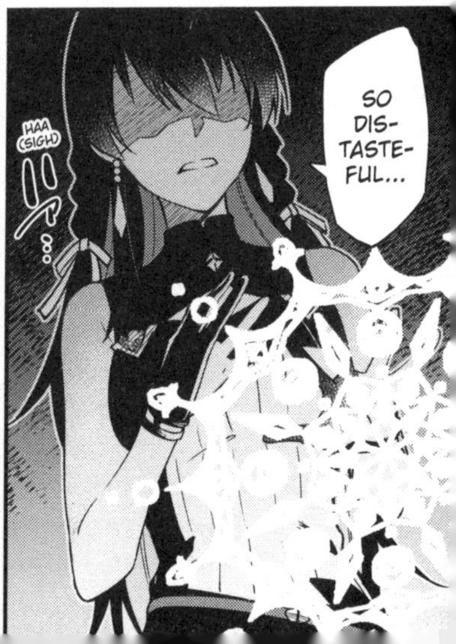
SO DIS-
TASTE-
FUL...
HAA (SIGH)

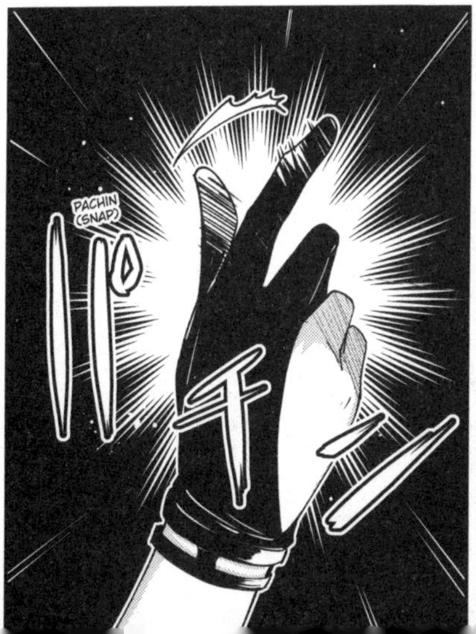
PACHIN (SNAP)

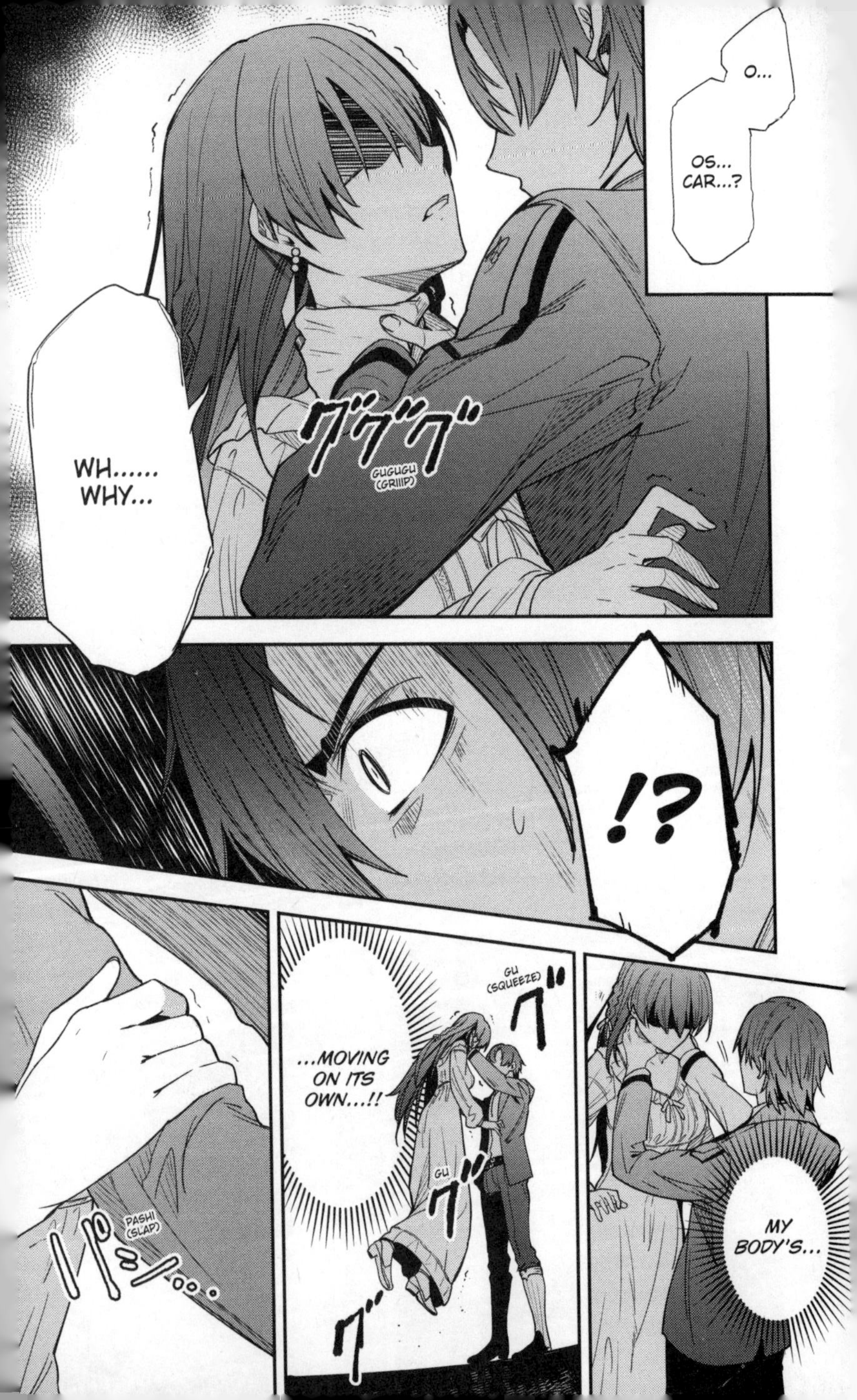
O...
OS... CAR...?
グググ
GUGUGU (GRIIIP)
WH...... WHY...
!?
MY BODY'S...
グッ
GU (SQUEEZE)
...MOVING ON ITS OWN...!!
グ
GU
PASHI (SLAP)

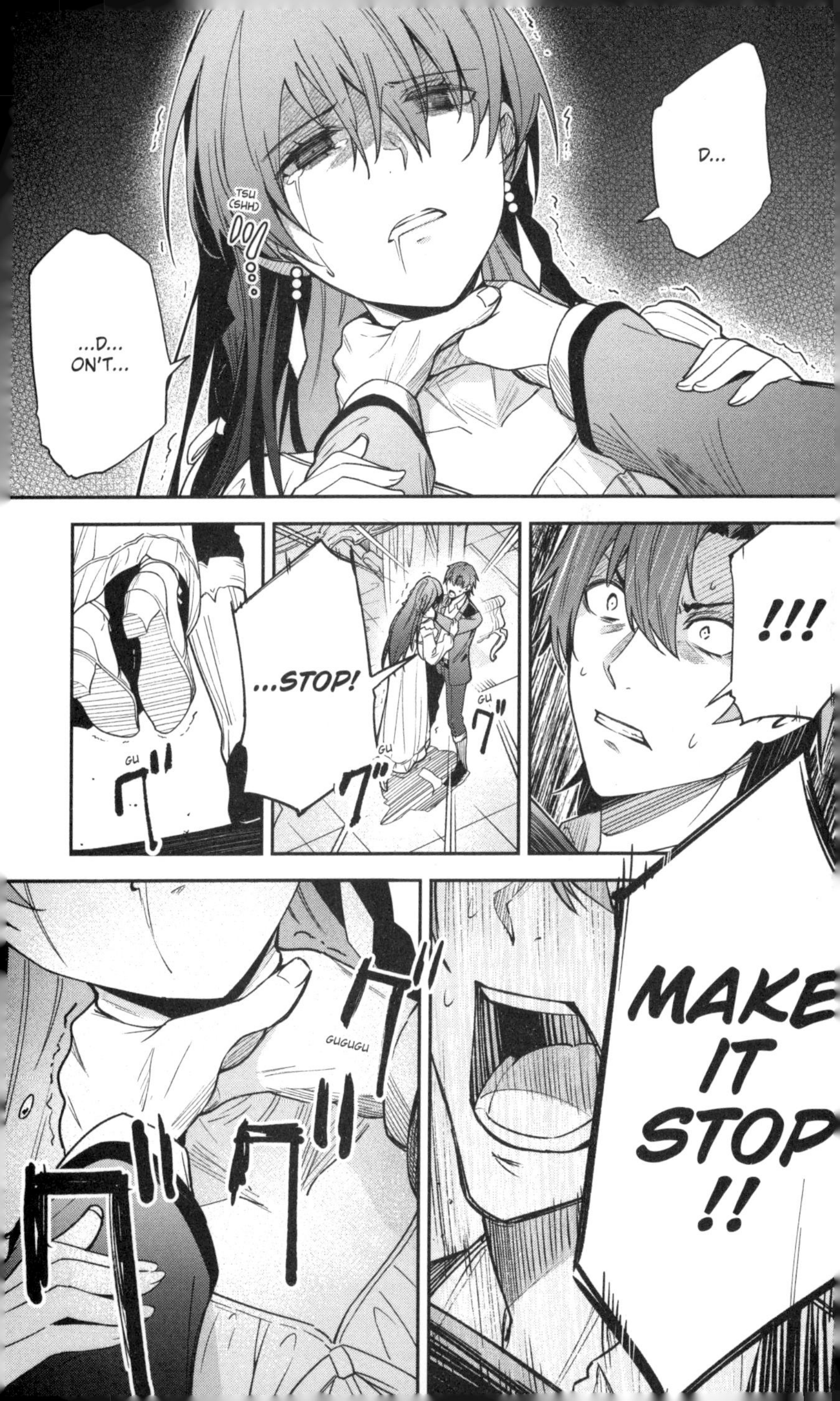
D...
TSU (SHH)
...D... ON'T...
!!!
...STOP!
GU
GU
GU
MAKE IT STOP!!
GUGUGU

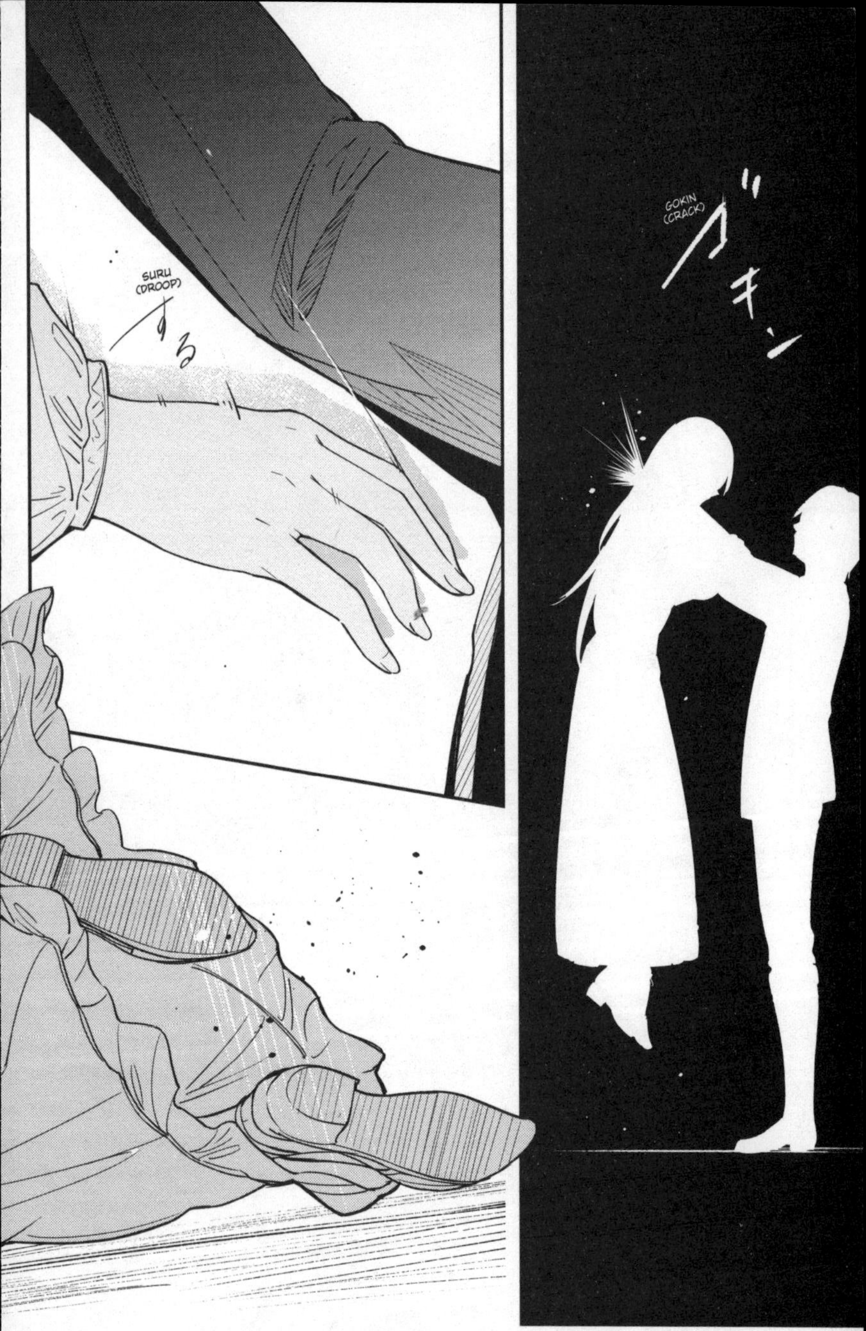
GOKIN (CRACK)
ゴキン
SURU (DROOP)
する

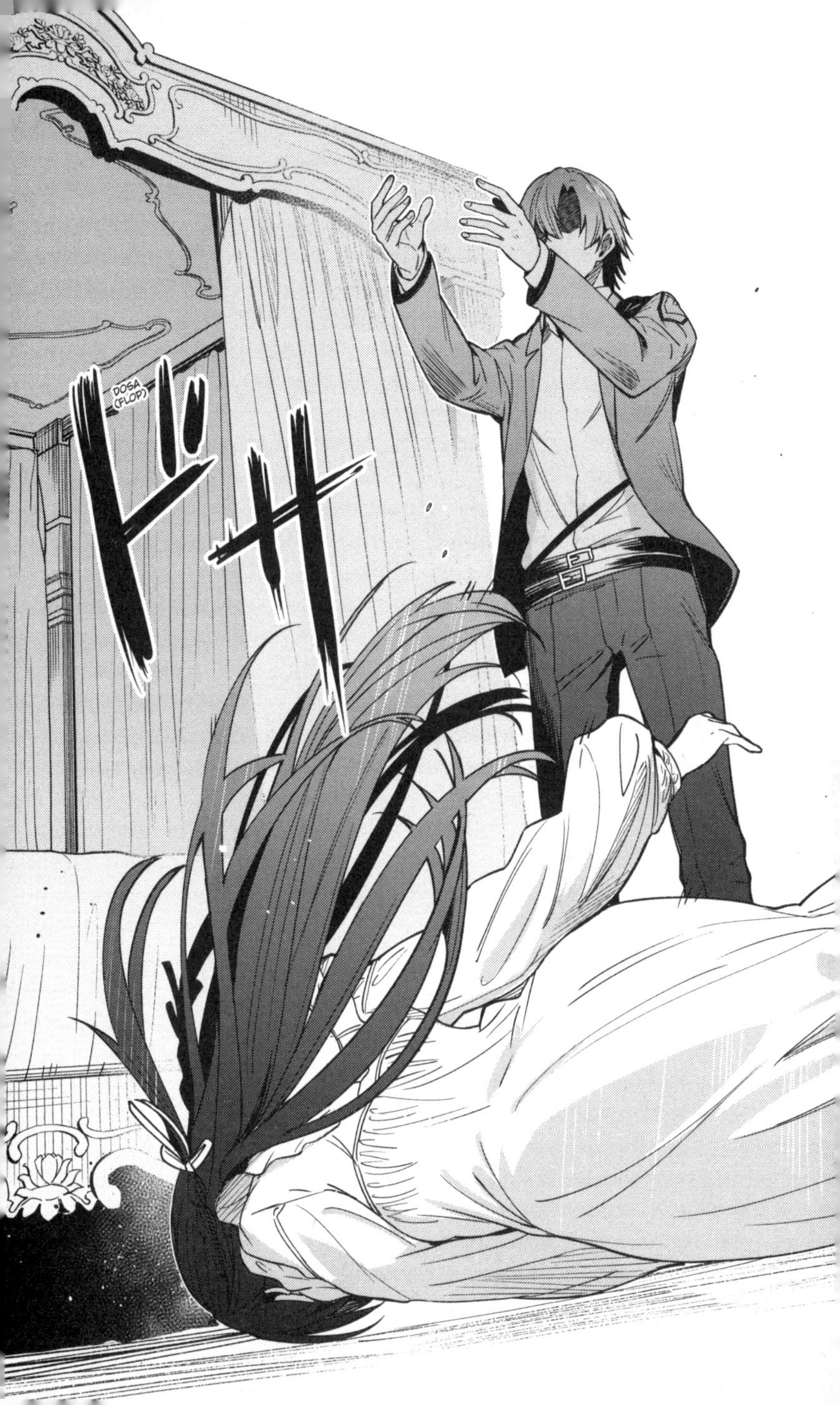

DOSA (FLOP)

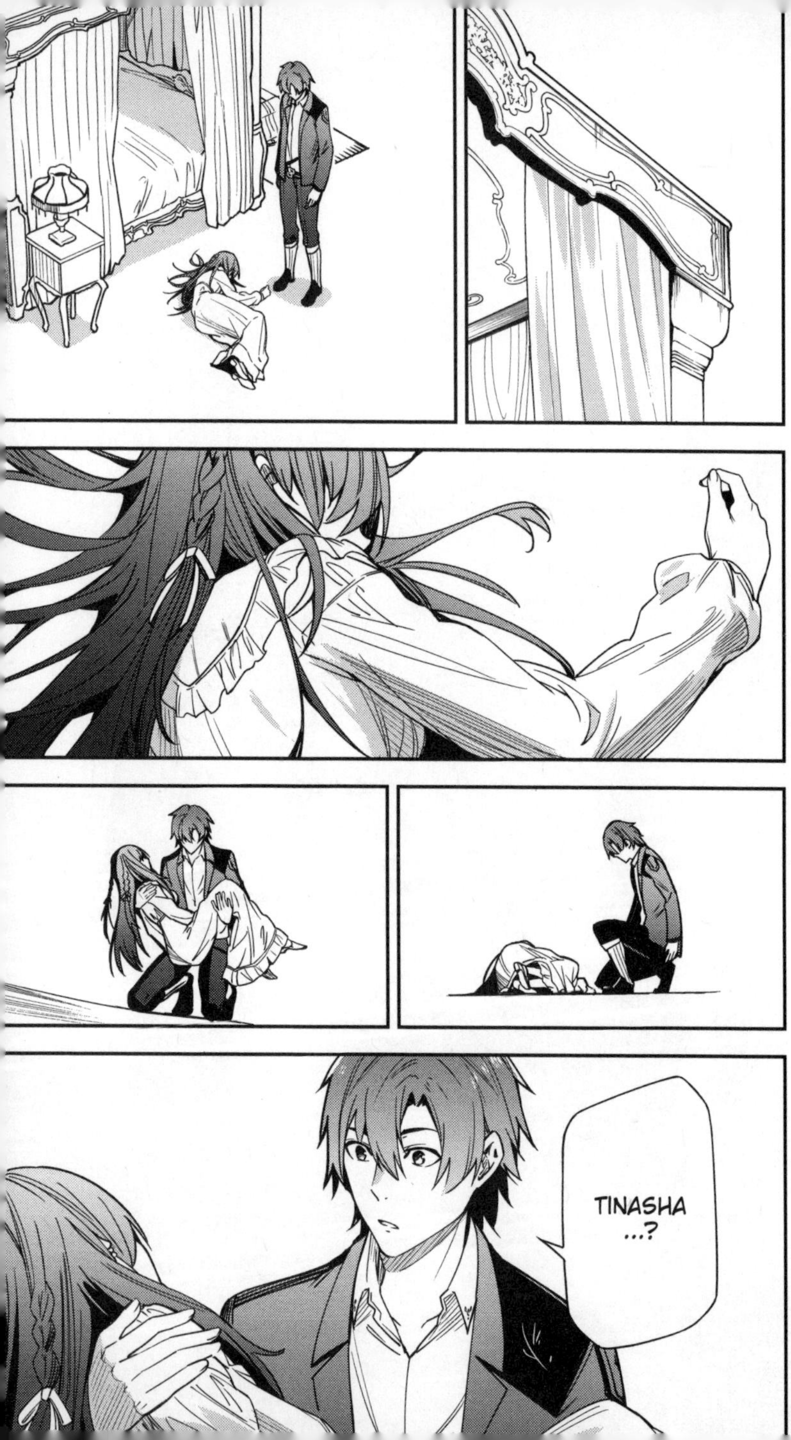
TINASHA ...?

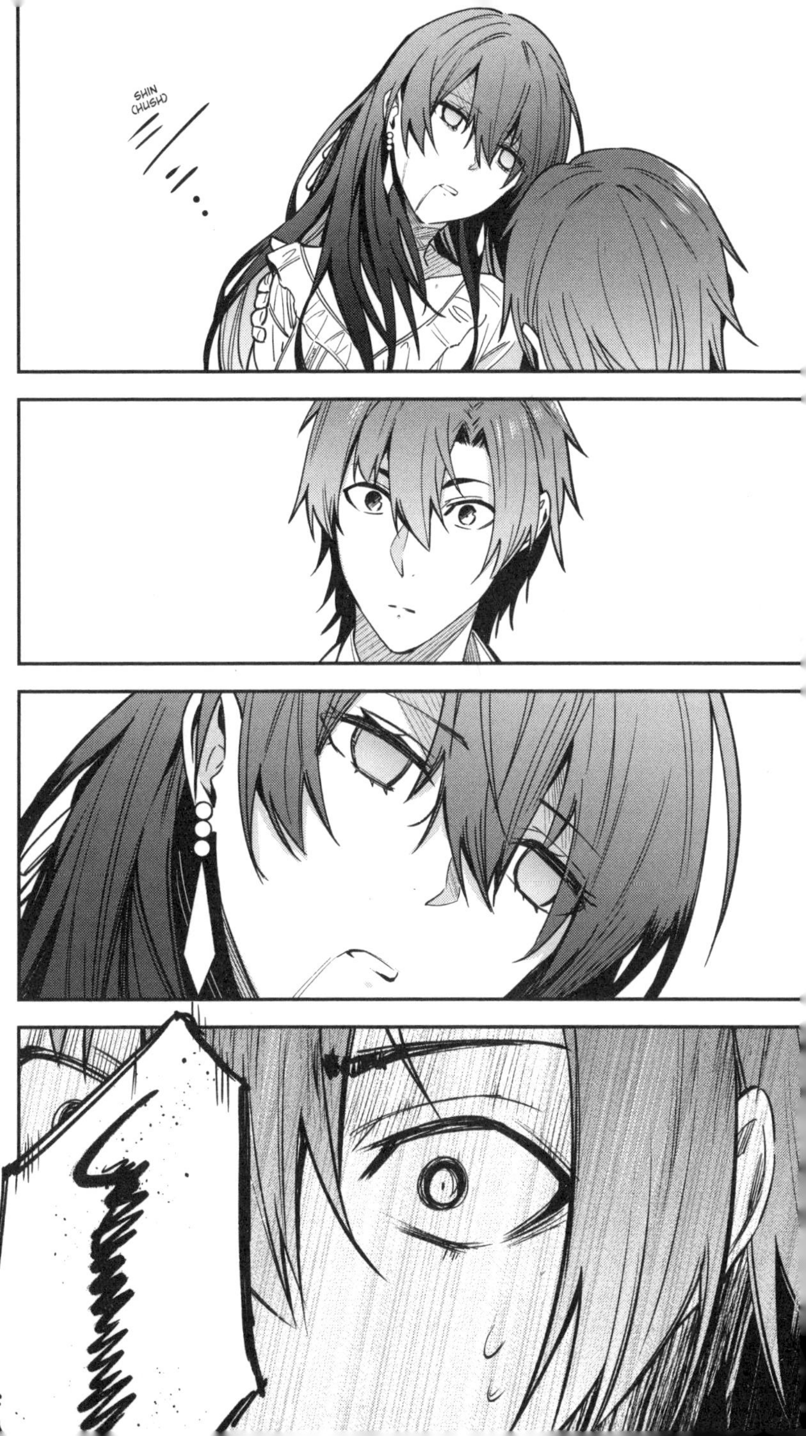
SHIN (HUSH)

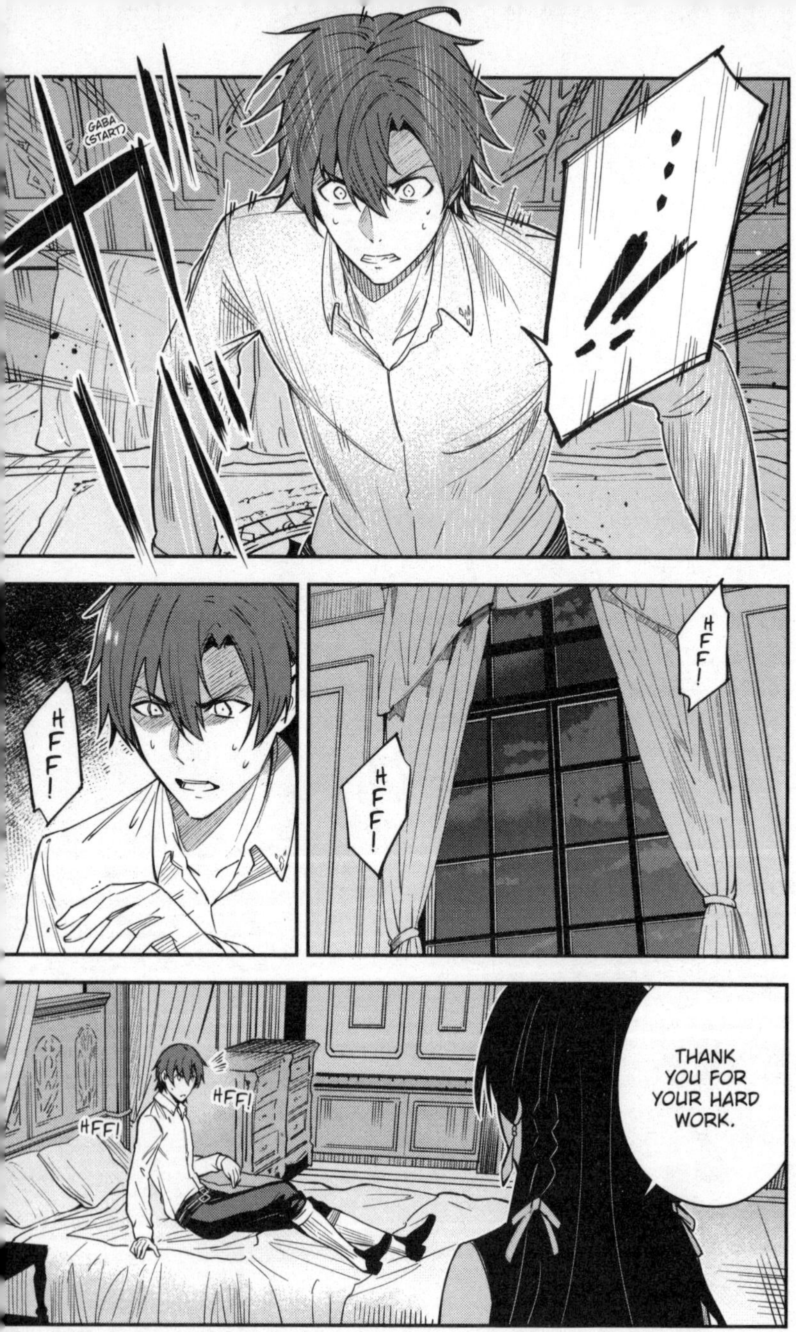
…!
GABA (START)
HFF!
HFF!
HFF!
THANK YOU FOR YOUR HARD WORK.
HFF!
HFF!

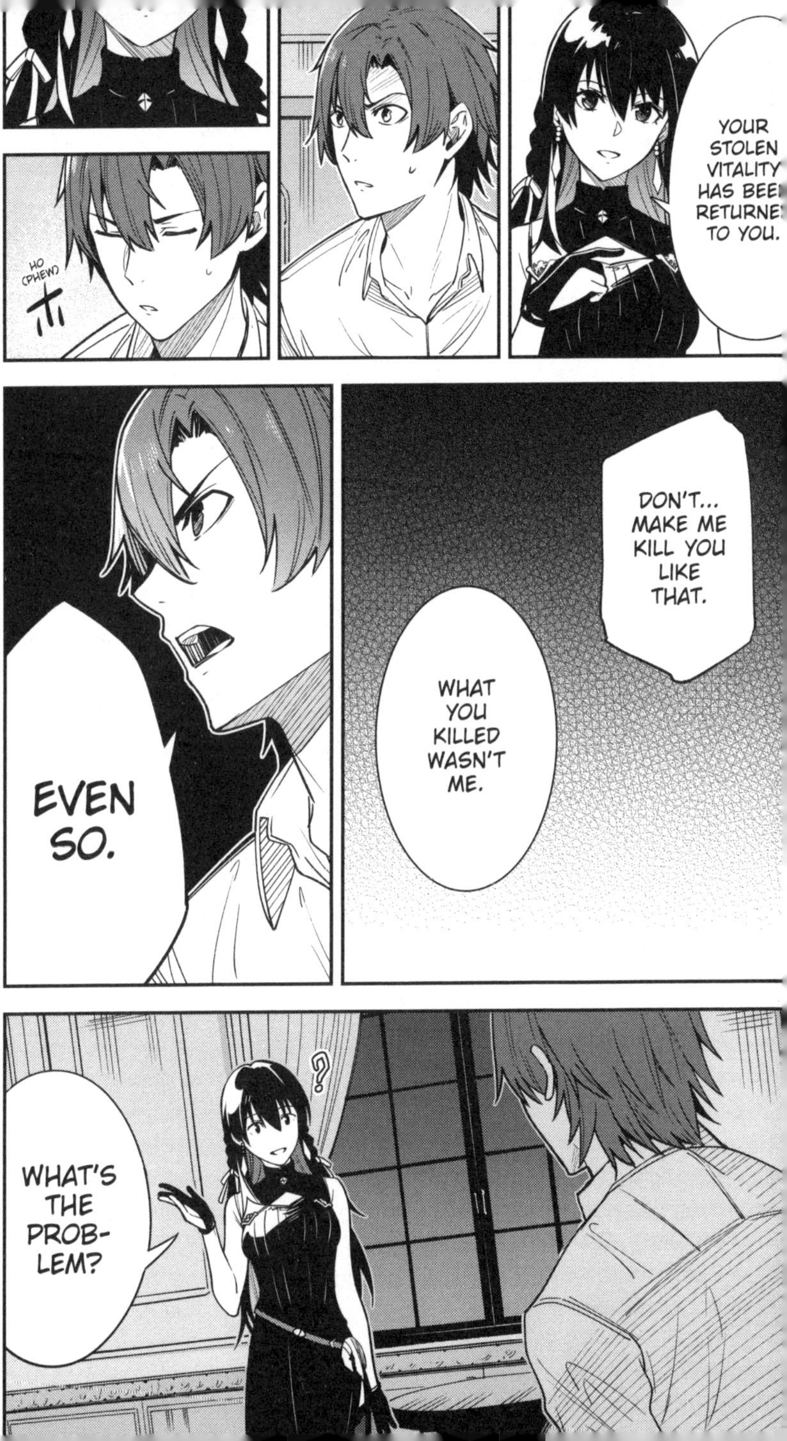
YOUR STOLEN VITALITY HAS BEE RETURNE TO YOU.
HO (PHEW)
DON'T... MAKE ME KILL YOU LIKE THAT.
WHAT YOU KILLED WASN'T ME.
EVEN SO.
?
WHAT'S THE PROB-LEM?

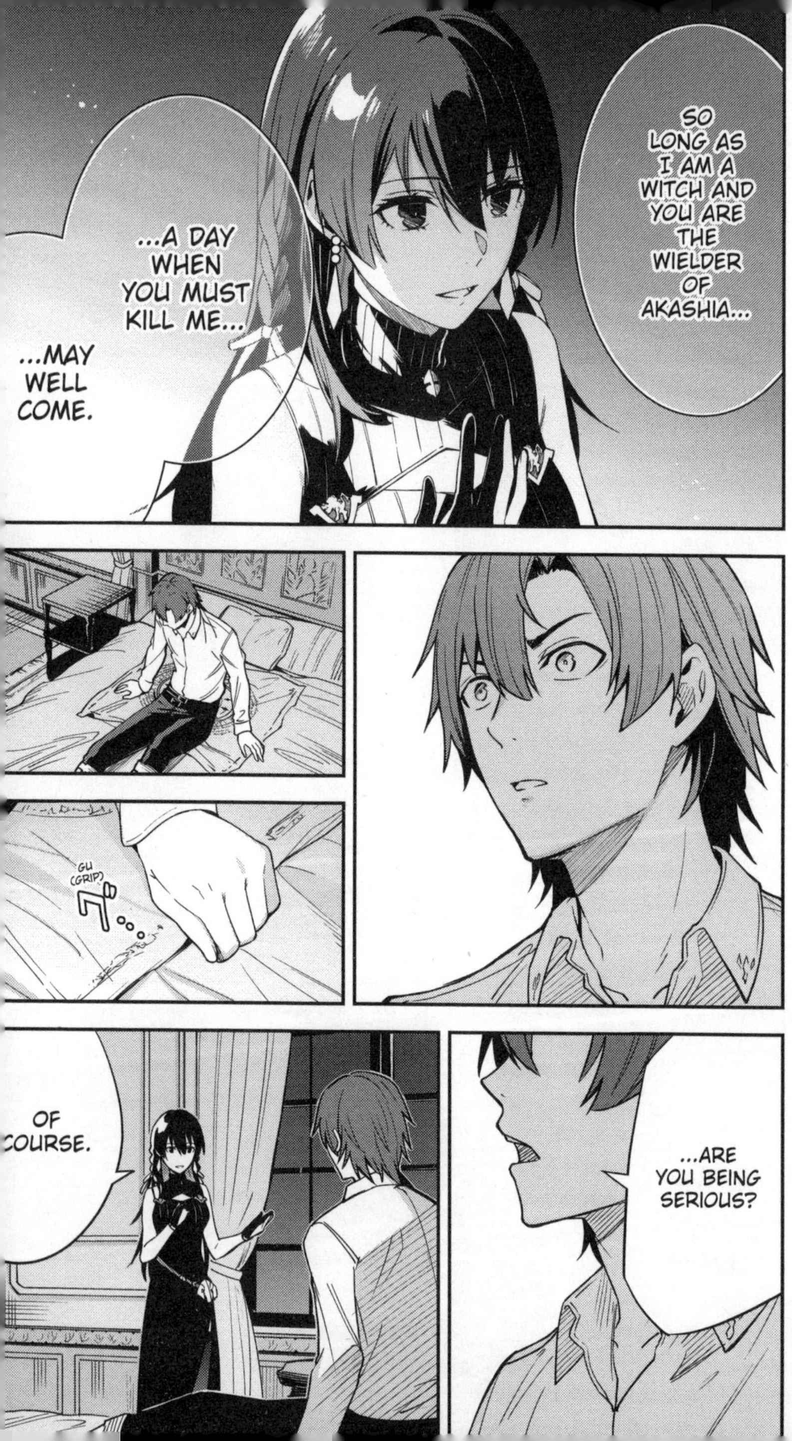
SO LONG AS I AM A WITCH AND YOU ARE THE WIELDER OF AKASHIA...
...A DAY WHEN YOU MUST KILL ME...
...MAY WELL COME.
GU (GRIP)
...ARE YOU BEING SERIOUS?
OF COURSE.

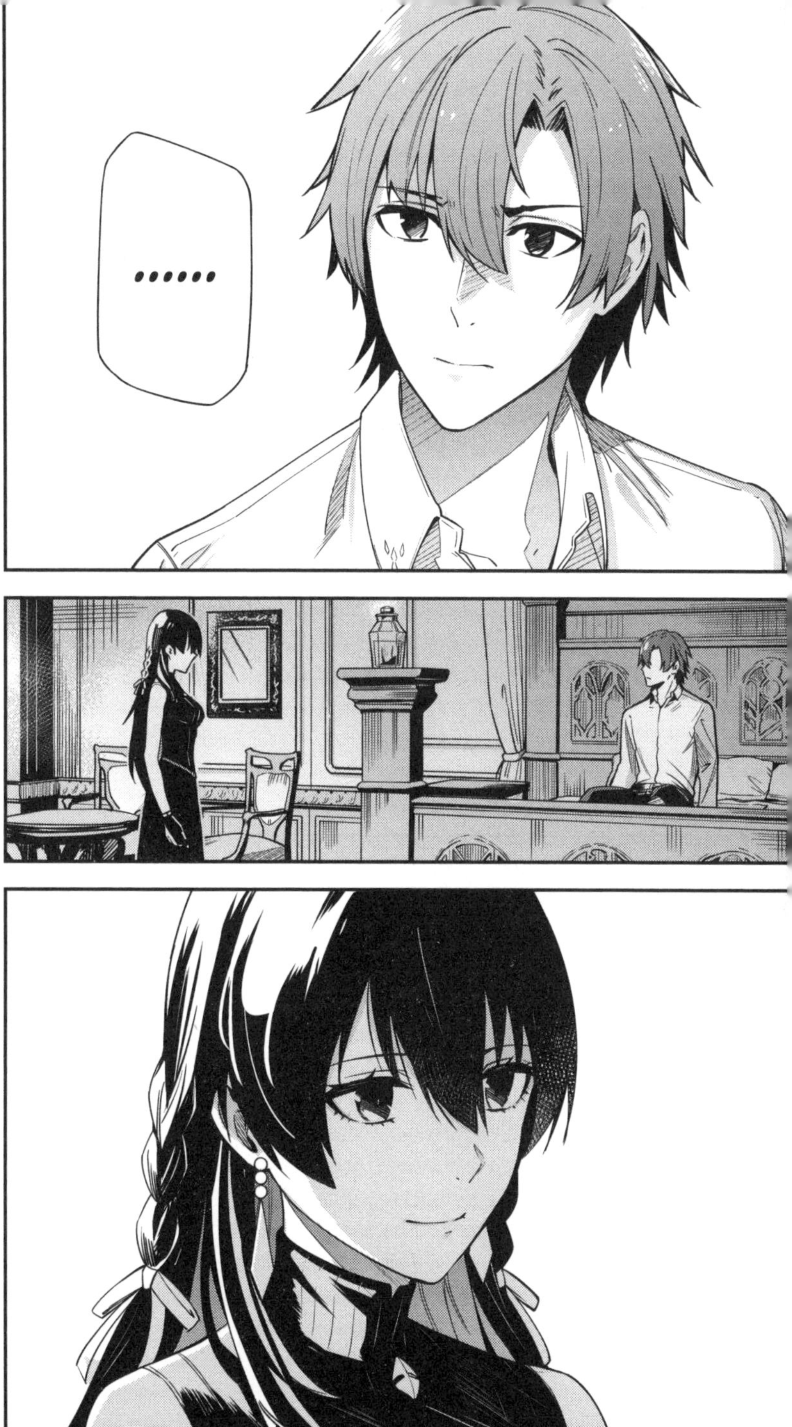
......

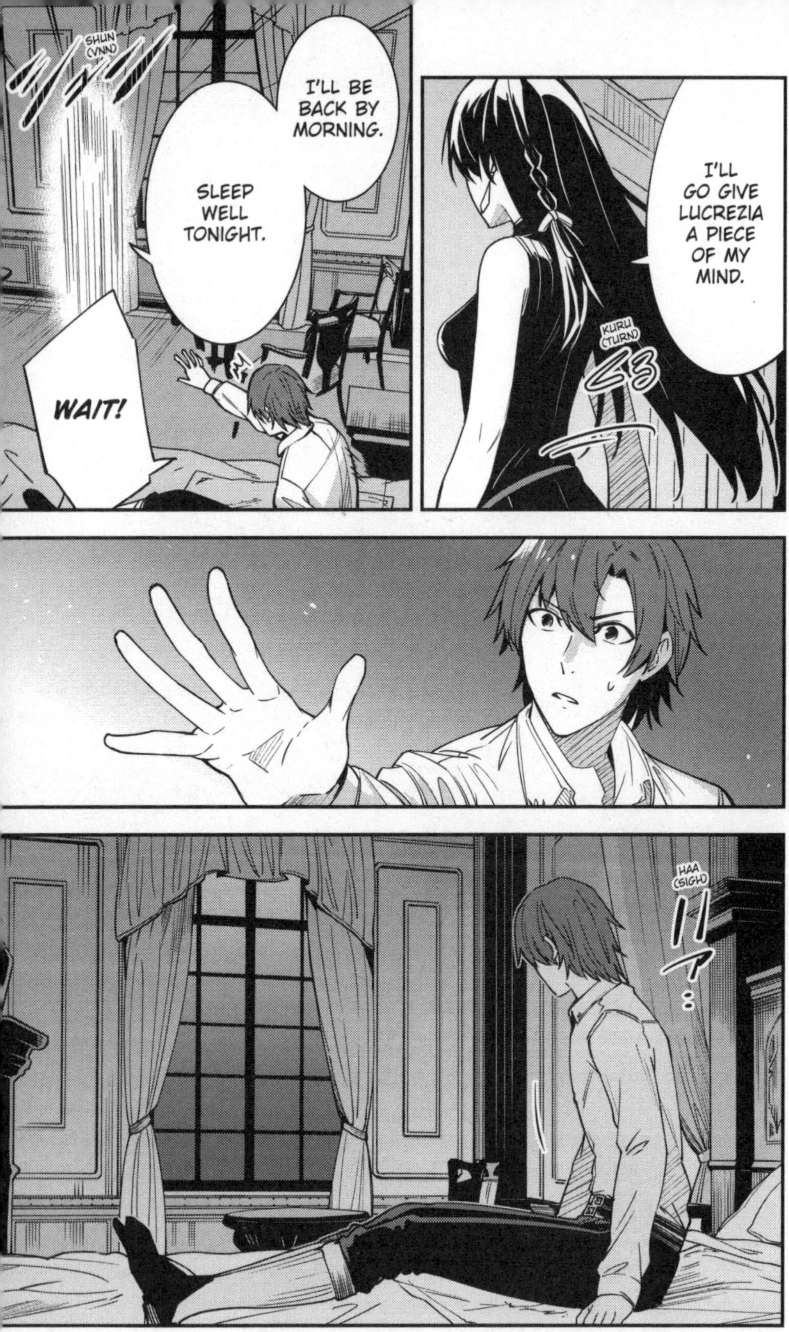
I'LL GO GIVE LUCREZIA A PIECE OF MY MIND.
KURU (TURN)
SHUN (VNN)
I'LL BE BACK BY MORNING.
SLEEP WELL TONIGHT.
WAIT!
HAA (SIGH)

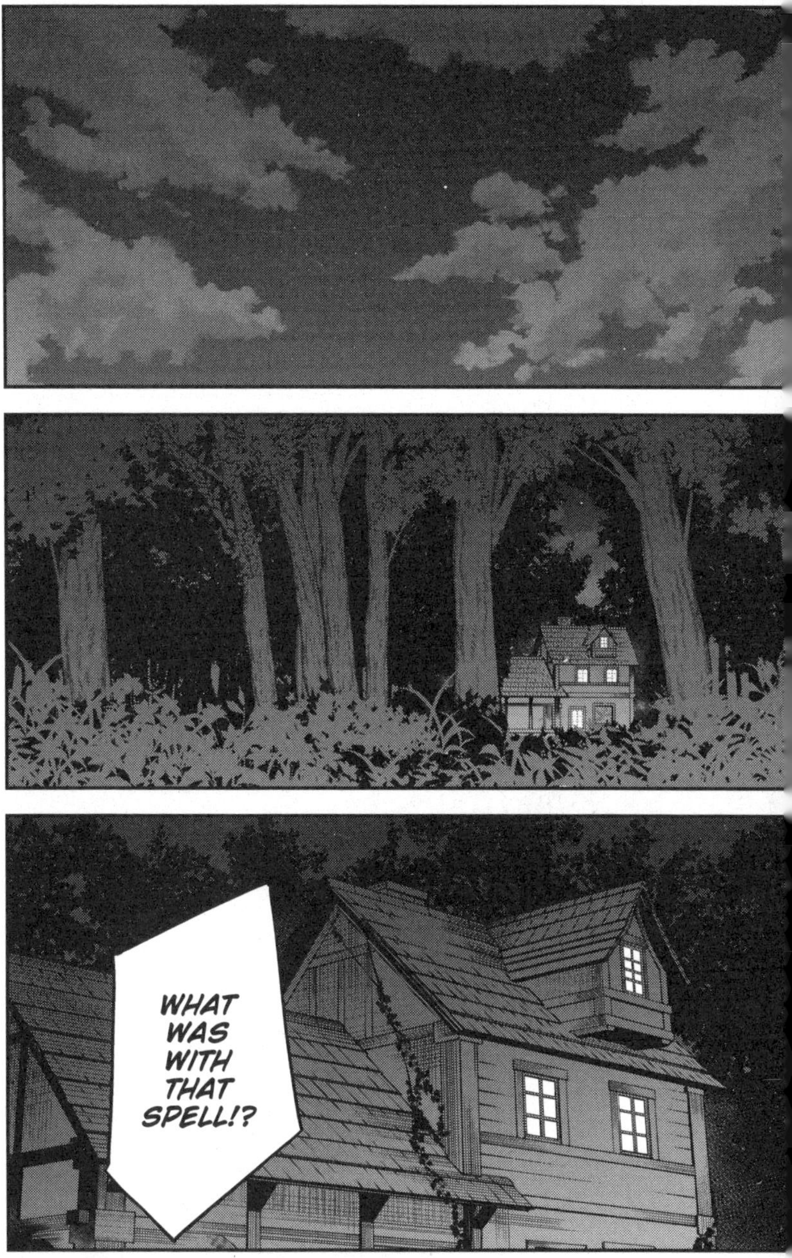
WHAT WAS WITH THAT SPELL!?

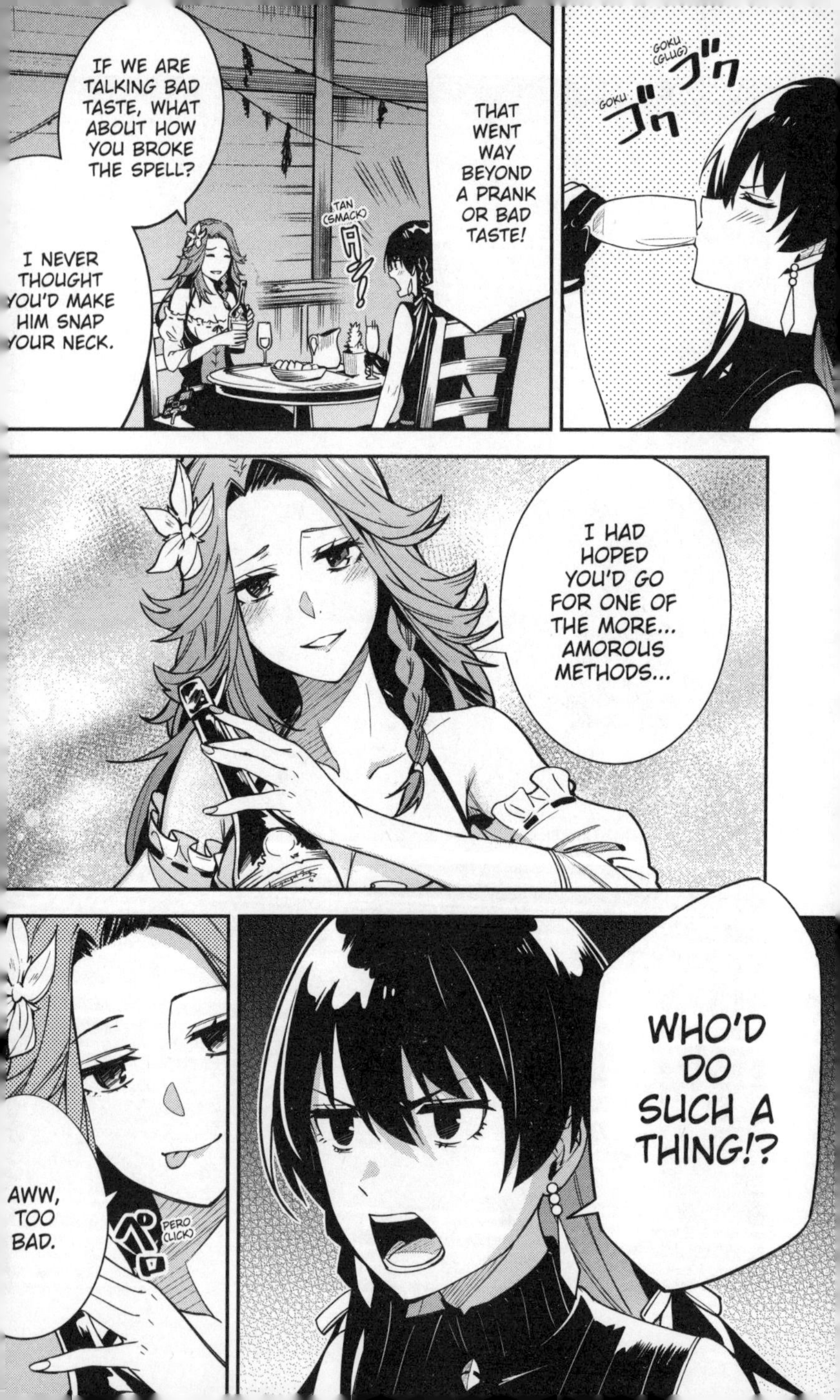
GOKU (GLUG) ゴク
GOKU ゴク
THAT WENT WAY BEYOND A PRANK OR BAD TASTE!
TAN (SMACK) タン!
IF WE ARE TALKING BAD TASTE, WHAT ABOUT HOW YOU BROKE THE SPELL?
I NEVER THOUGHT YOU'D MAKE HIM SNAP YOUR NECK.
I HAD HOPED YOU'D GO FOR ONE OF THE MORE... AMOROUS METHODS...
WHO'D DO SUCH A THING!?
AWW, TOO BAD.
PERO (CLICK) ペロ

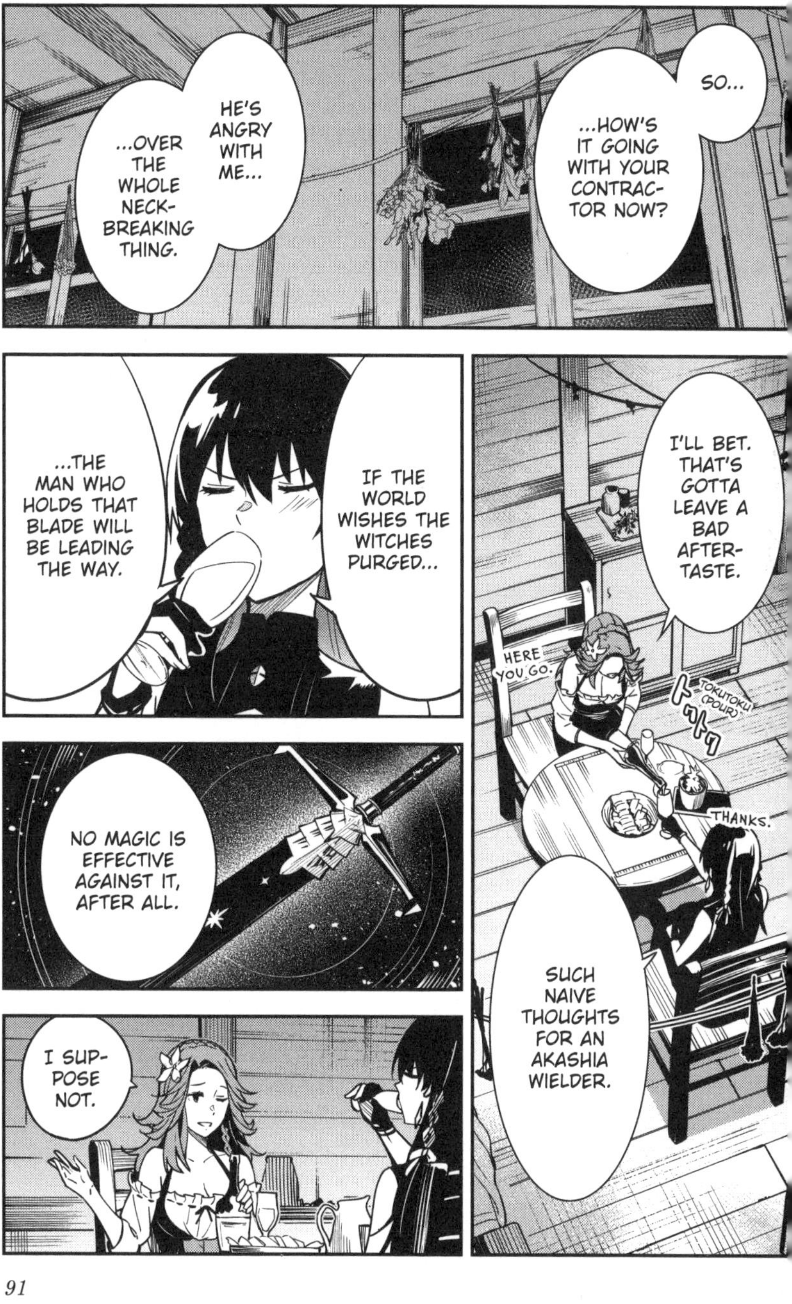
SO...
...HOW'S IT GOING WITH YOUR CONTRACTOR NOW?
HE'S ANGRY WITH ME...
...OVER THE WHOLE NECK-BREAKING THING.
I'LL BET. THAT'S GOTTA LEAVE A BAD AFTER-TASTE.
HERE YOU GO.
トクトク
TOKUTOKU (POUR)
THANKS.
SUCH NAIVE THOUGHTS FOR AN AKASHIA WIELDER.
IF THE WORLD WISHES THE WITCHES PURGED...
...THE MAN WHO HOLDS THAT BLADE WILL BE LEADING THE WAY.
NO MAGIC IS EFFECTIVE AGAINST IT, AFTER ALL.
I SUPPOSE NOT.

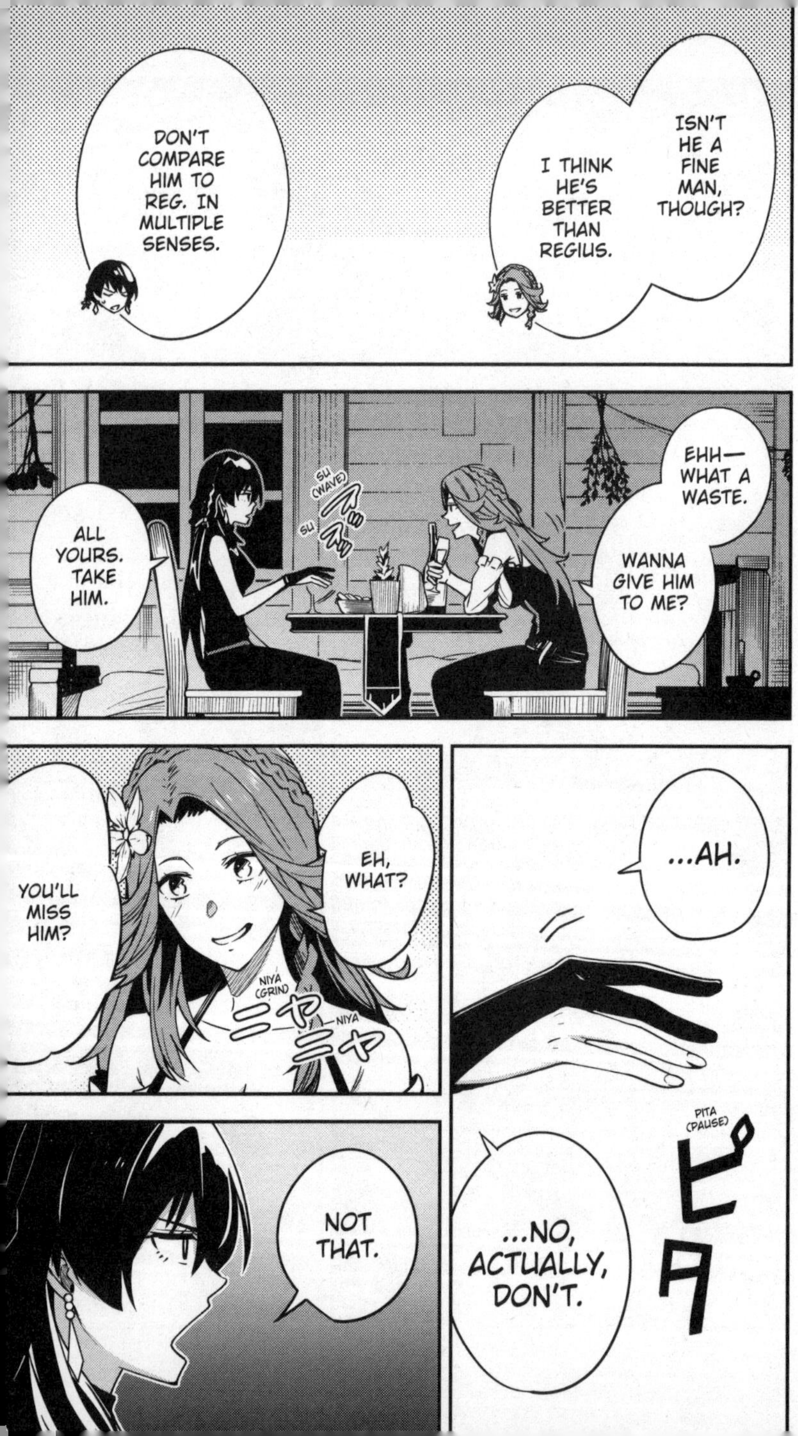
ISN'T HE A FINE MAN, THOUGH?
I THINK HE'S BETTER THAN REGIUS.
DON'T COMPARE HIM TO REG. IN MULTIPLE SENSES.
EHH— WHAT A WASTE.
WANNA GIVE HIM TO ME?
SU (WAVE)
SU
ALL YOURS. TAKE HIM.
...AH.
EH, WHAT?
YOU'LL MISS HIM?
NIYA (GRIN)
NIYA
PITA (PAUSE)
...NO, ACTUALLY, DON'T.
NOT THAT.

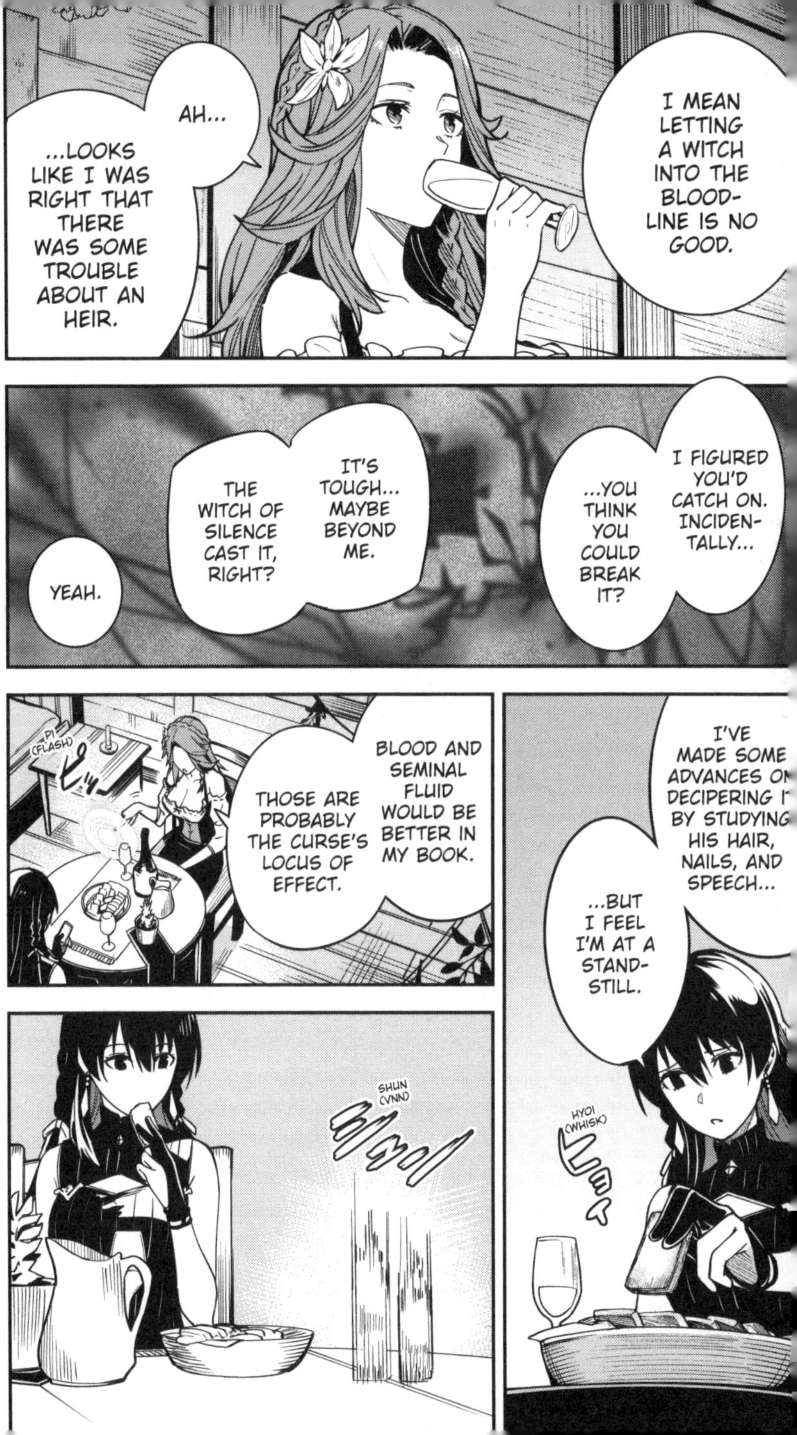
I MEAN LETTING A WITCH INTO THE BLOOD-LINE IS NO GOOD.
AH...
...LOOKS LIKE I WAS RIGHT THAT THERE WAS SOME TROUBLE ABOUT AN HEIR.
I FIGURED YOU'D CATCH ON. INCIDEN-TALLY...
...YOU THINK YOU COULD BREAK IT?
IT'S TOUGH... MAYBE BEYOND ME.
THE WITCH OF SILENCE CAST IT, RIGHT?
YEAH.
I'VE MADE SOME ADVANCES ON DECIPERING IT BY STUDYING HIS HAIR, NAILS, AND SPEECH...
...BUT I FEEL I'M AT A STAND-STILL.
HYOI (WHISK)
BLOOD AND SEMINAL FLUID WOULD BE BETTER IN MY BOOK.
THOSE ARE PROBABLY THE CURSE'S LOCUS OF EFFECT.
PI (FLASH)
SHUN (VNN)

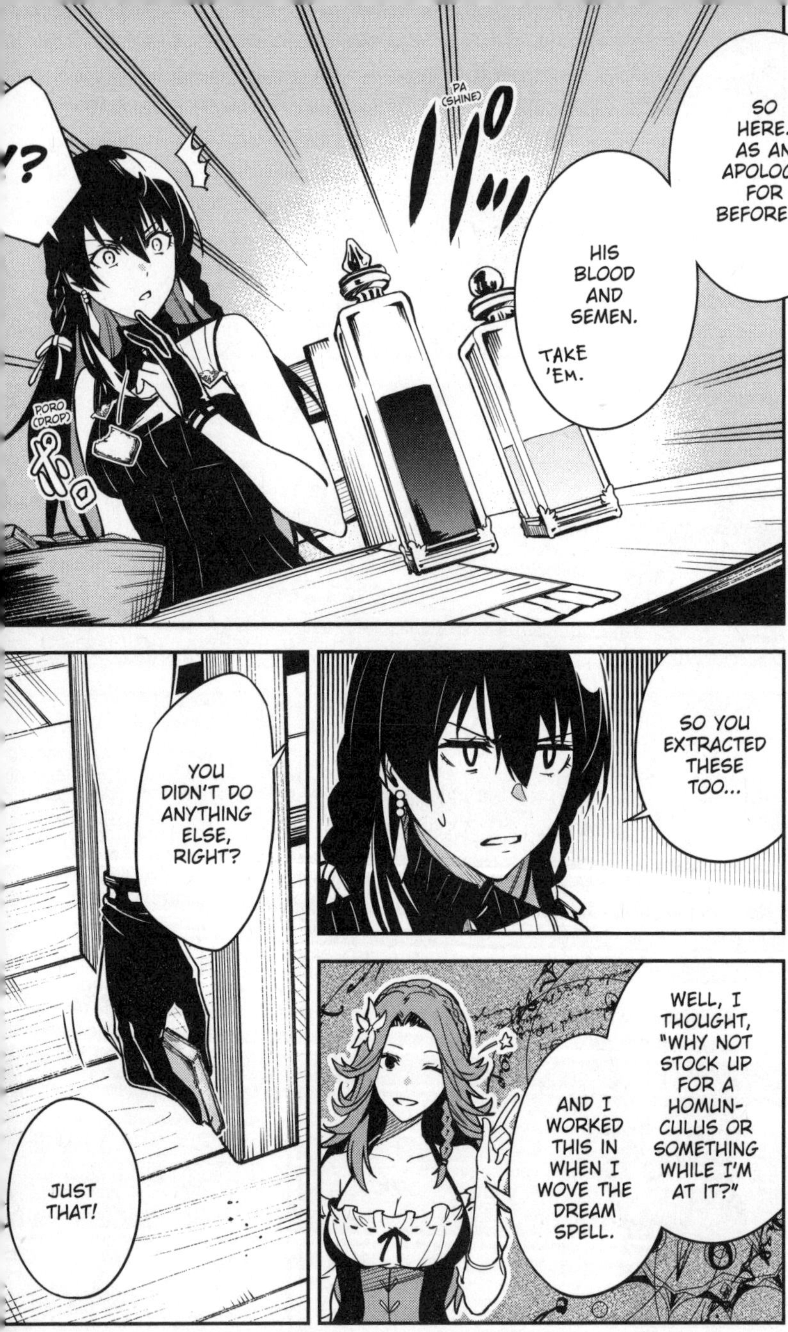
SO HERE. AS AN APOLOGY FOR BEFORE—
HIS BLOOD AND SEMEN.
TAKE 'EM.
PA (SHINE)
!?
PORO (DROP)
SO YOU EXTRACTED THESE TOO...
WELL, I THOUGHT, "WHY NOT STOCK UP FOR A HOMUN-CULUS OR SOMETHING WHILE I'M AT IT?"
AND I WORKED THIS IN WHEN I WOVE THE DREAM SPELL.
YOU DIDN'T DO ANYTHING ELSE, RIGHT?
JUST THAT!

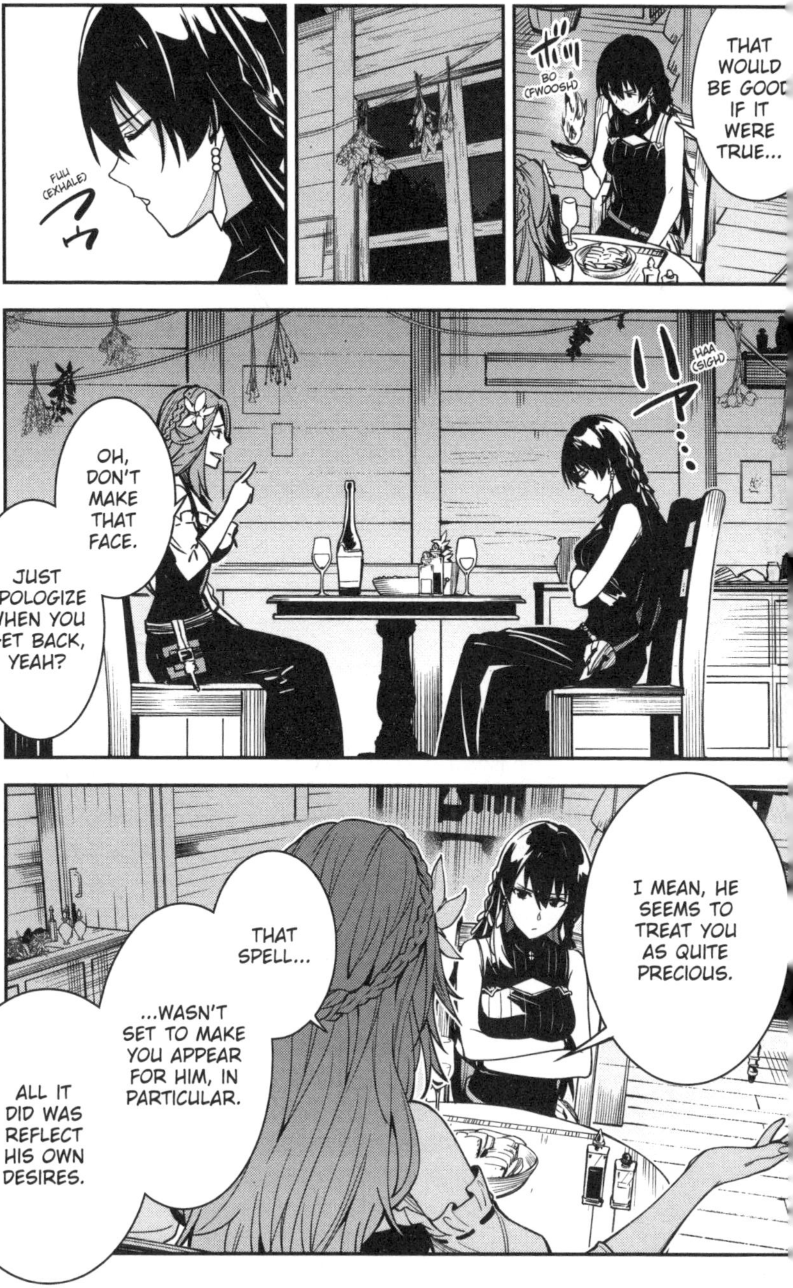
THAT WOULD BE GOOD IF IT WERE TRUE...
BO (FWOOSH)
FUU (EXHALE)
HAA (SIGH)
OH, DON'T MAKE THAT FACE.
JUST APOLOGIZE WHEN YOU GET BACK, YEAH?
I MEAN, HE SEEMS TO TREAT YOU AS QUITE PRECIOUS.
THAT SPELL...
...WASN'T SET TO MAKE YOU APPEAR FOR HIM, IN PARTICULAR.
ALL IT DID WAS REFLECT HIS OWN DESIRES.

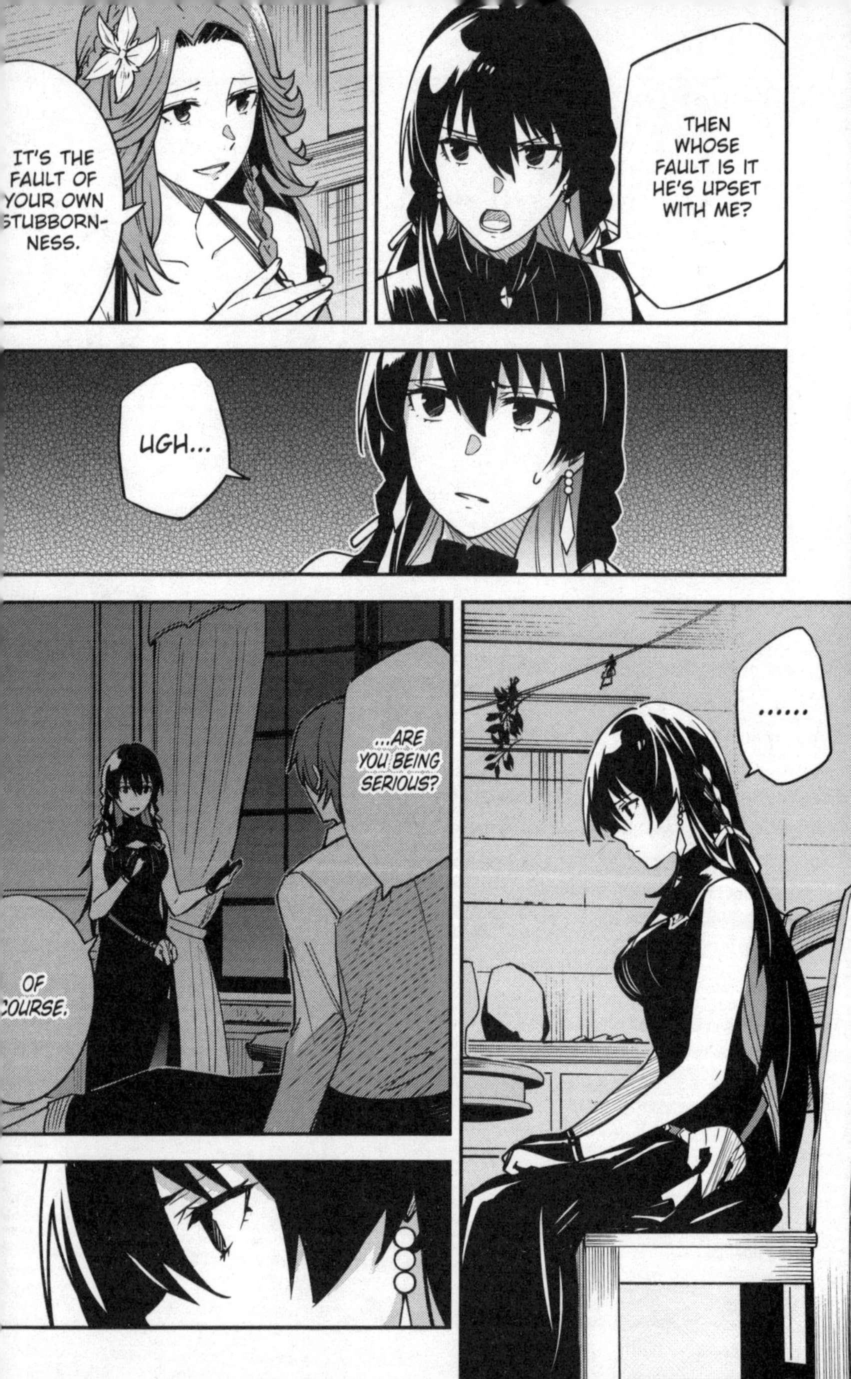
THEN WHOSE FAULT IS IT HE'S UPSET WITH ME?
IT'S THE FAULT OF YOUR OWN STUBBORN-NESS.
UGH...
......
...ARE YOU BEING SERIOUS?
OF COURSE.

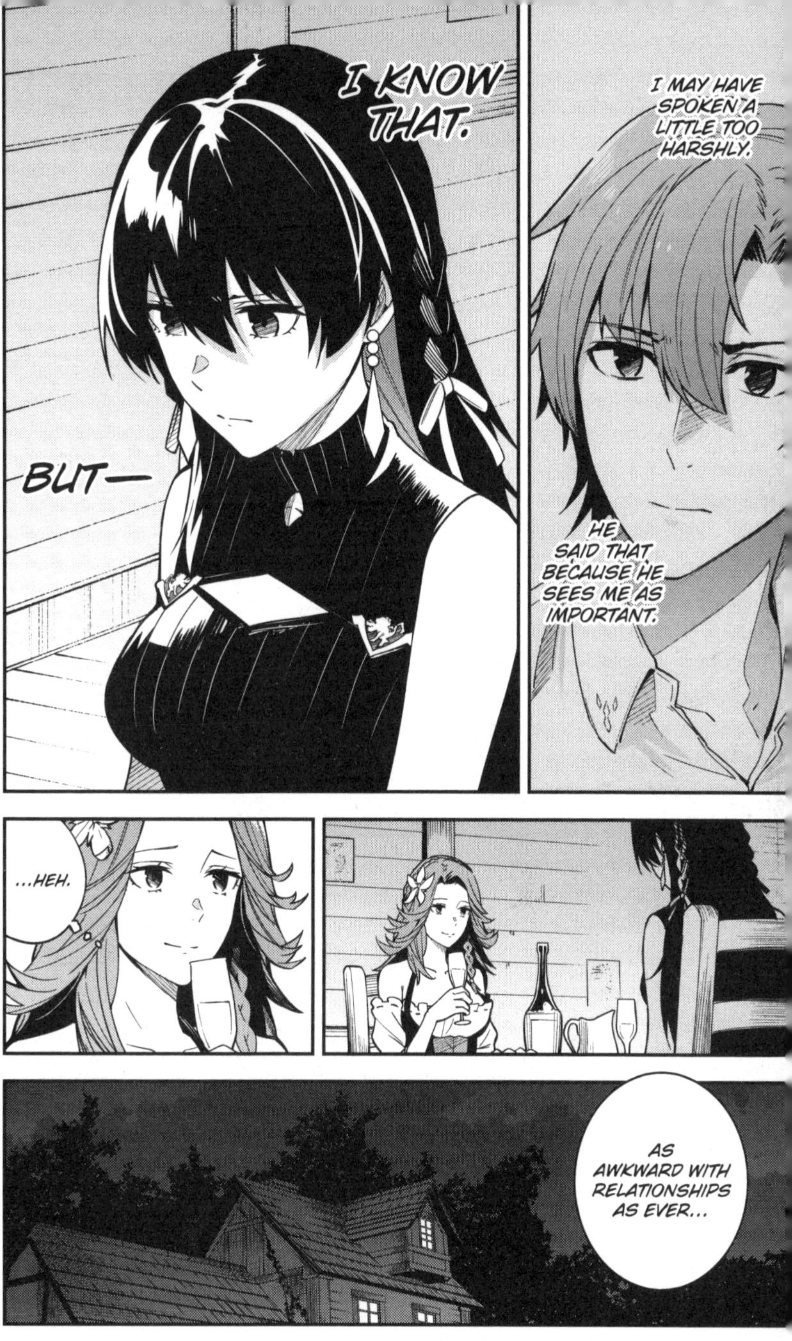
I MAY HAVE SPOKEN A LITTLE TOO HARSHLY.
HE SAID THAT BECAUSE HE SEES ME AS IMPORTANT.
I KNOW THAT.
BUT—
...HEH.
AS AWKWARD WITH RELATIONSHIPS AS EVER...

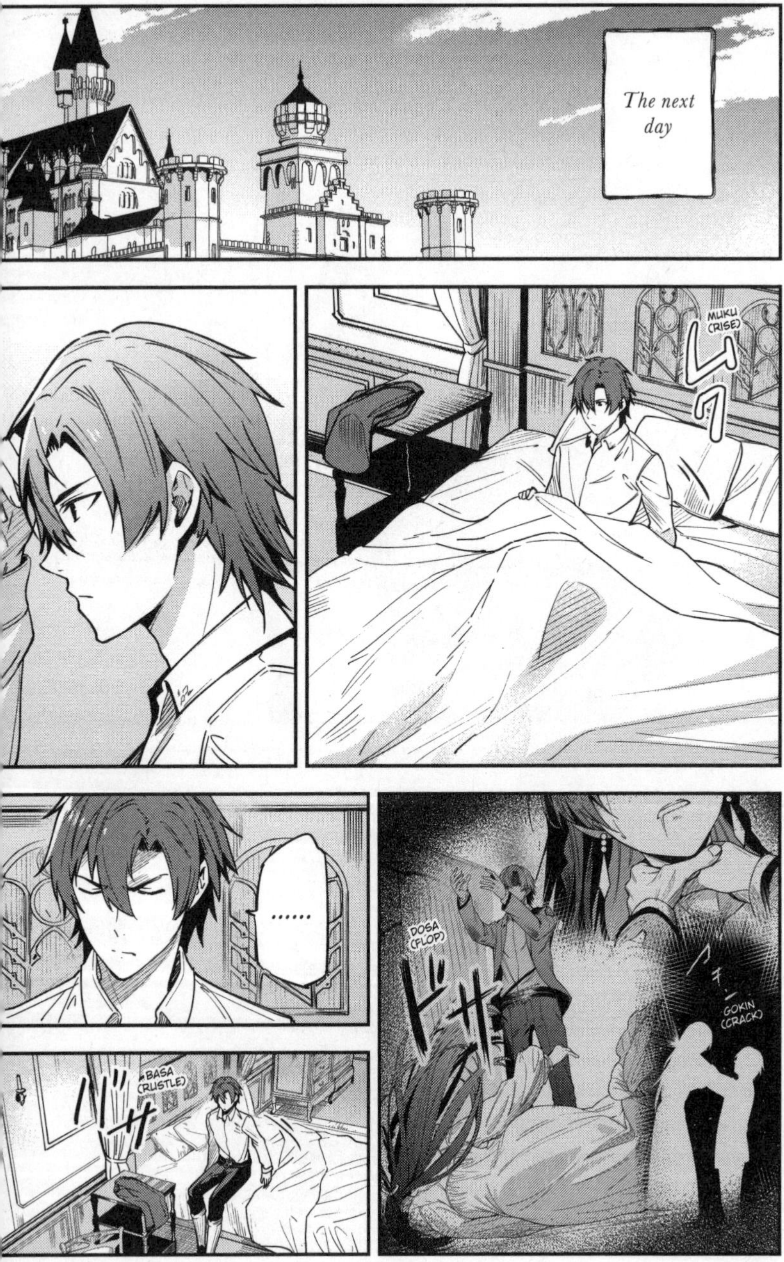

The next day
MUKU (RISE)
DOSA (FLOP)
GOKIN (CRACK)
....
BASA (RUSTLE)

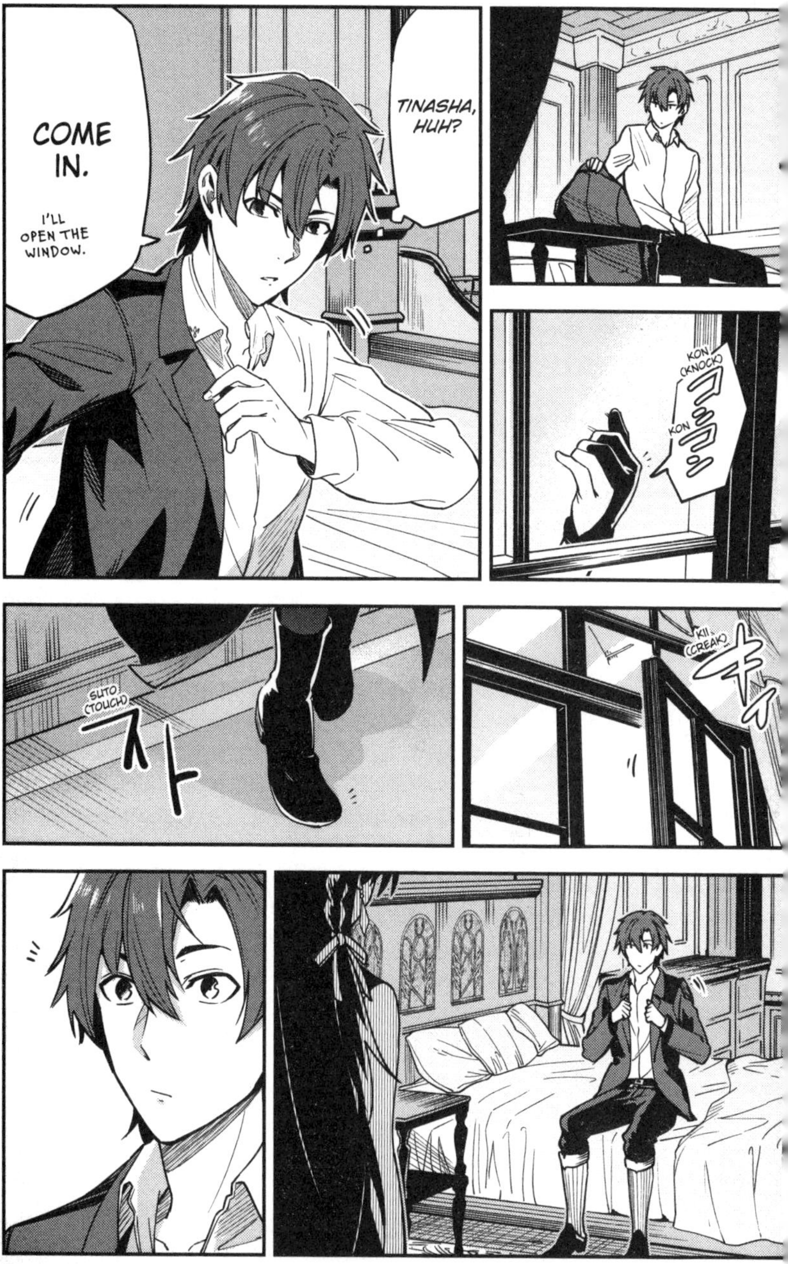
KON (KNOCK)
KON
TINASHA, HUH?
COME IN.
I'LL OPEN THE WINDOW.
KII (CREAK)
SUTO (TOUCH)

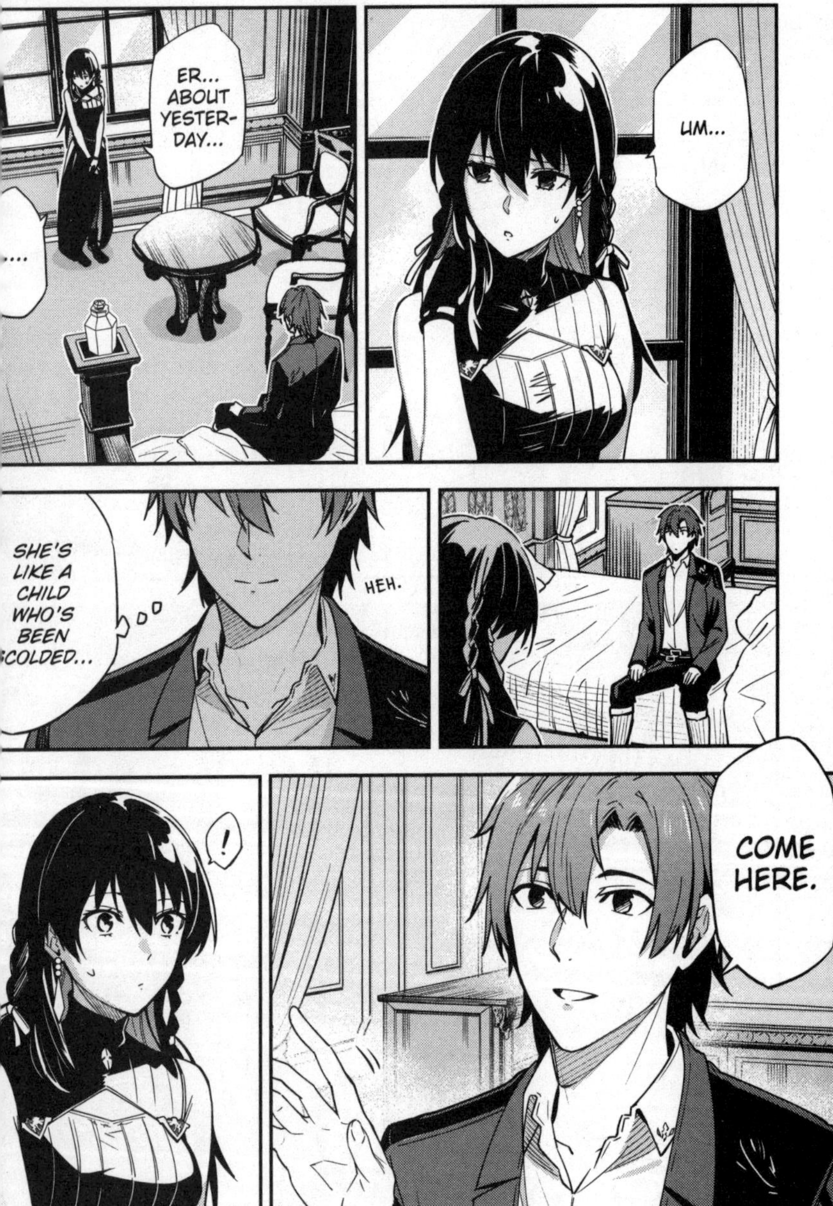
UM...
ER... ABOUT YESTER-DAY...
....
HEH.
SHE'S LIKE A CHILD WHO'S BEEN SCOLDED...
COME HERE.
!

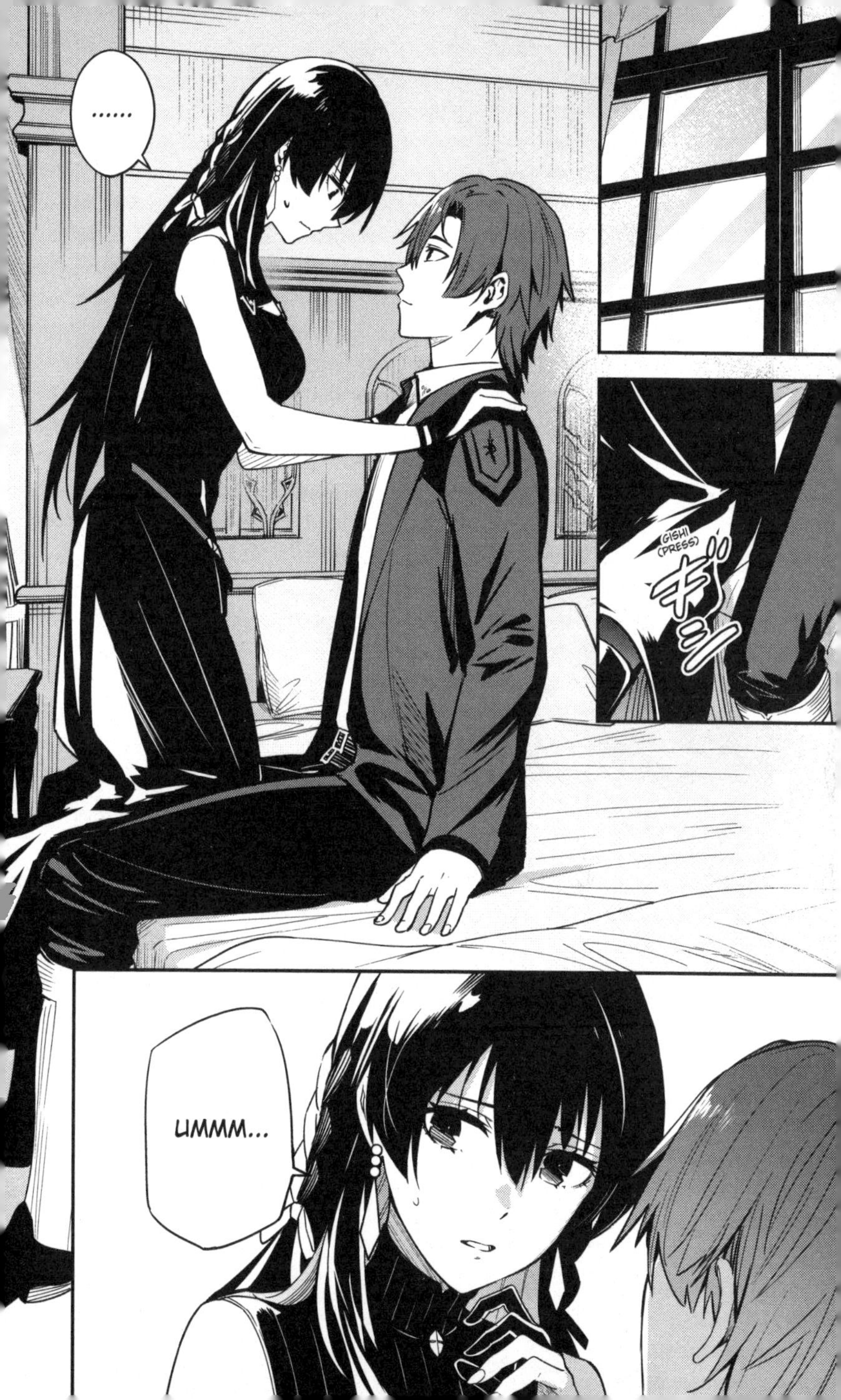
GISHI (PRESS)
ギシッ
......
UMMM...

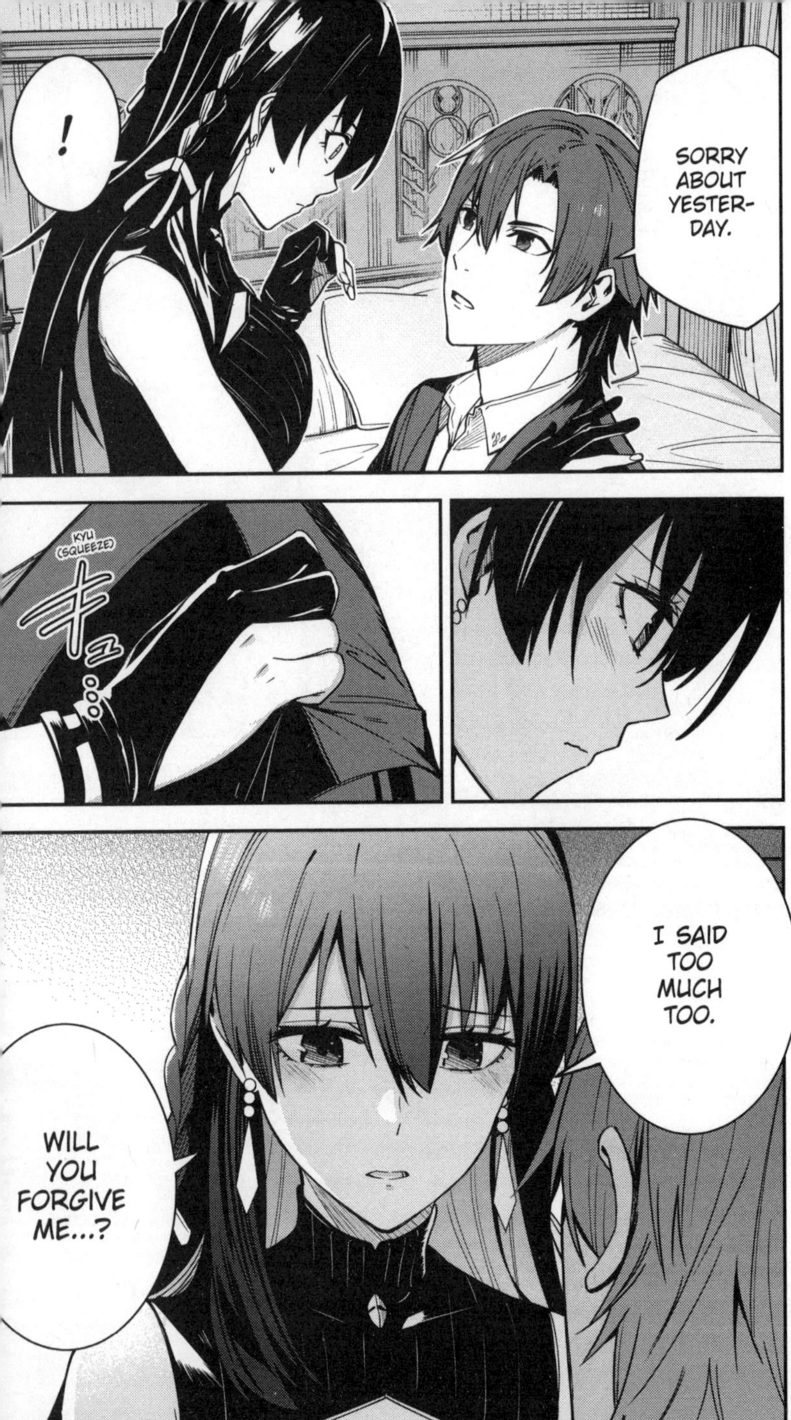
SORRY ABOUT YESTER-DAY.
!
KYU (SQUEEZE)
I SAID TOO MUCH TOO.
WILL YOU FORGIVE ME...?

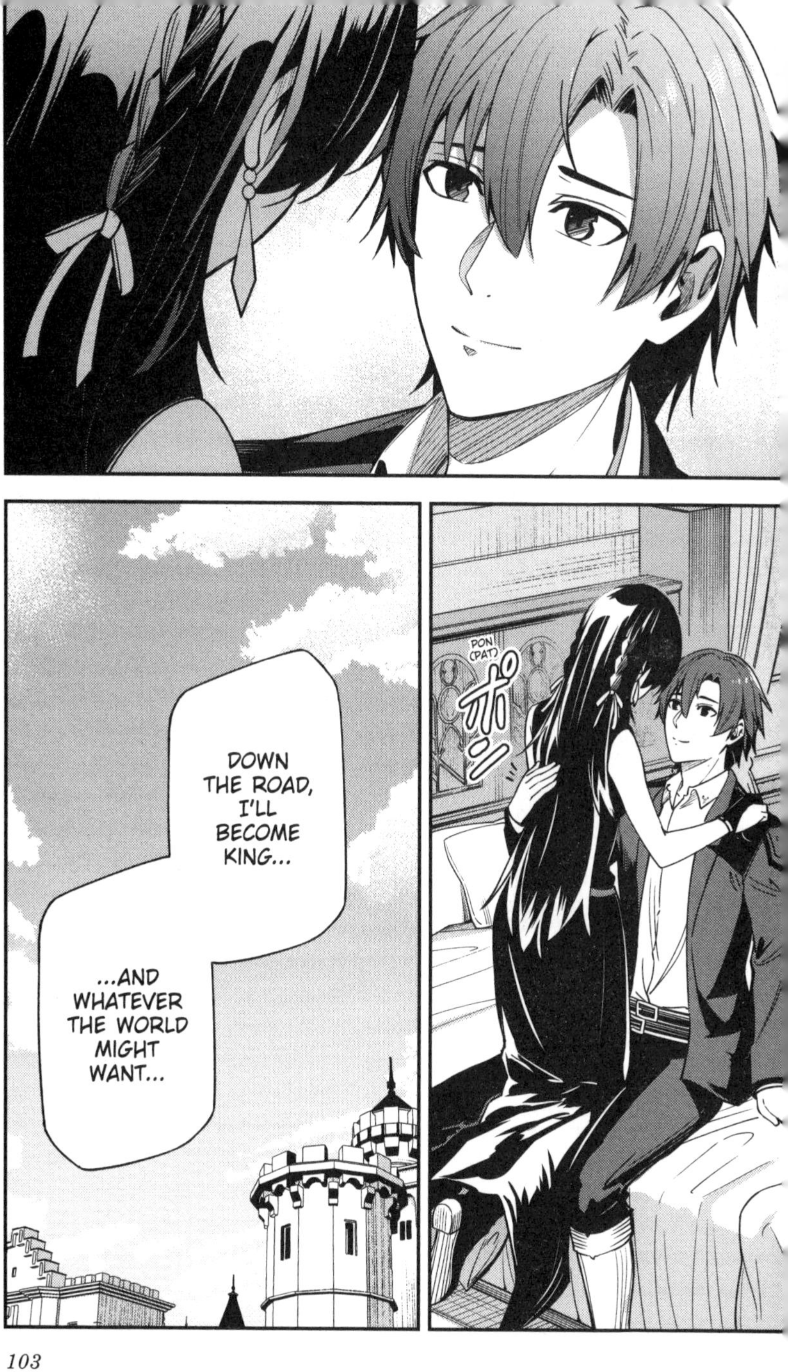
PON (PAT)
ポン
DOWN THE ROAD, I'LL BECOME KING...
...AND WHATEVER THE WORLD MIGHT WANT...

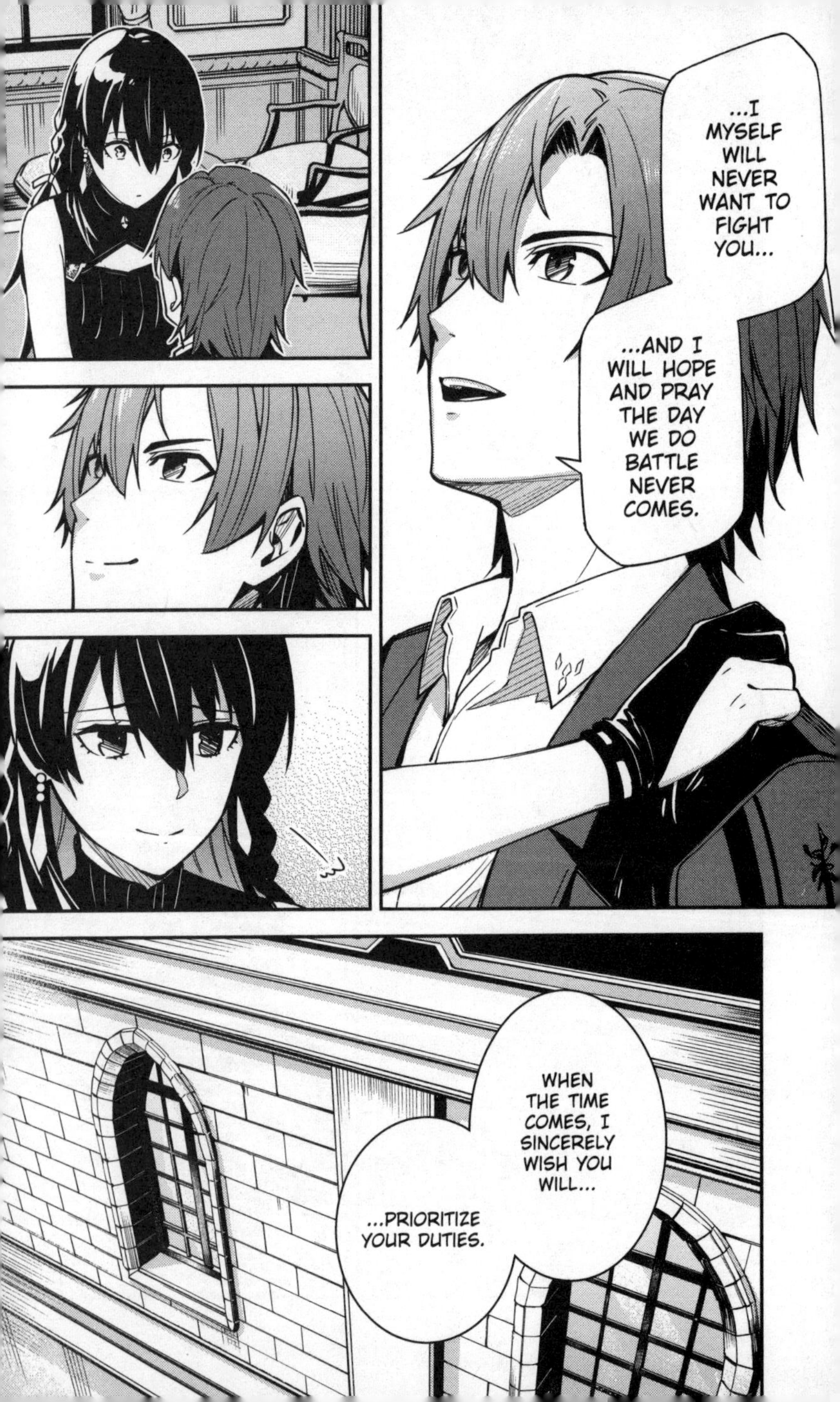
...I MYSELF WILL NEVER WANT TO FIGHT YOU...
...AND I WILL HOPE AND PRAY THE DAY WE DO BATTLE NEVER COMES.
WHEN THE TIME COMES, I SINCERELY WISH YOU WILL...
...PRIORITIZE YOUR DUTIES.

Unnamed Memory

Unnamed Memory

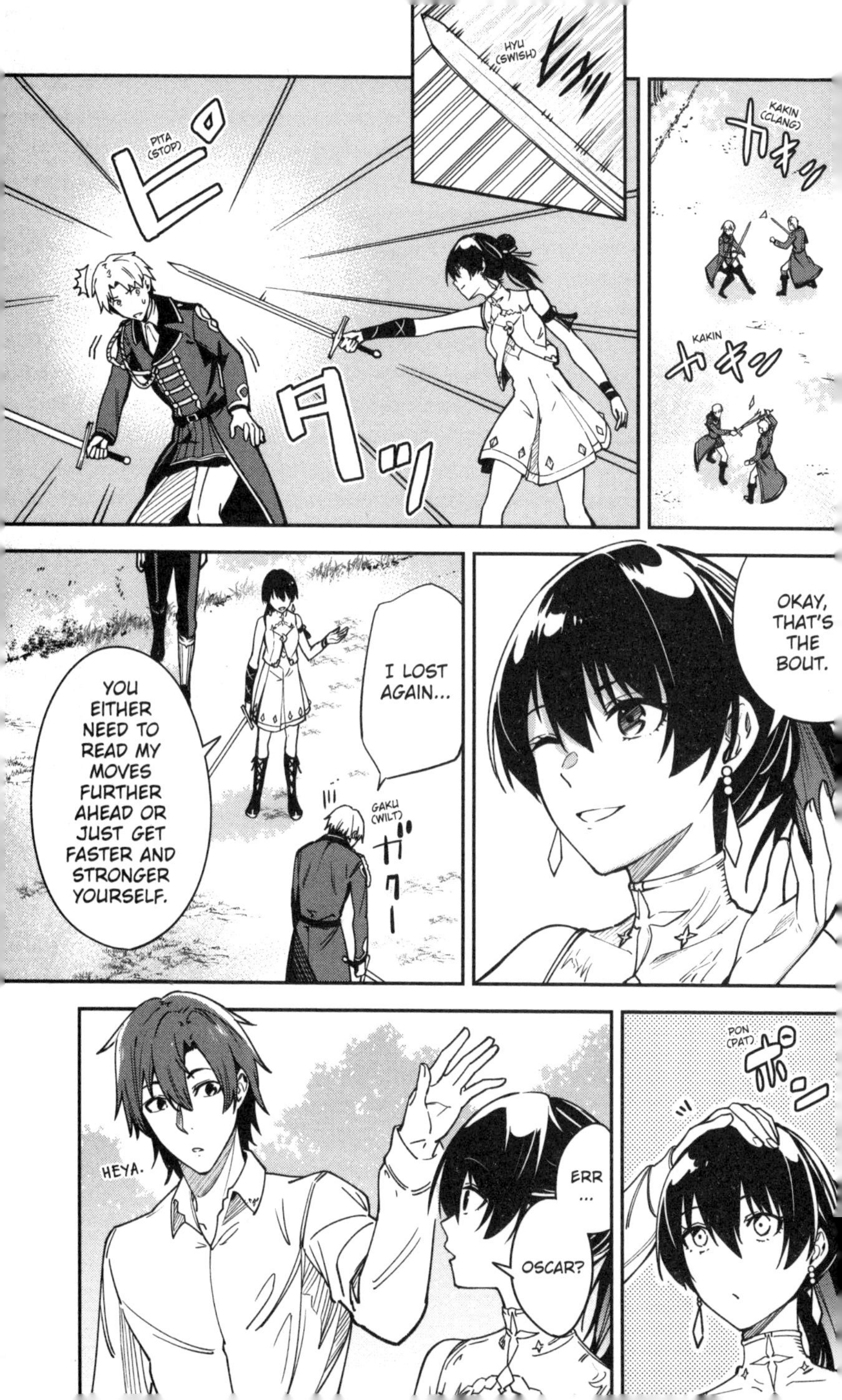
KAKIN (CLANG)
KAKIN
HYU (SWISH)
PITA (STOP)
OKAY, THAT'S THE BOUT.
I LOST AGAIN...
YOU EITHER NEED TO READ MY MOVES FURTHER AHEAD OR JUST GET FASTER AND STRONGER YOURSELF.
GAKU (WILT)
PON (PAT)
ERR...
OSCAR?
HEYA.

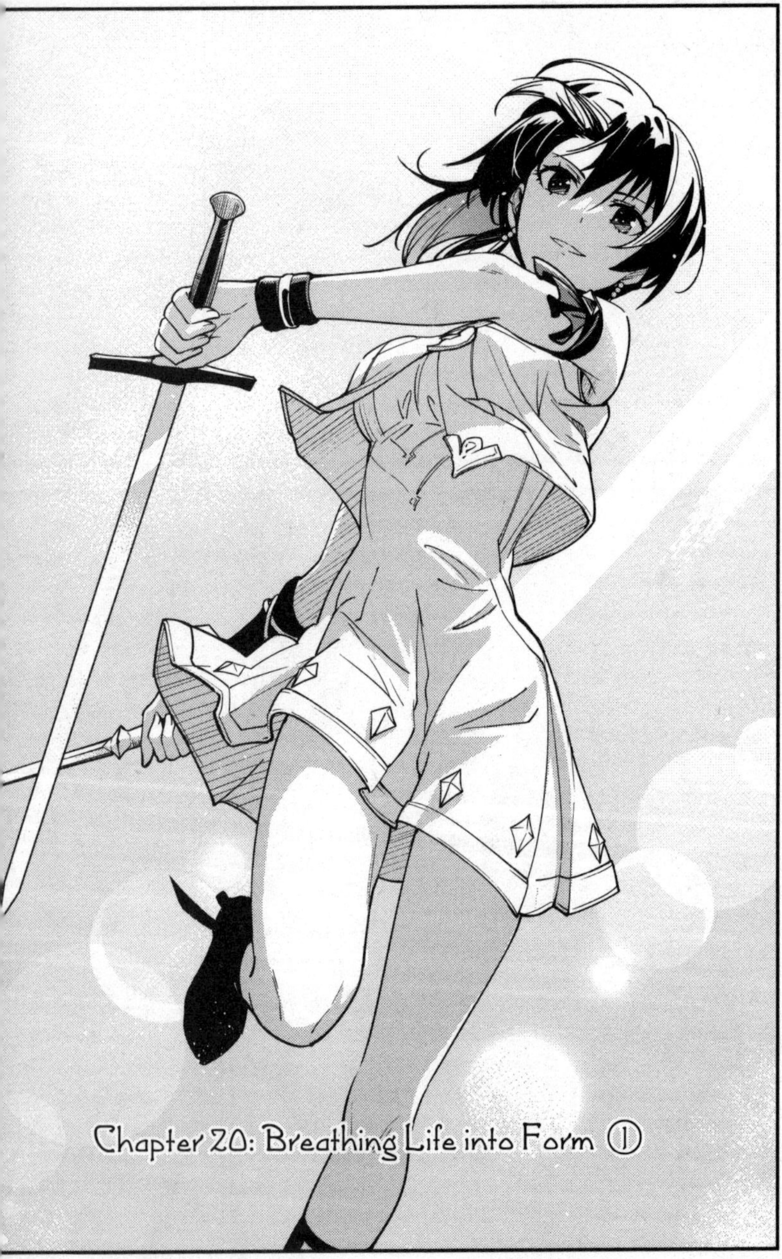
Chapter 20: Breathing Life into Form ①

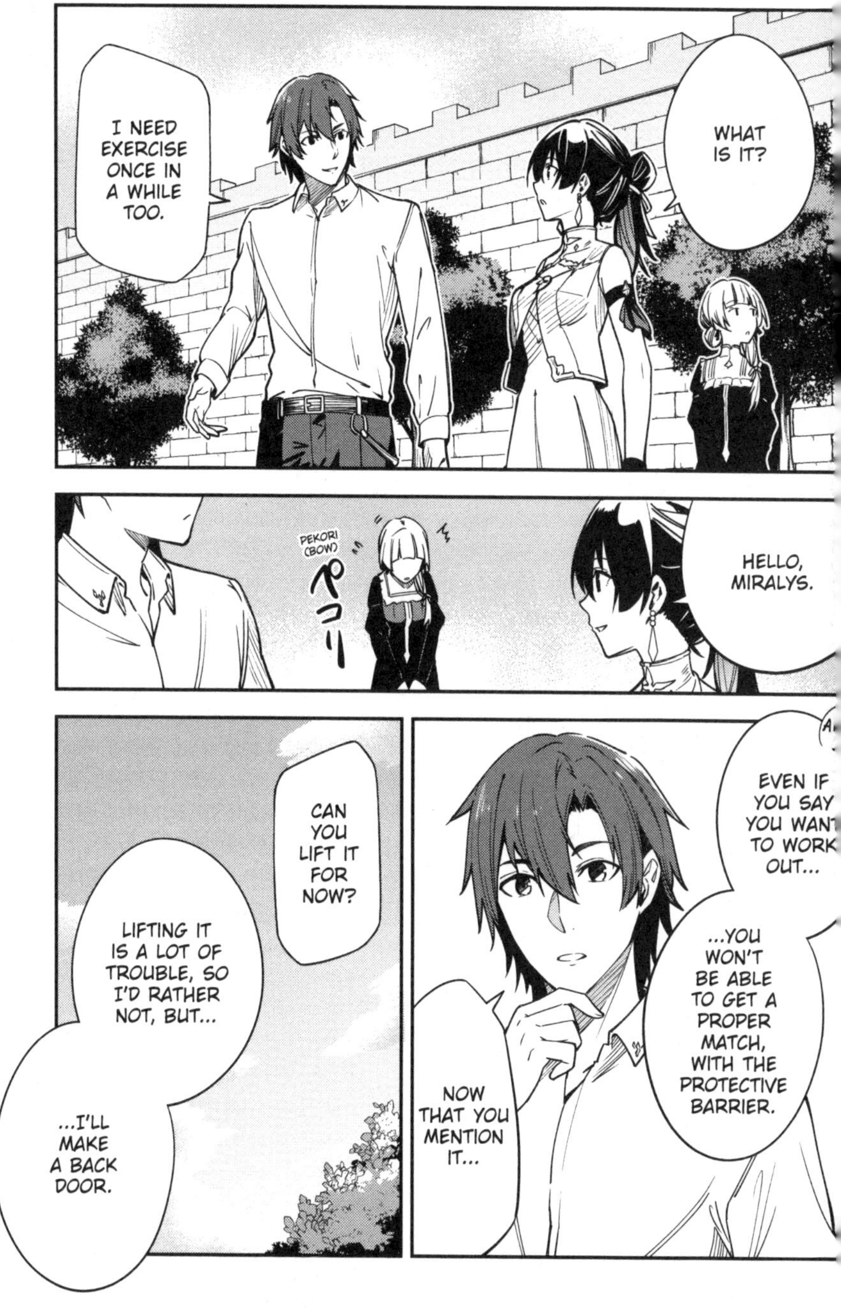
WHAT IS IT?
I NEED EXERCISE ONCE IN A WHILE TOO.
HELLO, MIRALYS.
PEKORI (BOW)
ペコリ
EVEN IF YOU SAY YOU WANT TO WORK OUT...
...YOU WON'T BE ABLE TO GET A PROPER MATCH, WITH THE PROTECTIVE BARRIER.
NOW THAT YOU MENTION IT...
CAN YOU LIFT IT FOR NOW?
LIFTING IT IS A LOT OF TROUBLE, SO I'D RATHER NOT, BUT...
...I'LL MAKE A BACK DOOR.

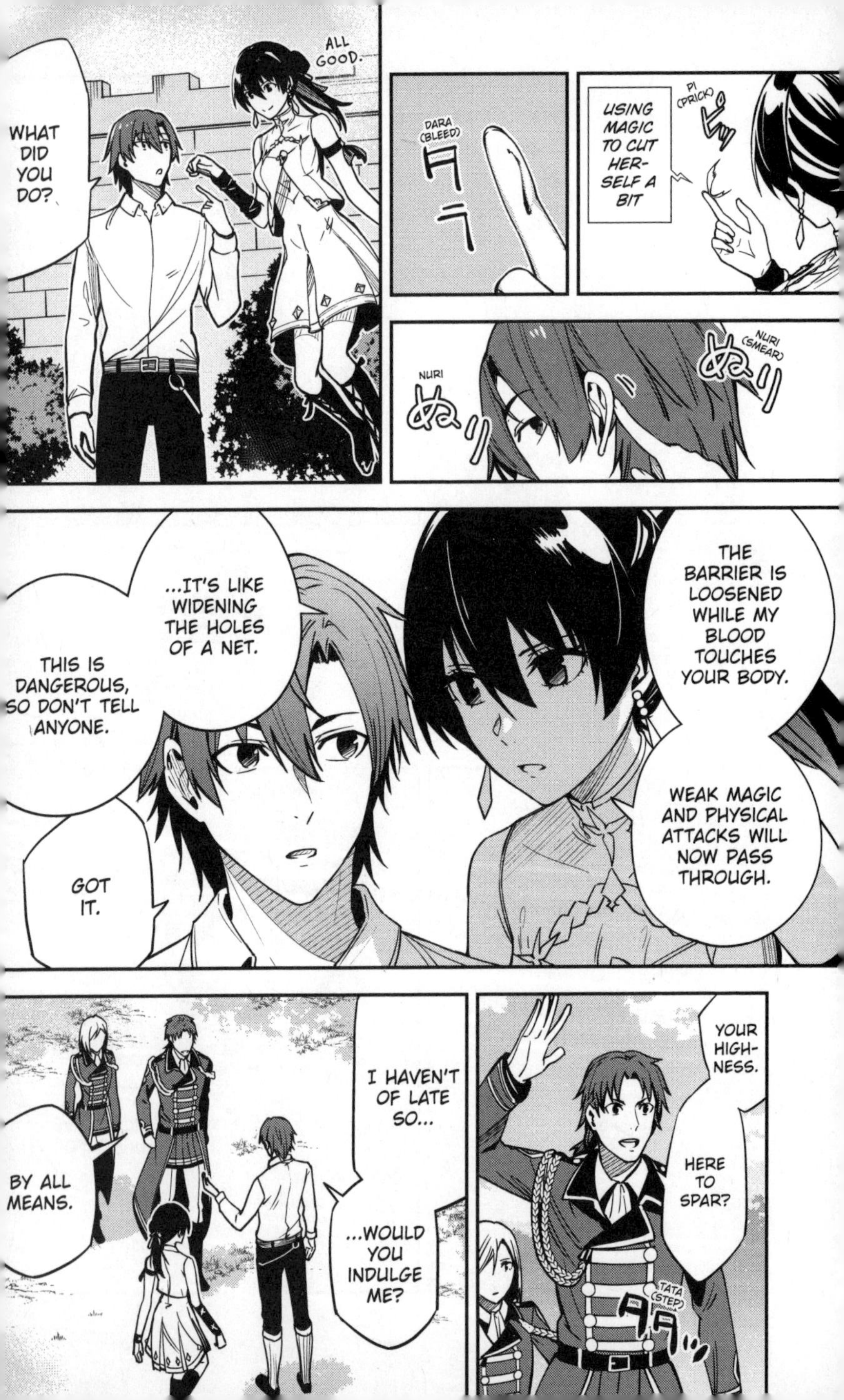
USING MAGIC TO CUT HER-SELF A BIT
PI (PRICK)
DARA (BLEED)
NURI (SMEAR)
NURI
ALL GOOD.
WHAT DID YOU DO?
THE BARRIER IS LOOSENED WHILE MY BLOOD TOUCHES YOUR BODY.
WEAK MAGIC AND PHYSICAL ATTACKS WILL NOW PASS THROUGH.
...IT'S LIKE WIDENING THE HOLES OF A NET.
THIS IS DANGEROUS, SO DON'T TELL ANYONE.
GOT IT.
YOUR HIGHNESS.
HERE TO SPAR?
TATA (STEP)
I HAVEN'T OF LATE SO...
...WOULD YOU INDULGE ME?
BY ALL MEANS.

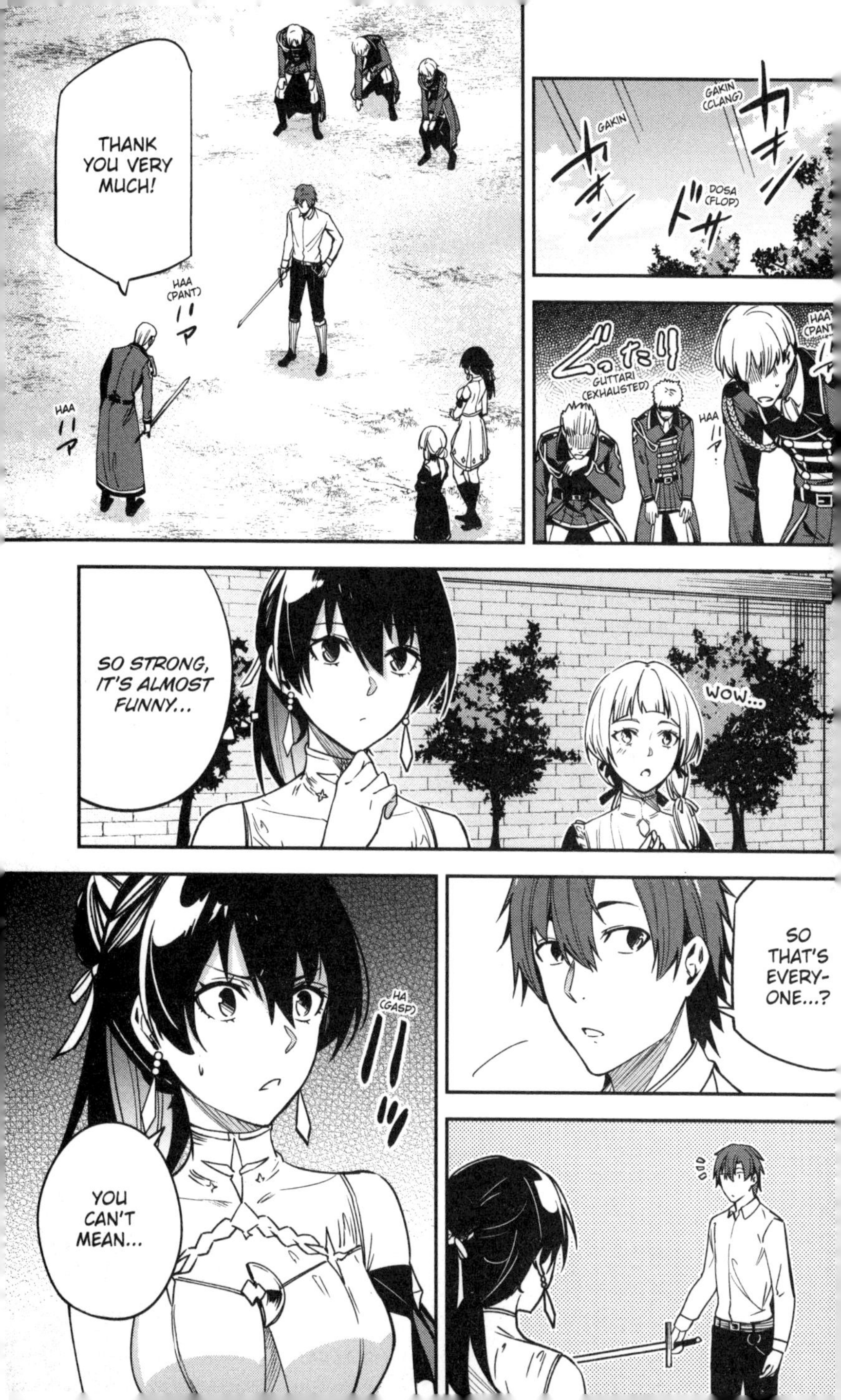

GAKIN (CLANG)
GAKIN
DOSA (FLOP)
HAA (PANT)
GUTTARI (EXHAUSTED)
HAA
THANK YOU VERY MUCH!
HAA (PANT)
HAA
WOW...
SO STRONG, IT'S ALMOST FUNNY...
SO THAT'S EVERY-ONE...?
HA (GASP)
YOU CAN'T MEAN...

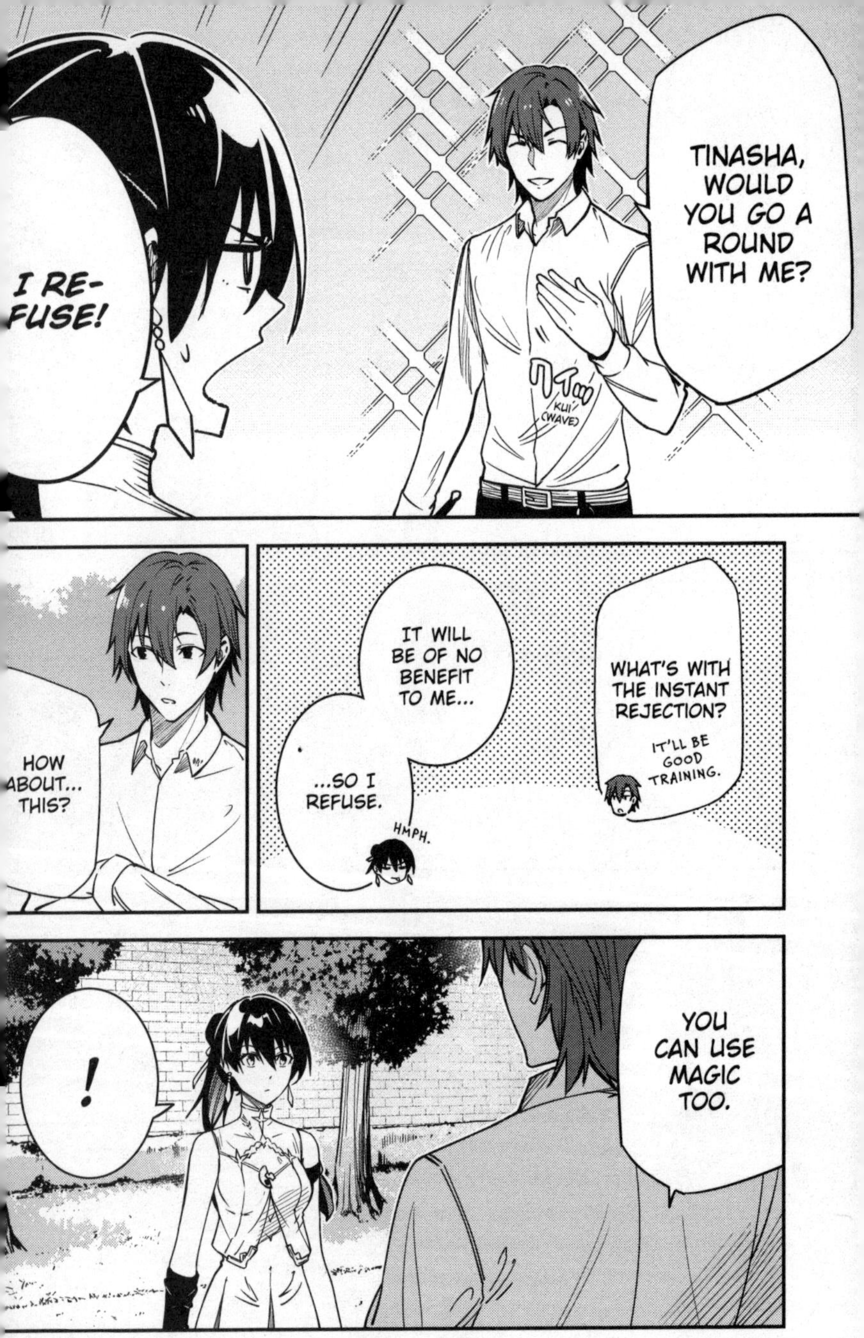
TINASHA, WOULD YOU GO A ROUND WITH ME?
KUI (WAVE)
I RE-FUSE!
WHAT'S WITH THE INSTANT REJECTION?
IT'LL BE GOOD TRAINING.
IT WILL BE OF NO BENEFIT TO ME...
...SO I REFUSE.
HMPH.
HOW ABOUT... THIS?
YOU CAN USE MAGIC TOO.
!

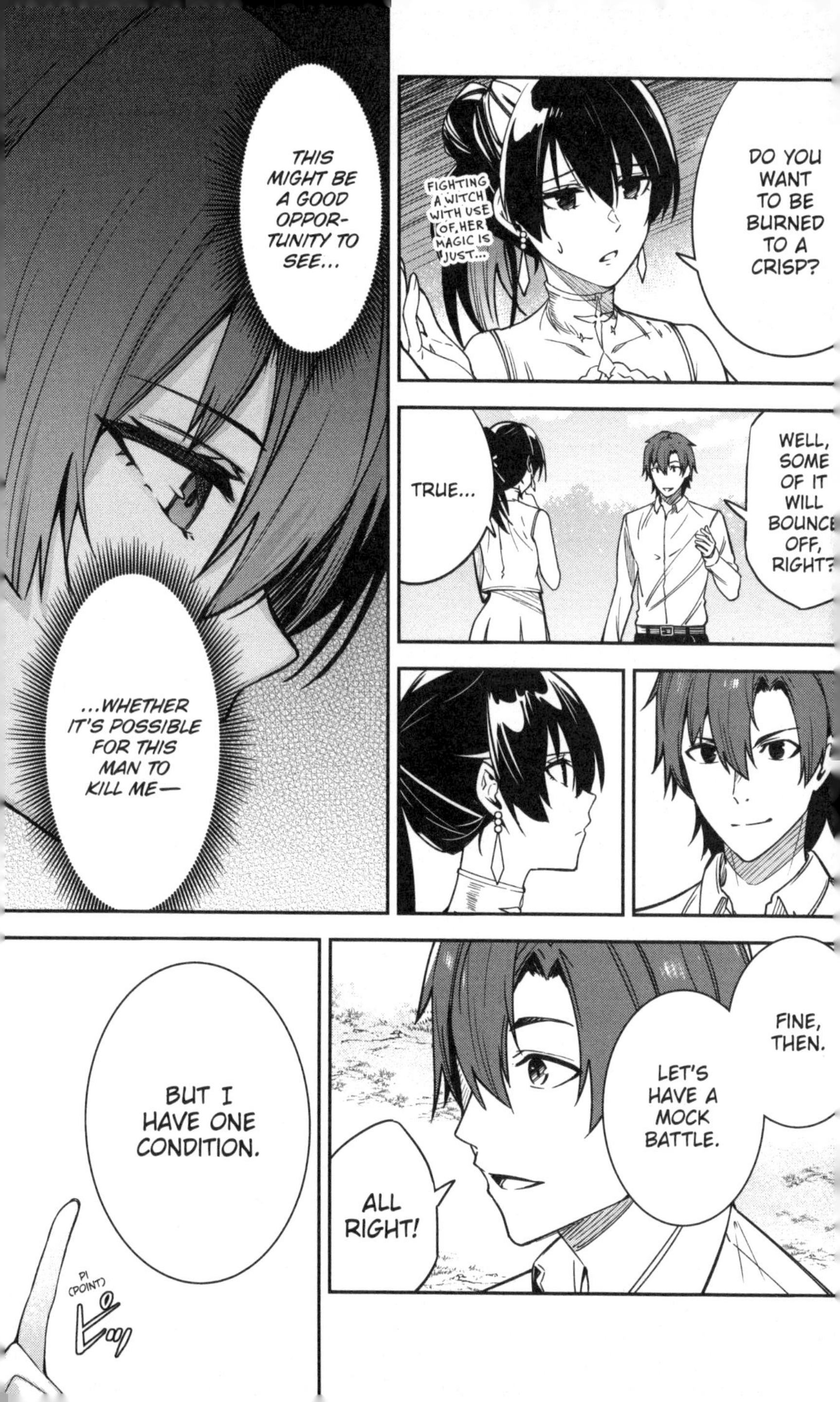
DO YOU WANT TO BE BURNED TO A CRISP?
FIGHTING A WITCH WITH USE OF HER MAGIC IS JUST...
WELL, SOME OF IT WILL BOUNCE OFF, RIGHT?
TRUE...
THIS MIGHT BE A GOOD OPPOR-TUNITY TO SEE...
...WHETHER IT'S POSSIBLE FOR THIS MAN TO KILL ME—
FINE, THEN.
LET'S HAVE A MOCK BATTLE.
ALL RIGHT!
BUT I HAVE ONE CONDITION.
PI (POINT)

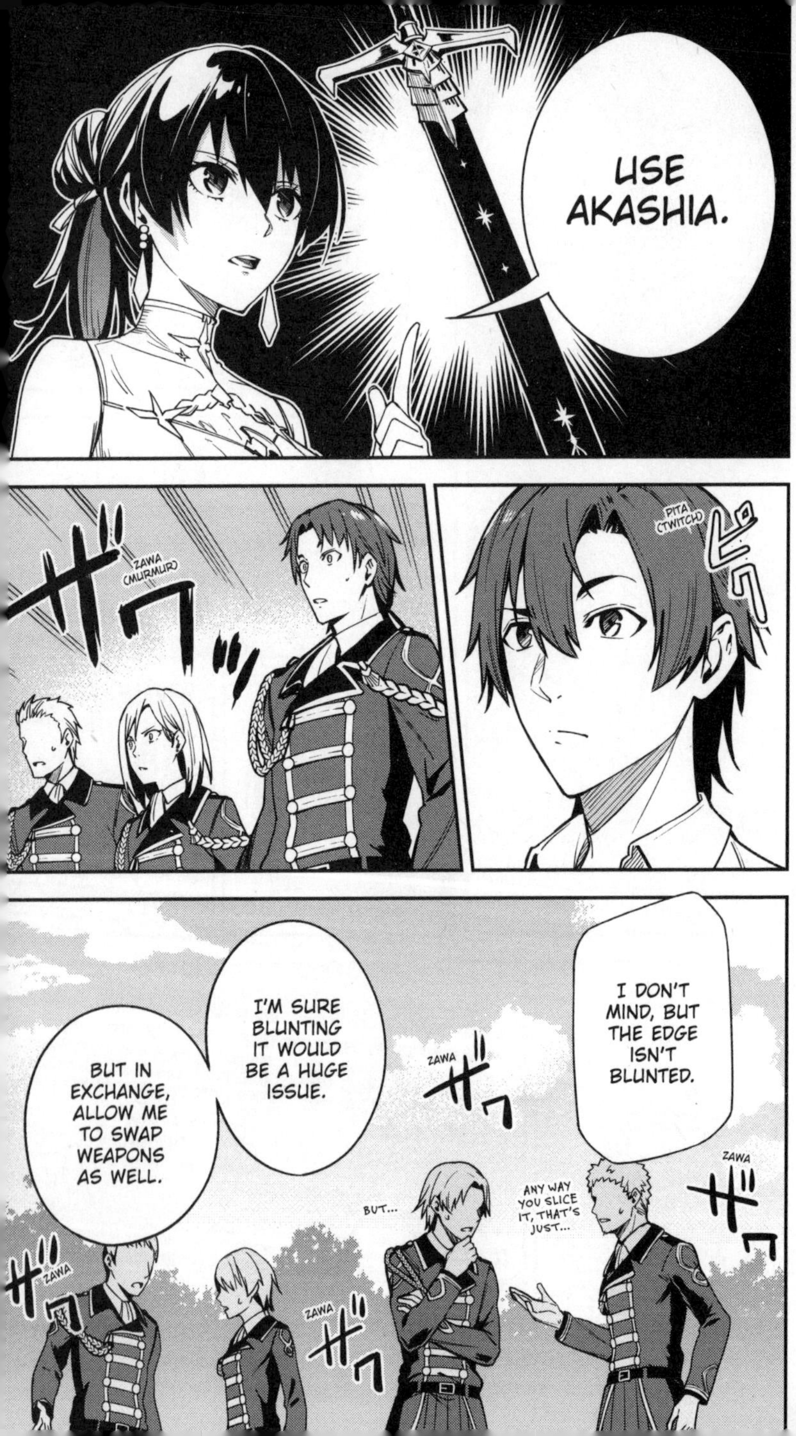
USE AKASHIA.
ピク
PITA (TWITCH)
ザワッ
ZAWA (MURMUR)
I DON'T MIND, BUT THE EDGE ISN'T BLUNTED.
ザワ
ZAWA
I'M SURE BLUNTING IT WOULD BE A HUGE ISSUE.
BUT IN EXCHANGE, ALLOW ME TO SWAP WEAPONS AS WELL.
ザワ
ZAWA
ANY WAY YOU SLICE IT, THAT'S JUST...
BUT...
ザワ
ZAWA
ザワ
ZAWA

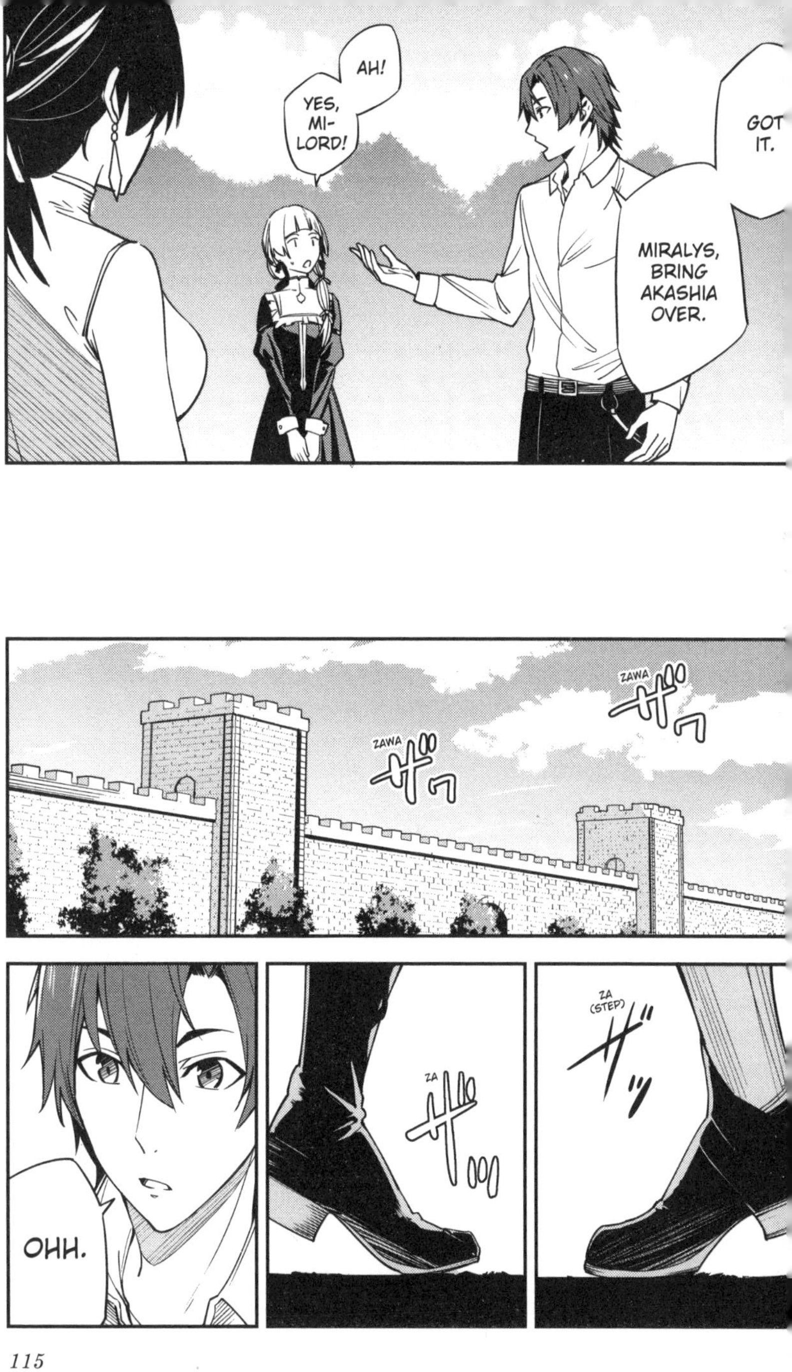
GOT IT.
MIRALYS, BRING AKASHIA OVER.
AH!
YES, MI-LORD!
ZAWA
ZAWA
ZA (STEP)
ZA
OHH.

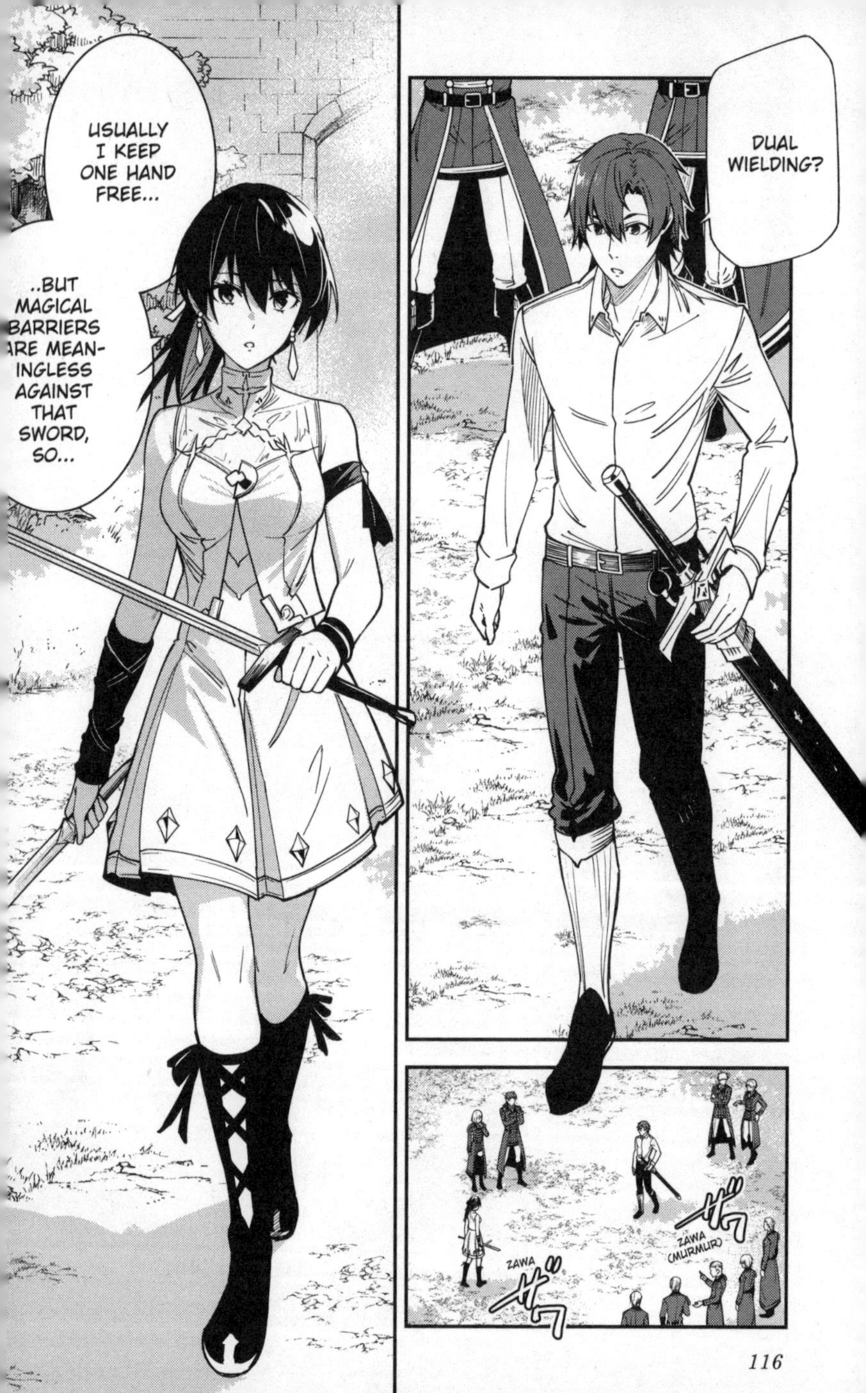
DUAL WIELDING?
ZAWA (MURMUR)
ZAWA
USUALLY I KEEP ONE HAND FREE...
..BUT MAGICAL BARRIERS ARE MEAN-INGLESS AGAINST THAT SWORD, SO...

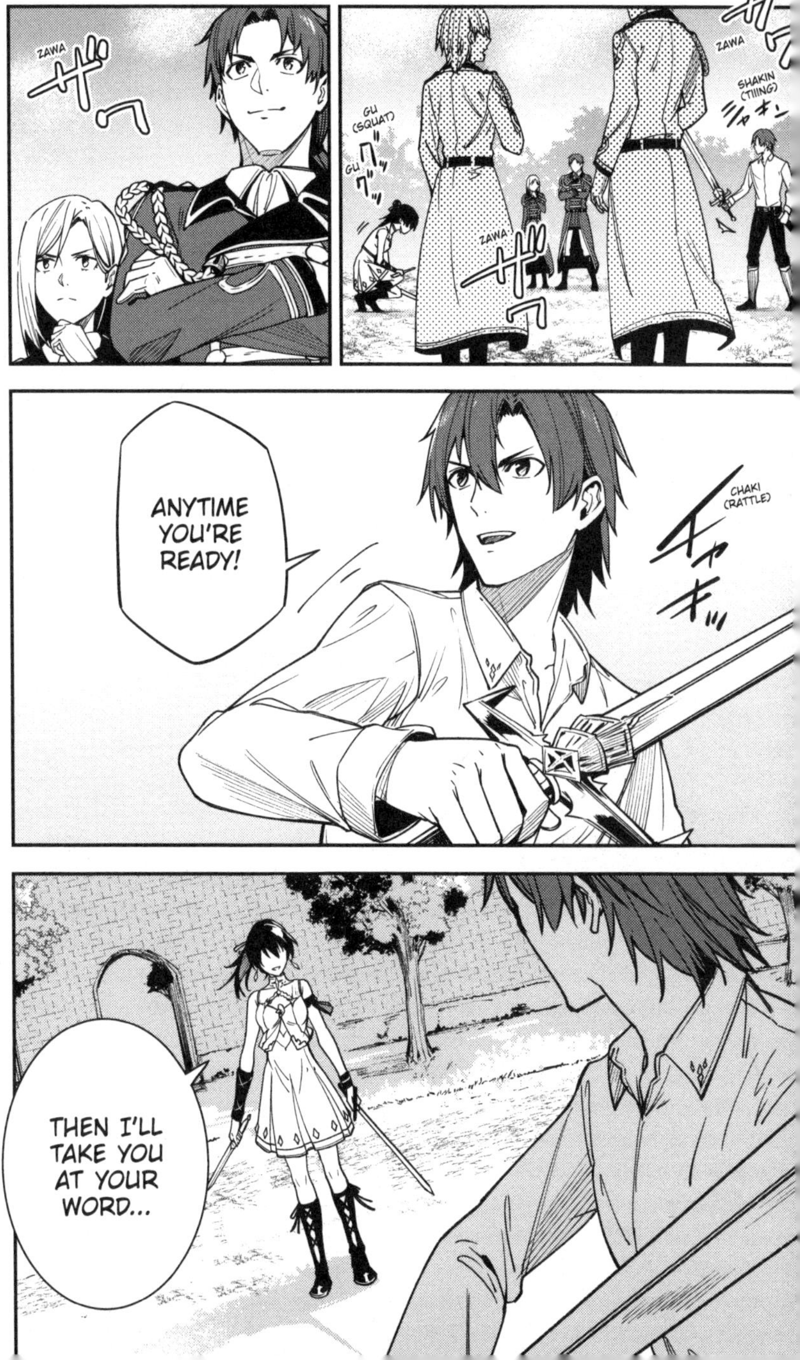
ZAWA
SHAKIN (TIIING)
GU (SQUAT)
GU
ZAWA
ZAWA
ANYTIME YOU'RE READY!
CHAKI (RATTLE)
THEN I'LL TAKE YOU AT YOUR WORD...

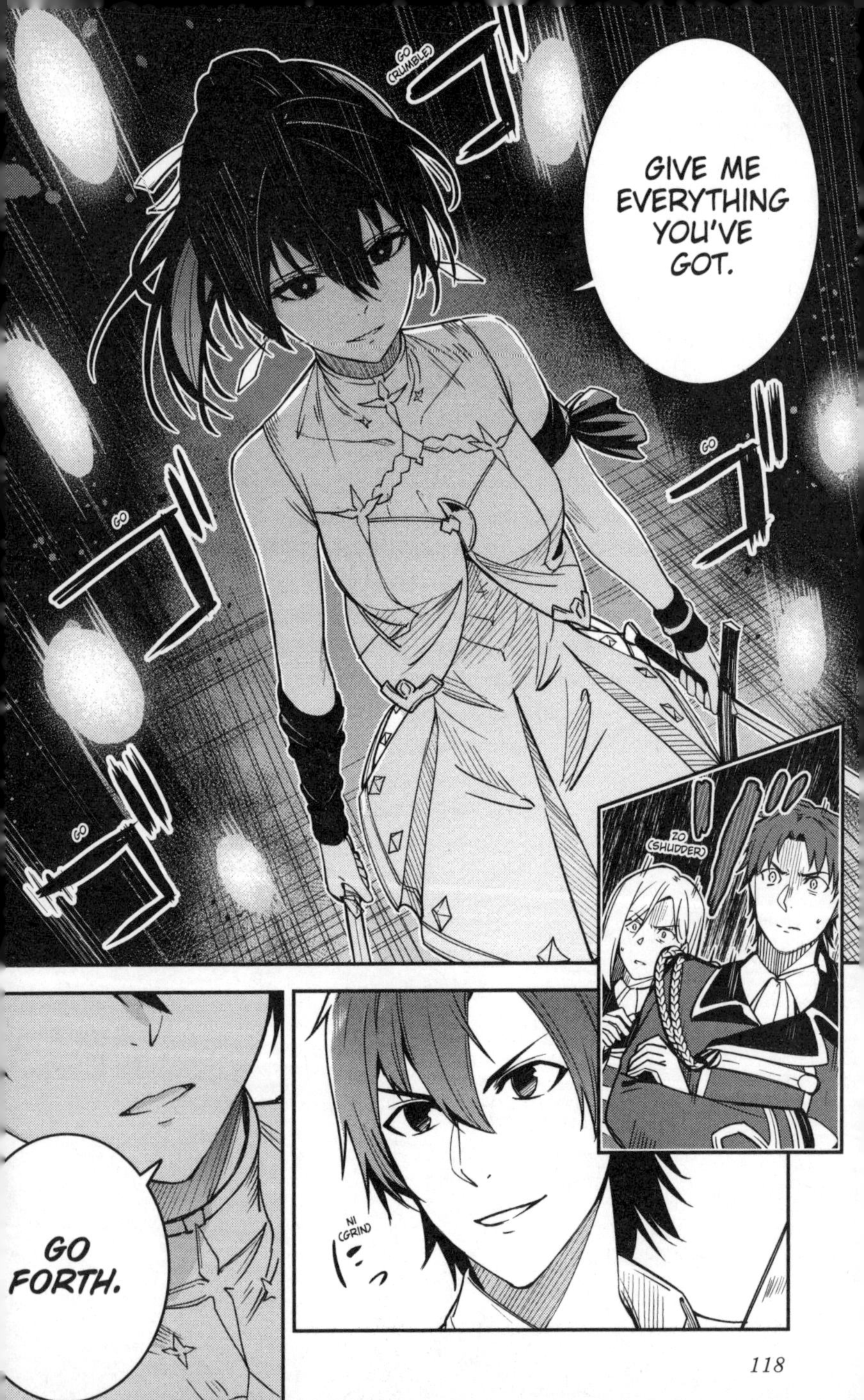
GO (RUMBLE)
GIVE ME EVERYTHING YOU'VE GOT.
GO
GO
GO
ZO (SHUDDER)
NI (GRIN)
GO FORTH.

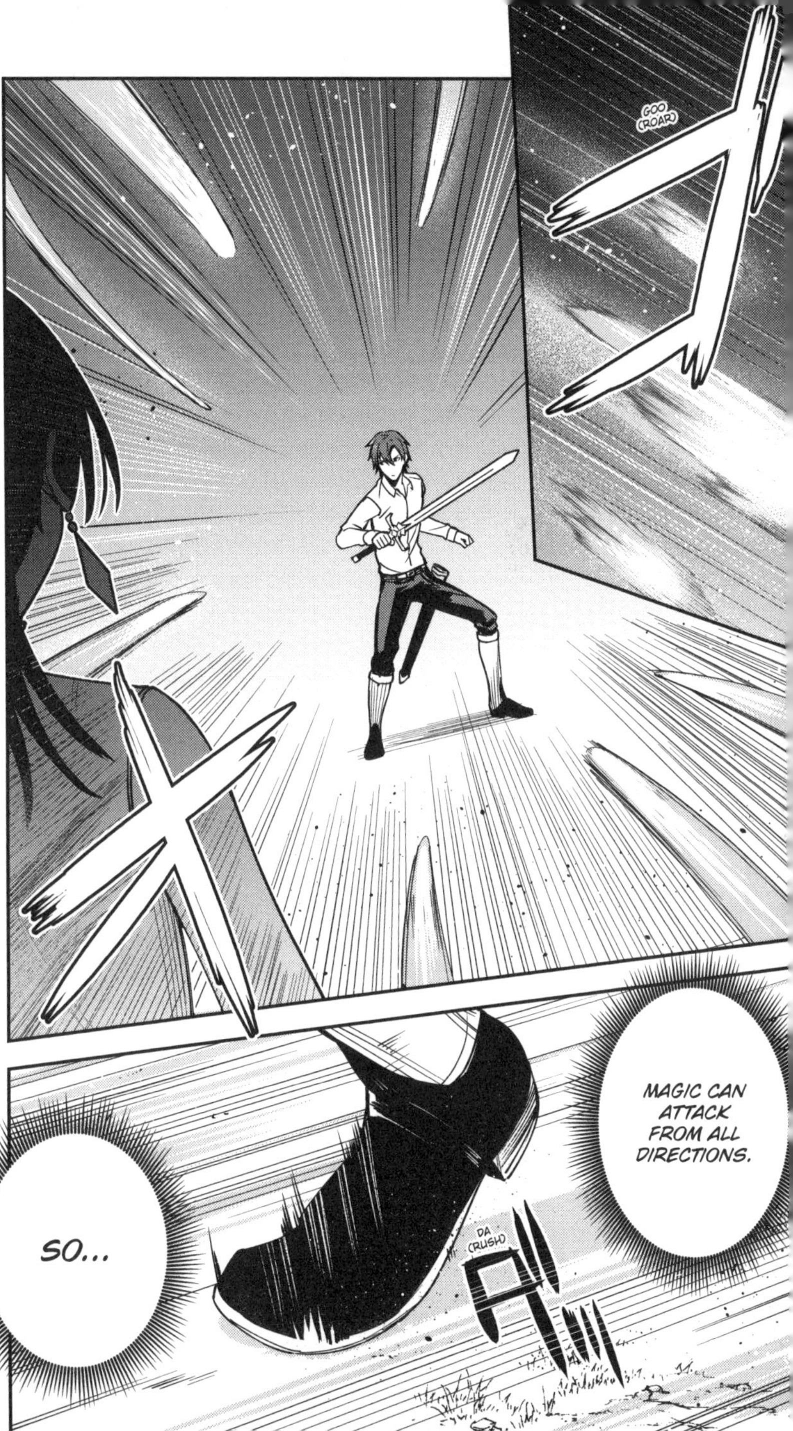
GOO
(ROAR)
MAGIC CAN ATTACK FROM ALL DIRECTIONS.
DA
(RUSH)
SO...

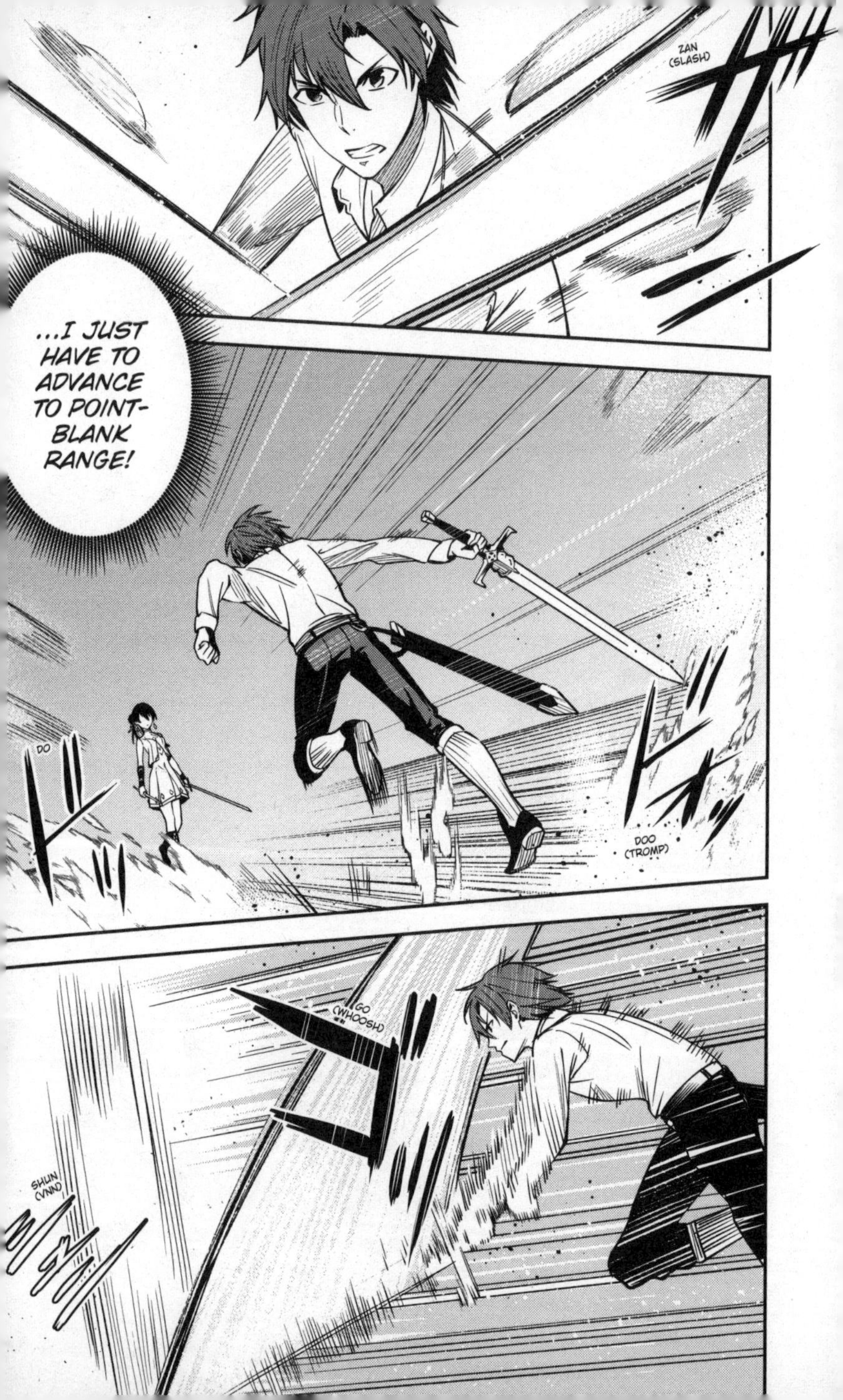
ZAN (SLASH)
...I JUST HAVE TO ADVANCE TO POINT-BLANK RANGE!
DOO (TROMP)
DO
GO (WHOOSH)
SHUN (VNN)

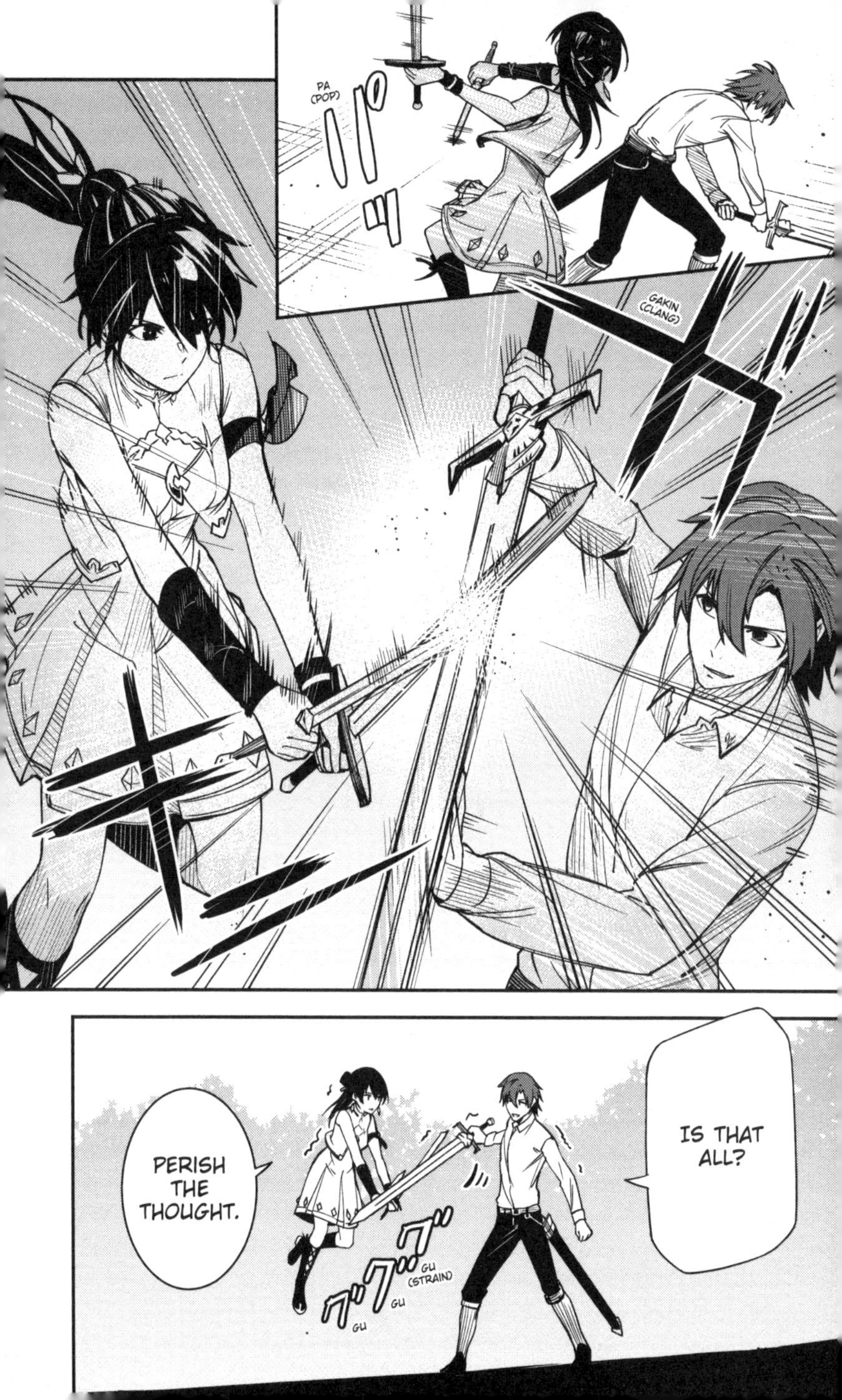
PA (POP)
GAKIN (CLANG)
IS THAT ALL?
PERISH THE THOUGHT.
GU (STRAIN)
GU
GU

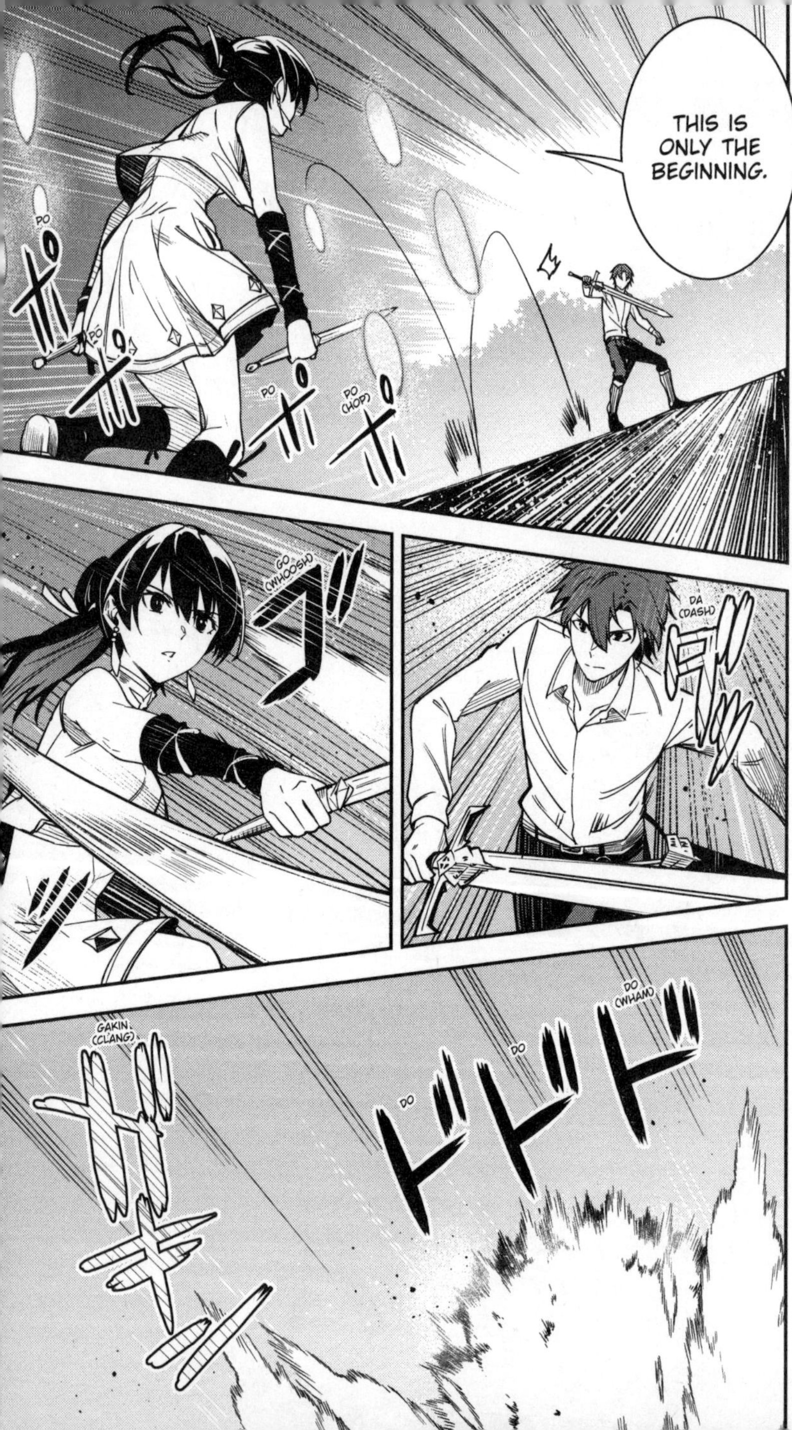
THIS IS ONLY THE BEGINNING.
PO (HOP)
PO
PO
PO
DA (DASH)
GO (WHOOSH)
DO (WHAM)
DO
DO
GAKIN (CLANG)

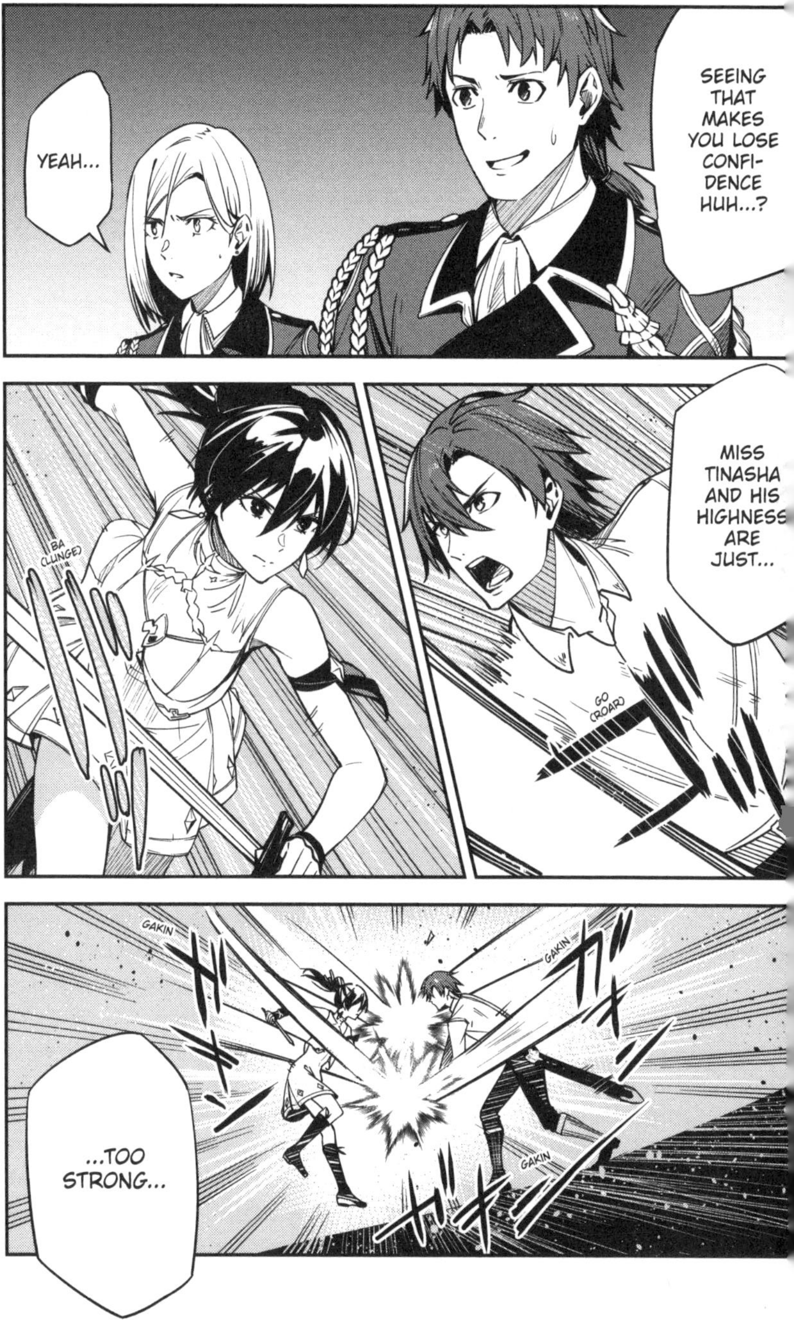
SEEING THAT MAKES YOU LOSE CONFI-DENCE HUH...?
YEAH...
MISS TINASHA AND HIS HIGHNESS ARE JUST...
GO (ROAR)
BA (LUNGE)
GAKIN
GAKIN
GAKIN
...TOO STRONG...

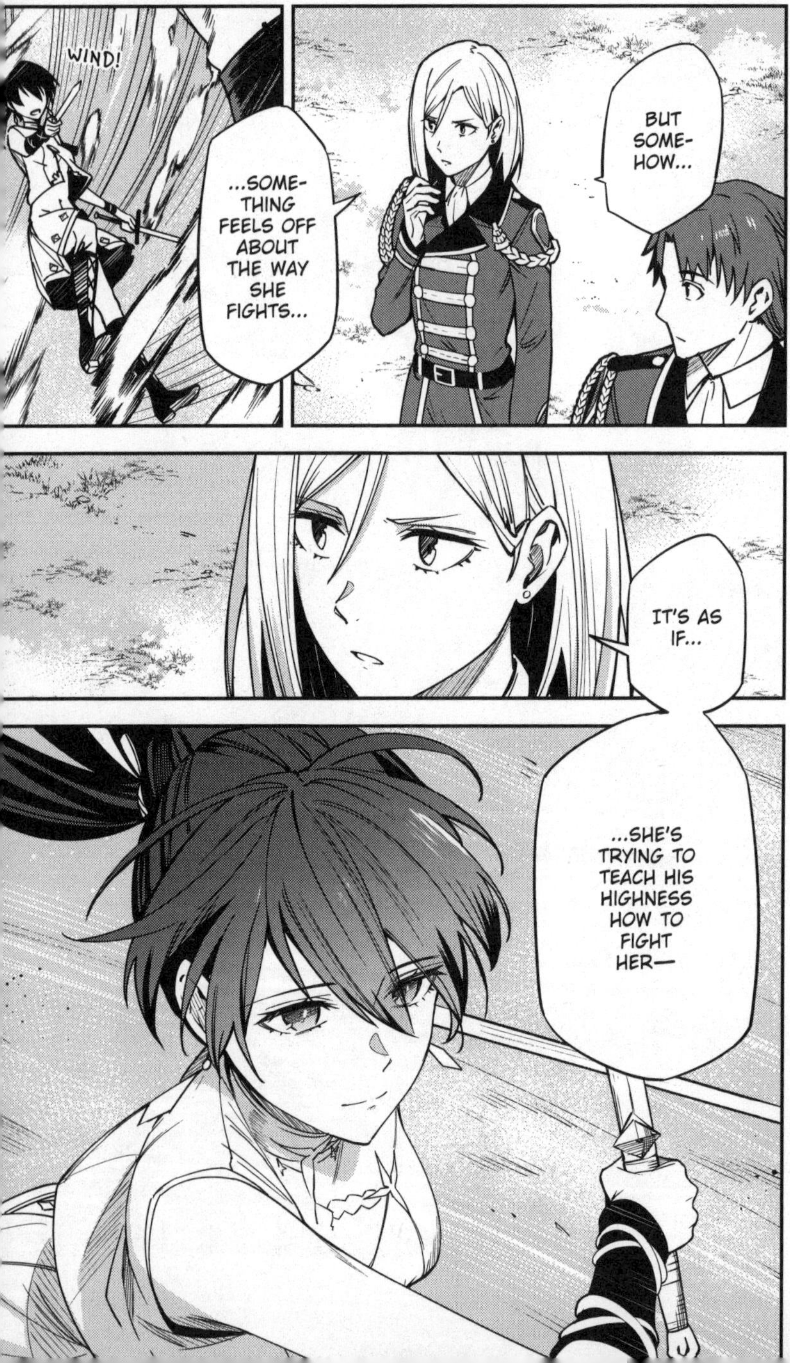
BUT SOMEHOW...
...SOMETHING FEELS OFF ABOUT THE WAY SHE FIGHTS...
WIND!
IT'S AS IF...
...SHE'S TRYING TO TEACH HIS HIGHNESS HOW TO FIGHT HER—

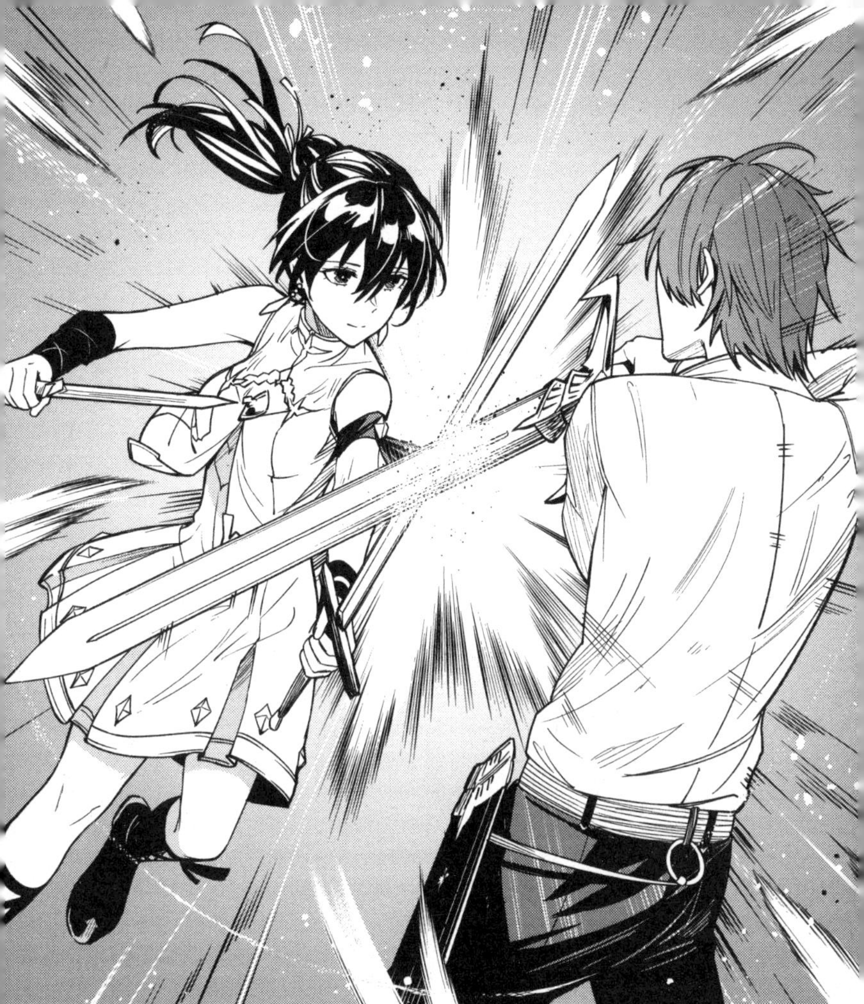

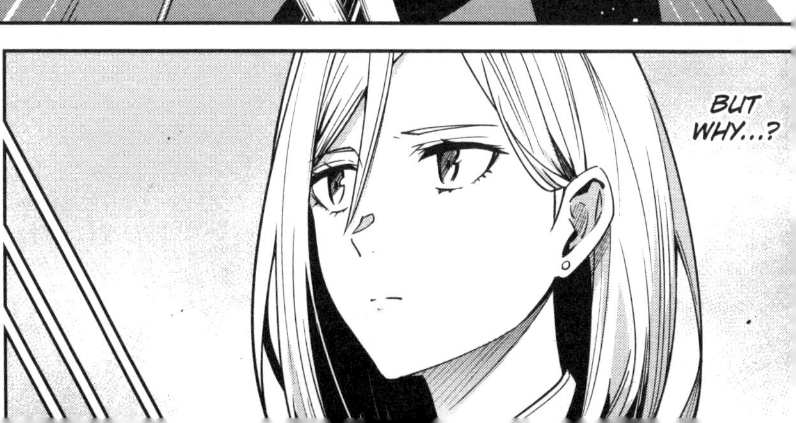
BUT WHY...?

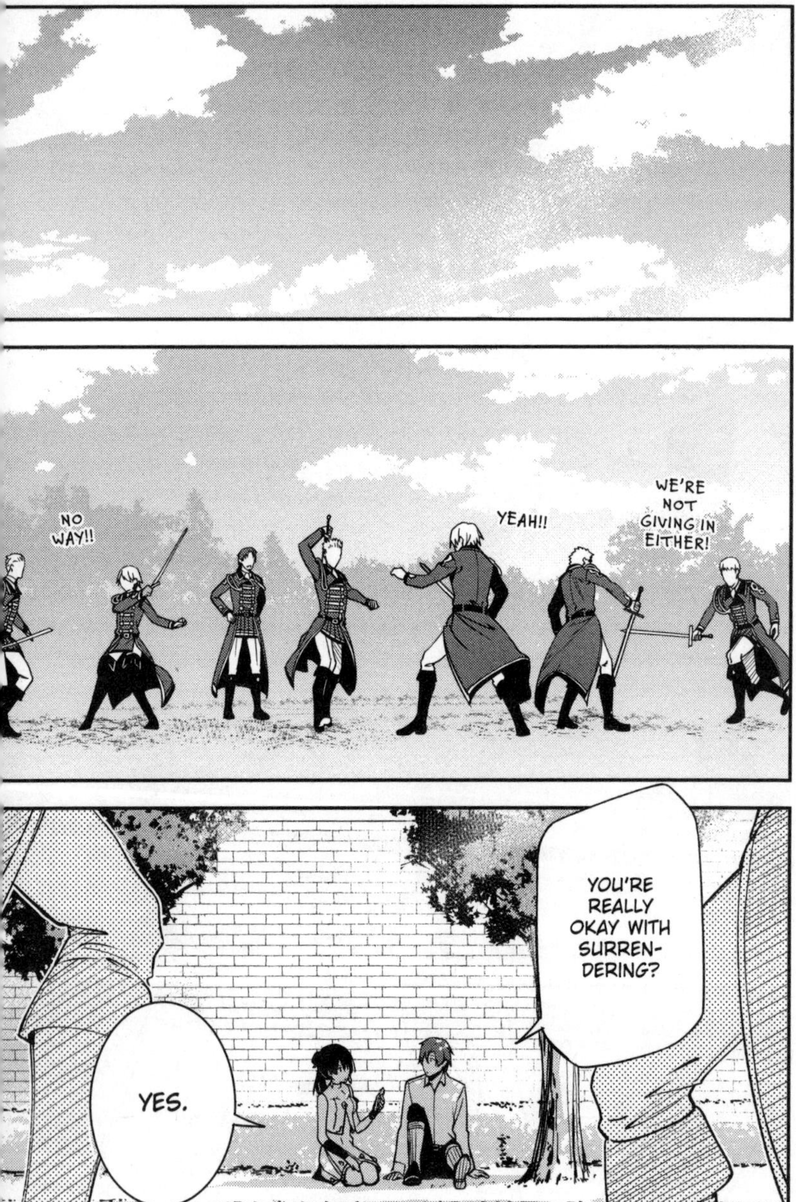
WE'RE NOT GIVING IN EITHER!
YEAH!!
NO WAY!!
YOU'RE REALLY OKAY WITH SURREN-DERING?
YES.

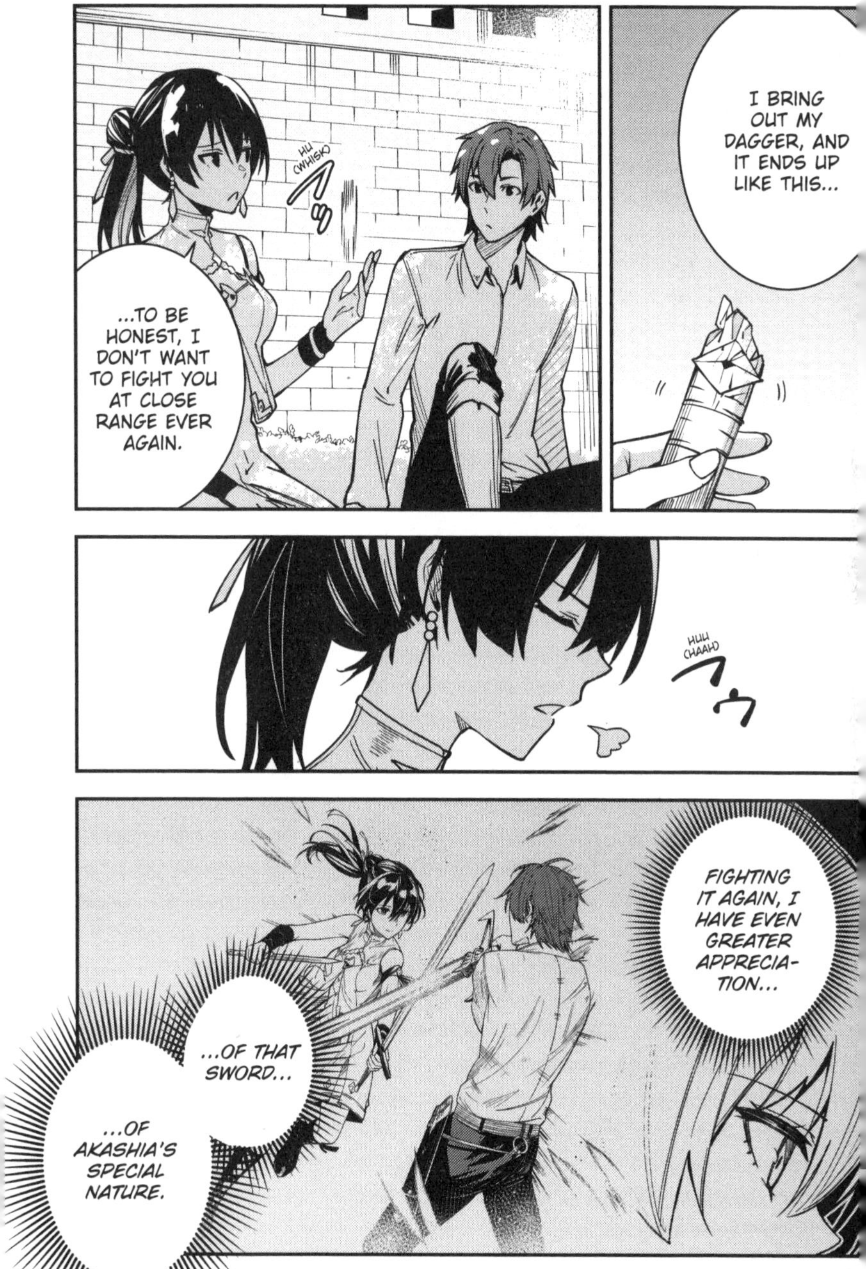
I BRING OUT MY DAGGER, AND IT ENDS UP LIKE THIS...
HU (WHISK)
...TO BE HONEST, I DON'T WANT TO FIGHT YOU AT CLOSE RANGE EVER AGAIN.
HUU (HAAH)
FIGHTING IT AGAIN, I HAVE EVEN GREATER APPRECIA-TION...
...OF THAT SWORD...
...OF AKASHIA'S SPECIAL NATURE.

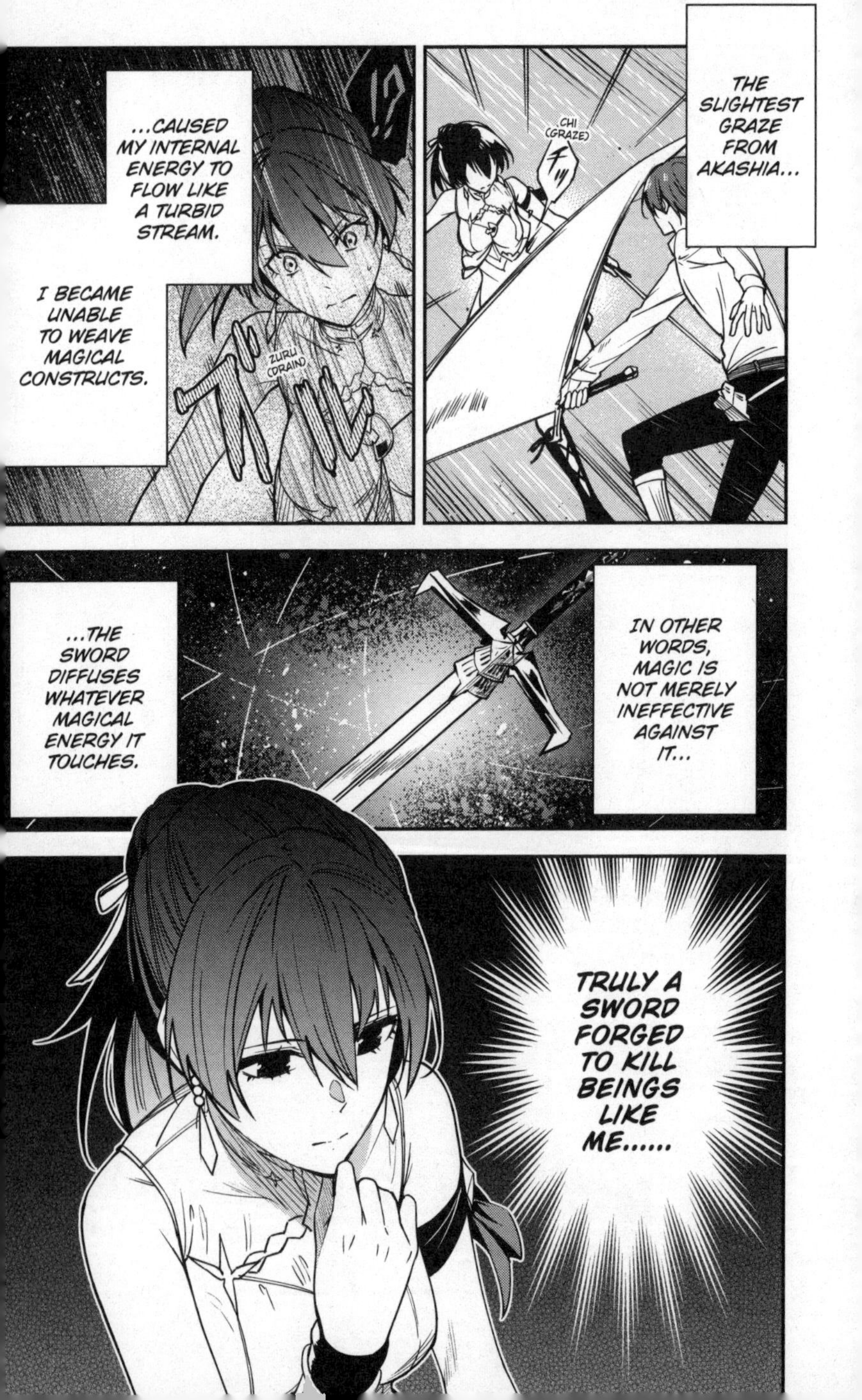
THE SLIGHTEST GRAZE FROM AKASHIA...
CHI (GRAZE)
!?
...CAUSED MY INTERNAL ENERGY TO FLOW LIKE A TURBID STREAM.
I BECAME UNABLE TO WEAVE MAGICAL CONSTRUCTS.
ZURU (DRAIN)
IN OTHER WORDS, MAGIC IS NOT MERELY INEFFECTIVE AGAINST IT...
...THE SWORD DIFFUSES WHATEVER MAGICAL ENERGY IT TOUCHES.
TRULY A SWORD FORGED TO KILL BEINGS LIKE ME......

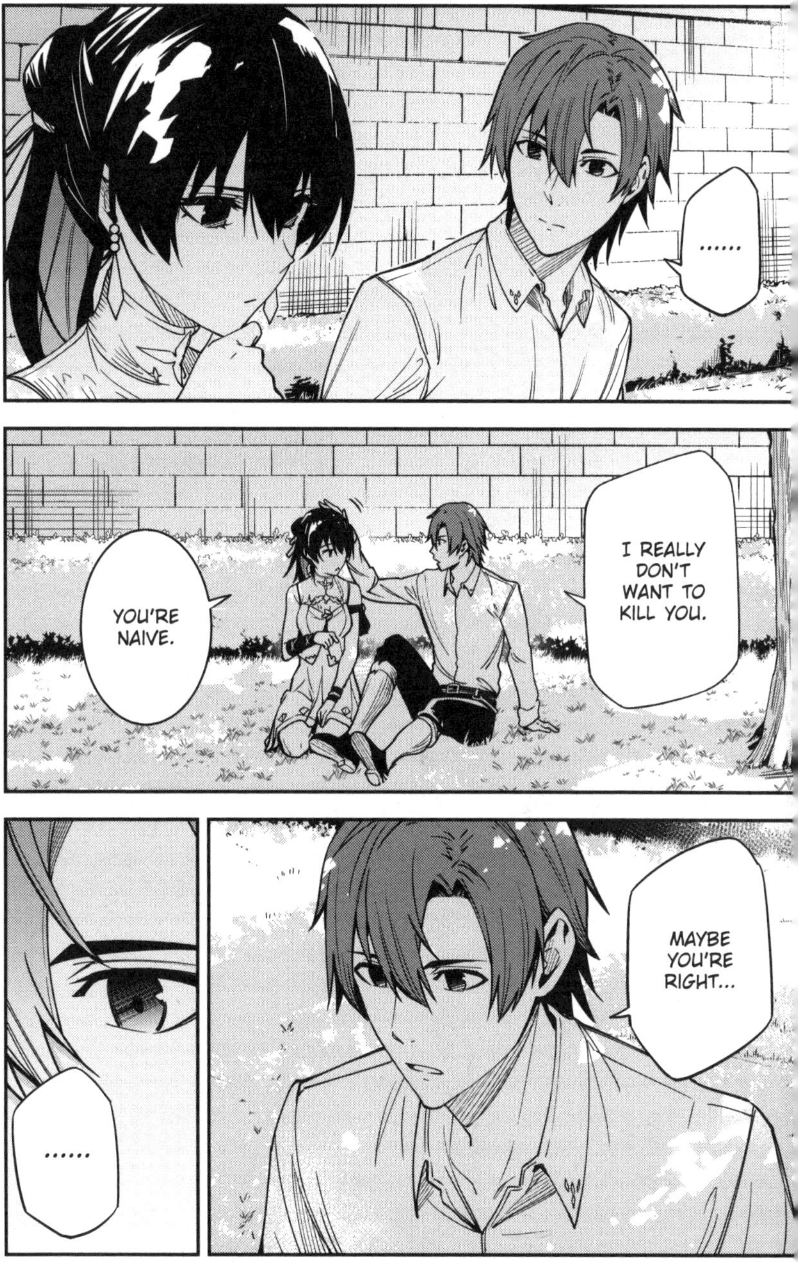
......
I REALLY DON'T WANT TO KILL YOU.
YOU'RE NAIVE.
MAYBE YOU'RE RIGHT...
......

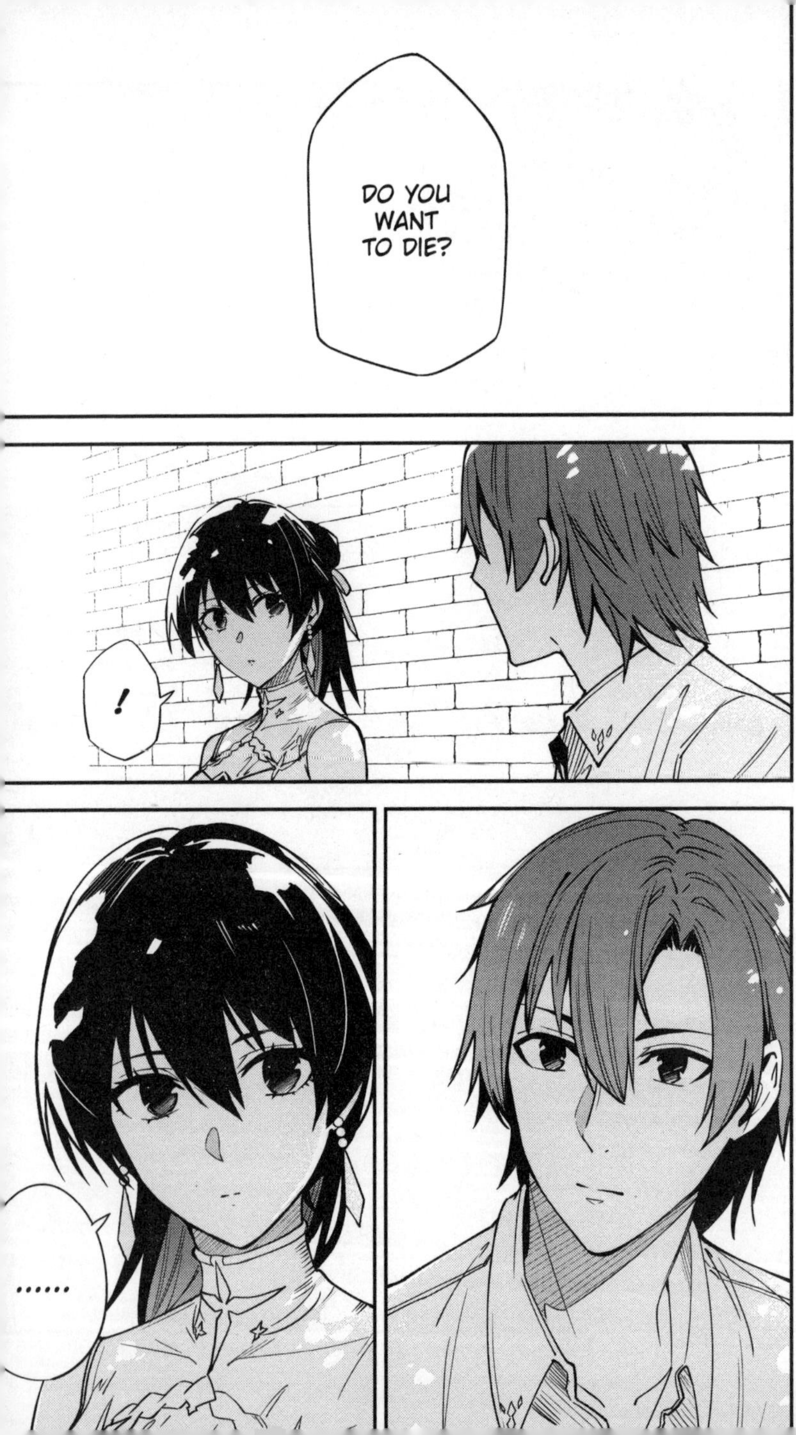
DO YOU WANT TO DIE?
!
......

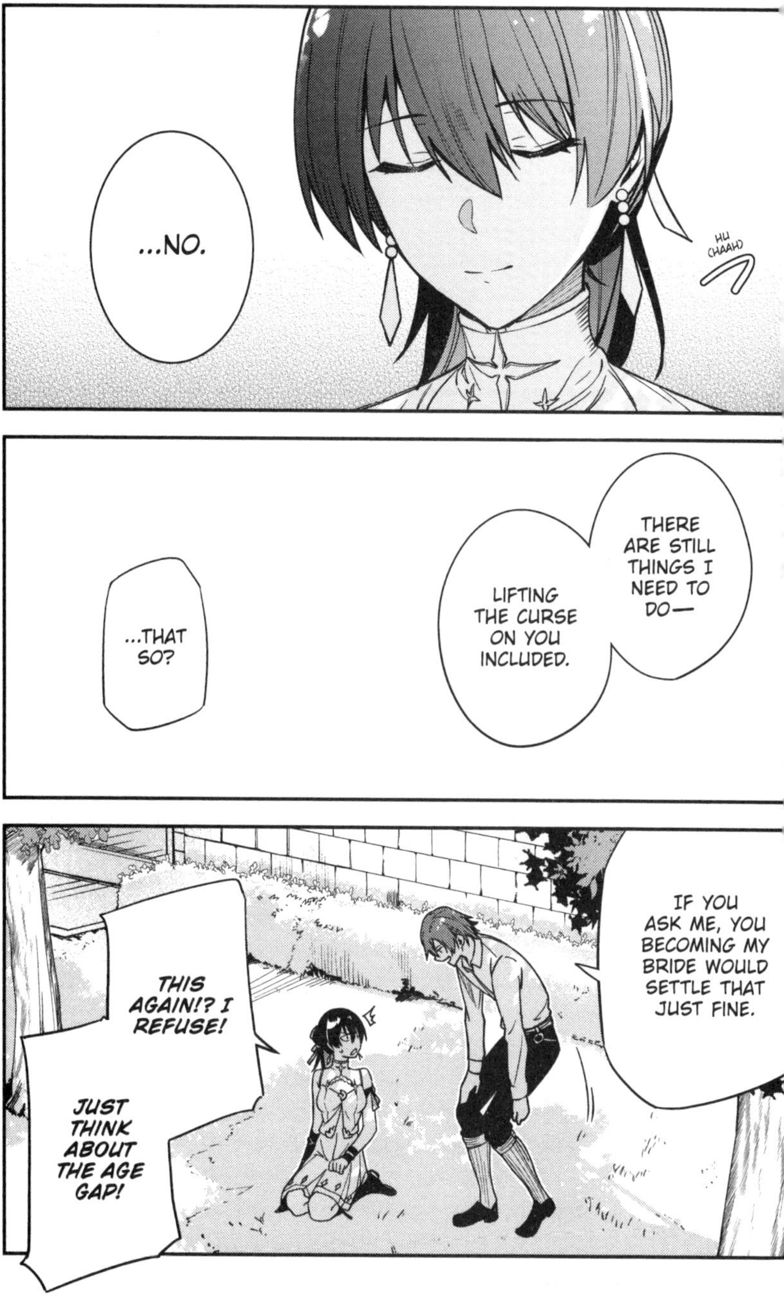
HU (HAAH)
...NO.
THERE ARE STILL THINGS I NEED TO DO—
LIFTING THE CURSE ON YOU INCLUDED.
...THAT SO?
IF YOU ASK ME, YOU BECOMING MY BRIDE WOULD SETTLE THAT JUST FINE.
THIS AGAIN!? I REFUSE!
JUST THINK ABOUT THE AGE GAP!

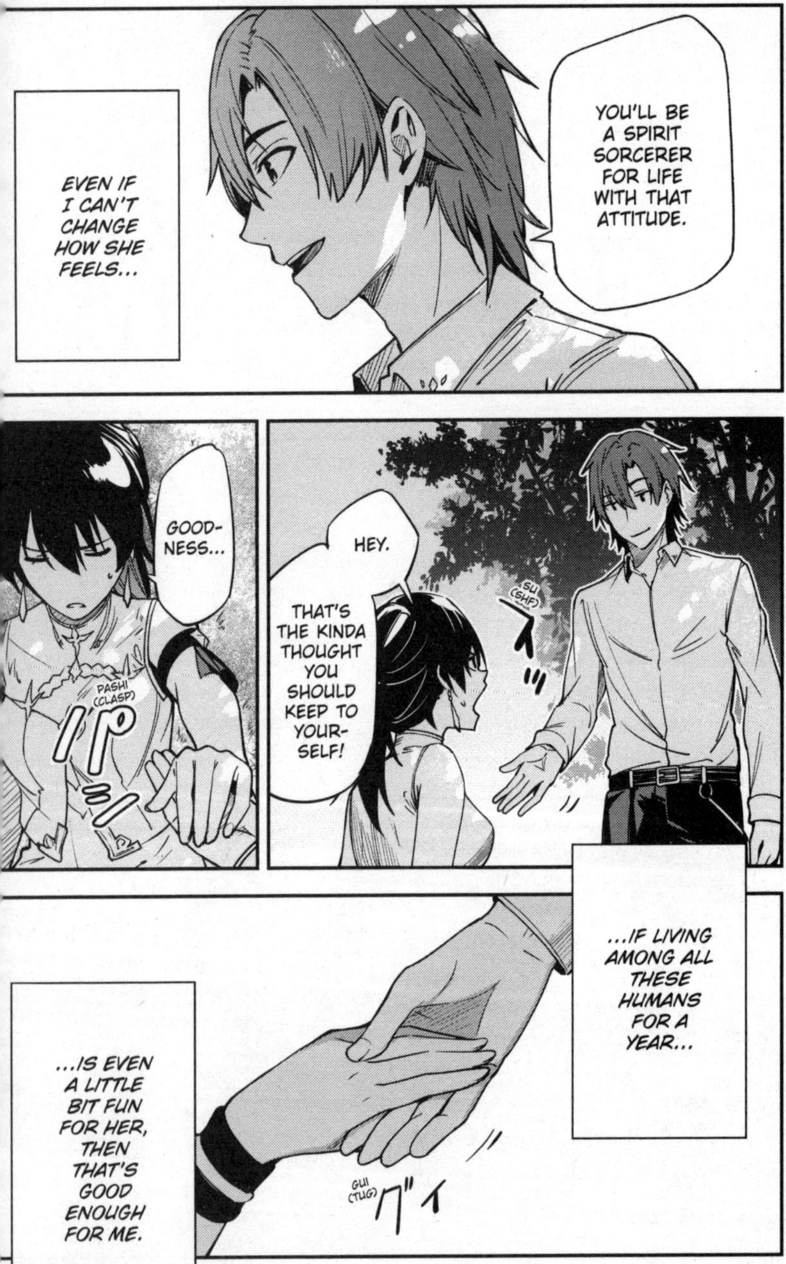
YOU'LL BE A SPIRIT SORCERER FOR LIFE WITH THAT ATTITUDE.
EVEN IF I CAN'T CHANGE HOW SHE FEELS...
SU (SHF)
HEY.
THAT'S THE KINDA THOUGHT YOU SHOULD KEEP TO YOURSELF!
GOODNESS...
PASHI (CLASP)
...IF LIVING AMONG ALL THESE HUMANS FOR A YEAR...
...IS EVEN A LITTLE BIT FUN FOR HER, THEN THAT'S GOOD ENOUGH FOR ME.
GUI (TUG)

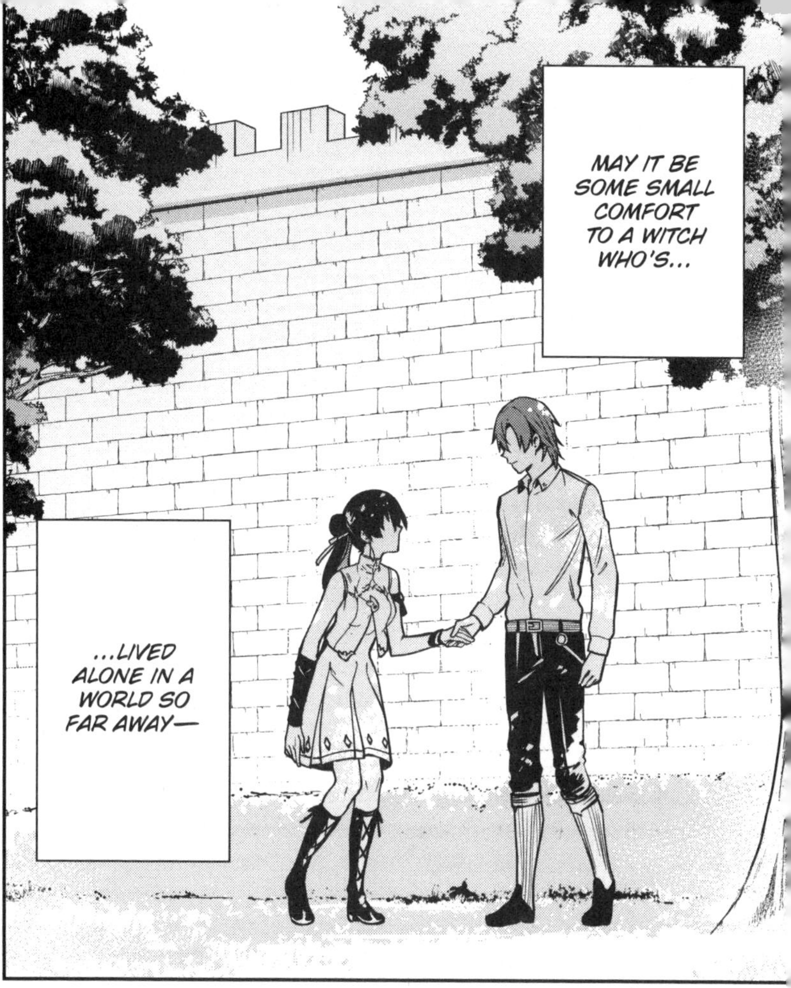
MAY IT BE SOME SMALL COMFORT TO A WITCH WHO'S...
...LIVED ALONE IN A WORLD SO FAR AWAY—

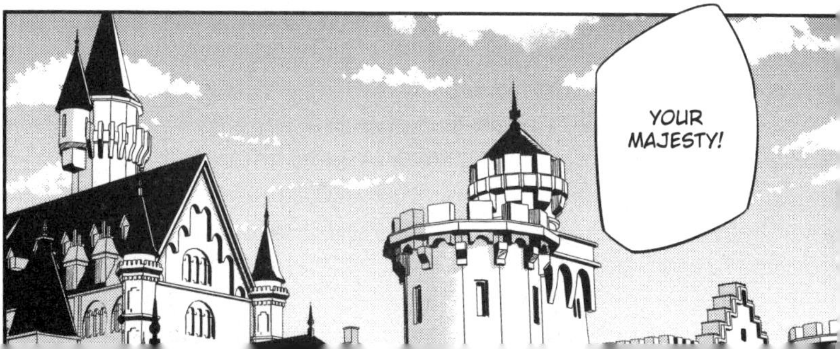
YOUR MAJESTY!

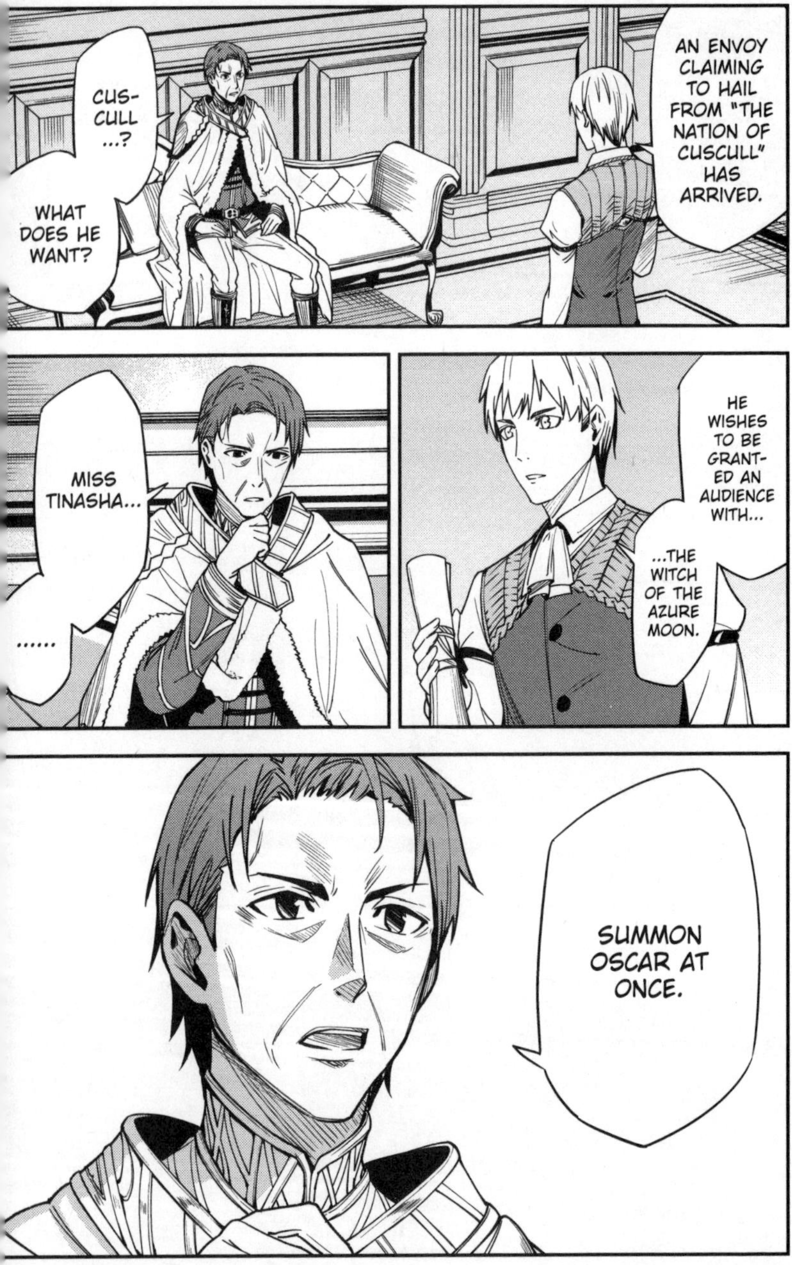
AN ENVOY CLAIMING TO HAIL FROM "THE NATION OF CUSCULL" HAS ARRIVED.
CUS-CULL ...?
WHAT DOES HE WANT?
HE WISHES TO BE GRANT-ED AN AUDIENCE WITH...
...THE WITCH OF THE AZURE MOON.
MISS TINASHA...
......
SUMMON OSCAR AT ONCE.

Unnamed Memory

Unnamed Memory

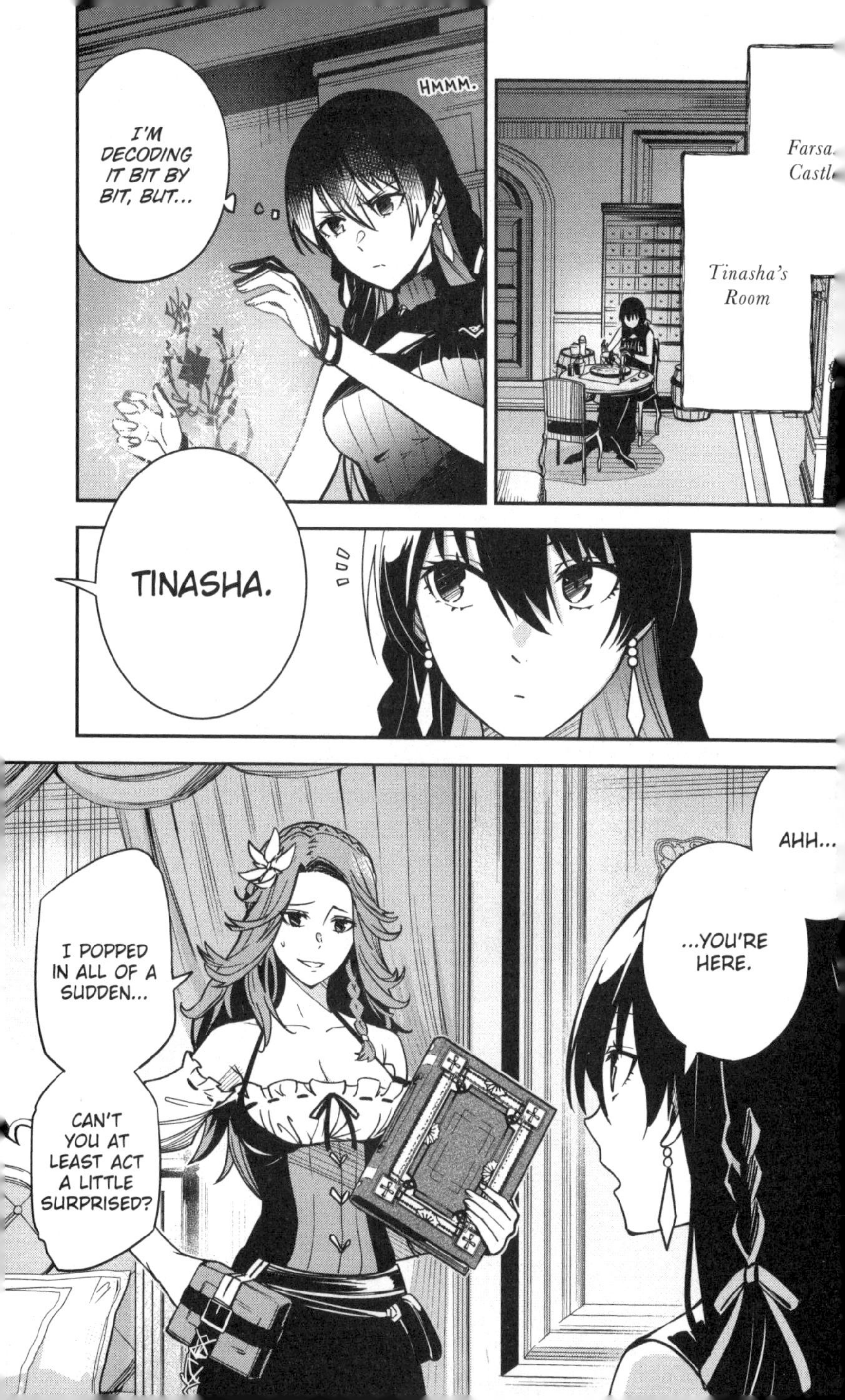

Farsa
Castl
Tinasha's Room
HMMM.
I'M DECODING IT BIT BY BIT, BUT...
TINASHA.
AHH...
...YOU'RE HERE.
I POPPED IN ALL OF A SUDDEN...
CAN'T YOU AT LEAST ACT A LITTLE SURPRISED?

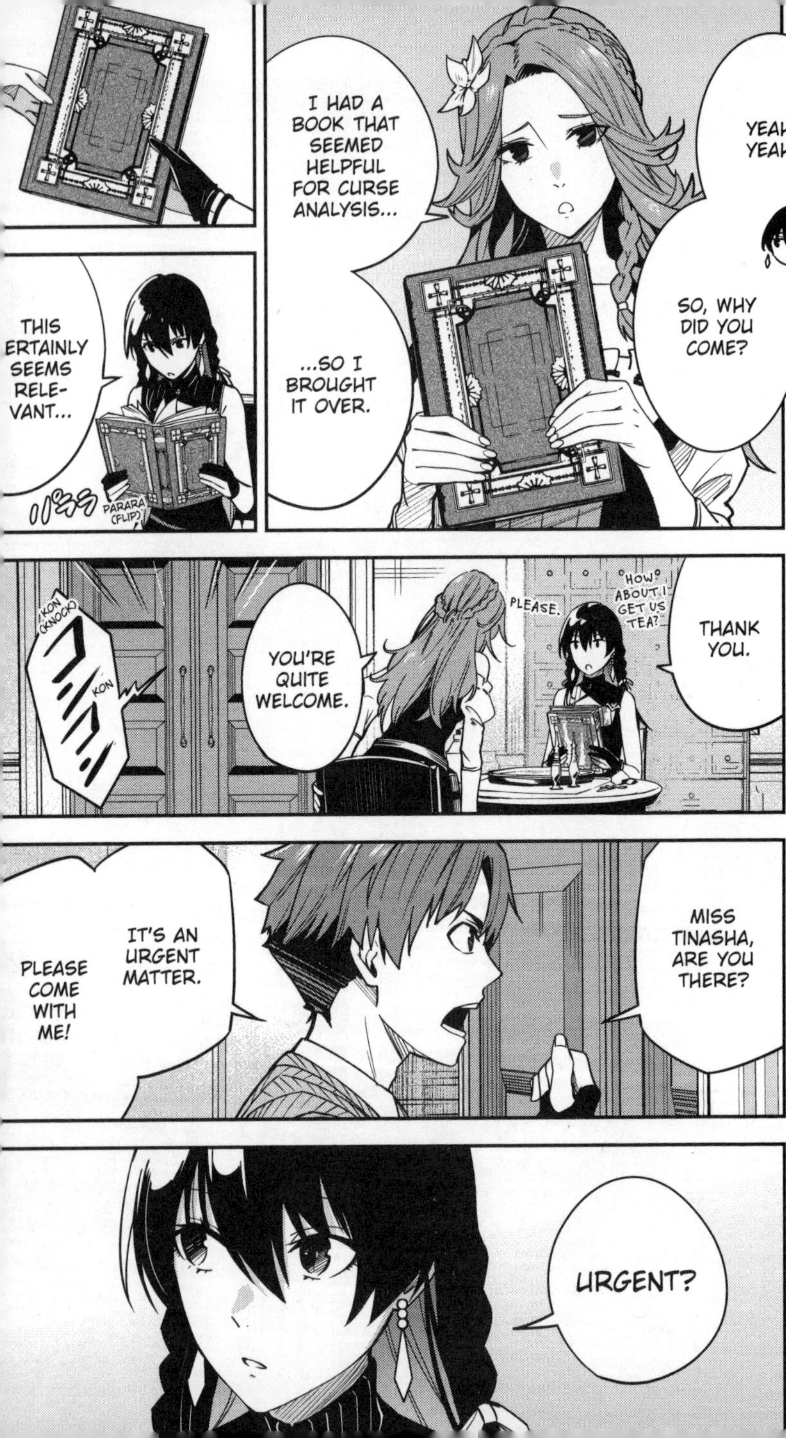
YEAH, YEAH.
SO, WHY DID YOU COME?
I HAD A BOOK THAT SEEMED HELPFUL FOR CURSE ANALYSIS...
...SO I BROUGHT IT OVER.
THIS ERTAINLY SEEMS RELE-VANT...
PARARA (FLIP)
THANK YOU.
HOW ABOUT I GET US TEA?
PLEASE.
YOU'RE QUITE WELCOME.
KON (KNOCK)
KON
MISS TINASHA, ARE YOU THERE?
IT'S AN URGENT MATTER.
PLEASE COME WITH ME!
URGENT?

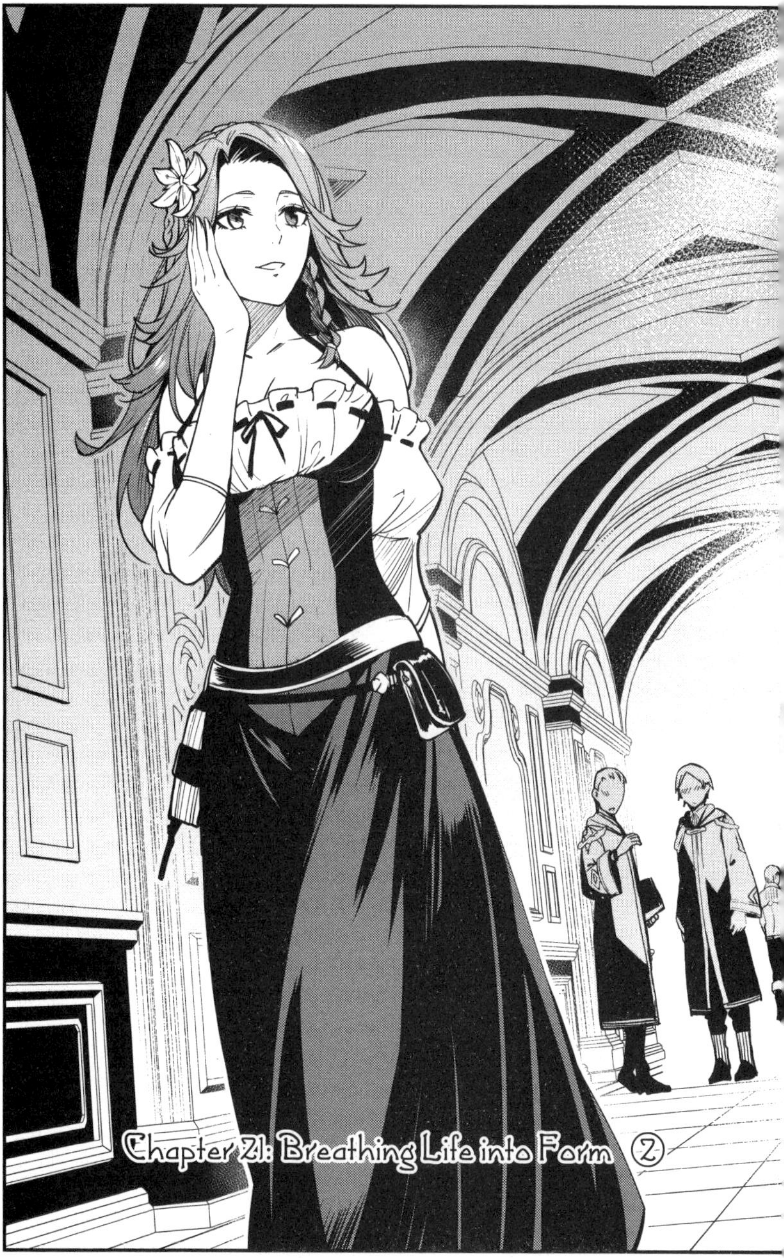
Chapter 21: Breathing Life into Form ②

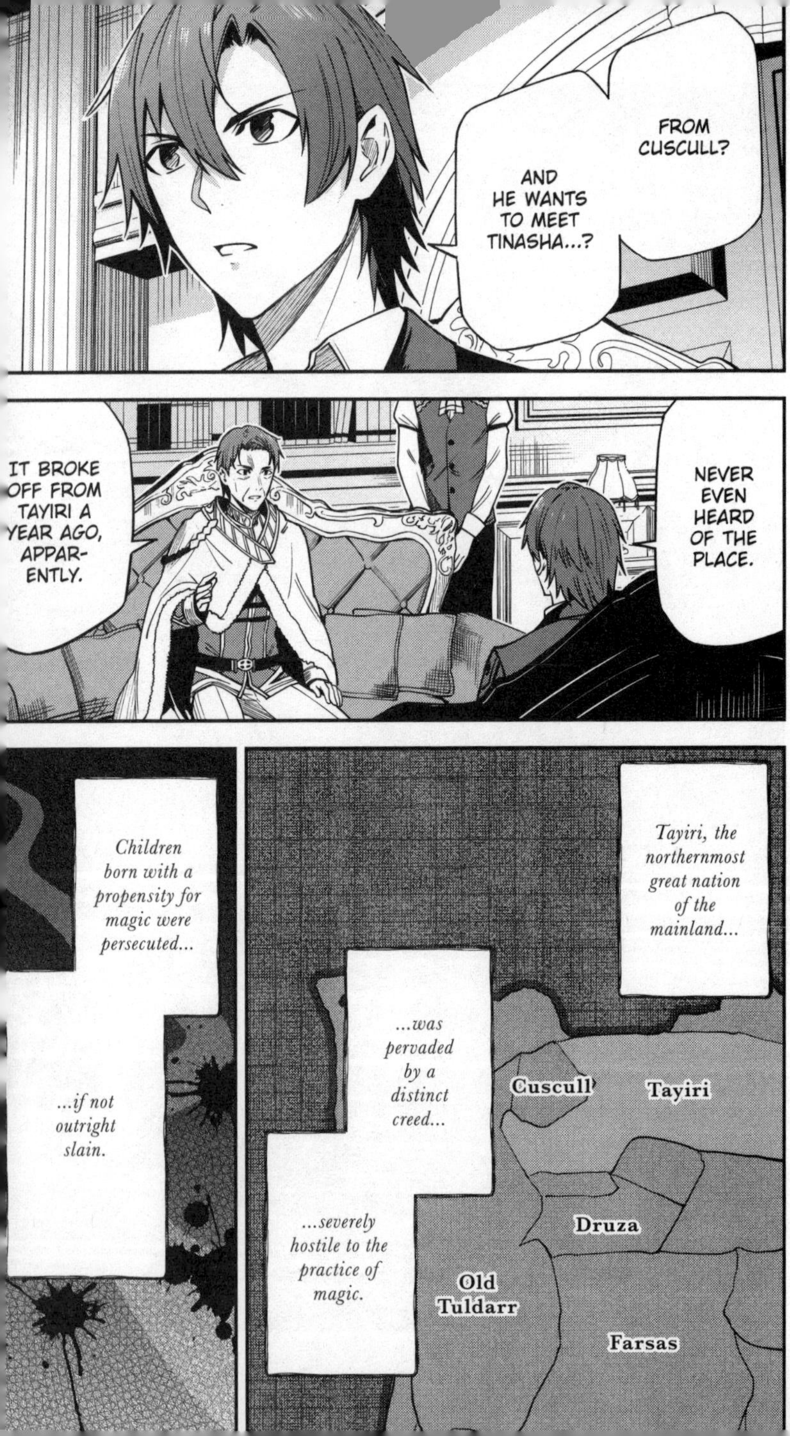
FROM CUSCULL?
AND HE WANTS TO MEET TINASHA...?
NEVER EVEN HEARD OF THE PLACE.
IT BROKE OFF FROM TAYIRI A YEAR AGO, APPARENTLY.
Tayiri, the northernmost great nation of the mainland...
...was pervaded by a distinct creed...
...severely hostile to the practice of magic.
Cuscull
Tayiri
Druza
Old Tuldarr
Farsas
Children born with a propensity for magic were persecuted...
...if not outright slain.

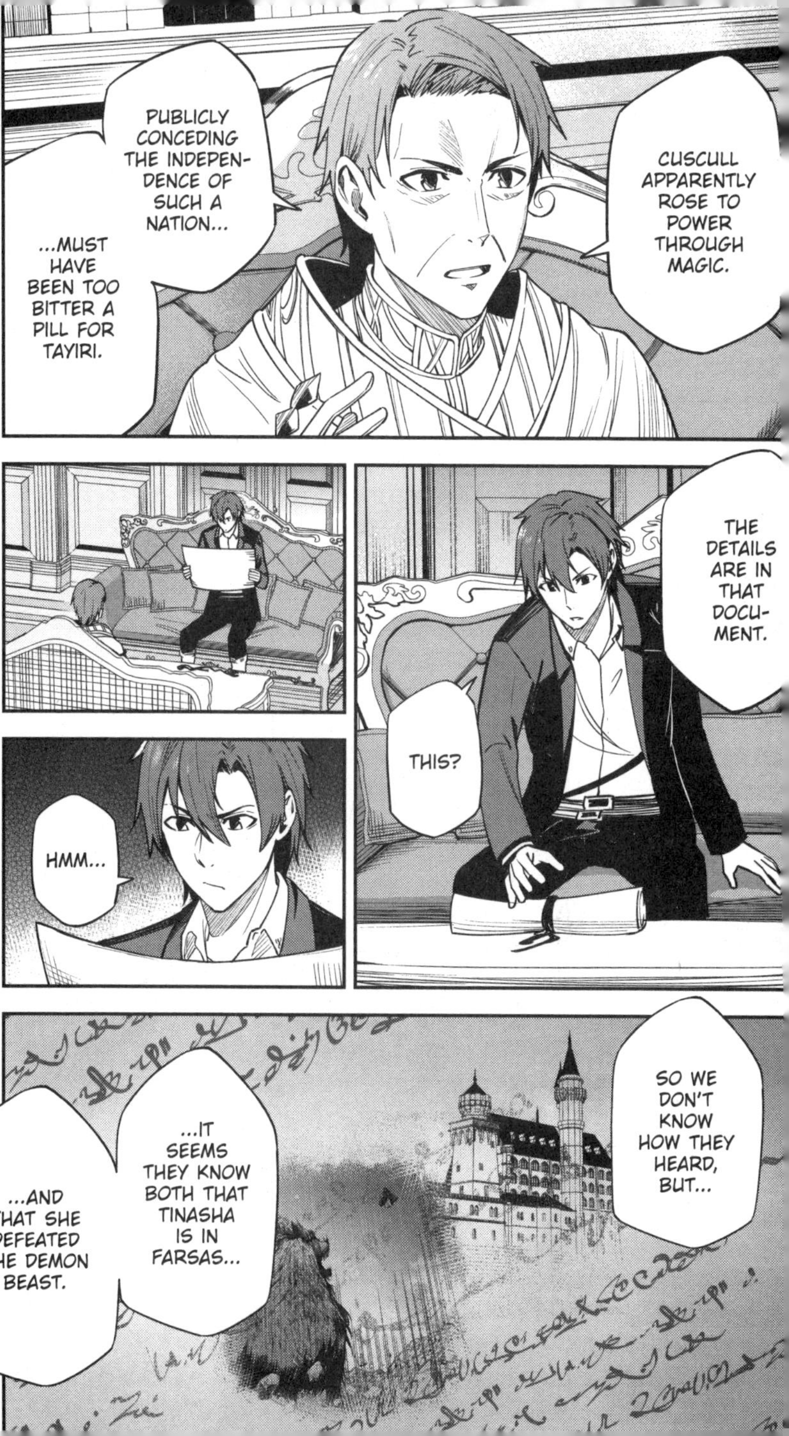
CUSCULL APPARENTLY ROSE TO POWER THROUGH MAGIC.
PUBLICLY CONCEDING THE INDEPENDENCE OF SUCH A NATION...
...MUST HAVE BEEN TOO BITTER A PILL FOR TAYIRI.
THE DETAILS ARE IN THAT DOCUMENT.
THIS?
HMM...
SO WE DON'T KNOW HOW THEY HEARD, BUT...
...IT SEEMS THEY KNOW BOTH THAT TINASHA IS IN FARSAS...
...AND THAT SHE DEFEATED THE DEMON BEAST.

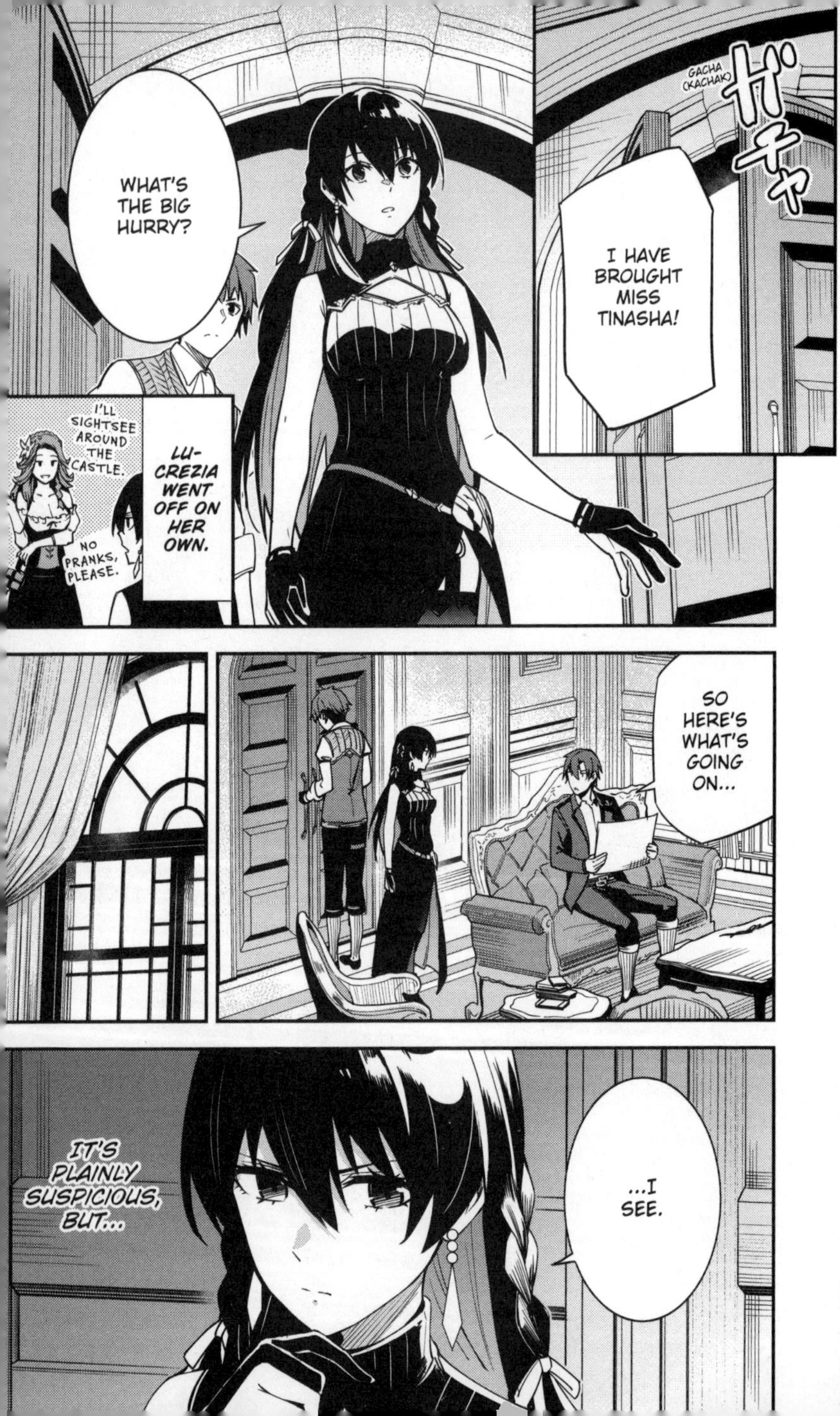
GACHA (KACHAK)
I HAVE BROUGHT MISS TINASHA!
WHAT'S THE BIG HURRY?
LUCREZIA WENT OFF ON HER OWN.
I'LL SIGHTSEE AROUND THE CASTLE.
NO PRANKS, PLEASE.
SO HERE'S WHAT'S GOING ON...
...I SEE.
IT'S PLAINLY SUSPICIOUS, BUT...

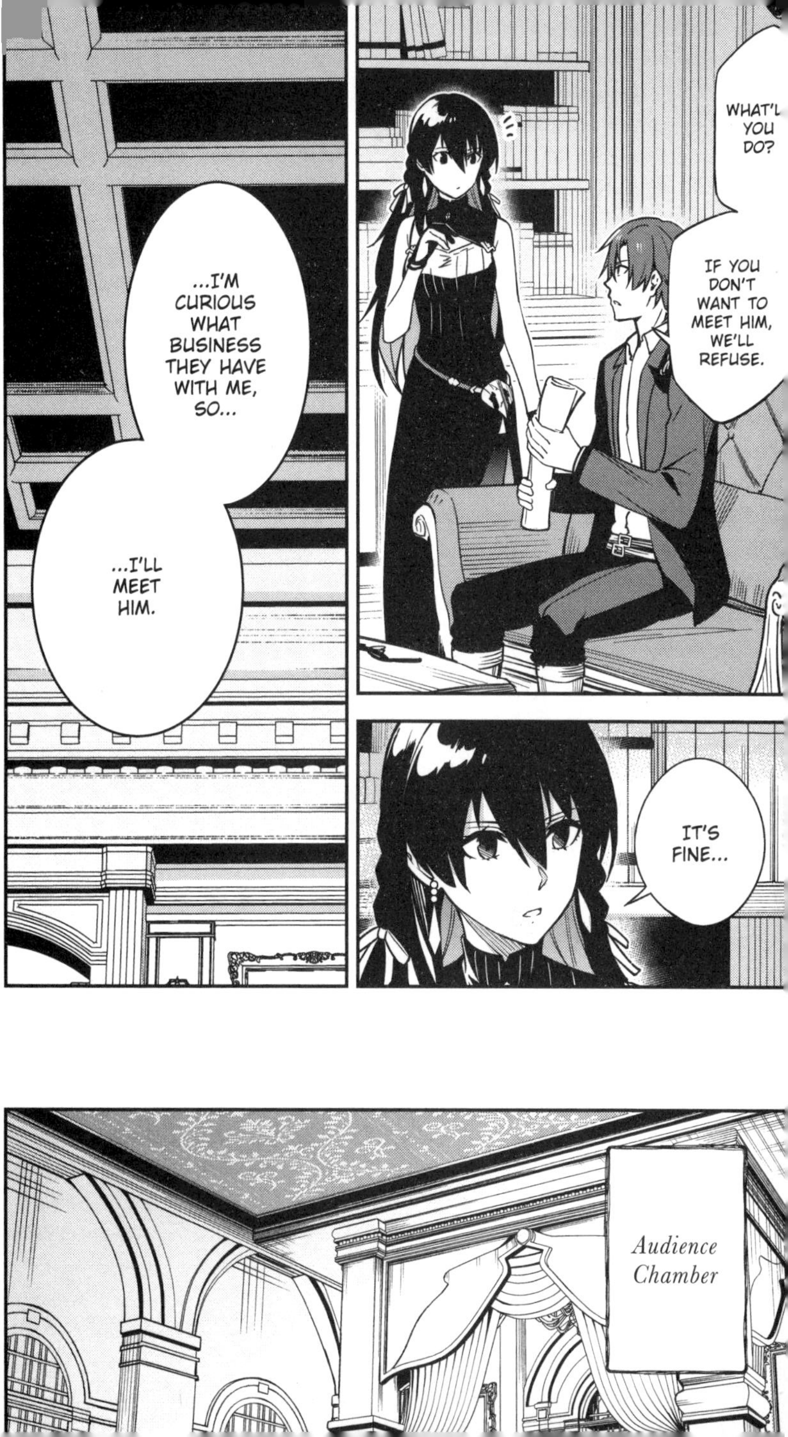
WHAT'L YOU DO?
IF YOU DON'T WANT TO MEET HIM, WE'LL REFUSE.
IT'S FINE...
...I'M CURIOUS WHAT BUSINESS THEY HAVE WITH ME, SO...
...I'LL MEET HIM.
Audience Chamber

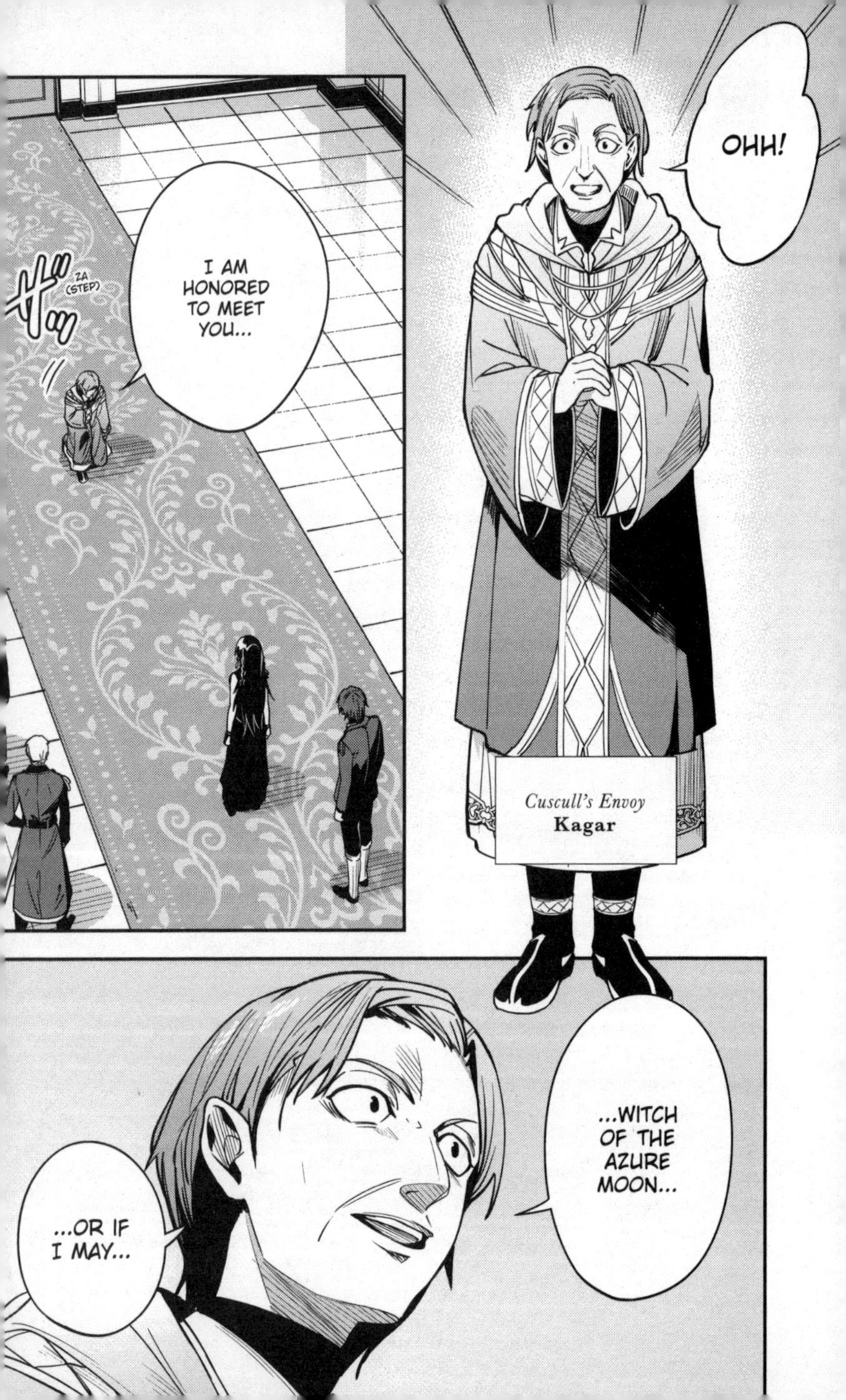
OHH!
Cuscull's Envoy
Kagar
ZA (STEP)
I AM HONORED TO MEET YOU...
...WITCH OF THE AZURE MOON...
...OR IF I MAY...

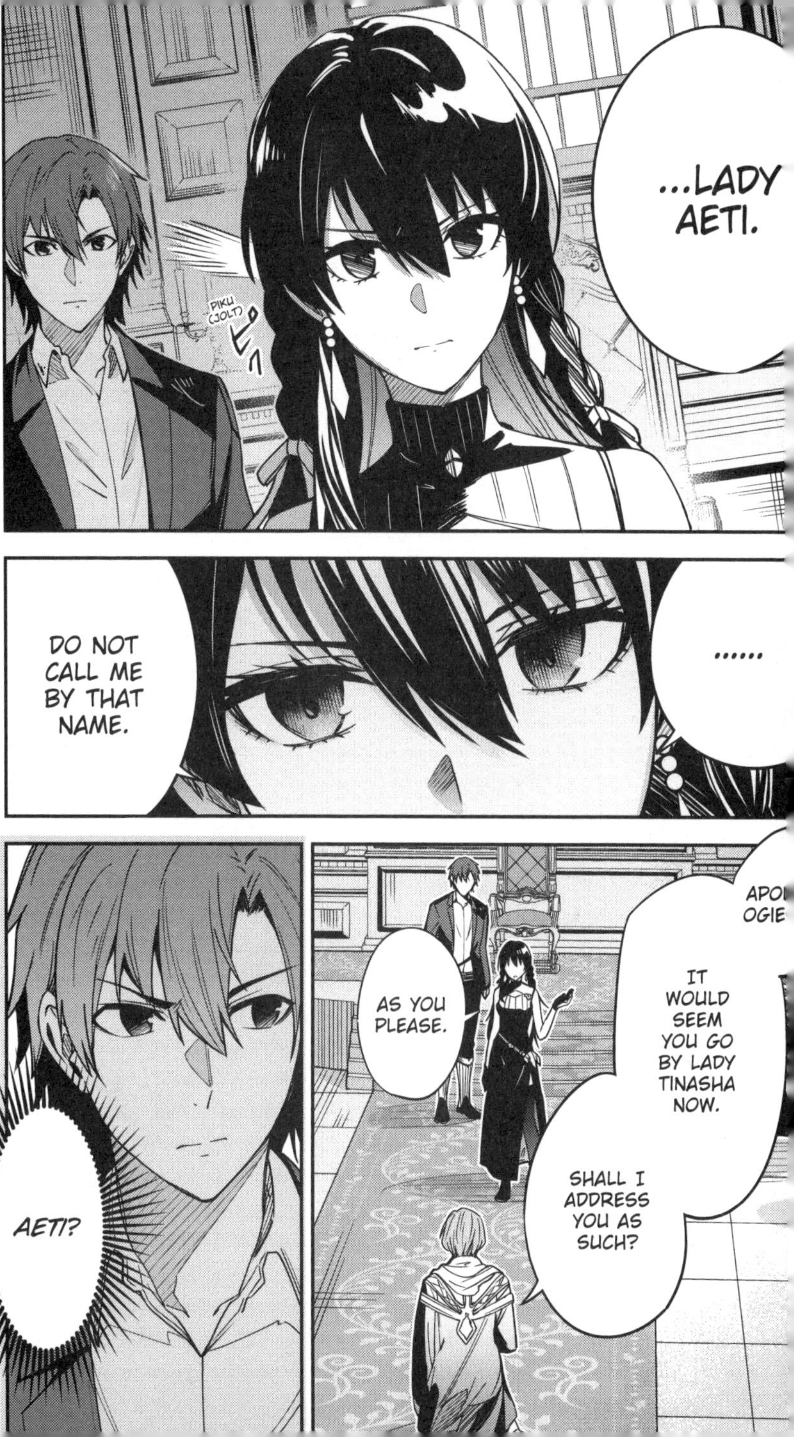
...LADY AETI.
PIKU (JOLT)
......
DO NOT CALL ME BY THAT NAME.
APOL OGIE
IT WOULD SEEM YOU GO BY LADY TINASHA NOW.
SHALL I ADDRESS YOU AS SUCH?
AS YOU PLEASE.
AETI?

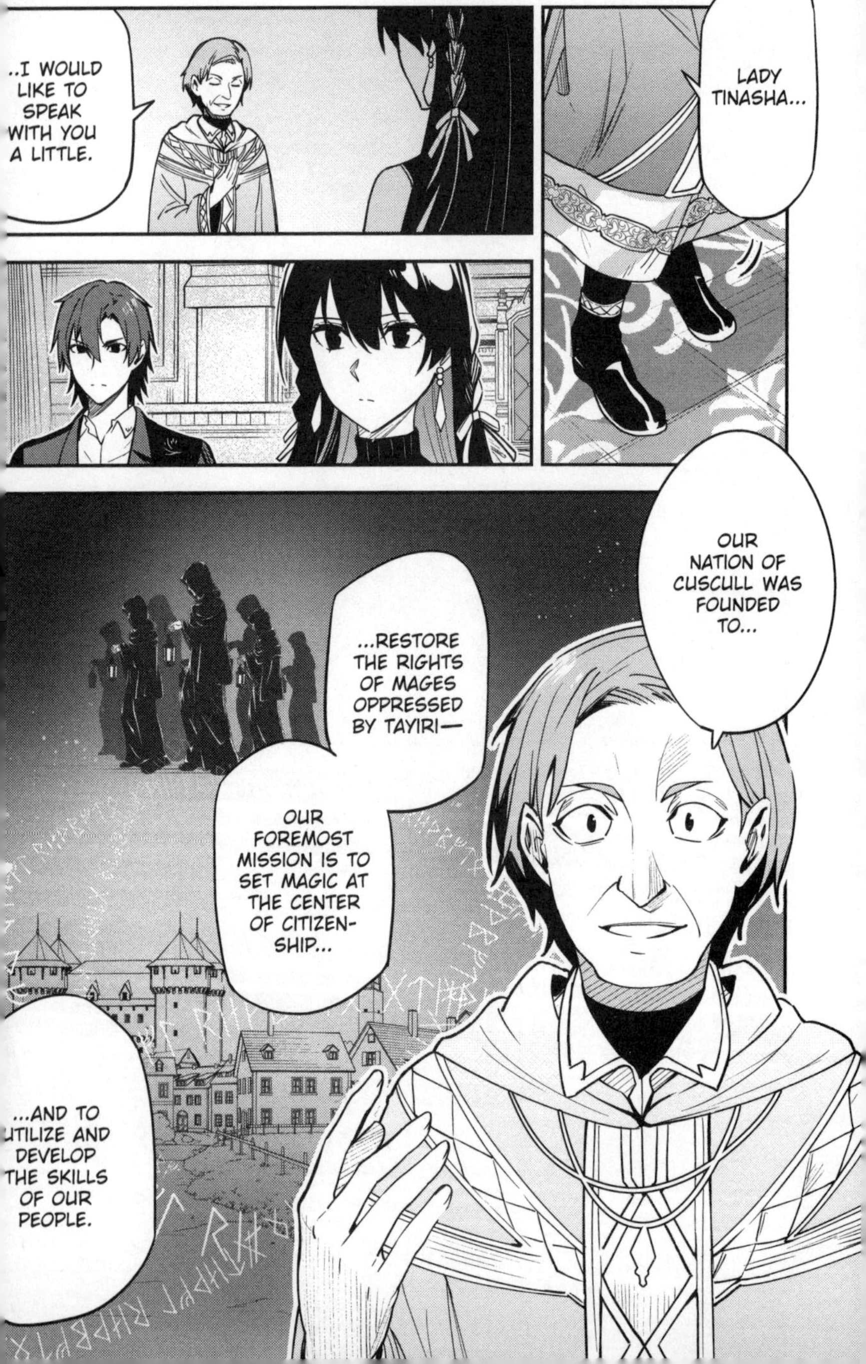
LADY TINASHA...
..I WOULD LIKE TO SPEAK WITH YOU A LITTLE.
OUR NATION OF CUSCULL WAS FOUNDED TO...
...RESTORE THE RIGHTS OF MAGES OPPRESSED BY TAYIRI—
OUR FOREMOST MISSION IS TO SET MAGIC AT THE CENTER OF CITIZEN-SHIP...
...AND TO UTILIZE AND DEVELOP THE SKILLS OF OUR PEOPLE.

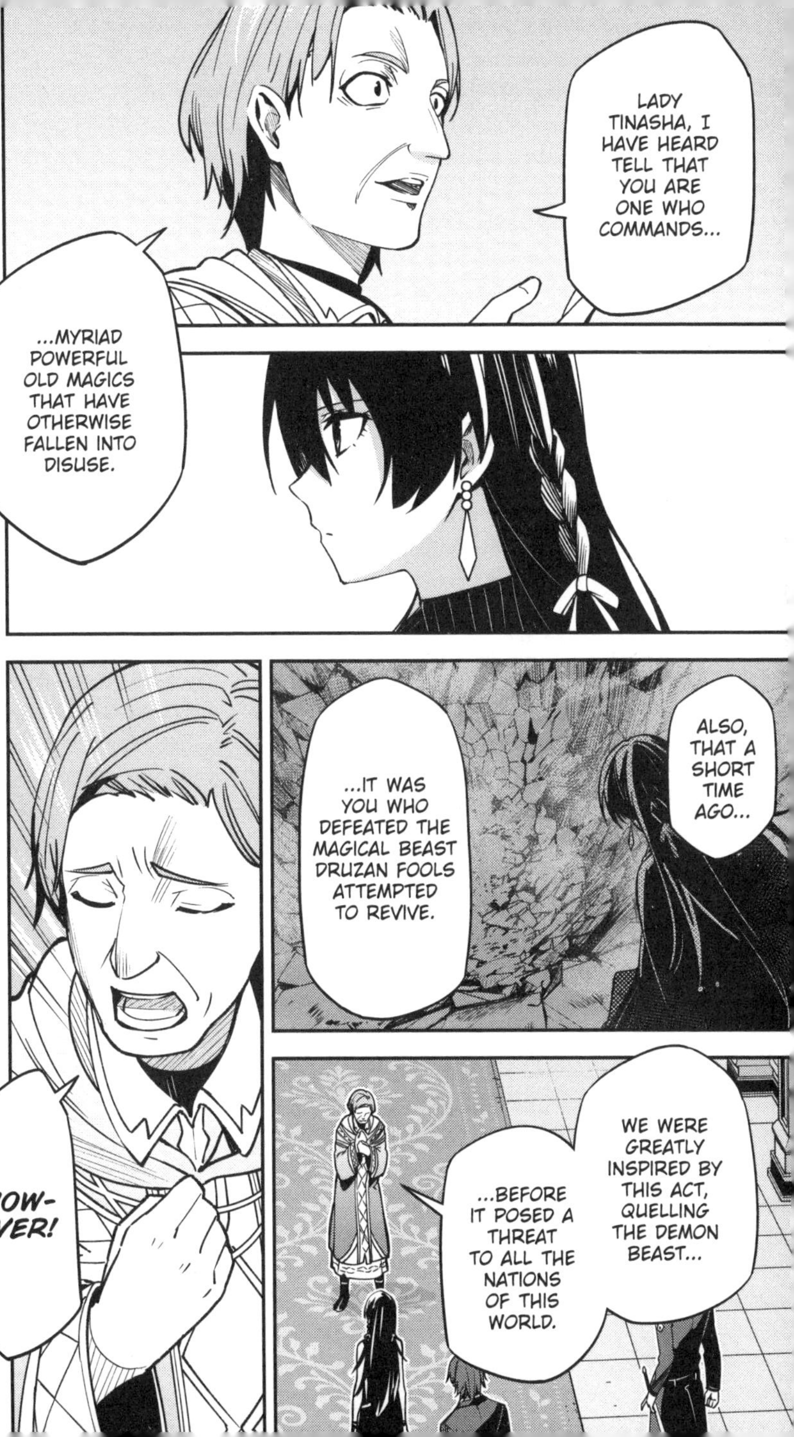
LADY TINASHA, I HAVE HEARD TELL THAT YOU ARE ONE WHO COMMANDS...
...MYRIAD POWERFUL OLD MAGICS THAT HAVE OTHERWISE FALLEN INTO DISUSE.
ALSO, THAT A SHORT TIME AGO...
...IT WAS YOU WHO DEFEATED THE MAGICAL BEAST DRUZAN FOOLS ATTEMPTED TO REVIVE.
WE WERE GREATLY INSPIRED BY THIS ACT, QUELLING THE DEMON BEAST...
...BEFORE IT POSED A THREAT TO ALL THE NATIONS OF THIS WORLD.
HOW-EVER!

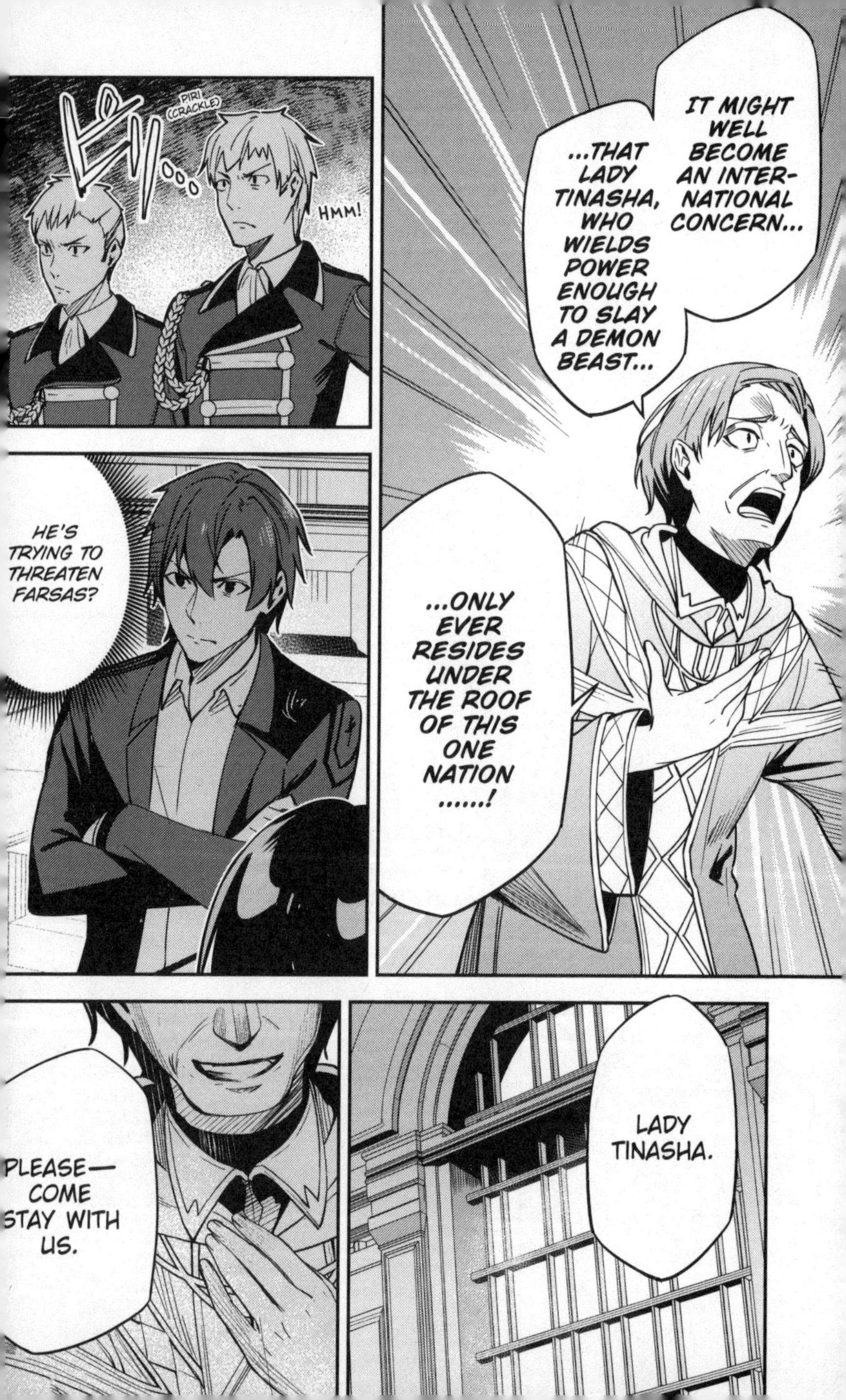
IT MIGHT WELL BECOME AN INTER-NATIONAL CONCERN...
...THAT LADY TINASHA, WHO WIELDS POWER ENOUGH TO SLAY A DEMON BEAST...
...ONLY EVER RESIDES UNDER THE ROOF OF THIS ONE NATION......!
ピリ
PIRI (CRACKLE)
HMM!
HE'S TRYING TO THREATEN FARSAS?
LADY TINASHA.
PLEASE— COME STAY WITH US.

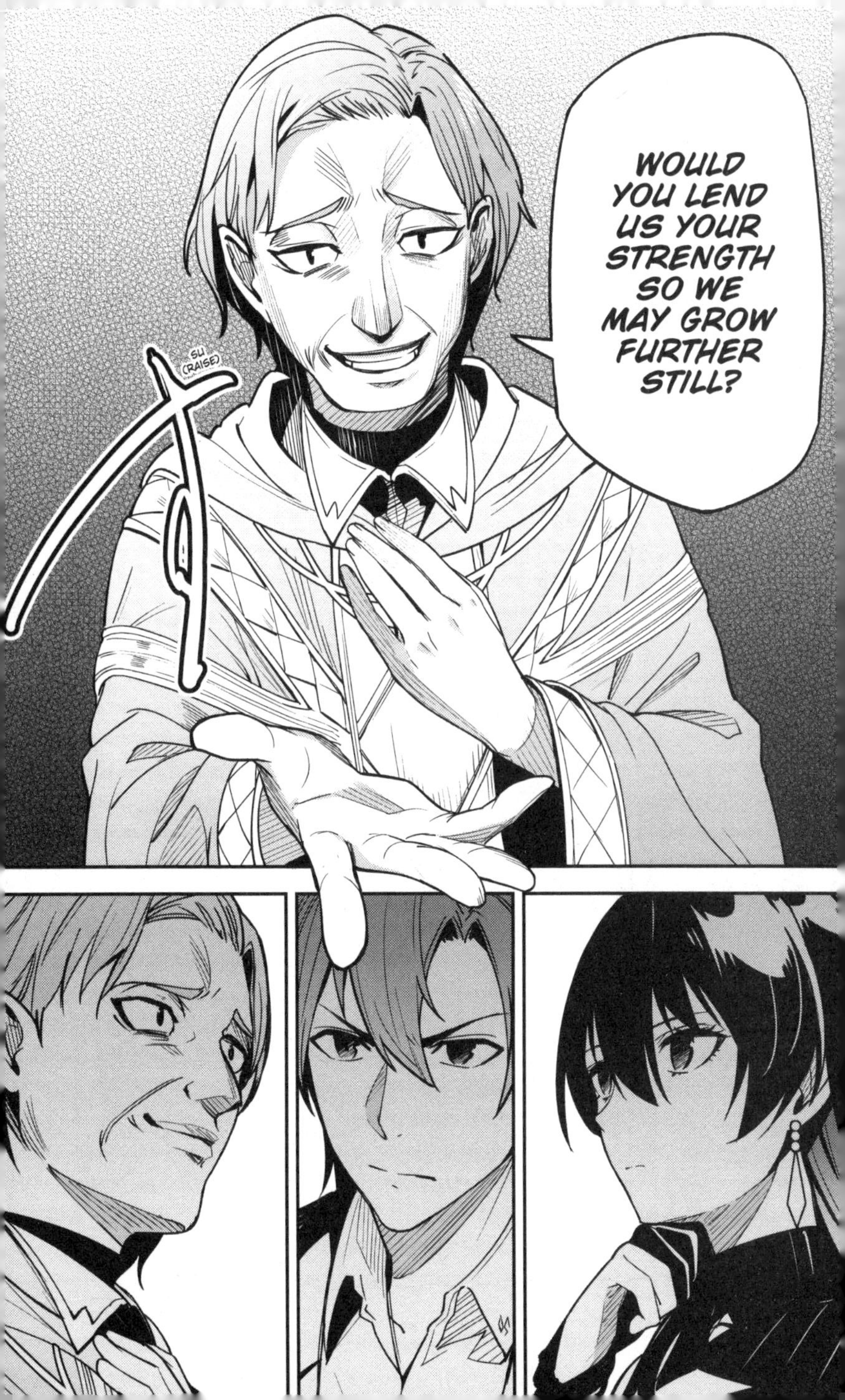
WOULD YOU LEND US YOUR STRENGTH SO WE MAY GROW FURTHER STILL?
SU (RAISE)

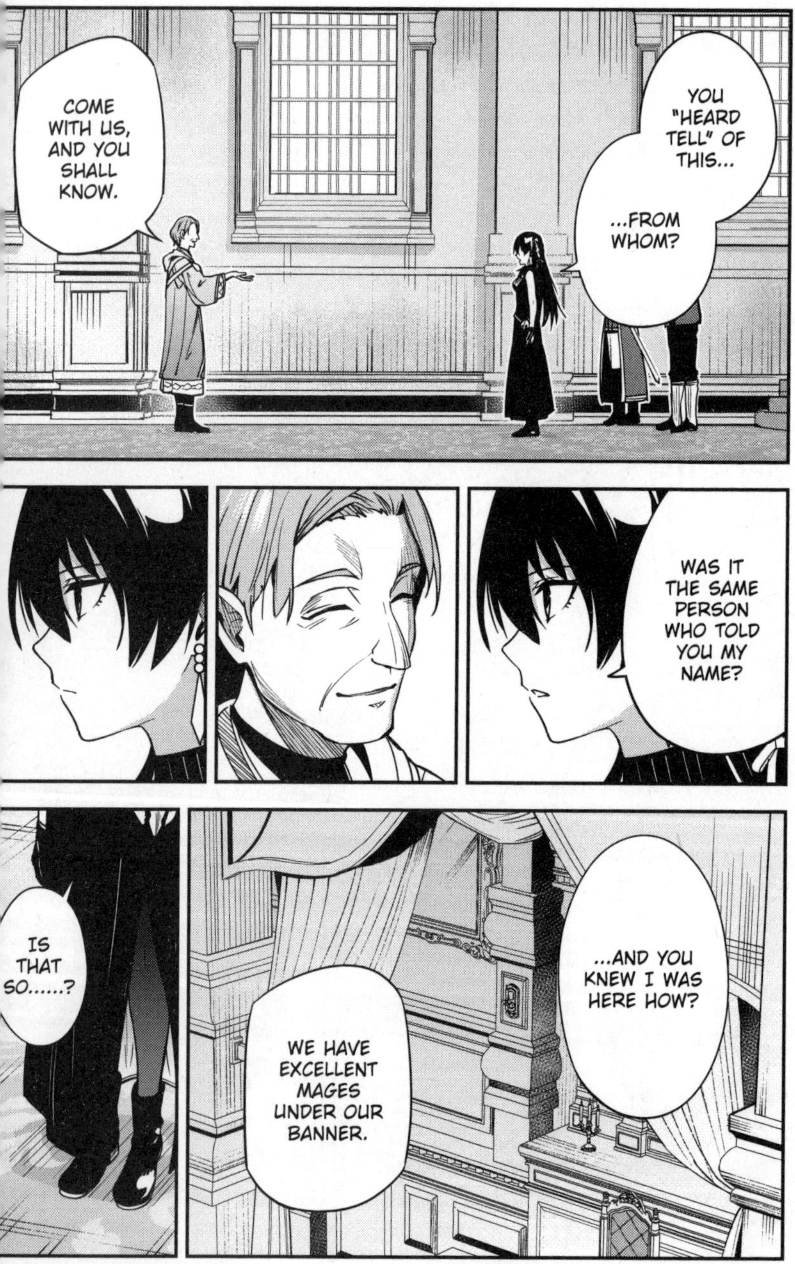
YOU "HEARD TELL" OF THIS...
...FROM WHOM?
COME WITH US, AND YOU SHALL KNOW.
WAS IT THE SAME PERSON WHO TOLD YOU MY NAME?
...AND YOU KNEW I WAS HERE HOW?
WE HAVE EXCELLENT MAGES UNDER OUR BANNER.
IS THAT SO......?

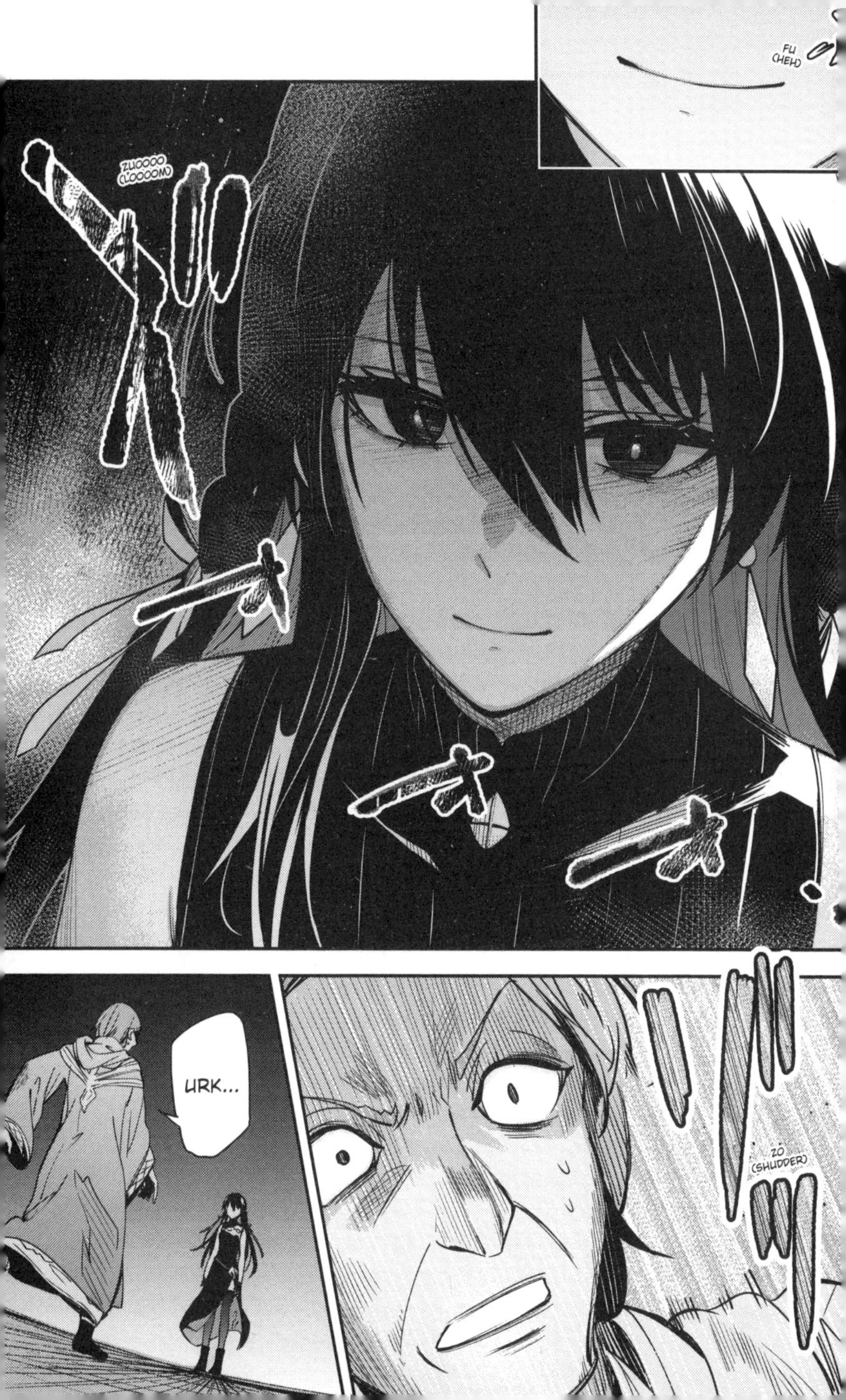
FU
(HEH)
ZUOOOO
(LOOOOM)
ZO
(SHUDDER)
URK...

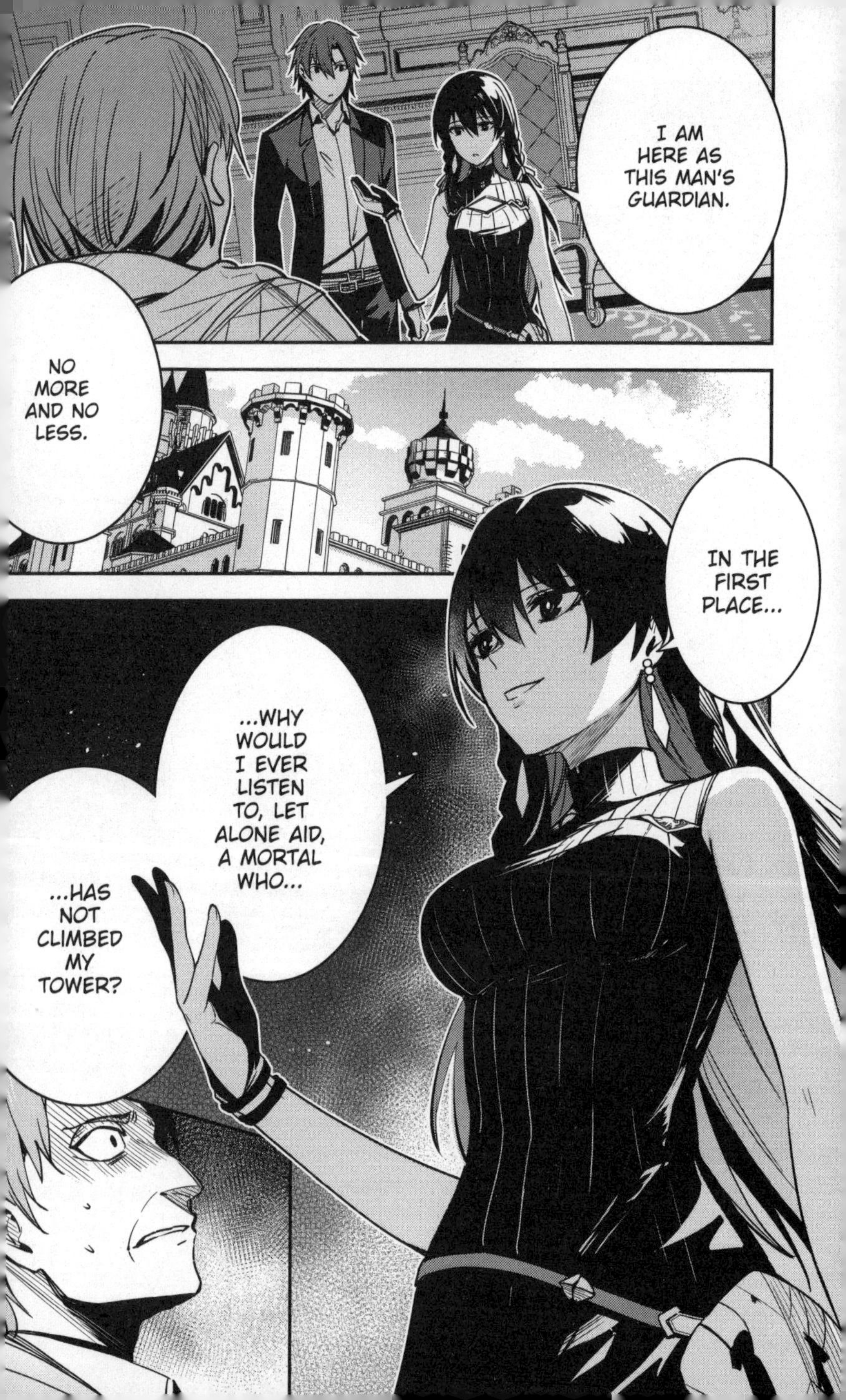
I AM HERE AS THIS MAN'S GUARDIAN.
NO MORE AND NO LESS.
IN THE FIRST PLACE...
...WHY WOULD I EVER LISTEN TO, LET ALONE AID, A MORTAL WHO...
...HAS NOT CLIMBED MY TOWER?

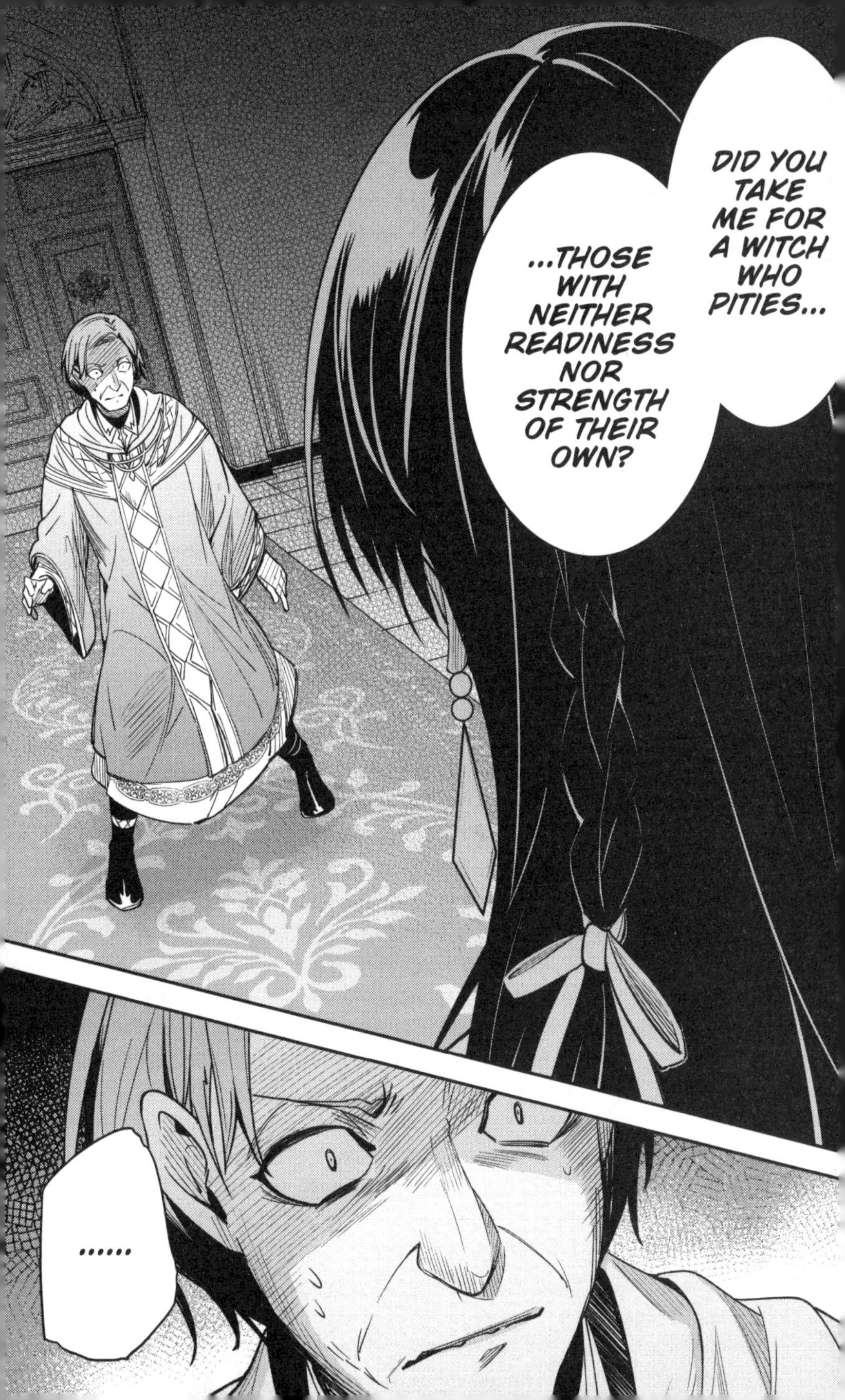

DID YOU TAKE ME FOR A WITCH WHO PITIES...
...THOSE WITH NEITHER READINESS NOR STRENGTH OF THEIR OWN?
......

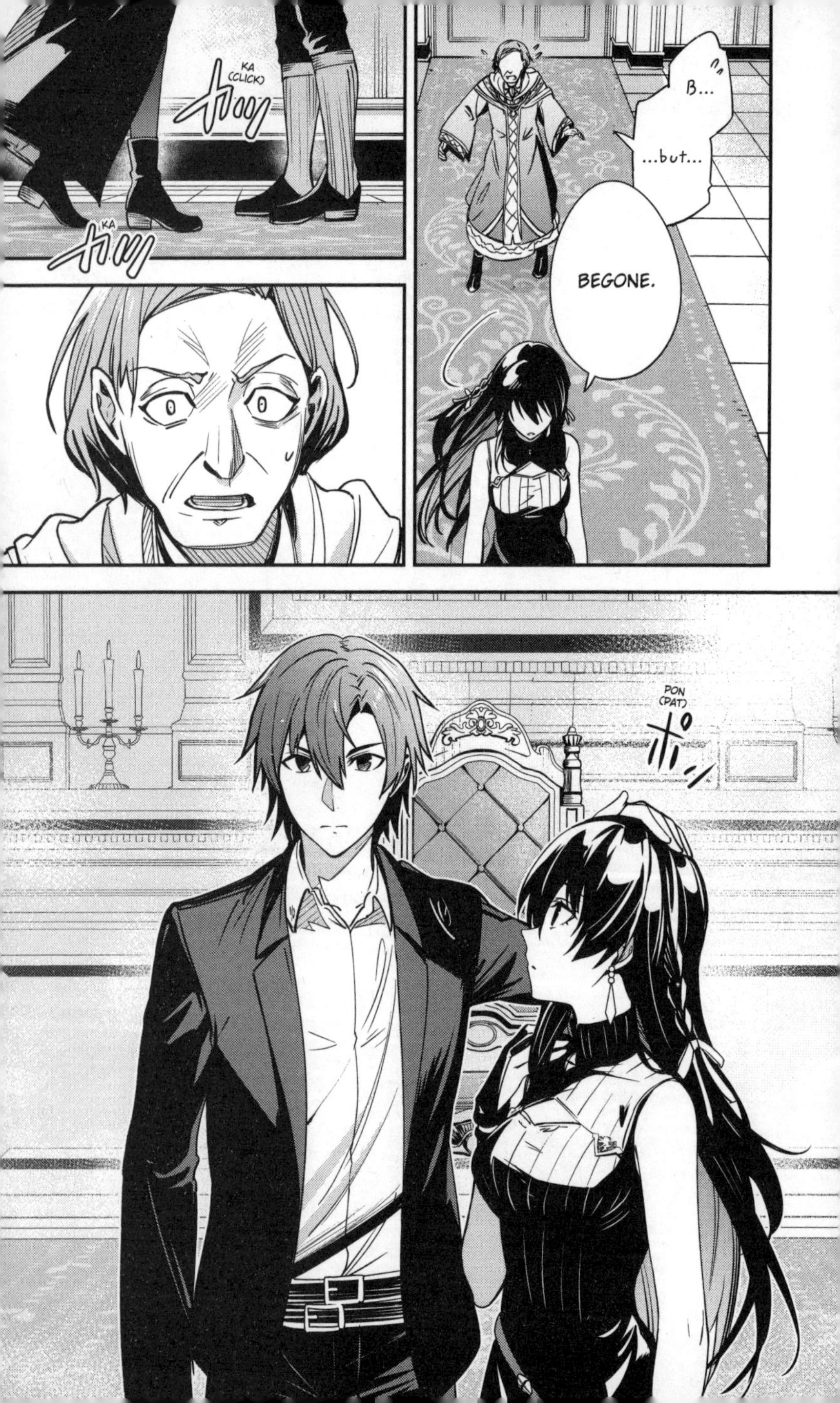
B...
...but...
BEGONE.
KA (CLICK)
KA
PON (PAT)

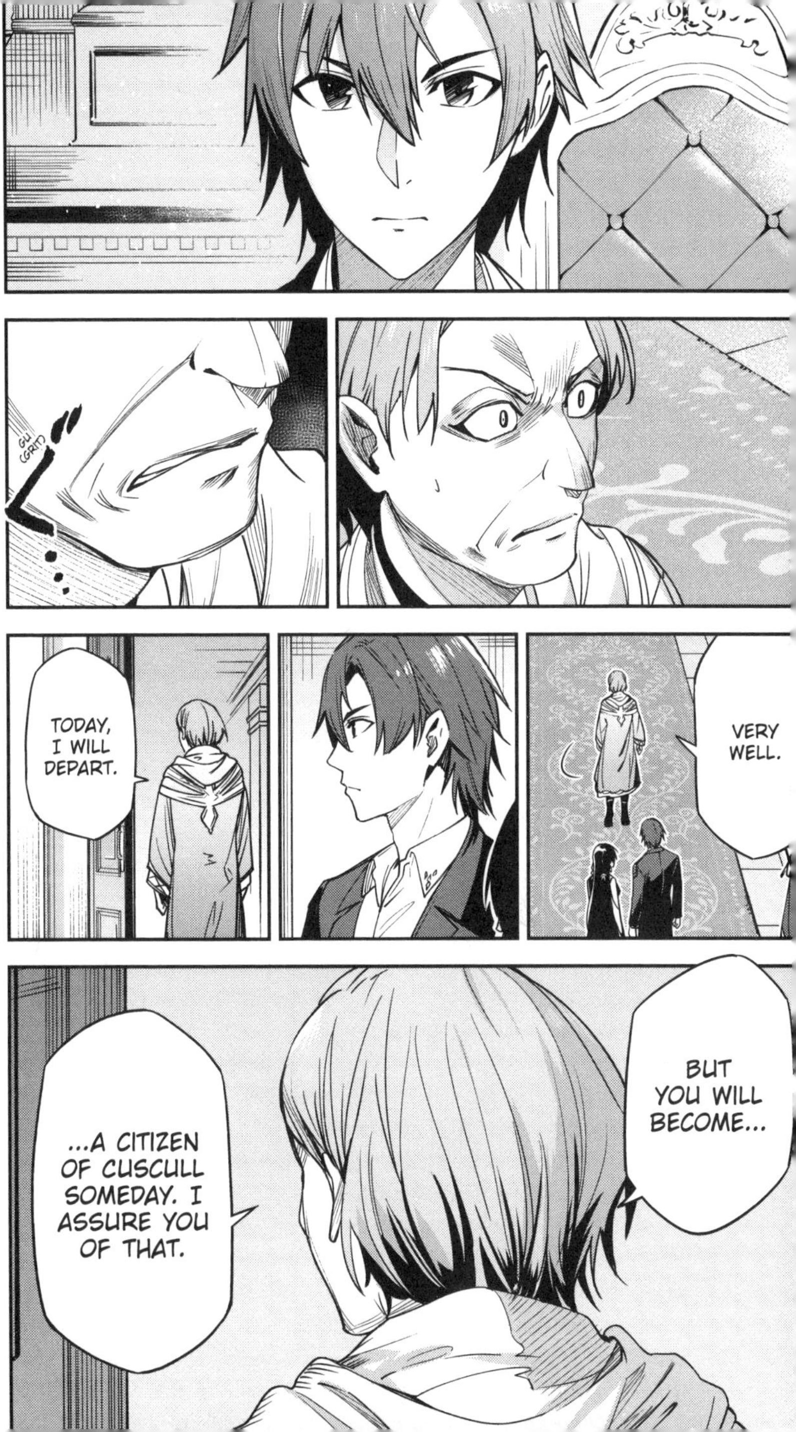
GU (GRIT)
VERY WELL.
TODAY, I WILL DEPART.
BUT YOU WILL BECOME...
...A CITIZEN OF CUSCULL SOMEDAY. I ASSURE YOU OF THAT.

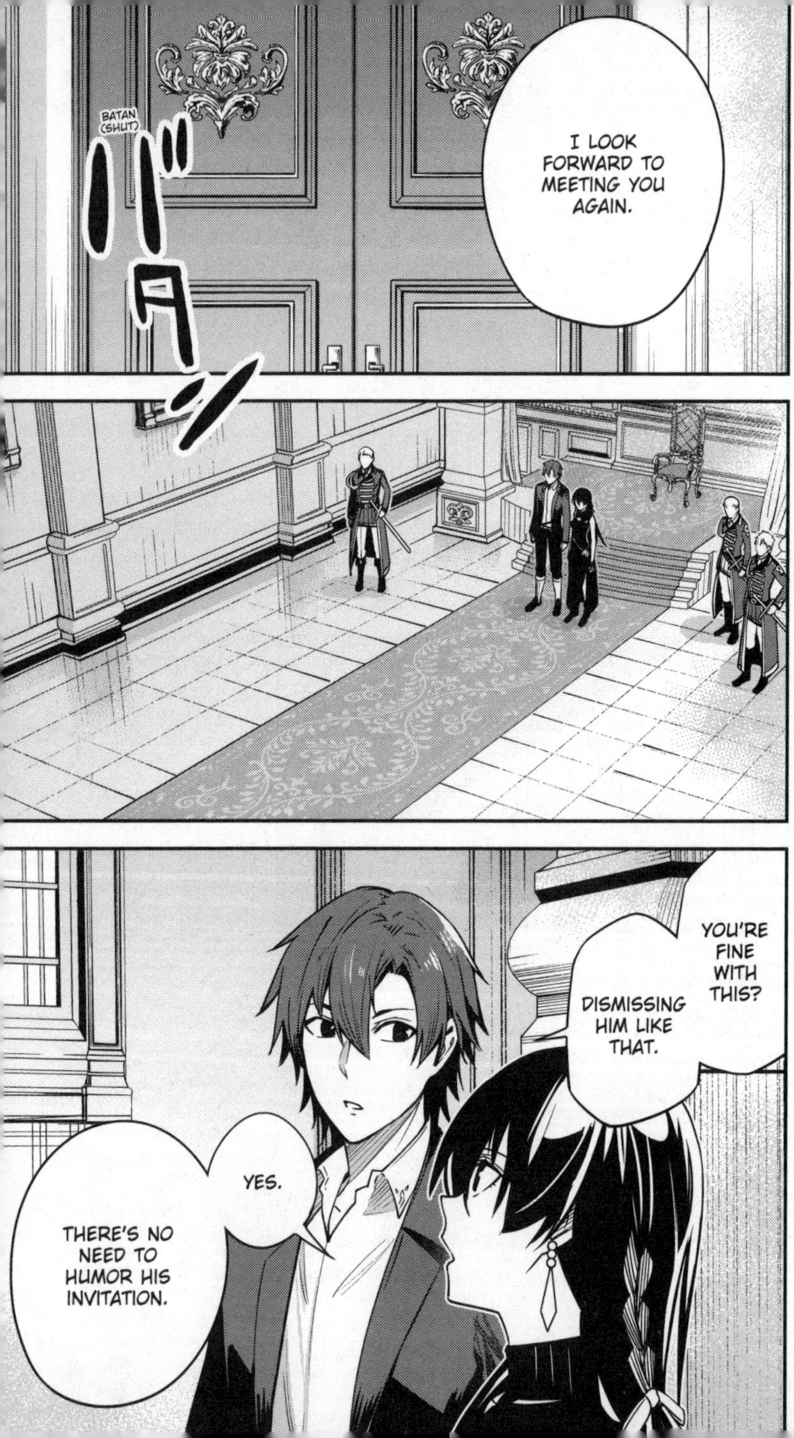
I LOOK FORWARD TO MEETING YOU AGAIN.
BATAN (SHUT)
YOU'RE FINE WITH THIS?
DISMISSING HIM LIKE THAT.
YES.
THERE'S NO NEED TO HUMOR HIS INVITATION.

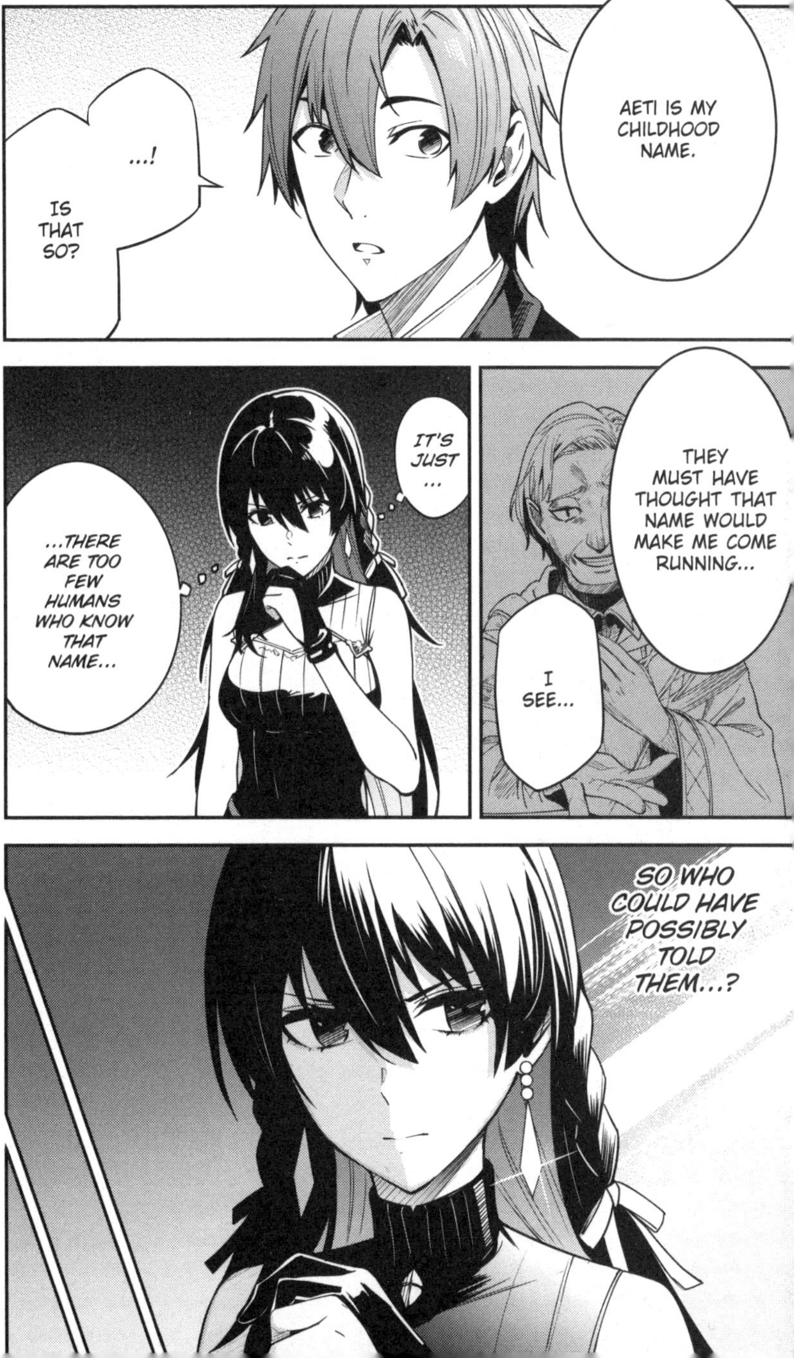
AETI IS MY CHILDHOOD NAME.
...! IS THAT SO?
THEY MUST HAVE THOUGHT THAT NAME WOULD MAKE ME COME RUNNING...
I SEE...
IT'S JUST...
...THERE ARE TOO FEW HUMANS WHO KNOW THAT NAME...
SO WHO COULD HAVE POSSIBLY TOLD THEM...?

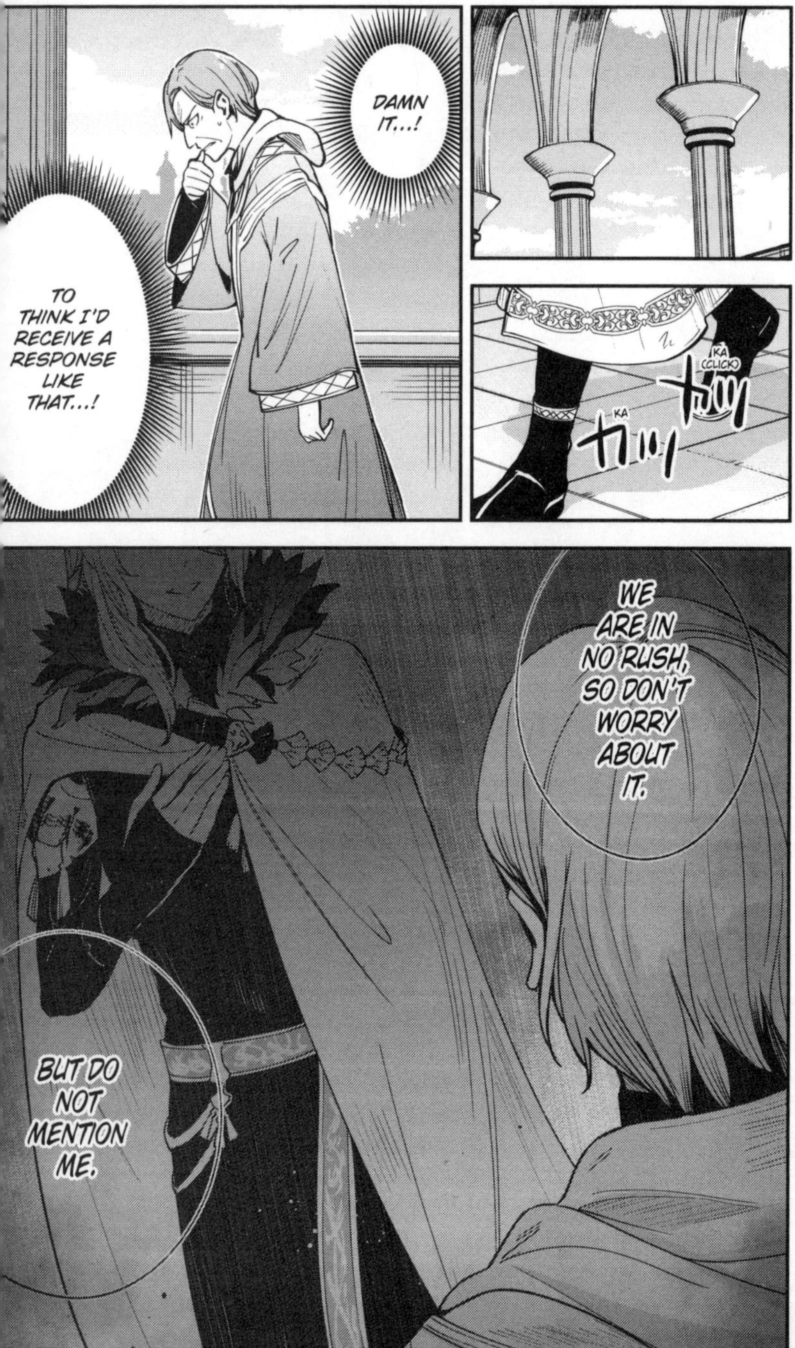
KA (CLICK)
KA
DAMN IT...!
TO THINK I'D RECEIVE A RESPONSE LIKE THAT...!
WE ARE IN NO RUSH, SO DON'T WORRY ABOUT IT.
BUT DO NOT MENTION ME.

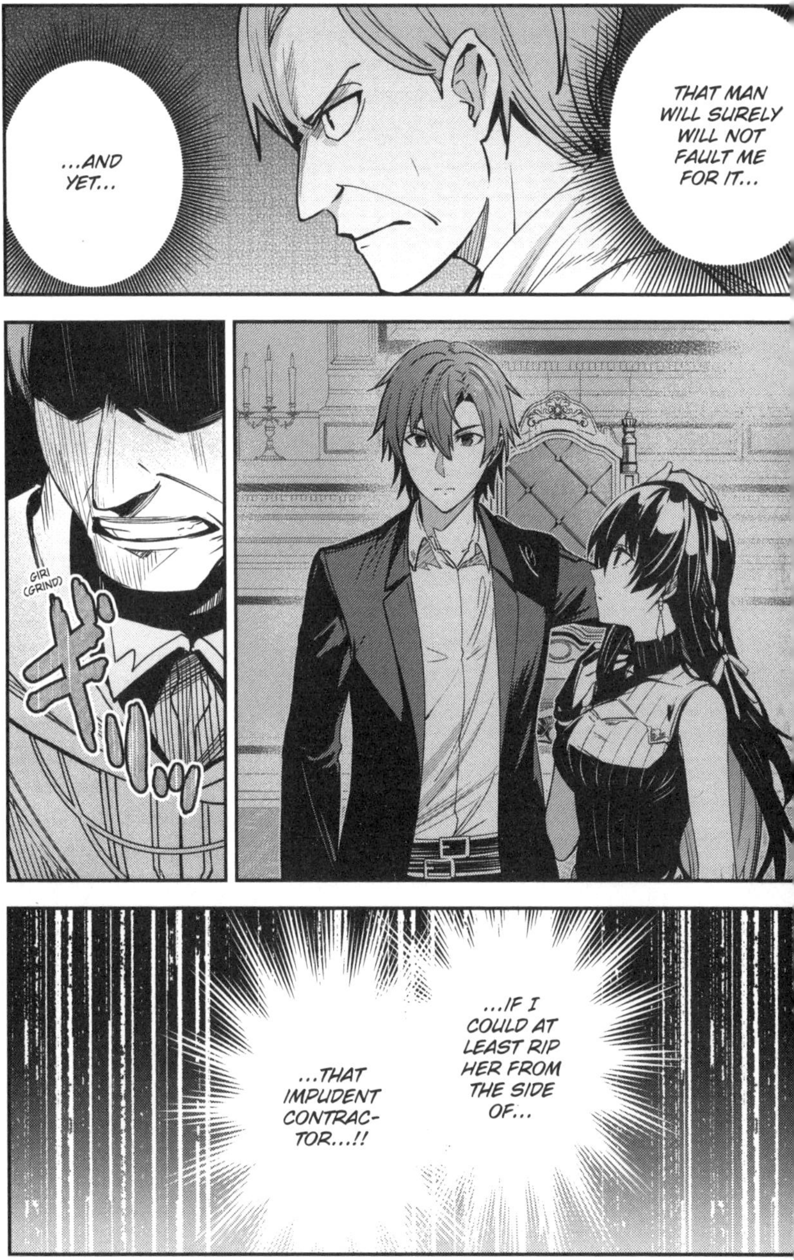
THAT MAN WILL SURELY WILL NOT FAULT ME FOR IT...
...AND YET...
GIRI (GRIND)
...IF I COULD AT LEAST RIP HER FROM THE SIDE OF...
...THAT IMPUDENT CONTRAC-TOR...!!

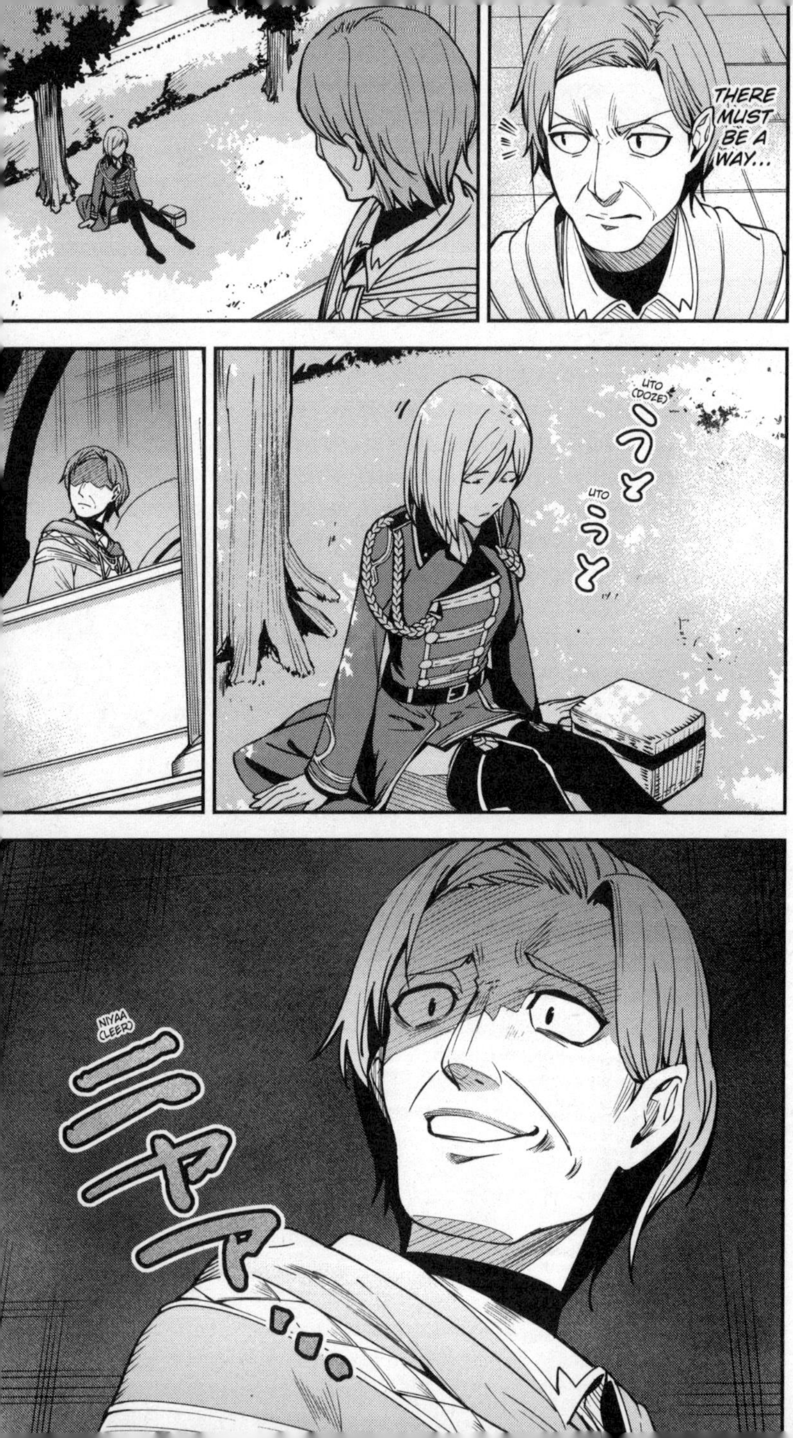
THERE MUST BE A WAY...
UTO (DOZE)
うと
UTO
うと
NIYAA (LEER)
ニヤア...

Unnamed Memory

Unnamed Memory

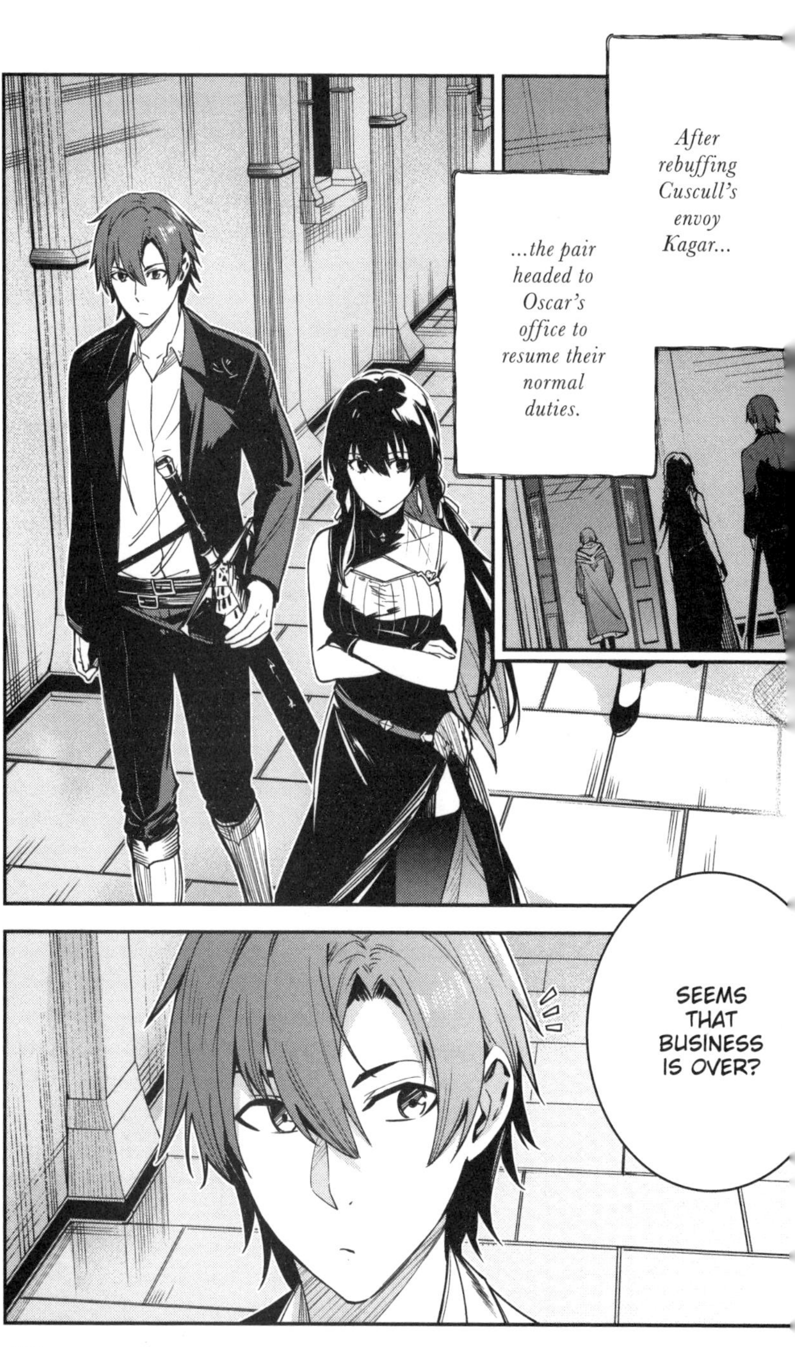
After rebuffing Cuscull's envoy Kagar...
...the pair headed to Oscar's office to resume their normal duties.
SEEMS THAT BUSINESS IS OVER?

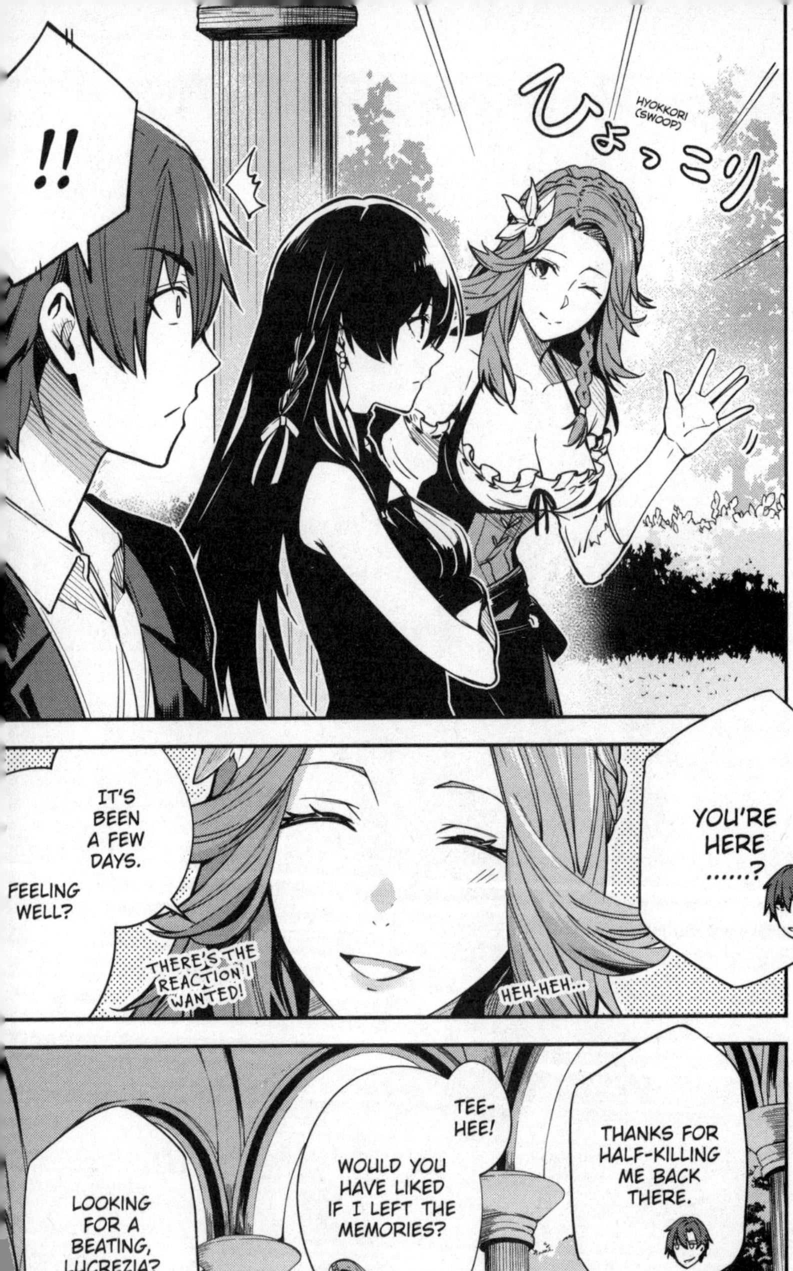
ひょっこり
HYOKKORI (SWOOP)
!!
YOU'RE HERE ......?
IT'S BEEN A FEW DAYS.
FEELING WELL?
HEH-HEH...
THERE'S THE REACTION I WANTED!
THANKS FOR HALF-KILLING ME BACK THERE.
TEE-HEE!
WOULD YOU HAVE LIKED IF I LEFT THE MEMORIES?
LOOKING FOR A BEATING, LUCREZIA?

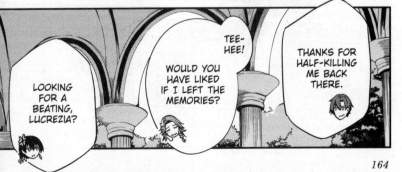

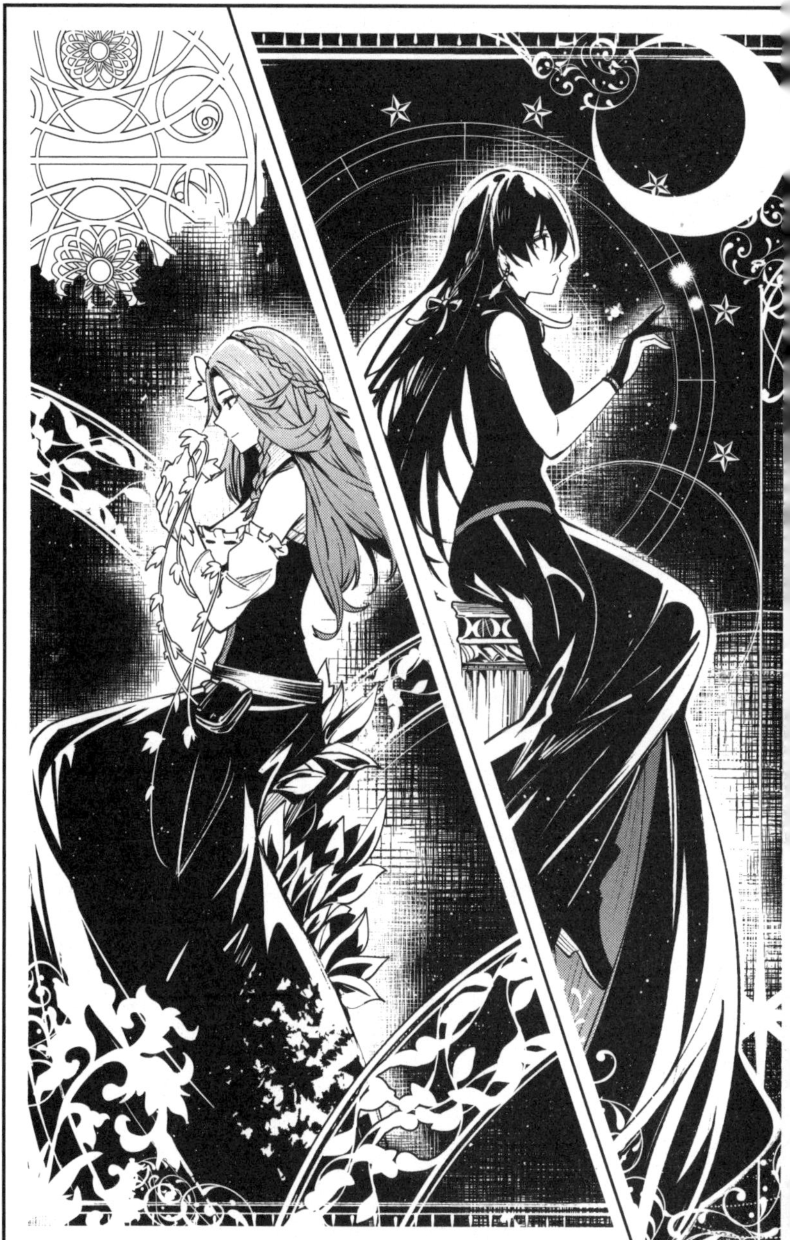

Chapter 22: Breathing Life into Form ③

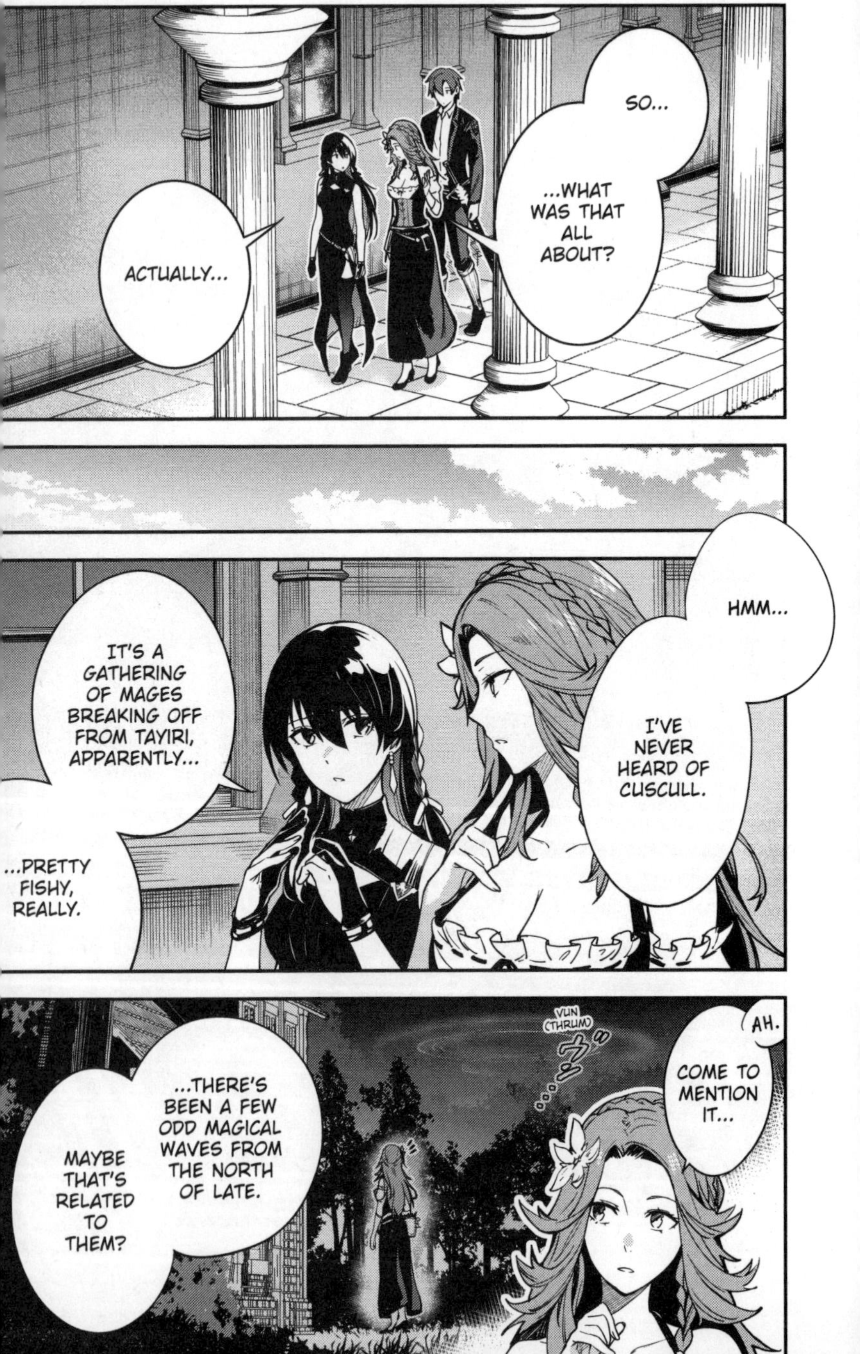
SO...
...WHAT WAS THAT ALL ABOUT?
ACTUALLY...
HMM...
I'VE NEVER HEARD OF CUSCULL.
IT'S A GATHERING OF MAGES BREAKING OFF FROM TAYIRI, APPARENTLY...
...PRETTY FISHY, REALLY.
AH.
COME TO MENTION IT...
VUN (THRUM)
...THERE'S BEEN A FEW ODD MAGICAL WAVES FROM THE NORTH OF LATE.
MAYBE THAT'S RELATED TO THEM?

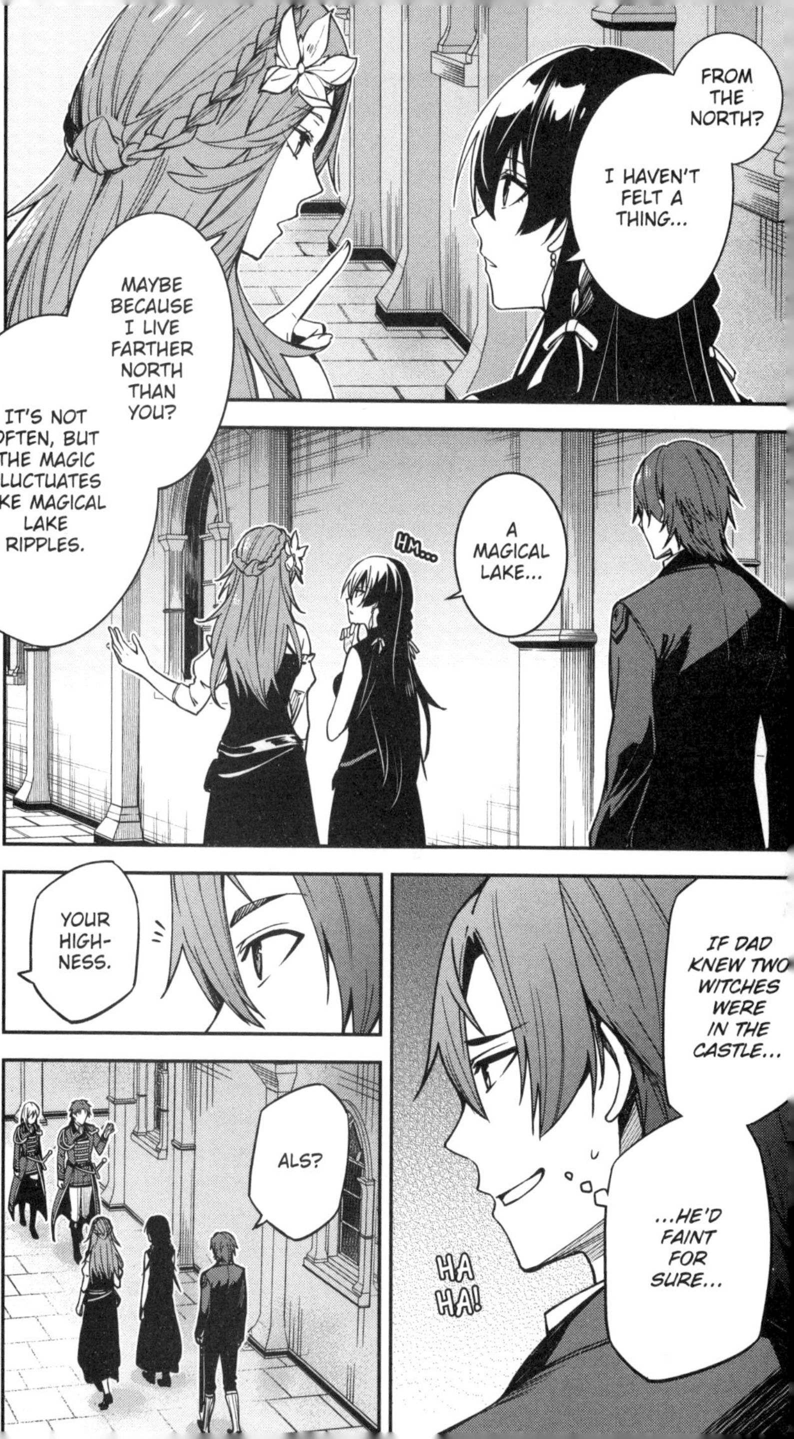
FROM THE NORTH?
I HAVEN'T FELT A THING...
MAYBE BECAUSE I LIVE FARTHER NORTH THAN YOU?
IT'S NOT OFTEN, BUT THE MAGIC FLUCTUATES LIKE MAGICAL LAKE RIPPLES.
A MAGICAL LAKE...
HM...
IF DAD KNEW TWO WITCHES WERE IN THE CASTLE...
...HE'D FAINT FOR SURE...
HA HA!
YOUR HIGH-NESS.
ALS?

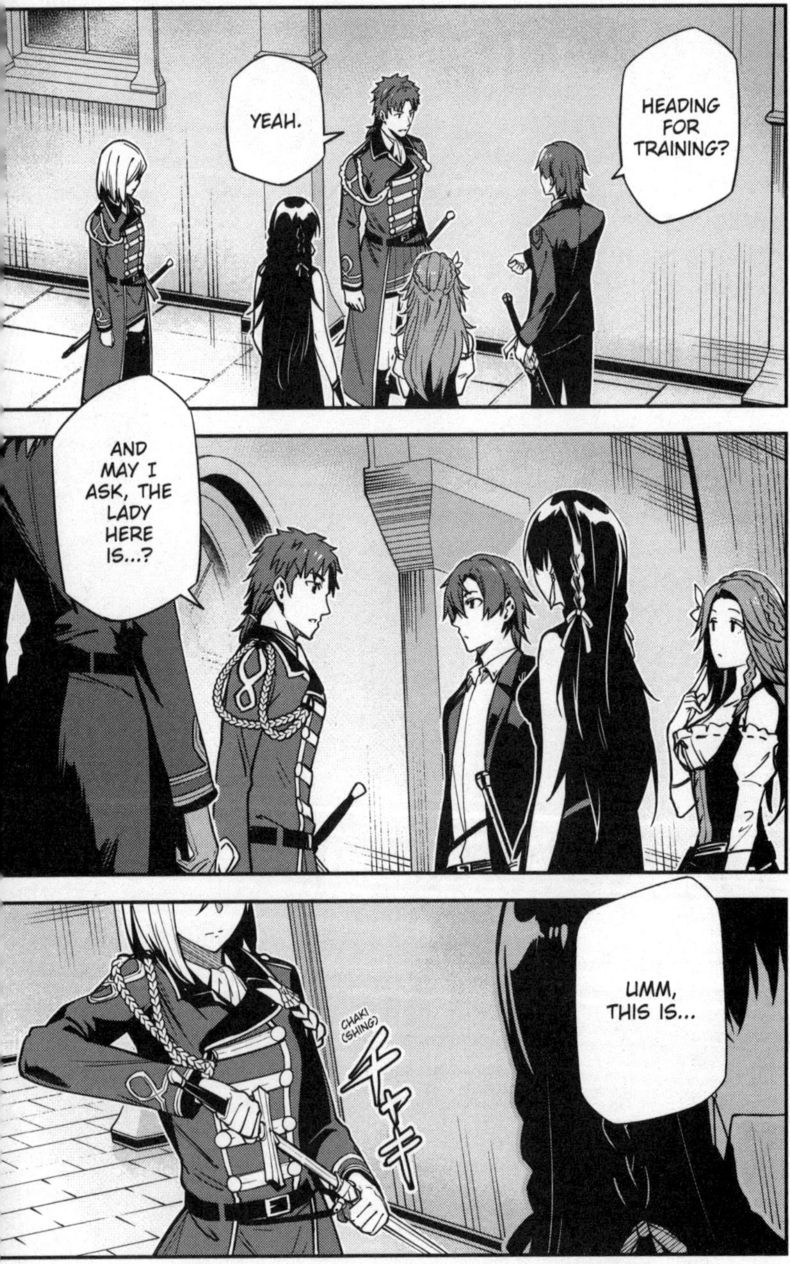
HEADING FOR TRAINING?
YEAH.
AND MAY I ASK, THE LADY HERE IS...?
UMM, THIS IS...
CHAKI (SHING)

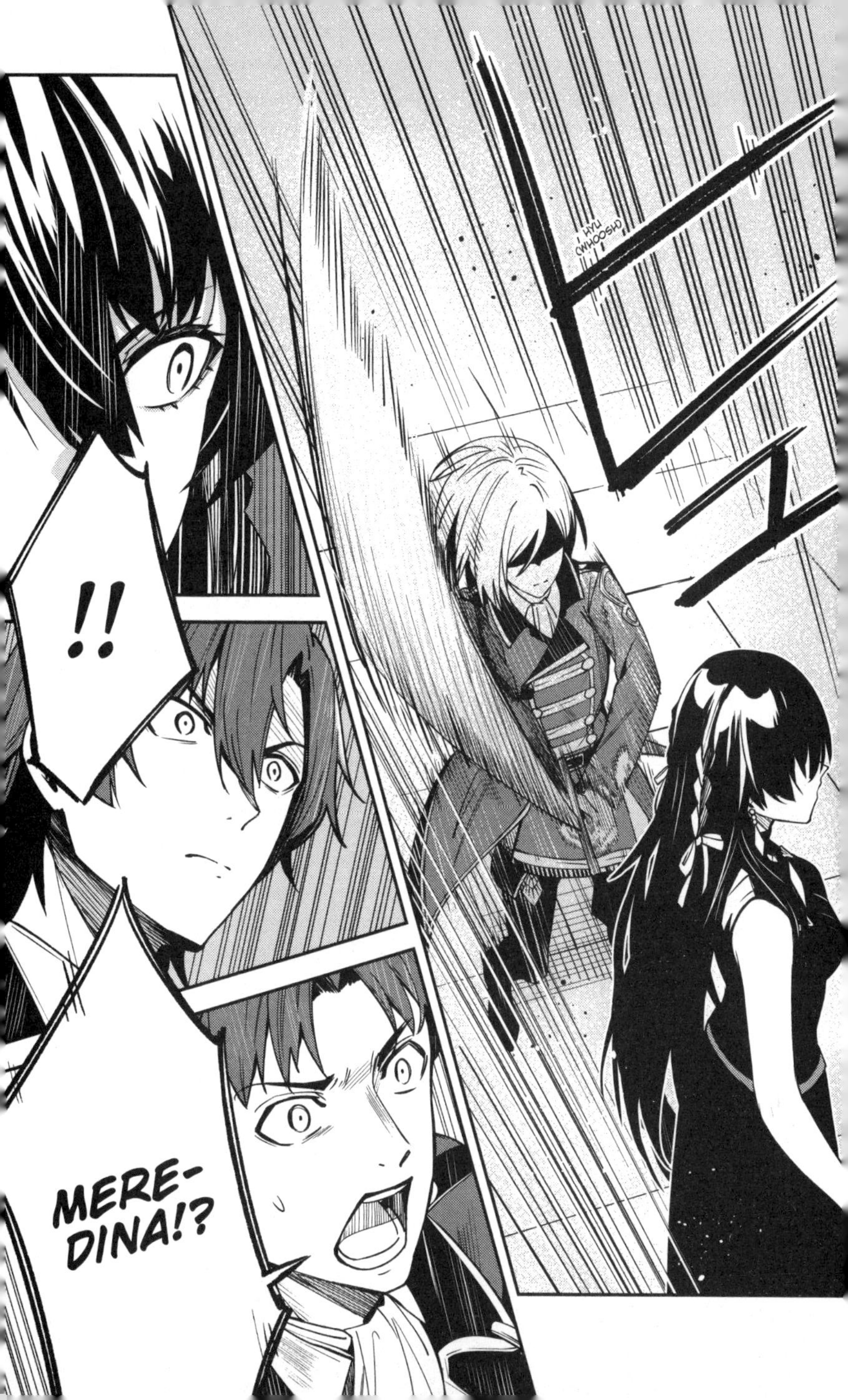
HYU (WHOOSH)
!!
MERE-DINA!?

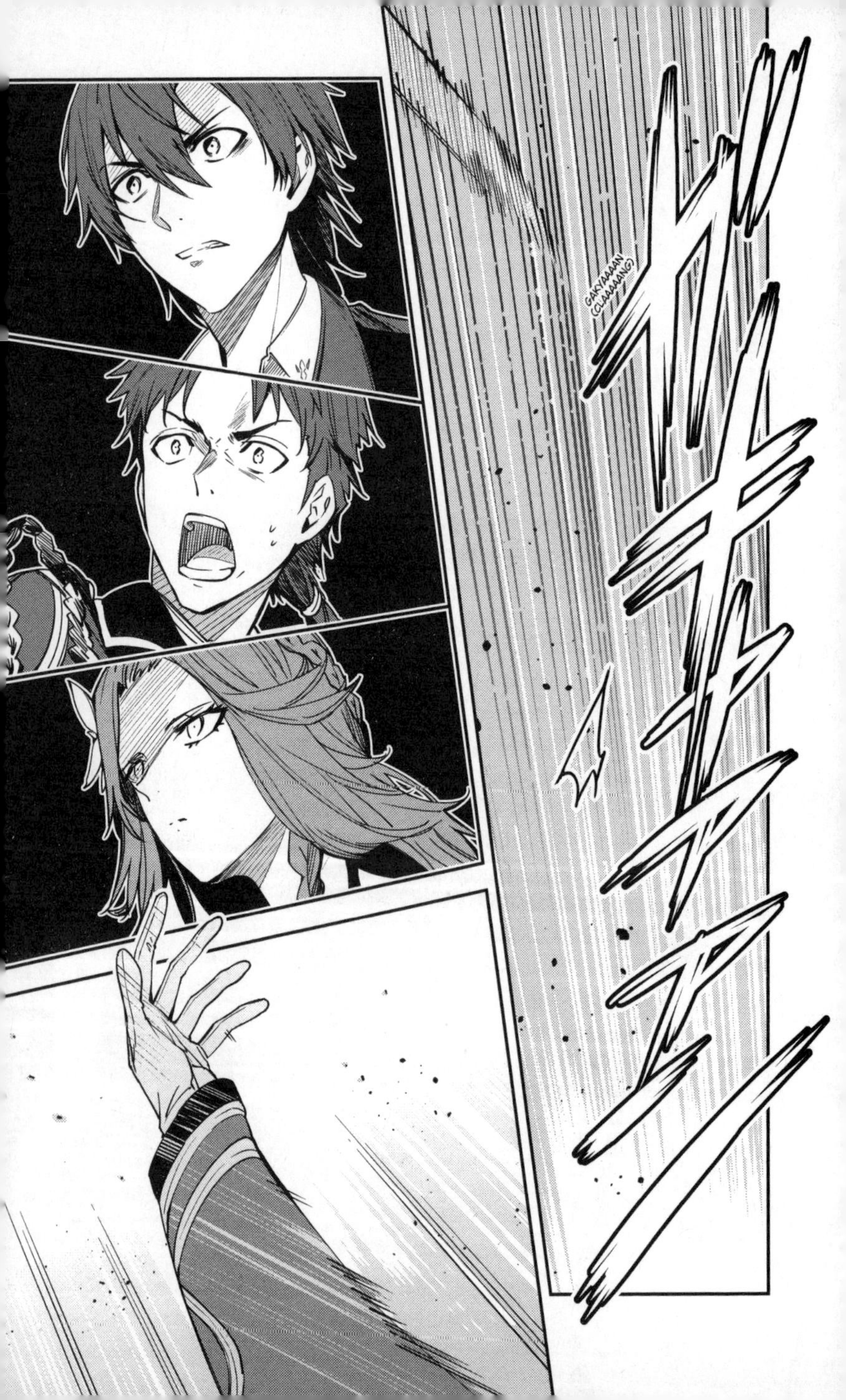
GAKYAAAAN
(CLAAAAANG)

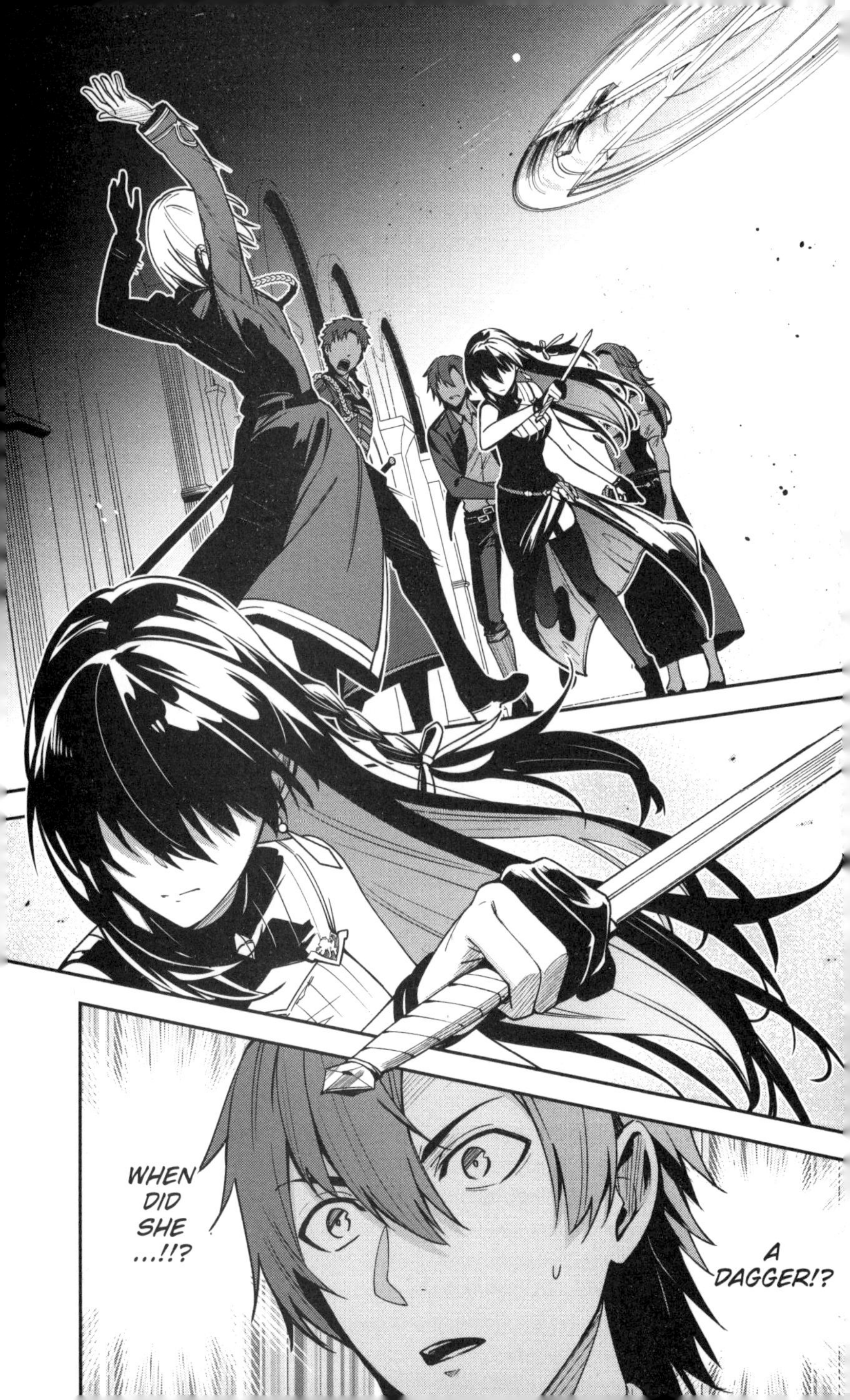
A DAGGER!?
WHEN DID SHE ...!!?

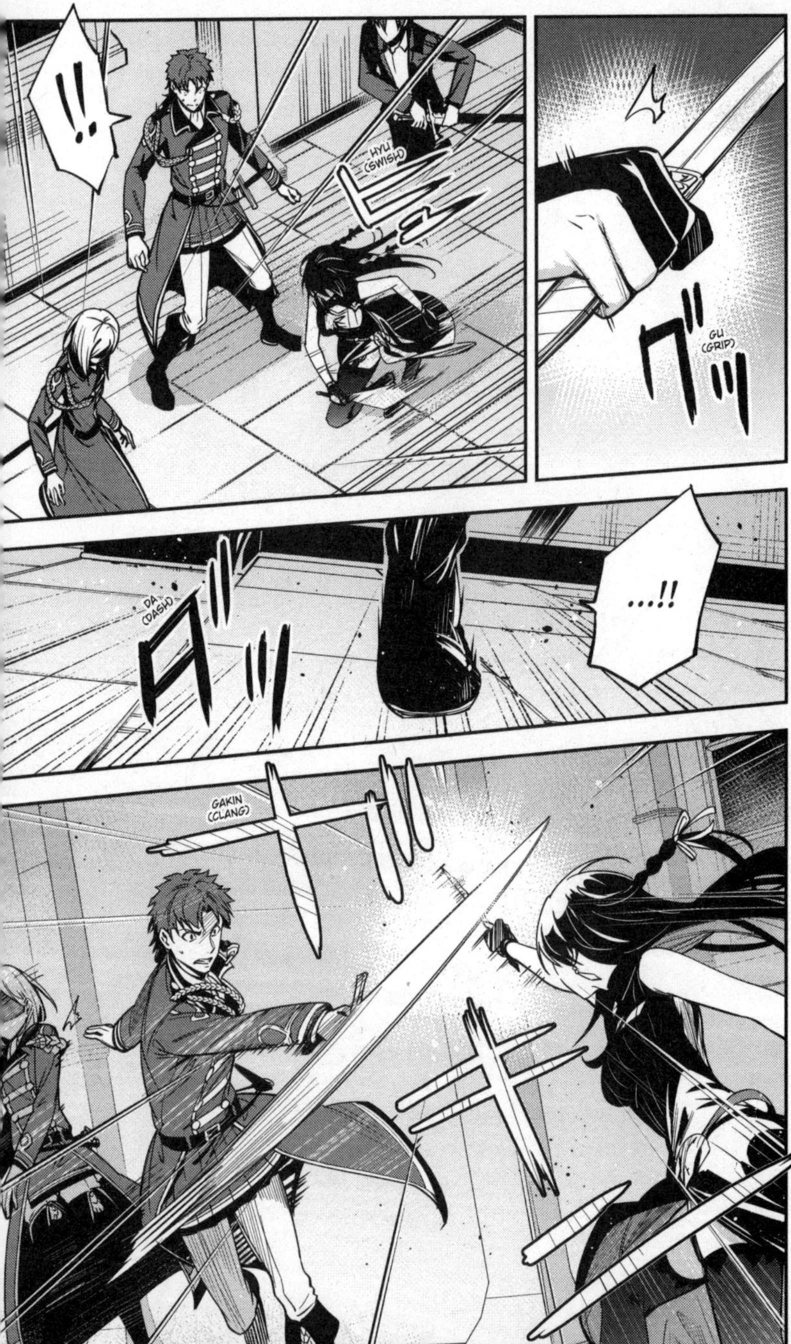
GU (GRIP)
!!
HYU (GWISH)
...!!
DA (DASH)
GAKIN (CLANG)

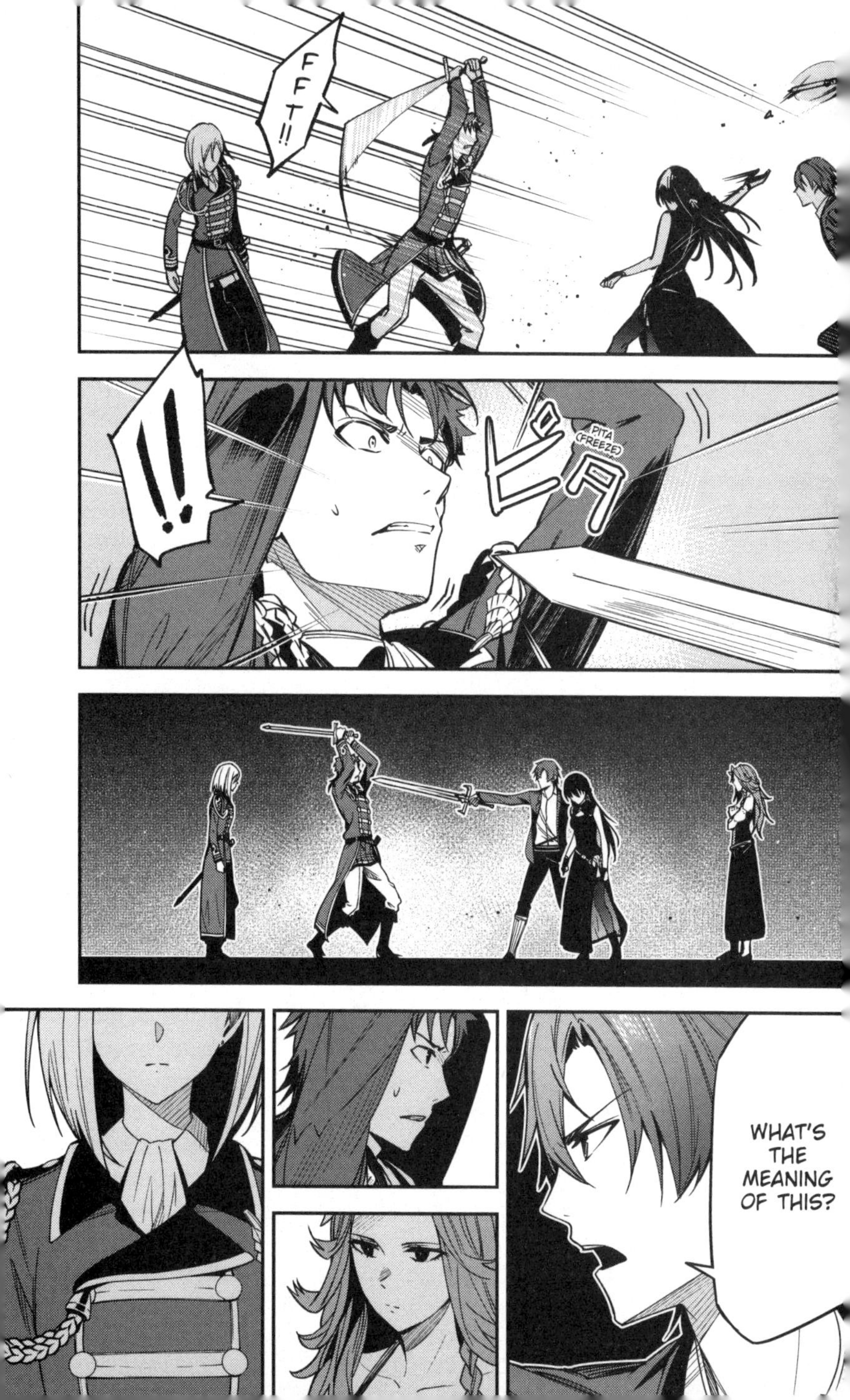
FFFT!!
!!
PITA (FREEZE)
WHAT'S THE MEANING OF THIS?

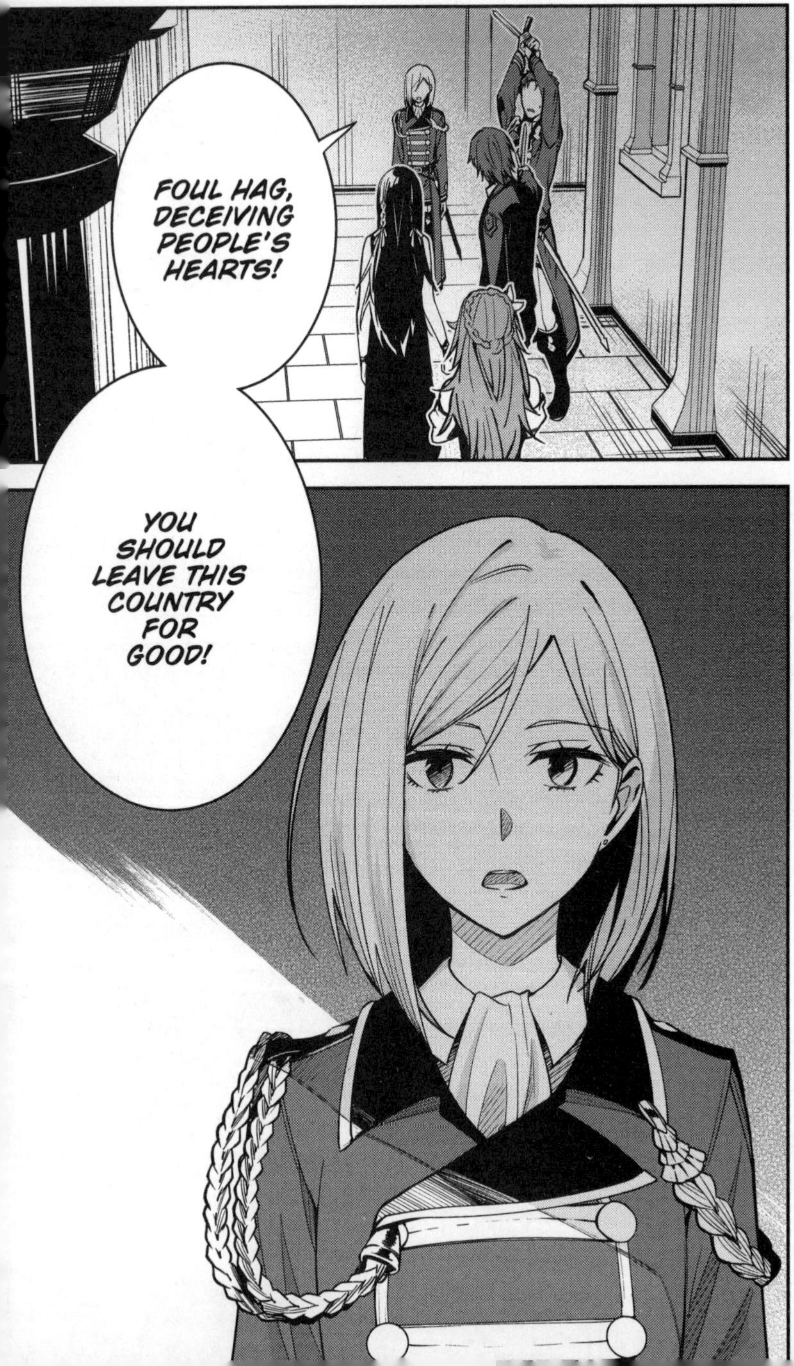
FOUL HAG, DECEIVING PEOPLE'S HEARTS!
YOU SHOULD LEAVE THIS COUNTRY FOR GOOD!

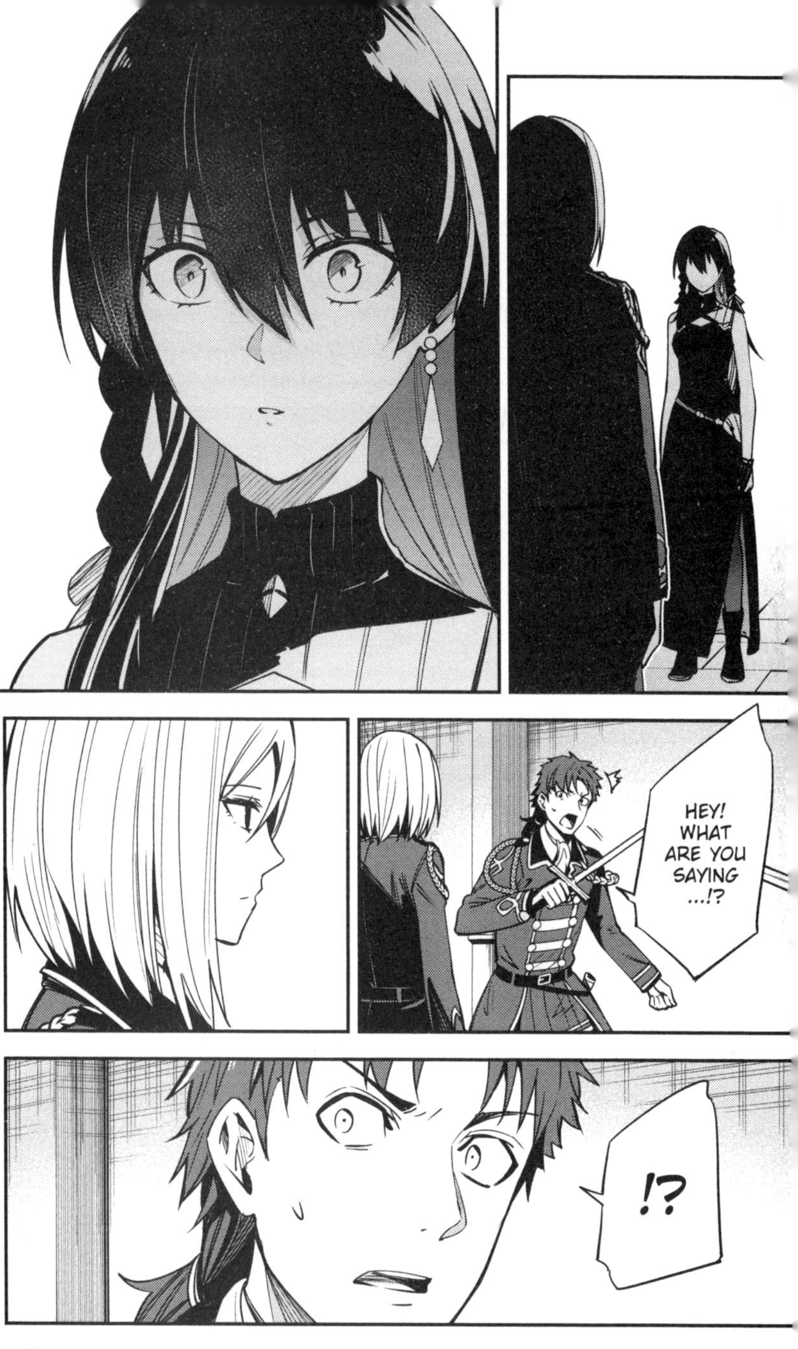
HEY! WHAT ARE YOU SAYING ...!?
!?

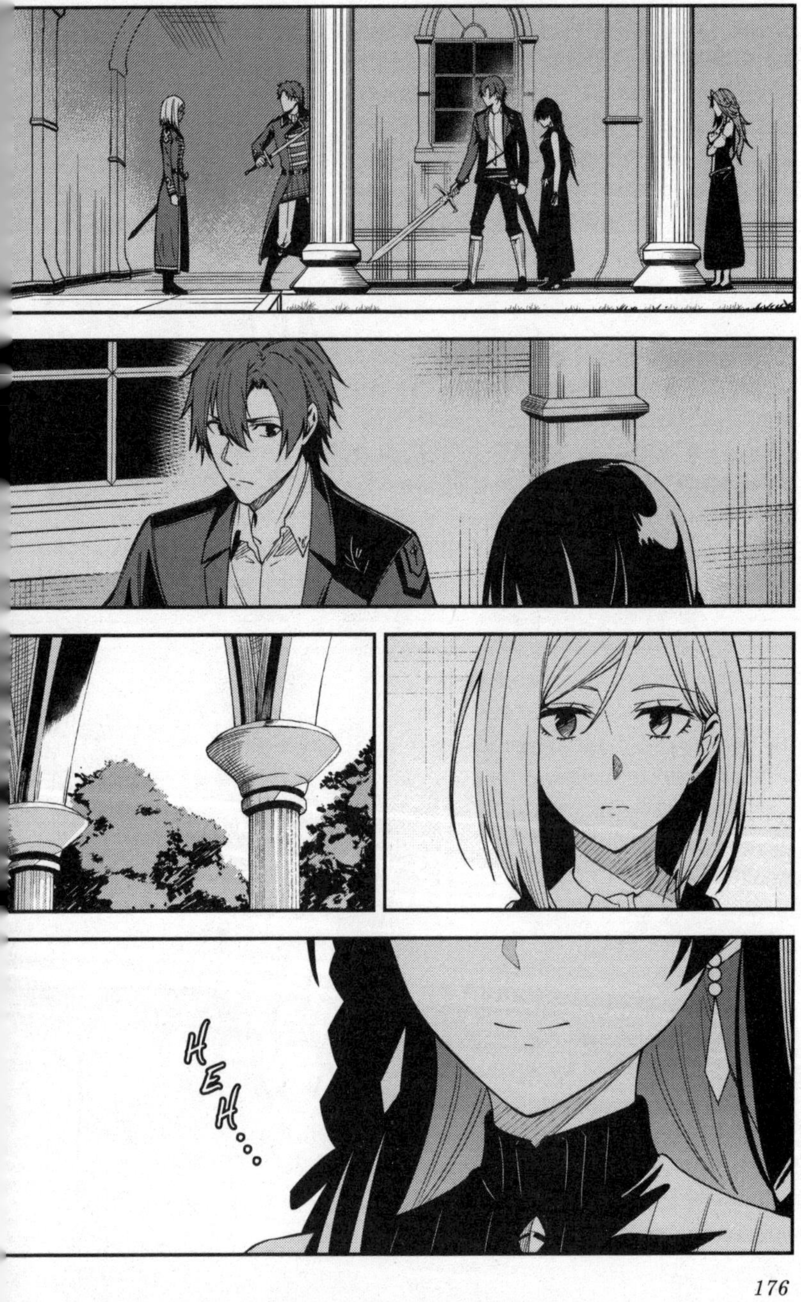
HEH...

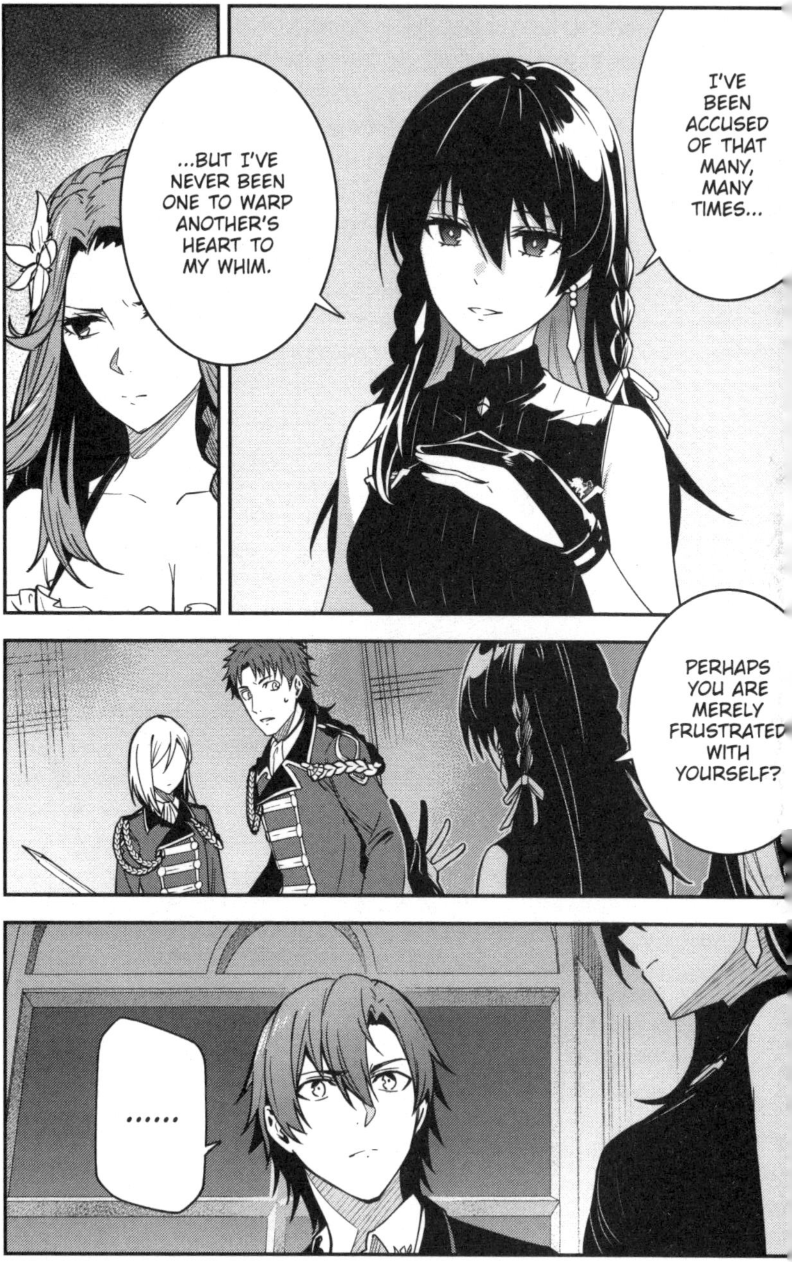
I'VE BEEN ACCUSED OF THAT MANY, MANY TIMES...
...BUT I'VE NEVER BEEN ONE TO WARP ANOTHER'S HEART TO MY WHIM.
PERHAPS YOU ARE MERELY FRUSTRATED WITH YOURSELF?
......

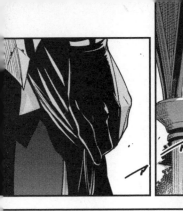

ZAAAAA
(RUUUSTLE)

TO HOLD ANOTHER'S HEART...

...HAS NO ALLURE TO ME.

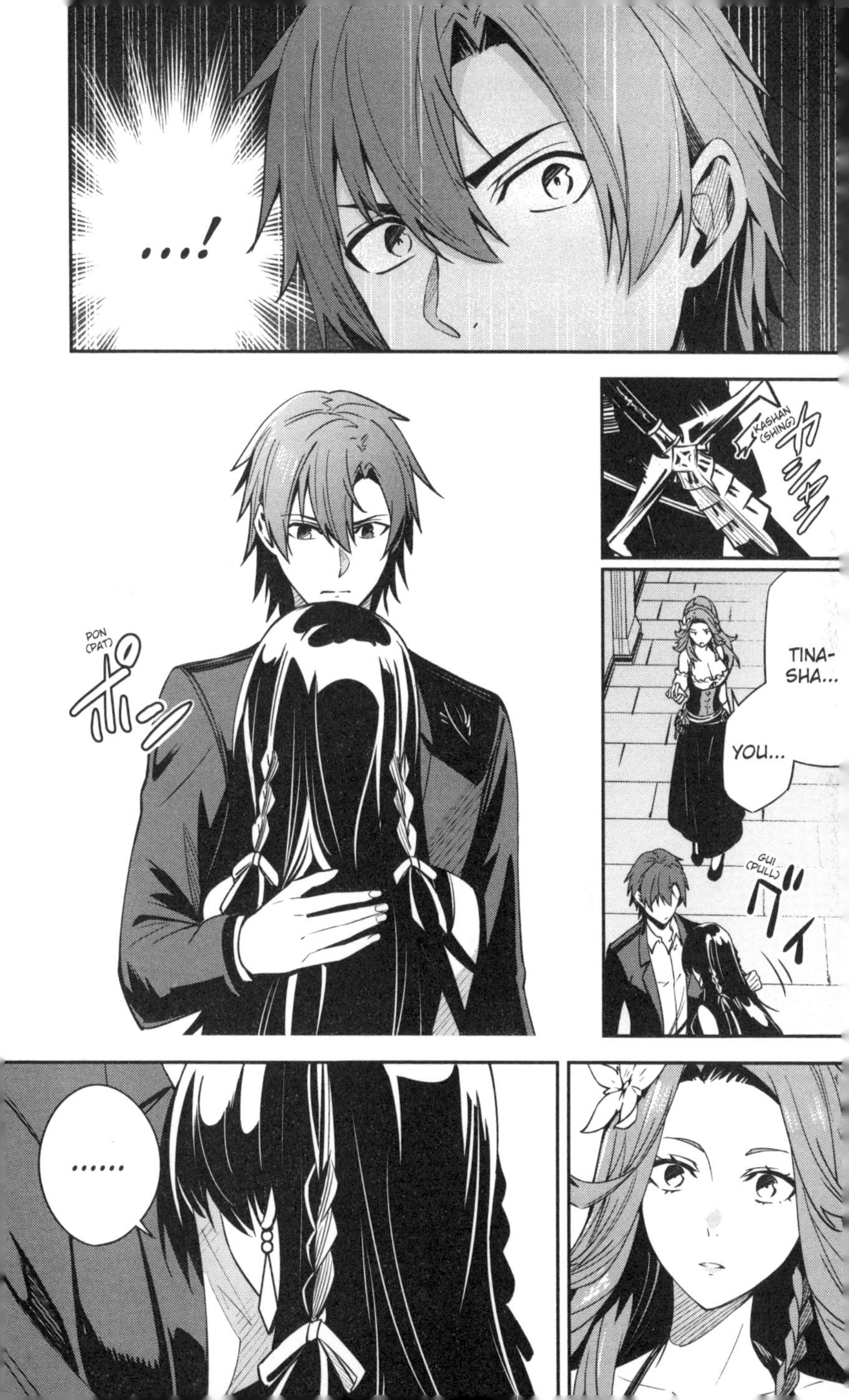
...!
KASHAN (SHING)
TINA-SHA...
YOU...
GUI (PULL)
PON (PAT)
......

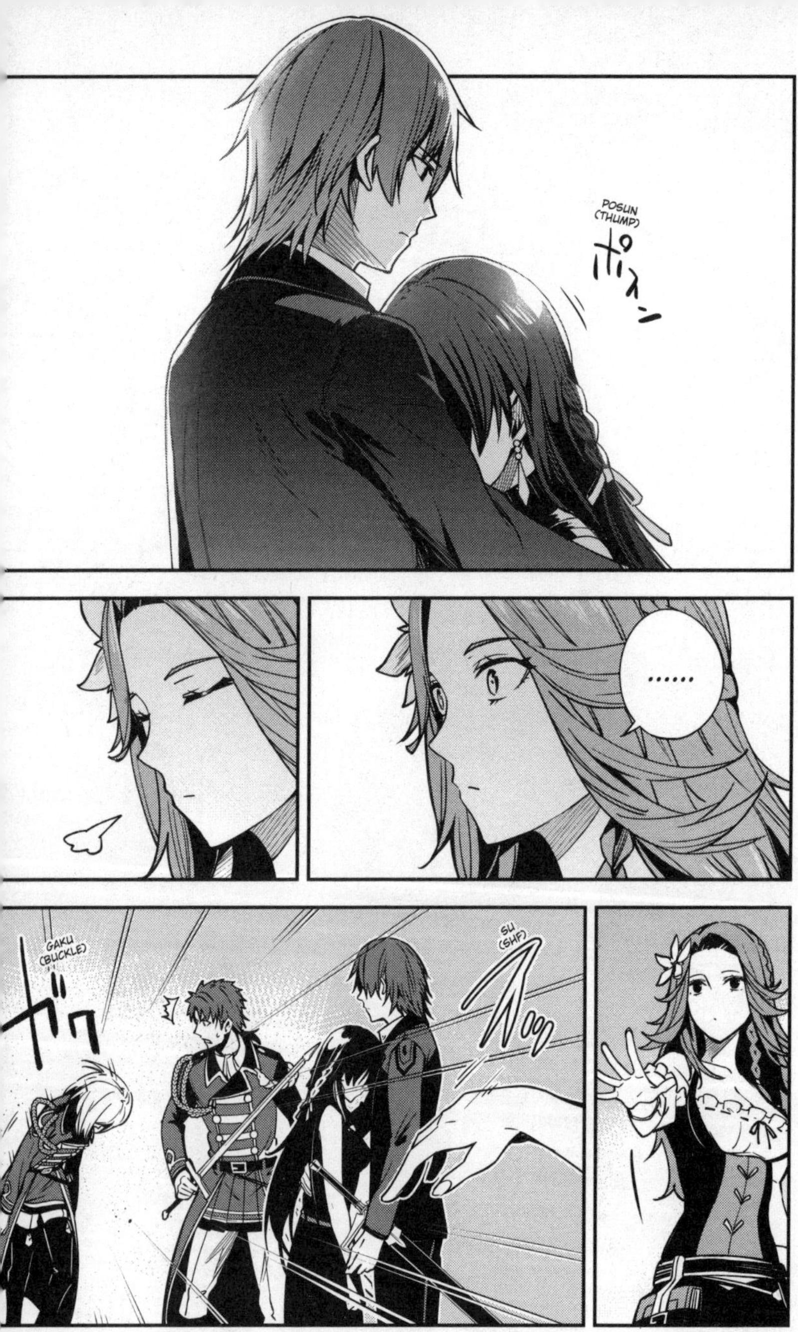
POSUN (THUMP)
ポスン
......
SU (SHF)
スッ
GAKU (BUCKLE)
ガク

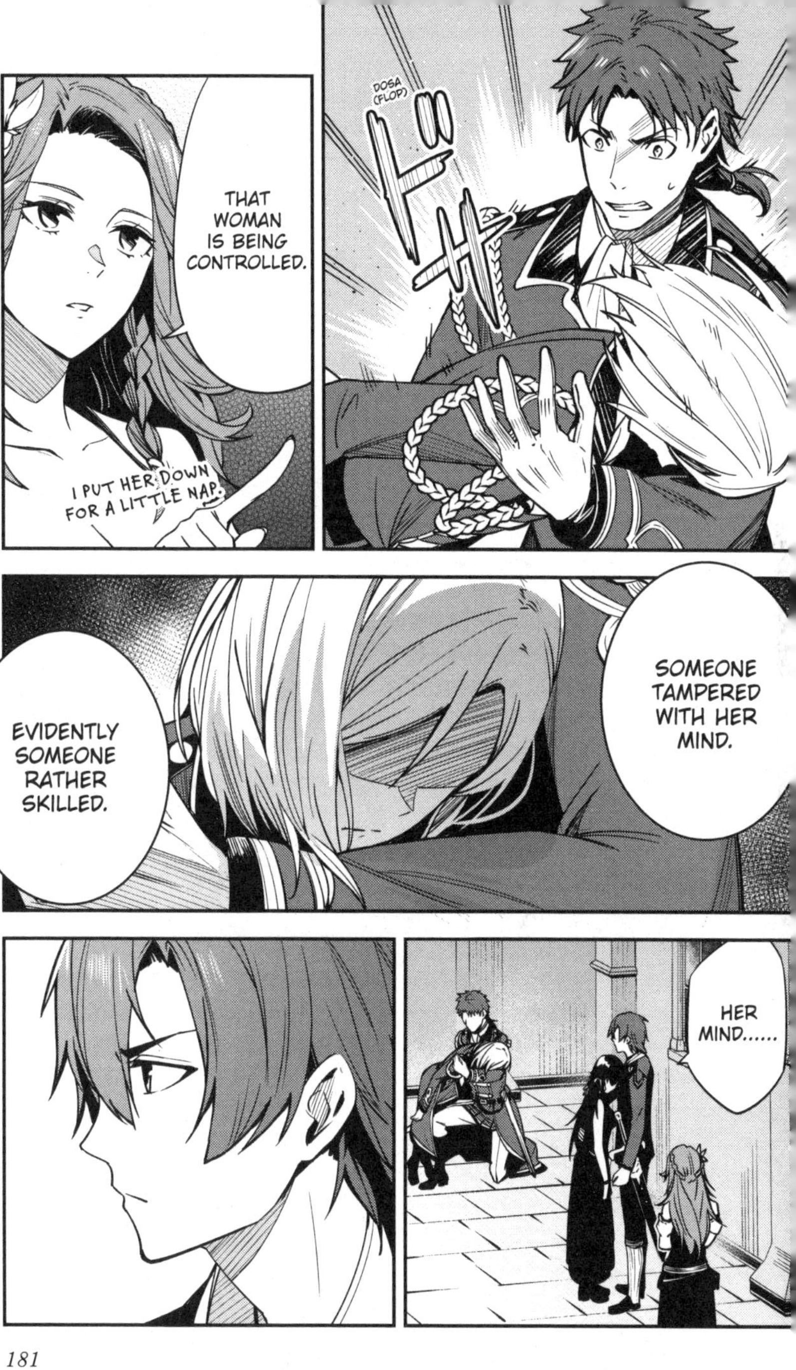
DOSA (FLOP)
THAT WOMAN IS BEING CONTROLLED.
I PUT HER DOWN FOR A LITTLE NAP.
SOMEONE TAMPERED WITH HER MIND.
EVIDENTLY SOMEONE RATHER SKILLED.
HER MIND......

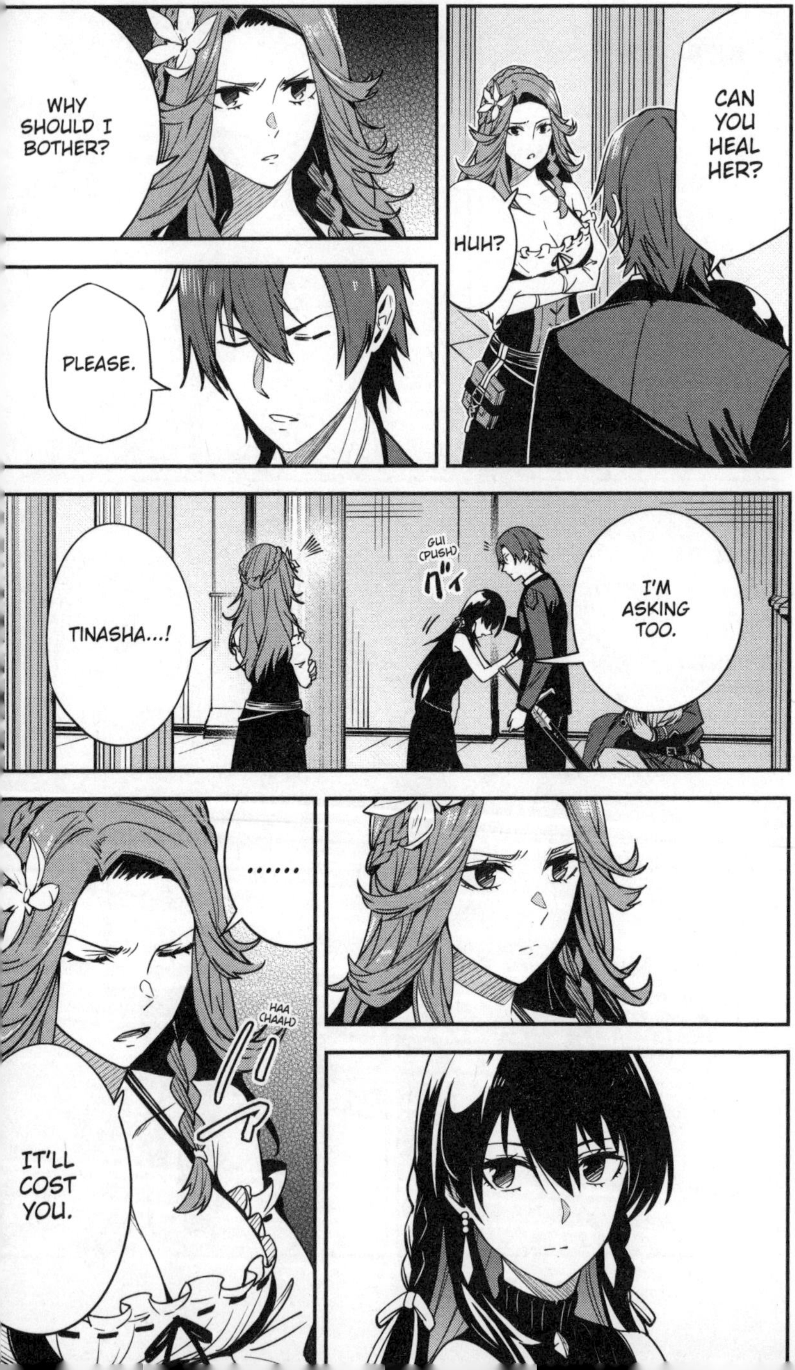
CAN YOU HEAL HER?
HUH?
WHY SHOULD I BOTHER?
PLEASE.
I'M ASKING TOO.
GUI (PUSH)
TINASHA...!
......
HAA (HAAH)
IT'LL COST YOU.

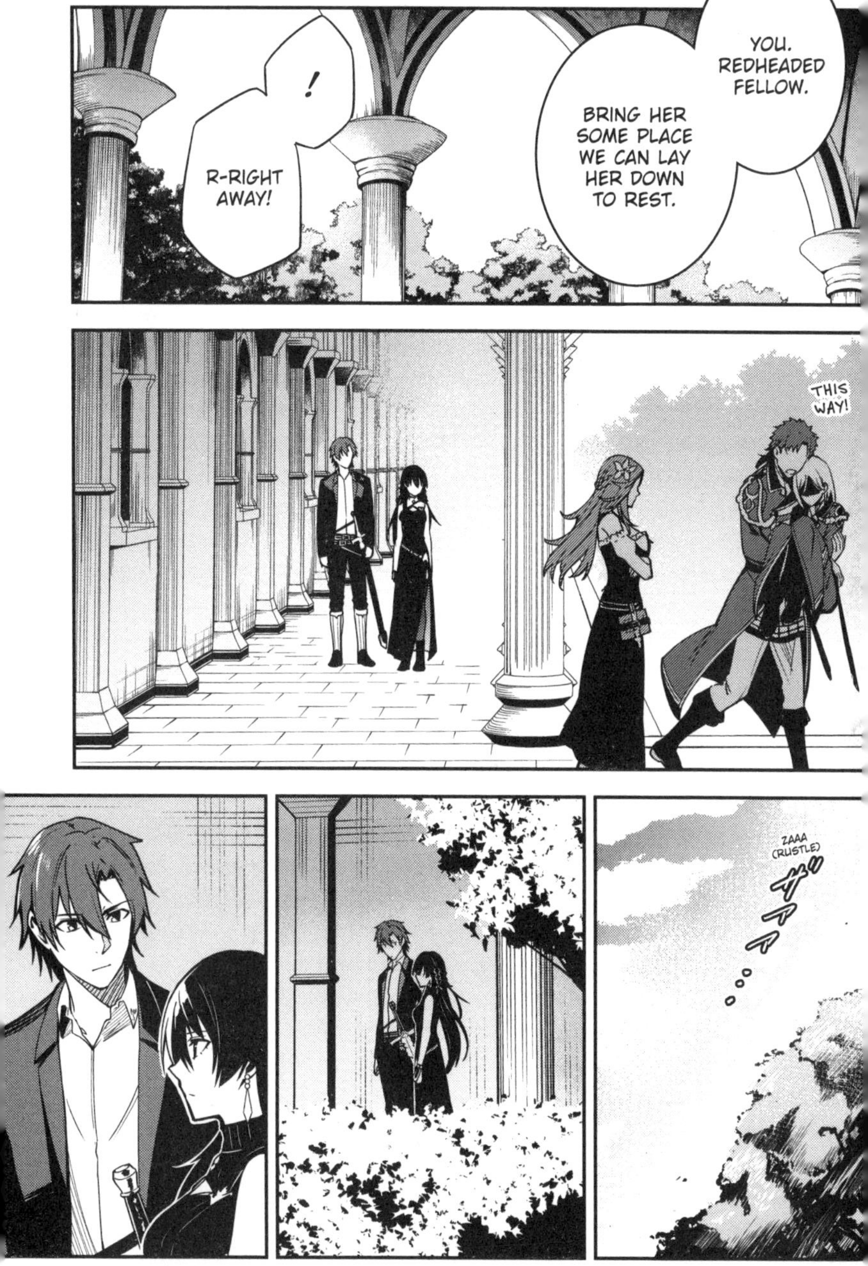
YOU. REDHEADED FELLOW.
BRING HER SOME PLACE WE CAN LAY HER DOWN TO REST.
!
R-RIGHT AWAY!
THIS WAY!
ZAAA (RUSTLE)

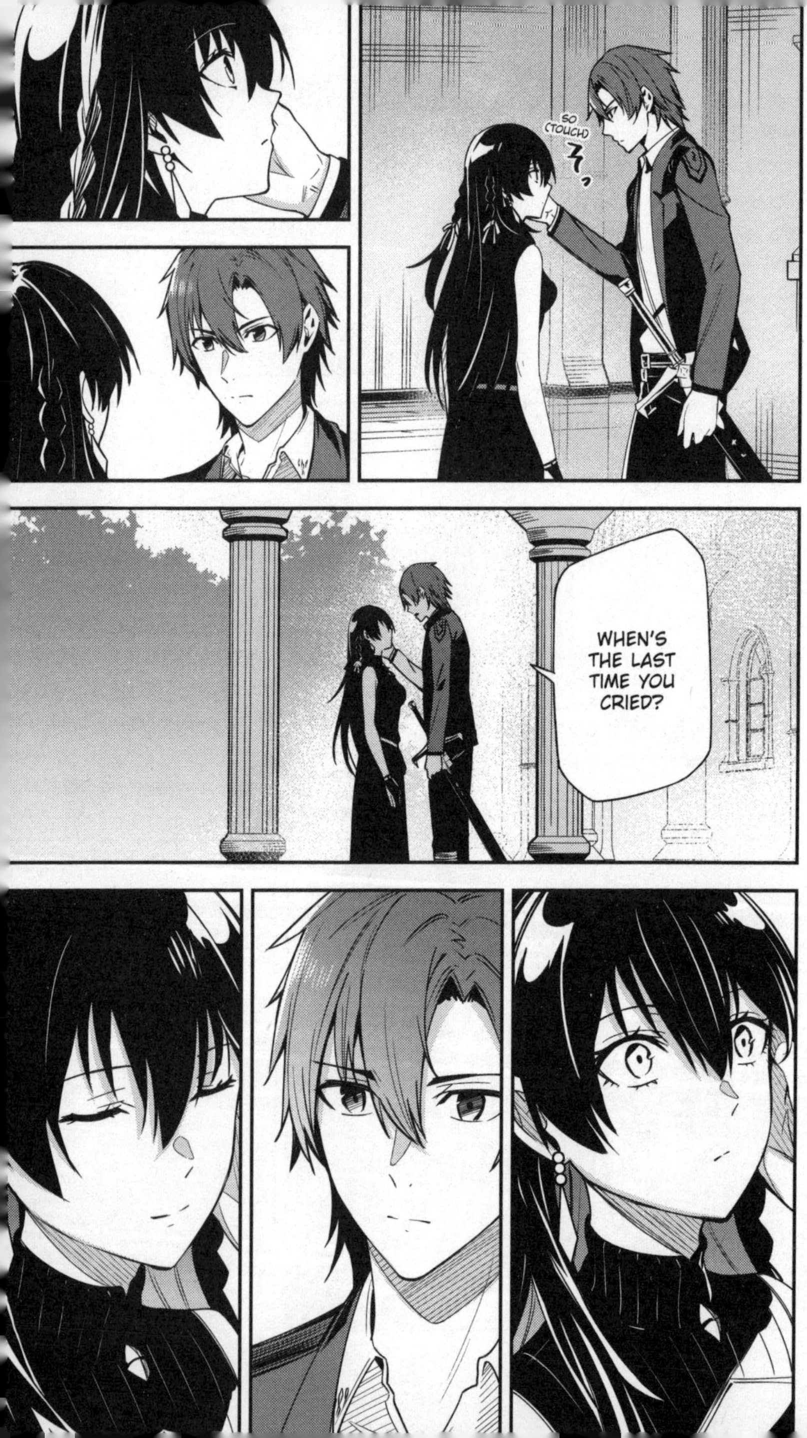
SO (TOUCH)
WHEN'S THE LAST TIME YOU CRIED?

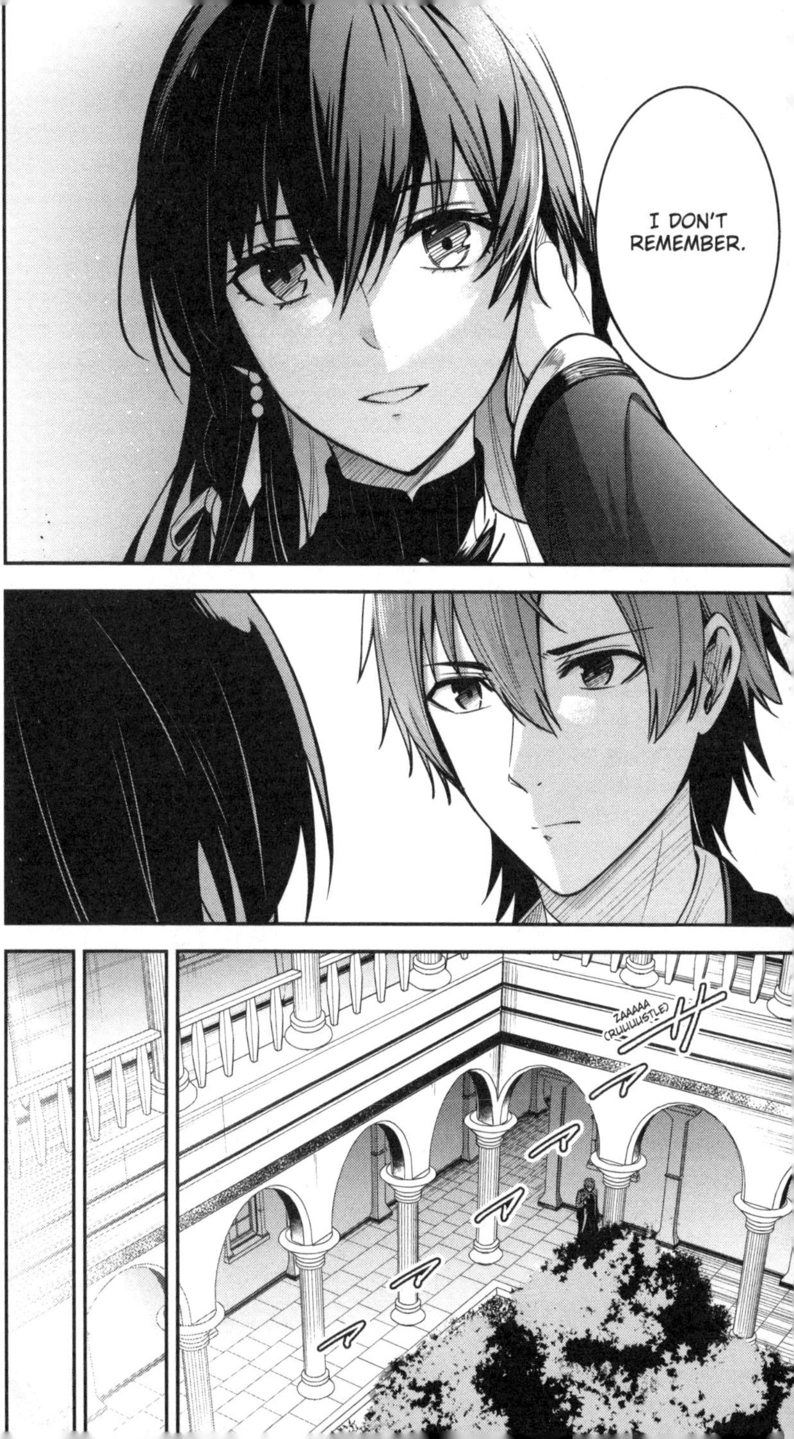
I DON'T REMEMBER.
ZAAAAA (RUUUUUSTLE)

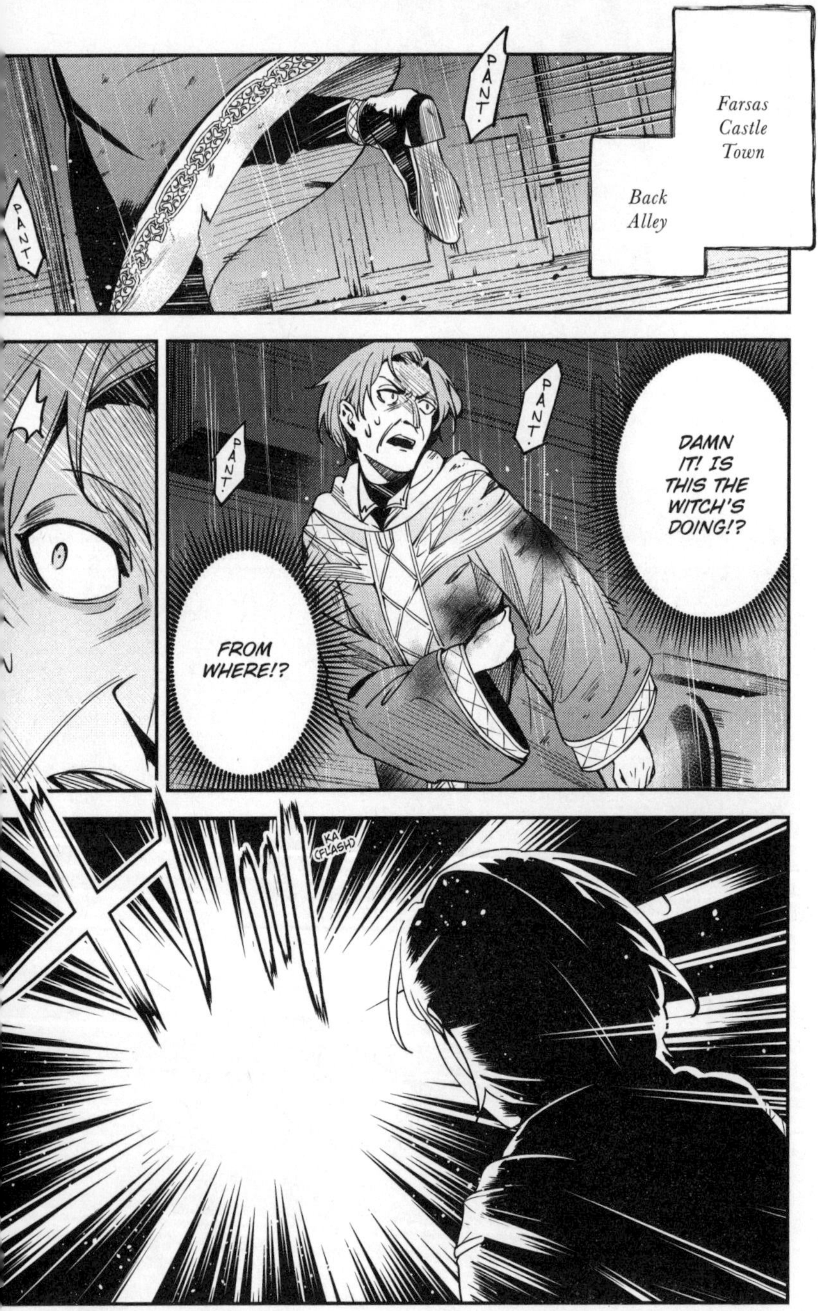
Farsas Castle Town
Back Alley
PANT.
PANT.
DAMN IT! IS THIS THE WITCH'S DOING!?
PANT.
PANT.
FROM WHERE!?
KA (FLASH)

AH...

GAH...

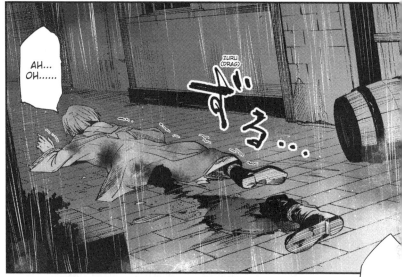

AH...
OH......

ZURU
(DRAG)

ME,
SAVE
YOU?

PU
(HEH)

...SAVE...

SOME-
ONE...

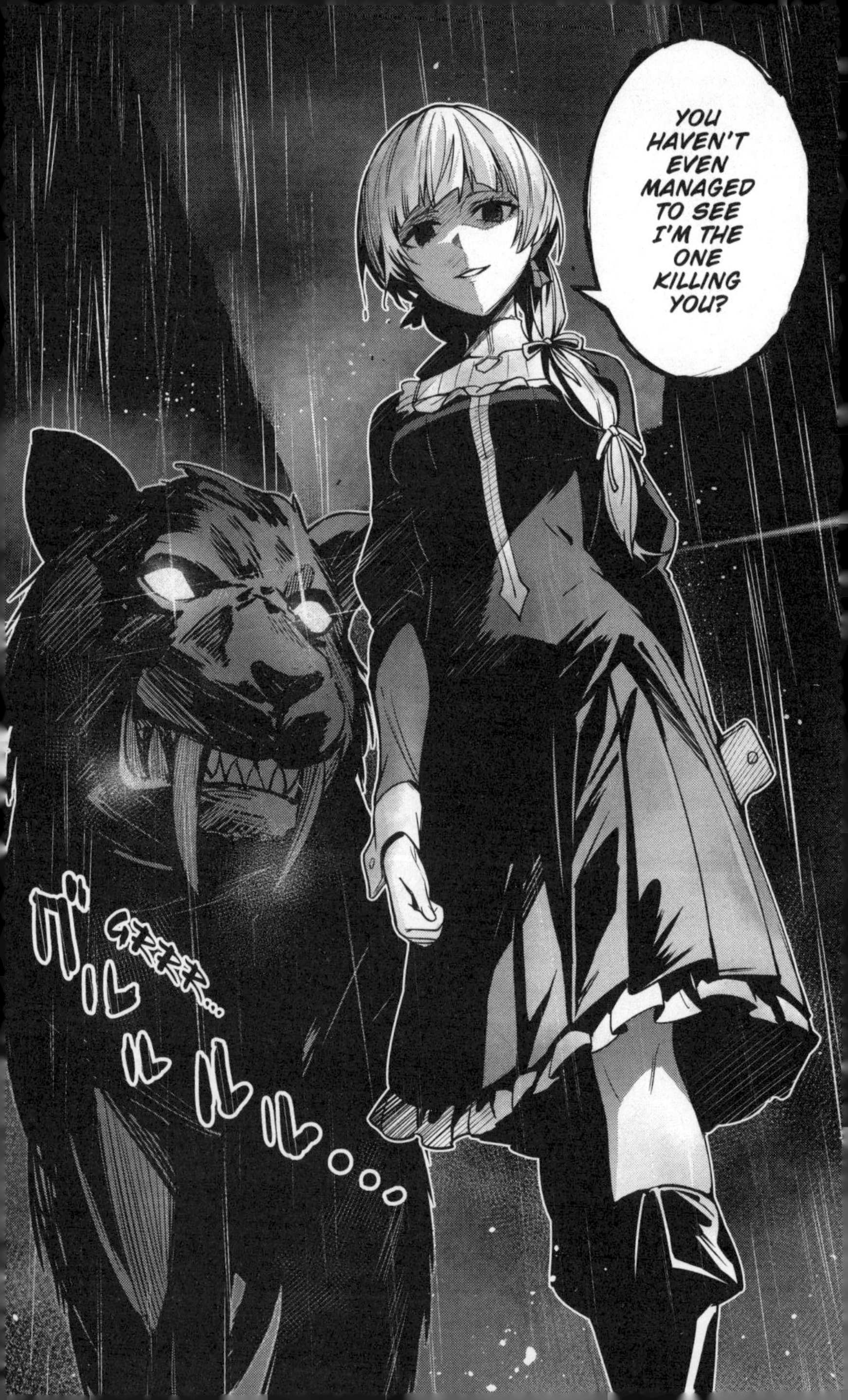
YOU HAVEN'T EVEN MANAGED TO SEE I'M THE ONE KILLING YOU?
ヴルルルル…

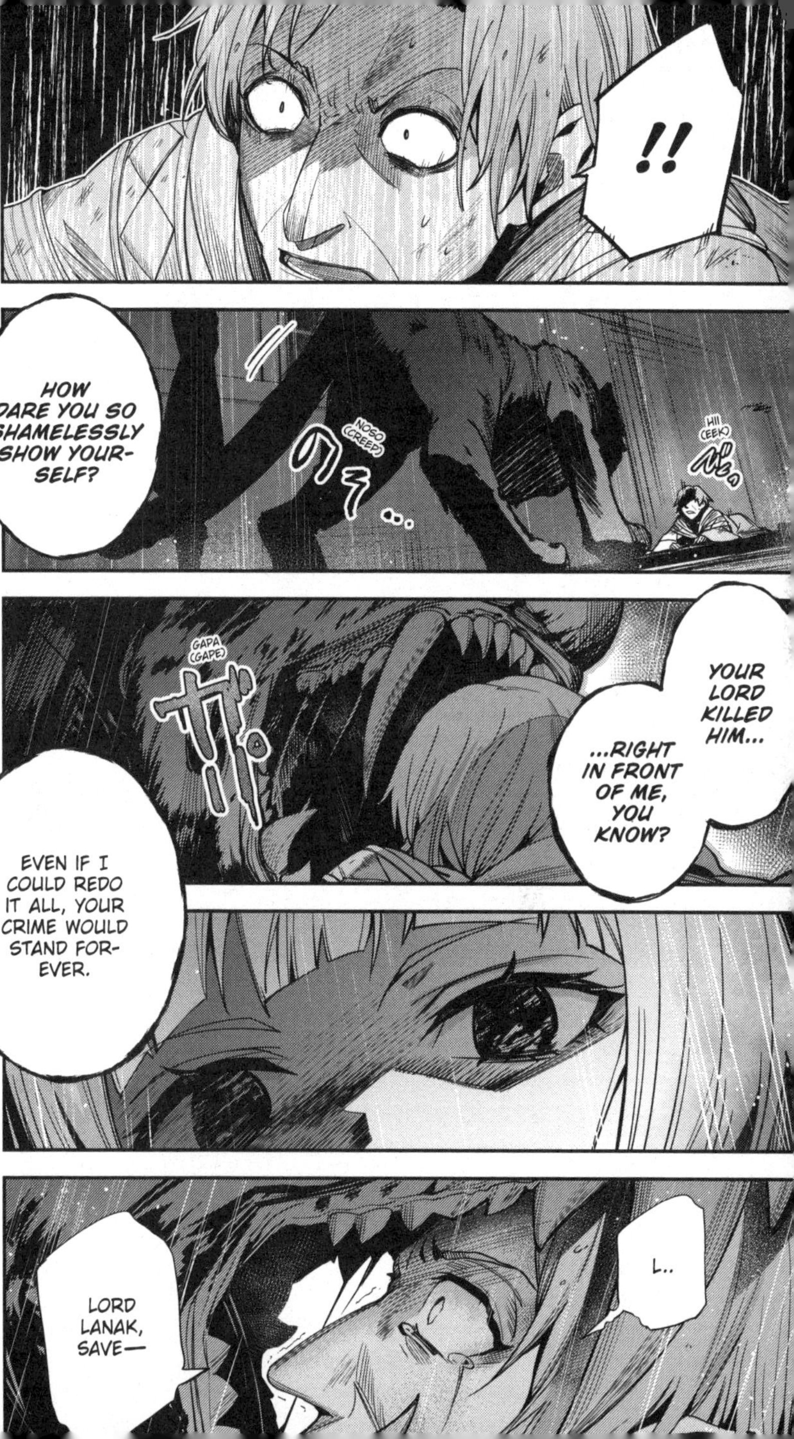
!!
HII (EEK)
NOSO (CREEP)
HOW DARE YOU SO SHAMELESSLY SHOW YOURSELF?
YOUR LORD KILLED HIM...
...RIGHT IN FRONT OF ME, YOU KNOW?
GAPA (GAPE)
EVEN IF I COULD REDO IT ALL, YOUR CRIME WOULD STAND FOREVER.
L..
LORD LANAK, SAVE—

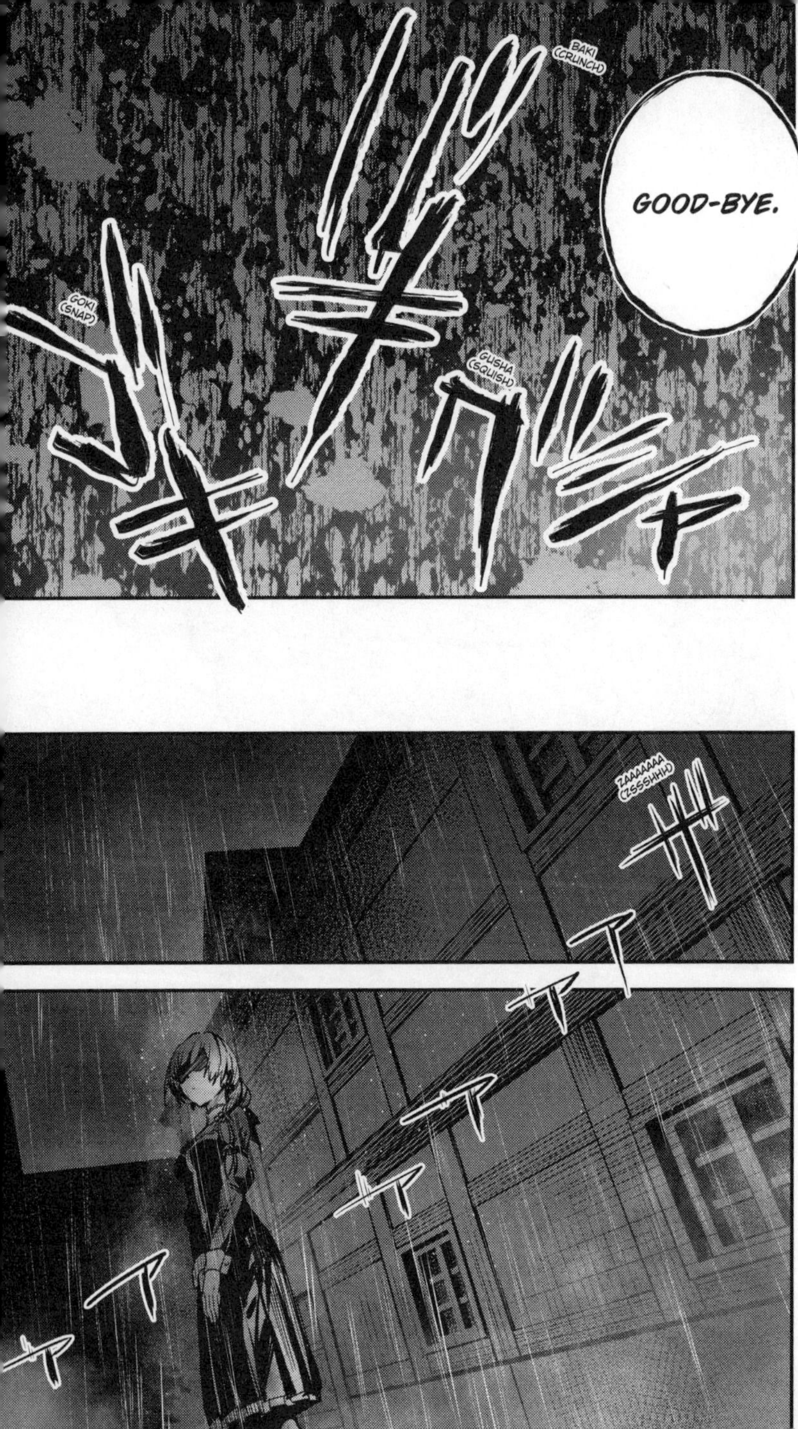
GOOD-BYE.
BAKI (CRUNCH)
GUSHA (SQUISH)
GOKI (SNAP)
ZAAAAAAA (ZSSSHHH)

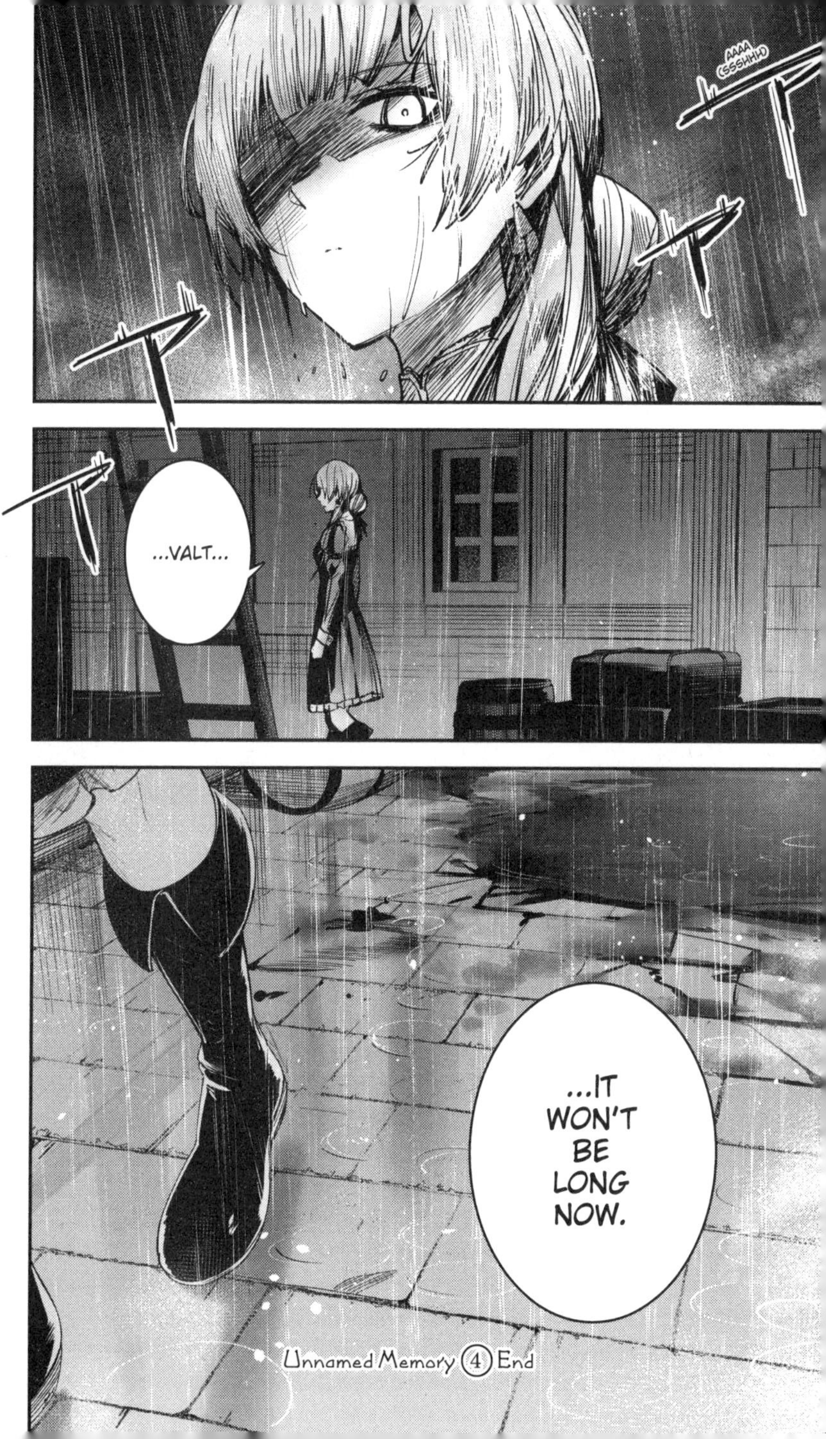
AAAA (SSSHHH)
...VALT...
...IT WON'T BE LONG NOW.
Unnamed Memory 4 End

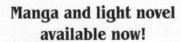

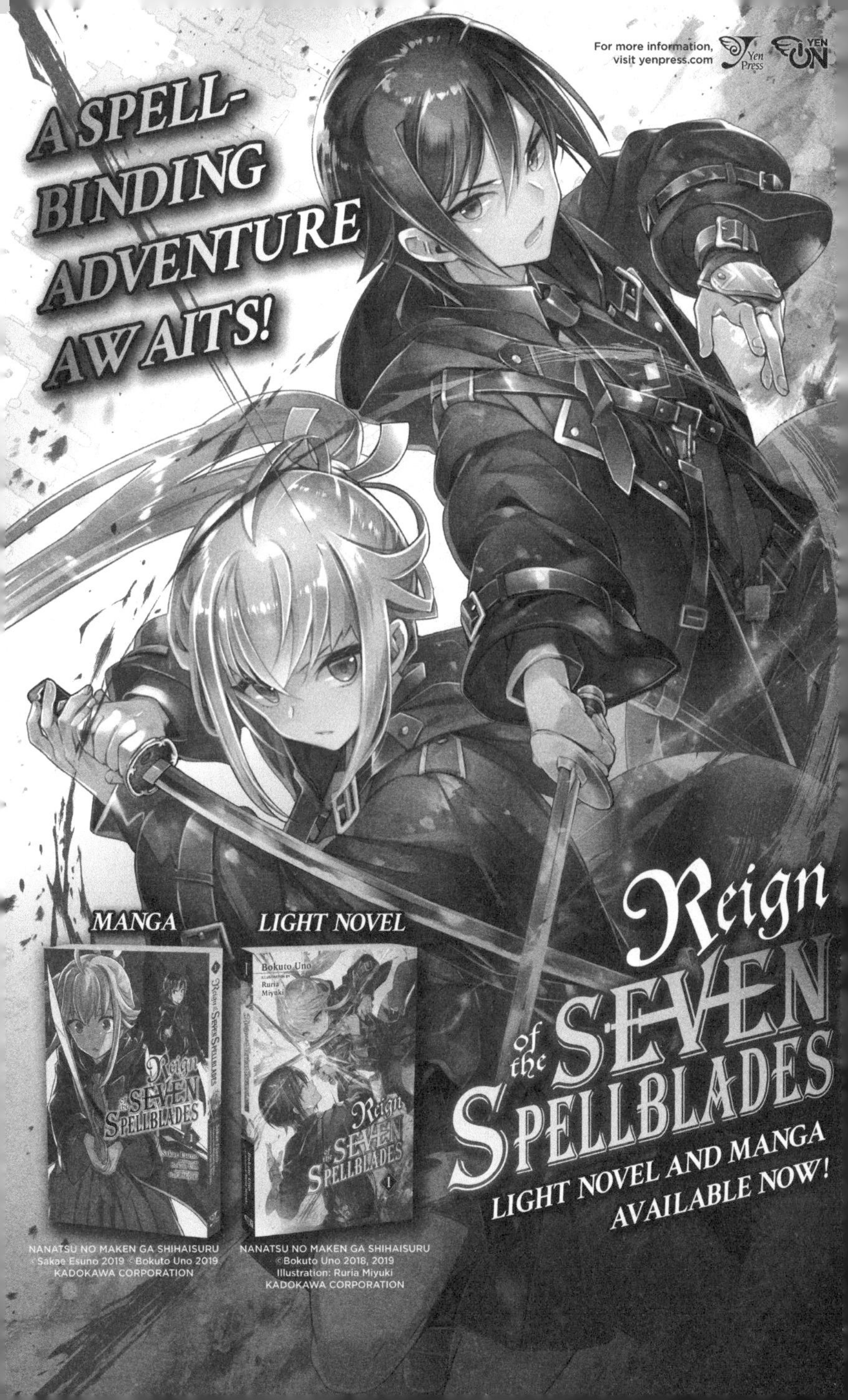

Unnamed Memory

04

Art by
NAOKI KOSHIMIZU

Original Story by
KUJI FURUMIYA

Character Design by
chibi

Translation: JEREMIAH BOURQUE
Lettering: CHIHO CHRISTIE

Unnamed Memory Vol. 4
©Koshimizu Naoki 2023 ©Furumiya Kuji 2023
First published in Japan in 2023 by KADOKAWA CORPORATION, Tokyo.
English translation rights arranged with KADOKAWA CORPORATION, Tokyo, through TUTTLE-MORI AGENCY, INC., Tokyo.

English translation © 2024 by Yen Press, LLC

Yen Press
150 West 30th Street, 19th Floor
New York, NY 10001

Visit us at yenpress.com
facebook.com/yenpress
twitter.com/yenpress
yenpress.tumblr.com
instagram.com/yenpress

First Yen Press Edition: January 2024
Edited by Yen Press Editorial: Rory Nevins, Carl Li
Designed by Yen Press Design: Eddy Mingki, Wendy Chan

Yen Press is an imprint of Yen Press, LLC.
The Yen Press name and logo are trademarks of Yen Press, LLC.

The publisher is not responsible for websites (or their content) that are not owned by the publisher.

Library of Congress Control Number: 2022937866

ISBNs: 978-1-9753-7561-4 (paperback)
        978-1-9753-7562-1 (ebook)

10 9 8 7 6 5 4 3 2 1

WOR

Printed in the United States of America